CAMBRIDGE STUDIES IN
ANGLO-SAXON ENGLAND

26

THE APOCRYPHAL GOSPELS OF MARY
IN ANGLO-SAXON ENGLAND

# CAMBRIDGE STUDIES IN ANGLO-SAXON ENGLAND

*Founding general editors*

MICHAEL LAPIDGE AND SIMON KEYNES

*Current general editors*

SIMON KEYNES AND ANDY ORCHARD

*Volumes published*

# THE APOCRYPHAL GOSPELS OF MARY IN ANGLO-SAXON ENGLAND

MARY CLAYTON

*Professor of Old and Middle English*
*University College, Dublin*

CAMBRIDGE
UNIVERSITY PRESS

PUBLISHED BY THE PRESS SYNDICATE OF THE UNIVERSITY OF CAMBRIDGE
The Pitt Building, Trumpington Street, Cambridge CB2 1RP, United Kingdom

CAMBRIDGE UNIVERSITY PRESS
The Edinburgh Building, Cambridge, CB2 2RU, United Kingdom
http://www.cup.cam.ac.uk
40 West 20th Street, New York, NY 10011–4211, USA    http://www.cup.org
10 Stamford Road, Oakleigh, Melbourne 3166, Australia

© Mary Clayton 1998

First published 1998

Printed in Great Britain at the University Press, Cambridge

Typeset in 11/13pt Garamond    [CE]

*A catalogue record for this book is available from the British Library*

*Library of Congress cataloguing in publication data*
Clayton, Mary, 1954–
The Apocryphal Gospels of Mary in Anglo-Saxon England / Mary Clayton.
p.   cm. – (Cambridge studies in Anglo-Saxon England : 26)
Includes bibliographical references and index.
ISBN 0 521 58168 0 (hardback)
1. Mary, Blessed Virgin, Saint – Legends – History and criticism.
2. Christian literature, English (Old) – History and criticism.
3. Apocryphal Gospels – Criticism, interpretation, etc. 4. Mary,
Blessed Virgin, Saint – Cult – England – History. 5. Manuscripts,
Medieval – England. 6. Manuscripts, English (Old) 7. Sermons,
English (Old)    I. Title.   II. Series.
BS2851.C55    1998
232.91′0942–dc21    98–17275    CIP

ISBN 0 521 58168 0 hardback

For Niall MacMonagle

# Contents

# Contents

# Acknowledgements

The beginnings of this book go back to 1979, when I produced an edition of the Old English *Gospel of Pseudo-Matthew*, under the supervision of Eric Stanley, for the M.Litt. Qualifying examination in Oxford; this was carefully corrected by the late Eric Dobson, whose comments were immensely helpful. Since then, many friends and scholars have been most generous with their help and support: I thank Rita Beyers, Carole Biggam, Kevin Cathcart, Catherine Clayton, Terry Dolan, Alan Fletcher, Jan Gijsel, Malcolm Godden, Tim Graham, Ananya Kabir, Peter Lucas, Hugh Magennis, Anne Middleton, Jennifer Miller, Bruce Mitchell, Jack Niles, Enrico Norelli, Jenny Rowland and Don Scragg. Michael Lapidge has, as always, been a most patient and helpful editor.

University College Dublin has helped with a grant towards the cost of microfilms and travel, and with a publication grant, as has the National University of Ireland. A grant from the Fulbright Commission of Ireland enabled me to spend six months in Berkeley in 1996, where much of the introduction was written. I should also like to thank the librarians of University College, Dublin, Trinity College, Dublin, the Parker Library, Corpus Christi College, Cambridge (where I should particularly like to thank Gill Cannell), Cambridge University Library, the Bodleian Library, Oxford, the British Library, the Berkeley University Library and the Graduate Theology Library, Berkeley.

The Pontificia Academia Mariana Internationalis has kindly granted permission to reproduce Monika Haibach-Reinisch's text of *Transitus B²* in Appendix 2.

ix

# Sigla

B    Blickling Homilies
D    Cambridge, Corpus Christi College, 41
F    Cambridge, Corpus Christi College, 198
I    Oxford, Bodleian Library, Bodley 343
O    Oxford, Bodleian Library, Hatton 114
N    London, British Library, Cotton Nero E. i
P    Cambridge, Pembroke College 25
R    Vatican City, Biblioteca Apostolica Vaticana, Reginensis lat. 537
f$^a$    Cambridge, Corpus Christi College, 367, Part II, fols. 3–6, 11–29

# Abbreviations

*AB*      *Analecta Bollandiana*
*ASE*     *Anglo-Saxon England*
*BT*      Bosworth, J., and Northcote Toller, T., *An Anglo-Saxon Dic-tionary* (London, 1898)
CC       Corpus Christianorum
EEMF     Early English Manuscripts in Facsimile
EETS     Early English Text Society
*MCOE*    *A Microfiche Concordance to Old English*, ed. R. Venezky and A. Healey (Toronto, 1980)
MGH      Monumenta Germaniae Historica
PG       Patrologia Graeca
PL       Patrologia Latina
*RES*     *Review of English Studies*

# Editorial conventions

In the Old English texts edited here, punctuation, word-division and the capitalization of proper and sacred names are modernized.
Abbreviations have been expanded without notice. The following signs are used:

[[ ]] encloses letters or words that a scribe has deleted or subpuncted in the manuscript
/ indicates a page break in the manuscript
\/ indicates insertions by scribes
*om.* indicates omitted

# Introduction

The texts edited in this volume are Old English versions of Latin texts on the birth, childhood, death and assumption of Mary. These Old English texts are late descendants of much older traditions, going back, in the case of the text on Mary's birth and childhood, to the second century after Christ. They are generally classed among the New Testament apocrypha of the Christian church, so called because they are writings associated in some way with the New Testament, either in genre or content. They are, therefore, not part of the canon of the New Testament, in which the Virgin features hardly at all, but they supply what were perceived as gaps in the biblical accounts of Mary. In origin these texts also address christological problems which troubled the contemporary church. Their designation as apocrypha goes back largely to the so-called Gelasian decree, one section of which contains a long list of works to be rejected by the faithful: the origin of this section is disputed, but it seems to have been compiled around 500, perhaps in Italy or Gaul. The list of works forbidden as apocryphal includes a 'liber de infantia Saluatoris' and a 'liber de natiuitate Saluatoris et de Maria uel obstetrice',[1] as well as a 'liber qui appellatur Transitus S. Mariae', with textual variants including 'adsumptio' and 'revelatio'.[2] Although the decree does not seem to have

---

[1] Dobschütz, ed., *Das Decretum Gelasianum*, p. 11. Dobschütz thinks that the first of these refers to the *Gospel of Pseudo-Matthew* and the second perhaps a different version of *Pseudo-Matthew* or a mixed version drawing on *Pseudo-Matthew* and the *De natiuitate Mariae* (*ibid.*, pp. 296–7). A translation of the *Proteuangelium* is more likely, at least for the second text mentioned; the beginning of this deals with Mary's birth and childhood.

[2] *Ibid.*, pp. 12 and 203. For a discussion of the *transitus* texts as apocrypha, see Mimouni, 'Les Transitus Mariae sont-ils vraiment des apocryphes?' See also Manns, *Le récit*, pp. 230–2.

1

been an official document of the church, it was influential and had an effect on readers of and writers about the apocrypha. Later Western writers, such as Paschasius Radbertus in Carolingian Gaul and Ælfric in England, show unease about the Marian apocrypha, an attitude they probably derived from the Gelasian decree, but the texts were enormously popular in both the Eastern and Western churches, influencing liturgy, art and literature throughout the Middle Ages and beyond. Mimouni suggests that they should be viewed as hagiographic writings[3] and such a perspective would better explain their penetration of the liturgy and their survival in large numbers of manuscripts, often legendaries and homiliaries. The manuscript contexts of the Anglo-Saxon texts would certainly also support such a description, as they are found in homiletic and hagiographic collections.

The particular circumstances of the origins of the birth and death apocrypha will be treated in more detail in the relevant chapters of this book, but what is striking about both families of texts is the degree to which they are preoccupied with the body of Mary and its foundational role in Christian theology: the divinity can become incarnate in her only if she is a pure virgin, which determines almost all aspects of the stories of Mary's infancy, and since her origins and upbringing 'prove' her to be a sinless virgin, then her body has to be spared the ignominy of decaying in the tomb while awaiting the Last Judgement. In this way, Mary offers a model of the recuperated Christian body and the apocrypha are constantly concerned to establish her perfect purity: she is conceived during her father's absence, brought up in the temple, eating only food brought by an angel, and entrusted from there to the care of an old man, before conceiving Jesus miraculously. At her death the fate of her soul is naturally assured and all attention centres on her body; as it is being washed and prepared for burial, it is protected from any impure gaze by a blinding light and is then, in many texts, resurrected and assumed after three days as a sign of its physical perfection. The corruption attendant on sin is inappropriate for this extraordinary body.

The apocryphal treatments of Mary's origin and end are modelled on that of Christ and of other biblical figures. The texts most influential on the accounts of Mary's birth and childhood include the canonical infancy gospels, while Old Testament accounts are also heavily drawn upon. Mary's

---

[3] Mimouni, 'Les Transitus Mariae sont-ils vraiment des apocryphes?' p. 128.

birth is miraculous, although not to the same degree as Christ's, and it is announced in advance to her parents by an angel, just as Christ's birth was announced to her. Pagan influences have been detected also, especially from the cult of Cybele, and it has been argued that the aim of the author of the first of these texts, the *Proteuangelium*, was to elevate Mary to the level of the virgin-goddesses of the Greco-Roman world.[4] After her death, also preceded by an Annunciation scene modelled on that preceding the Incarnation, Mary generally spends three days in the tomb (a new tomb, like that of Christ, in many of the texts) before being resurrected (in some texts only) and assumed from the site of the tomb, the Mount of Olives, the same place from where Christ ascended. Her death is attended by hostilities on the part of the Jews, again probably modelled on the circumstances of Christ's death. Just as Christ descended into hell after his death, so the accounts of Mary's death originally included an account of her being brought to view hell. The birth story of John the Baptist and the death of John the Evangelist, also thought by many to have been assumed, were important too in the development of the Marian legends.[5]

This volume contains editions of three Old English texts and three Latin texts preserved in manuscripts from Anglo-Saxon England. The Old English texts are a version of part of the Latin *Gospel of Pseudo-Matthew*, of the assumption narrative known as *Transitus B²* or the *Transitus of Pseudo-Melito* and a composite account, combining most of *Transitus W* with a different translation of the end of *Transitus B²*. The Latin texts are a translation of part of the Greek *Proteuangelium*, a version of the *Gospel of Pseudo-Matthew* and a version of *Transitus W*. They are valuable indications of the kinds of Latin texts circulating in Anglo-Saxon England, many others of which must have been lost. No text of *Transitus B* survives in a manuscript from Anglo-Saxon England, although it was known in England from at least the time of Bede and was used as source for two of the vernacular homilies. As it is difficult to obtain, I have, with the kind permission of the Pontificia Academia Mariana Internationalis, included a copy of Haibach-Reinisch's edition of this version, without apparatus or notes.

---

[4] See S. Benko, *The Virgin Goddess: Studies in the Pagan and Christian Roots of Mariology*, Studies in the History of Religions 59 (Leiden, 1993), pp. 196–206.

[5] On the death of John the Evangelist, see the appendix 'La mort et l'assomption de saint Jean l'Evangéliste' in Jugie, *La mort*, pp. 708–26.

There is also in Old English a version of a further part of the *Gospel of Pseudo-Matthew*, in a Christmas homily known as Vercelli VI, dealing with the miracles on the flight into Egypt. I have not included this here, partly because of the recent edition of the Vercelli Book by Donald Scragg,[6] but also because, due to a lacuna in the manuscript, the part of this homily dependent on *Pseudo-Matthew* is fragmentary and Mary's role is not prominent. I have also not edited, though I have quoted in full, the highly condensed account of Mary's birth and childhood in the *Old English Martyrology*, even though this is drawn exclusively from the *Pseudo-Matthew*.[7] Again, there is an excellent modern edition of this text and the *Martyrology*'s account is an abbreviation rather than a translation. Three anonymous Old English homilies include an account of an episode which appears to be drawn ultimately from an apocalypse of Mary, in which Mary, Michael and the apostles, after Mary's assumption, are taken to view hell, where they plead for the sinners imprisoned there. Such episodes are originally found attached to *transitus* texts and are later found as self-contained apocalypses. Again, these texts are not edited here, as the Old English treatments are abbreviated, isolated incidents, set into a different context, and I have discussed them elsewhere.[8]

The sigla used for the manuscripts containing the Old English texts are those devised by Scragg for the anonymous homilies, 'designed to show both the relation between manuscripts in respect of their anonymous content and the importance of individual manuscripts in the information they offer on the early tradition'.[9]

Although all of the Old English texts have been edited already,[10] only

---

[6] *The Vercelli Homilies.*    [7] Kotzor, ed., *Das altenglische Martyrologium.*

[8] See my 'Delivering the Damned'. See also T. Hill, 'Delivering the Damned in Old English Anonymous Homilies and Jon Arason's *Ljomur*', *Medium Ævum* 61 (1992), 75–82, and S. Cutforth, 'Delivering the Damned in Old English Homilies: an Additional Note', *Notes and Queries* 40 (1993), 435–7.

[9] Scragg, 'The Corpus of Vernacular Homilies', p. 224. Lees, 'Working with Patristic Sources', pp. 163–5, critically discusses the different sigla assigned to Old English homiletic manuscripts.

[10] The Old English *Gospel of Pseudo-Matthew* was edited, using two of the three manuscripts, by Assmann, *Angelsächsische Homilien und Heiligenleben*, pp. 117–37; the version of *Transitus B²* in Cambridge, Corpus Christi College 41 was edited by Grant, *Three Homilies*, pp. 18–31, and by Tristram, *Vier altenglische Predigten*, pp. 125–51; and the assumption homily in CCCC 198 and in the Blickling Homilies manuscript was edited from the latter manuscript by Morris, *Blickling Homilies*, pp. 136–59.

one of them has been edited in this century and the two nineteenth-century editions do not take all the now-available manuscript evidence into account. This is also the first edition to present the texts as a group, to give an extended account of the background to the Marian apocrypha, to look at the texts in the context of the development of that tradition and to examine in detail the sources of all the Old English texts.

# 1

# The birth and childhood of Mary: the development of a tradition

The bible contains nothing on the origins, birth and childhood of Mary, or on her last days and her death, but from a very early period a wish to know more about the mother of Christ, both in relation to her son and in her own life, is evident. Of the gospels only Matthew and Luke contain infancy narratives: Matthew has Mary's pregnancy by the Holy Spirit, Joseph's wish to put her away, his dream with its promise of the birth of Jesus, the chaste marriage of Mary and Joseph until after the birth, then a description of the visit of the Magi, the murder of the innocents in Bethlehem, the flight into Egypt and the return to Nazareth; while Luke recounts first the conception of John the Baptist, then the Annunciation to Mary, with her response referring to her virginity, the reference to the Holy Spirit coming upon her, Elizabeth's witness, Mary's *Magnificat*, the birth in Bethlehem, the tidings to the shepherds, the Circumcision, the presentation in the temple, the prophecies of Simeon and Anna and the episode of the twelve-year-old child Jesus in the temple. Mary naturally features in these chapters of the gospels, but then, as in Mark and John, almost drops out of sight as the account of Jesus's adult ministry gets under way. These biblical infancy narratives are chiefly concerned with christological issues, particularly with Christ's divine nature, which they 'prove' by means of the conception by the Holy Spirit and the virgin birth, with Joseph viewed as the adoptive, rather than natural, father. They seek too to show Jesus's fulfilment of Old Testament prophecy: both Matthew and Luke include genealogies tracing Jesus's ancestry back to David through Joseph, and Luke's accounts of the presentation and of the twelve-year-old Jesus in the temple emphasize the fulfilment of the priesthood in him. The importance of agreement with the Old Testament is evident too in the concern with establishing Bethlehem as the place of birth, even though Jesus was known to have come from Nazareth. The poverty of the circumstances of Jesus's birth in Luke is typical of that evangelist's concern with the ideal of poverty, and the story of the Magi and of the flight into Egypt is intended to show that Jesus's kingship was universal and not restricted to the Jews.[1]

## THE *PROTEUANGELIUM JACOBI*

Mary is significant in these canonical accounts of the nativity only in relation to her son Jesus, and as soon as her role in his life diminishes, she ceases to feature in the gospels. Popular interest in her and in other figures who were peripheral to the gospels' accounts was not satisfied with this scant information, however, and the gospels did not suffice either to counter all of the attacks on Christian teachings in relation to Jesus in the first centuries of Christianity. Already by the second century, before the canon of the New Testament was entirely fixed, further texts were being composed, based on oral and written traditions, on the gospels themselves and on the Old Testament. As the four-gospel canon was being consolidated from the second century onwards, these texts did not become part of the canon (a term not attested as a designation for the bible until the middle of the fourth century) and were recognized as a problem for the church.[2] They were designated as apocrypha, which originally meant something 'kept hidden because of its costliness or because of the objectionable nature of its content', then 'of hidden origin'[3] and was a

---

[1] On the New Testament infancy narratives, see O. Cullmann, 'Infancy Gospels', in *New Testament Apocrypha*, ed. Schneemelcher, I, 414–16, and R. Laurentin, *Les Evangiles de l'enfance du Christ. Vérité de Noël au-delà des mythes. Exégèse et sémiotique. Historicité et théologie* (Paris, 1982).

[2] On the growth of the canon, see the general introduction by Schneemelcher in *New Testament Apocrypha*, I, 9–33, and the texts translated on pp. 34–50, and B. M. Metzger, *The Canon of the New Testament: its Origin, Development and Significance* (Oxford, 1987).

[3] Schneemelcher, ed., *New Testament Apocrypha*, I, 14. For bibliography on the apocrypha, see J. Charlesworth and J. Mueller, *The New Testament Apocrypha and Pseudepigrapha: a Guide to Publications, with Excursus on Apocalypses*, Atla Bibliography Series 17 (Metuchen, NJ, and London, 1987); Geerard, *Clauis Apocryphorum* and 'Bibliographie Générale', *Apocrypha* 1 (1990), 13–67.

term associated especially with gnosticism. When Christian writers took over the term they associated it with the rejected gnostic texts and used it pejoratively, and by about 400 the word designated texts regarded as disreputable or even heretical, which could not be read in church. The so-called *Decretum Gelasianum de libris recipiendis et non recipiendis*, probably dating from around 500, gives a catalogue of 'apocrypha' and other rejected texts, including those dealing with the birth and death of Mary.[4]

As the apocryphal gospels describing the life of Mary grew out of a desire to fill gaps left by the canonical gospels, one of their main sources was those gospels themselves. This can clearly be seen in the earliest surviving account, the so-called *Proteuangelium Iacobi*, which is the basis for much of the later apocryphal Marian literature, profoundly influenced the development of Mariology and Christian art and gave rise to a series of Marian feasts.[5] I shall summarize it in detail here as it is of such importance for subsequent accounts.

The *Proteuangelium*, written in Greek, has been described as a midrashic exegesis[6] of the birth narratives in Matthew and Luke and it begins with

---

[4] Dobschütz, ed., *Das Decretum Gelasianum*, translated in Schneemelcher, ed. *New Testament Apocrypha*, I, 38–40. See above, pp. 1–2.

[5] It was called the *Proteuangelium* because it related events before those recounted in the canonical gospels: the title is a sixteenth-century one, given by the French Jesuit Guillaume Postel who published a Latin translation in 1552. The standard edition was for a long time Tischendorf, ed., *Evangelia Apocrypha*, pp. 1–50, which is based on seventeen manuscripts, dating from the ninth to the sixteenth centuries. M. Testuz, *Papyrus Bodmer V* (Cologny-Geneva, 1958), edited the earliest manuscript of the text (fourth century) and de Strycker, *La forme*, has produced a provisional critical edition based on the earliest manuscripts, on Tischendorf's collations and on early translations into other languages. It is translated by O. Cullmann using Tischendorf's and de Strycker's editions in Schneemelcher, ed., *New Testament Apocrypha*, I, 426–37, and by Elliott, using Tischendorf only, in *The Apocryphal New Testament*, pp. 57–67. A valuable overview of the problems of the text is provided by E. de Strycker, 'Le Protévangile de Jacques: Problèmes critiques et exégétiques', in *Studia Evangelica* III, ed. F. L. Cross, Texte und Untersuchungen 88 (Berlin, 1964), pp. 339–59. On Postel's text, see I. Backus, 'Guillaume Postel, Théodore Bibliander et le "Protévangile de Jacques"', *Apocrypha* 6 (1995), 7–65.

[6] Smid, *Protevangelium Jacobi: a Commentary*, p. 8; Cothenet, 'Le Protèvangile de Jacques'; but see also M. McNamara, 'Midrash, Apocrypha, Culture Medium and Development of Doctrine: Some Facts in Quest of a Terminology', *Apocrypha* 6 (1995), 127–64.

details about Mary's pious parents, Joachim and Anna, who are childless. When Joachim's offering at the temple is refused on the grounds that he has no offspring, he retires to the wilderness and fasts for forty days. His wife Anna, in the meantime, laments her twofold sorrow, the loss of her husband and her childlessness. While walking in her garden lamenting that she alone is not fruitful, an angel appears and tells her that she will conceive and that her offspring shall be spoken of in the whole world, and Anna promises to dedicate the child to God. Two further angels announce the return of her husband to her, and an angel has also told Joachim that his wife will conceive (or has conceived, depending on the manuscript). When Anna meets Joachim on his return she declares that she, who was childless, will conceive or has conceived, again depending on which manuscript is followed.

After six (or seven or nine) months, Anna gives birth and the child is called Mary. At six months she walks seven steps and returns to her mother, who then vows that she shall walk no more on the ground until she is dedicated to the temple. A sanctuary is made in Mary's bedroom and the undefiled daughters of the Hebrews serve her there. On her first birthday Joachim holds a great feast where Mary is blessed by the priests and chief priests and Anna afterwards sings a song of praise to the Lord. At three years old Mary is dedicated to God in the temple, where she dances on the steps of the altar and does not look back at her parents. She receives food from the hand of an angel and, when she is twelve years old and can remain no longer in the temple, an angel appears to the high-priest Zacharias and orders him to assemble all of the widowers of the people in order to choose a husband for Mary. The high-priest takes all the widowers' rods and prays with them in the temple, but when he gives them back there is no sign from the Lord until Joseph receives the last rod. A dove flies out on to Joseph's head and the priest tells him that he has been chosen by lot to receive the virgin of the Lord. When Joseph answers that he already has sons and is old, the priest warns him of the consequences of a refusal and Joseph takes Mary as his ward. He leaves her in his house and goes away to work on his buildings, as he is a carpenter, and Mary is chosen by lot to weave the pure purple and scarlet for the temple veil, a task reserved for those descended from David.

When Mary is sixteen (or fourteen or fifteen) she goes to draw water one day and a voice says 'Hail, thou that art highly favoured, the Lord is with thee, blessed art thou among women'.[7] Trembling and unable to see where the voice comes from, she returns to the house where an angel of the Lord appears and tells her that she will conceive by the word of God and that her son will be called Jesus, the son of the Most High. Mary replies, as in Luke, that she is the handmaid of the Lord, 'be it to me according to your word'. When she has finished the purple and the scarlet, she brings them to the priest, who blesses her, and then goes to Elizabeth, in whose womb John the Baptist leaps. Mary, unaccountably, 'forgot the mysteries which the archangel Gabriel had told her, and raised a sigh towards heaven and said, 'Who am I, Lord, that all the women [generations] of the earth count me blessed?'[8] She remains three months with Elizabeth, hiding herself from the children of Israel as her pregnancy becomes evident. When Mary is six months pregnant, Joseph returns and is distraught when he finds her with child. He does not believe Mary's protestations of innocence until an angel appears in a dream, as in Matthew I.20. When Mary's pregnancy is discovered by the scribes and priests, both she and Joseph are made to drink the 'water of the conviction of the Lord' and both are declared innocent in front of the entire people.

Augustus then declares a census in Bethlehem and Joseph, his sons and Mary set out, with Mary on a she-ass. On the way, she has visions of two peoples, one weeping and one rejoicing, and half-way to Bethlehem the birth begins and Joseph brings her to a cave. Leaving Mary in the care of his sons, Joseph sets out to seek a midwife. A passage in the first person follows in which Joseph describes the standstill of all nature and, when motion is resumed, he finds a midwife and brings her to the cave. A bright cloud overshadows the cave and the midwife announces that salvation is born to Israel. The cloud then disappears and a great light shines; when it withdraws the baby appears and takes Mary's breast. The midwife comes out of the cave and meets Salome, who refuses to believe that a virgin has given birth without inserting her finger to test Mary's virginity, an episode which seems to be modelled on that of the disbelieving Thomas. After Salome has tested and believed, her hand is consumed by fire and is healed only when an angel instructs her to touch the child. The Magi then come to Herod and to the child in the cave and

---

[7] Schneemelcher, ed., *New Testament Apocrypha*, I, 430. I quote from Cullmann as he gives the reading of Bodmer Papyrus V and of Tischendorf, where these diverge.

[8] *Ibid.*, I, 431.

the massacre of the innocents is described, with Elizabeth and John the Baptist saved by a mountain which opens for them. Zacharias, John's father, is killed by Herod's soldiers. The text ends with the epilogue: 'Now I, James, who wrote this history, when a tumult arose in Jerusalem on the death of Herod, withdrew into the desert until the tumult in Jerusalem ceased. And I will praise the Lord, who gave me the wisdom to write this history. Grace shall be with all those who fear the Lord.'[9] The text therefore purports to have been written when Jesus was still a child.

The earliest manuscript of the *Proteuangelium* is Geneva, Bibliotheca Bodmeriana, Papyrus Bodmer 5 of the first half of the fourth century[10] and this already shows signs of revision and cutting.[11] Altogether 140 Greek manuscripts are known[12] and the work was translated into Syriac (fifth century), Ethiopic, Coptic (Sahidic), Georgian, Old Church Slavonic, Armenian, Arabic, Latin and Irish.[13] There is debate about the initial scope of the work and whether some parts of the text are later additions, particularly as the earliest manuscript has a shorter version in several places, but de Strycker argues convincingly that it has been abbreviated, clumsily, from the long text which we find in other early witnesses.[14]

The *Proteuangelium* probably dates from the second half of the second century and the first incontestable reference to it is by Origen (*d.* 254), but Clement of Alexandria (*d.* 215) seems to refer to it also.[15] Clement of

---

[9] *Ibid.*, I, 437.

[10] Its editor, Testuz, dated it to the third century, but de Strycker, *La forme*, pp. 195–7, presents good arguments for a fourth-century date.

[11] See de Strycker, *La forme*, esp. pp. 377–92.

[12] De Strycker, 'Die griechischen Handschriften'.

[13] See Geerard, *Clauis Apocryphorum*, pp. 27–9, for a list of editions of these various versions. On the Irish, see M. McNamara, *The Apocrypha in the Irish Church* (Dublin, 1975), pp. 42–7.

[14] De Strycker, *La forme*, pp. 376–92; he also argues, however, that all surviving forms of the text preserve anomalies and inconsequences which suggest that an even longer form of the text was originally composed and then abbreviated in such a way as to leave traces (pp. 404–12).

[15] See de Strycker, *La forme*, pp. 412–18; P. A. van Stempvoort, 'The Protevangelium Jacobi, the Sources of its Theme and Style and their Bearing on its Date', in *Studia Evangelica* III, ed. F. L. Cross, Texte und Untersuchungen zur Geschichte der altchristlichen Literatur 88 (Berlin, 1964), pp. 410–26; and Smid, *Protevangelium Jacobi: a Commentary*, pp. 22–4, for a summary of the evidence for the dating of the text and de Strycker, *La forme*, pp. 393–4 and p. 412, for a discussion of Origen's use of the apocryphon.

Alexandria's reference, in bk VII of his *Stromates*, is to the story of a midwife who examined Mary and found her to be a virgin; as no other text of this period refers to this episode, it is most likely with the *Proteuangelium* that he was familiar and that he was conflating the midwife and Salome. Clement also refers to the brothers of Jesus as being the sons of Joseph. Origen similarly refers to the brothers of Jesus as the sons of Joseph and attributes this to the *Gospel of Peter* or to the *Book of James*: the latter must be the *Proteuangelium*. In the earliest manuscript the title of the *Proteuangelium* is *The Birth of Mary: Revelation of James* (*Génésis Marias. Apokalypsis Jakôb*).[16] This James is presumably to be taken as the step-brother of Jesus by Joseph's supposed first marriage and the Gelasian decree identifies him with James the Less in Mark XV.40.[17] As the text describes the sons of Joseph as present at the birth of Jesus, this would make James an eyewitness. The real author is not known, but is not likely to have been a Jew as the text demonstrates ignorance of Palestinian geography and Jewish customs. De Strycker argues that Egypt was the place of origin of the text, but Smid proposes Syria as a possibility, while saying that countries other than Egypt and Syria should not be left out *a priori*.[18] Cothenet, too, argues for Syria, on the grounds that the author must have lived in a milieu close to Judeo-Christianity because of his use of midrashic techniques: in Syria there were constant contacts between Jews and Christians, and the way in which Mary's relationship with Joseph is described makes her very similar to the *uirgines subintroductae* who were common in Syria.[19] These were women who, in the period when there were as yet no monasteries, took refuge in the houses of male ascetics in order to live as virgins. Cothenet points as well to the analogies between the praise of Mary's virginity in the *Proteuangelium* and the exhortations to chastity in the apocryphal acts of the apostles, which also seem to originate in Syria.[20]

While the most important sources of the *Proteuangelium* are the New Testament infancy gospels of Matthew and Luke, from which the author

---

[16] See de Strycker, *La forme*, p. 14, n. 4 and pp. 208–16, for this title.

[17] See Cullmann in Schneemelcher, ed., *New Testament Apocrypha*, I, 423.

[18] See de Strycker, *La forme*, pp. 419–23, and Smid, *Protevangelium Jacobi: a Commentary*, pp. 20–2.

[19] Cothenet, 'Le Protévangile de Jacques', pp. 4267–8. On Judeo-Christianity and the *Proteuangelium*, see also F. Manns, *Essais sur le Judéo-Christianisme*, Studium Biblicum Franciscanum Analecta 12 (Jerusalem, 1977), pp. 69–114.

[20] Cothenet, 'Le Protévangile de Jacques', p. 4267.

selected to give a sequential narrative, the influence of the Old Testament is profound. Old Testament texts which influenced the author of the *Proteuangelium* include the story of Abraham and Sarah in Genesis XVIII and XXI, the story of Samson's parents in Judges XIII, the story of Hannah and Elkanah and their son Samuel in 1 Samuel I–II (this is the account on which the story of the birth of Mary is most clearly modelled), the story of Susanna in the Greek Book of Daniel, the Book of Judith and the Book of Tobias; the New Testament story of Elizabeth and Zachariah in Luke I is another analogue to the conception of Mary.[21] The name of Mary's father, Joachim, seems to come from the name of the husband of the chaste Susanna in Daniel and that of Anna from Hannah, the mother of Samuel. The work clearly aims to praise and glorify Mary in all respects and in this it can be seen to take issue with anti-Christian polemic. In Jewish circles of the second century an alternative version of the story of Jesus was circulating, which can be reconstructed from quotations from the *Logos Alèthès* of the pagan, anti-Christian author Celsus, writing *c.* 178. Celsus's arguments were explicitly quoted and combated by Origen in his *Contra Celsum*[22] (written between 246 and 248): 'But now let us return to where the Jew is introduced, speaking of the mother of Jesus, and saying that "when she was pregnant she was turned out of doors by the carpenter to whom she had been betrothed, as having been guilty of adultery, and that she bore a child to a certain soldier named Pantera . . ."' (bk I, ch. xxxii): 'For he [Celsus] represents him [a Jew] disputing with Jesus, and confuting him, as he thinks, on many points; and in the first place, he accuses Him of having "invented his birth from a virgin", and upbraids Him with being "born in a certain Jewish village, of a poor woman of the country, who gained her subsistence by spinning,

---

[21] See van Stempvoort, 'The Protevangelium Jacobi', pp. 415–25, and Smid, *Protevangelium Jacobi: a Commentary, passim*, but also W. S. Vorster, 'The Protevangelium of James and Intertextuality', in *Text and Testimony: Essays on New Testament and Apocryphal Literature in Honour of A. J. F. Klijn* (Kampen, 1988), pp. 262–75.

[22] Origen against Celsus in *The Ante-Nicene Fathers: Translations of the Fathers down to A. D. 325*, IV, ed. A. Roberts and J. Donaldson (Edinburgh, 1885). See also van Stempvoort, 'The Proteuangelium Jacobi', p. 414; Smid, *Protevangelium Jacobi: a Commentary*, pp. 15–17; Cullmann in Schneemelcher, ed., *New Testament Apocrypha*, I, 417; Erbetta, ed., *Gli Apocrifi del Nuovo Testamento*, I, 2, 15–17; Cothenet, 'Le Protévangile de Jacques', pp. 4257–8; and H. L. Strack, *Jesus, die Häretiker und die Christen nach den ältesten jüdischen Angaben* (Leipzig, 1910) on rabbinical anti-Christian views.

and who was turned out of doors by her husband, a carpenter by trade, because she was convicted of adultery; that after being driven away by her husband, and wandering about for a time, she disgracefully gave birth to Jesus, an illegitimate child, who having hired himself out as a servant in Egypt on account of his poverty, and having there acquired some miraculous powers, on which the Egyptians greatly pride themselves, returned to his own country, highly elated on account of them, and by means of these proclaimed himself a God"' (bk I, ch. xxviii).

While Origen sets out to refute this account point by point, implicitly the same claims are countered in the *Proteuangelium*'s very detailed account of the virgin birth, the chastity of Mary and Joseph's marriage and Joseph's adoptive paternity, and by the way in which the priests and all the people witness Mary's vindication from accusations of adultery. Joseph's advanced age also seems intended as a guarantee of Mary's virginity. The emphasis on the wealth of Mary's parents, who possess herds and servants, and Joseph's work as a building contractor of some kind (unlike Luke's stress on poverty in the *Magnificat* and in the birth story) seems likewise intended to combat the view that Mary was a poor spinning girl: in the *Proteuangelium* her spinning is sacred, unpaid work on the temple veil and only those of the tribe of David are allowed do this work. This, of course, also establishes Mary's Davidic descent, so that Jesus's connection with David is no longer dependent on Joseph; this tradition is already found in the second-century theologian Justin.[23] Mary's virginity *ante*, *in* and *post partum* is emphasized. Her purity before the birth is evident from the way in which she is kept from the world in her bedroom, served only by virgins, and in her subsequent sojourn in the temple, where she is fed by an angel. The birth of Jesus, while understood as a real birth (Mary is big with child and Jesus immediately takes Mary's breast) in distinction to the docetic view that Christ descended directly from heaven, is described in such a way that Mary's virginity can be seen to remain intact, as is evident also from Salome's testing. The birth is without pain, as in other early apocrypha such as the *Ascension of Isaiah* and the *Odes of Solomon*.[24] The Salome episode provides, too, a Jewish

---

[23] Cullmann in Schneemelcher, ed., *New Testament Apocrypha*, I, 417.

[24] The *Ascension of Isaiah* is translated in *New Testament Apocrypha*, ed. W. Schneemelcher, English translation ed. R. McL. Wilson (Cambridge and Louisville, KY, 1992), II, 603–20; the Odes of Solomon are translated in *The Odes of Solomon: the Syriac Texts*, ed. J. H. Charlesworth (Oxford, 1973), p. 82.

witness to the virgin birth, important because this very issue was one of the most contentious between Jews and Christians.[25] The four brothers and the sisters of Jesus, mentioned in Mark VI.3, who are most naturally regarded as the children of Mary and Joseph, here become the children of the widower Joseph's former marriage, so that Mary's virginity is also maintained after the birth of Christ. The *Proteuangelium* also contains the idea of Mary as second Eve, reversing the actions of the first.[26]

All of these details can be seen to issue from a desire to defend the purity and nobility of Mary against Jewish and pagan detractors; the unknown author has drawn on Old and New Testament stories to create the fictitious *uita* of an unblemished heroine. The preservation of authentic Jewish tradition is ruled out by such un-Jewish details as the upbringing of Mary in the temple. The question of the author's view of the nature of Anna's conception of Mary, however, is a difficult and debated one. The manuscript readings differ at crucial points (indicated in the summary above) on whether Joachim has a part in this conception or not. If one accepts the reading of the oldest manuscript, and some other manuscripts, and of the Syriac and Ethiopic translations, as well as the fourth-century testimony of St Epiphanius and the later Latin adaptation, the *Gospel of Pseudo-Matthew*, it appears that the angel announces to Joachim that his wife has already conceived, presumably therefore in the absence of her husband, as the angel's announcement to Anna was that she would conceive. Other manuscripts have instead of the perfect a future tense in the announcement to Joachim, reflecting unease at the theological implications of the perfect form.[27] When Anna greets Joachim on his return, the versions just listed again have a perfect form, while the majority of manuscripts has a future tense here also. Epiphanius attempted to get around the problem of the perfect form familiar to him

---

[25] See the discussion by K. Schreiner, *Maria. Jungfrau, Mutter, Herrscherin* (Munich and Vienna, 1994), pp. 415–23.

[26] *Proteuangelium*, 13.1, and see G. Kretschmar, ' "Natus ex Maria virgine": *Zur Konzeption und Theologie des Protevangelium Jacobi*', in *Anfänge der Christologie: Festschrift für Ferdinand Hahn zum 65. Geburtstag*, ed. C. Breytenbach and H. Paulsen (Göttingen, 1991), pp. 423–8.

[27] See de Strycker, *La forme*, pp. 81–3, 87–9 and 409–10; de Strycker, 'Die griechischen Handschriften', pp. 581–2; Smid, *Protevangelium Jacobi: a Commentary*, p. 41; M. Jugie, 'Le Protévangile de Jacques et l'Immaculée Conception', *Echos d'Orient* 14 (1911), 16–20.

15

by arguing that it must have a future reference, and the differing lengths of Anna's pregnancy in the manuscripts suggest disquiet as well, but it seems fairly certain that the perfect reading was the original one and this suggests that the author meant to imply a miraculous conception. This cannot, of course, be equated with the fully-fledged doctrine of Mary's immaculate conception, formulated a thousand years later, but it does stress the author's view of the extraordinary nature of her birth: her purity seems to date for him from her very conception.

The unknown second-century author of the *Proteuangelium*, therefore, seems to have drawn motifs for his account of Mary's birth and childhood from Old Testament infancy stories, in response to anti-Christian versions of Jesus's origins; the work is polemic in the guise of biography. So passionate is his defence of Mary's virginity that even some canonical details are omitted in the interest of exalting Mary's purity: there is no account of the Purification of Mary, for example, though Luke includes this and Anna is purified after the birth of Mary.[28]

## THE *PROTEUANGELIUM* IN LATIN

The *Proteuangelium* was translated into Latin, as well as the other languages listed above, but a complete Latin text has not survived. Parts, some of them very substantial, of different translations do survive, however, several of them incorporated in other texts.[29] Extracts from the *Proteuangelium* are included in the Barbarus Scaligeri, an Alexandrian compilation of the first half of the fifth century, which was translated into Latin in the fifth or sixth century.[30] About half of the text is incorporated in the Latin infancy gospel published by James from a thirteenth-century and a fourteenth-century manuscript, which draws also on the *Gospel of Pseudo-Matthew*, the *Libellus de natiuitate Sanctae Mariae*, pseudo-Augustine *Sermo* cxcv, the canonical gospels of Matthew and Luke and another unknown source; its version of the *Proteuangelium* was probably

---

[28] Cothenet, 'Le Protévangile de Jacques', p. 4266.

[29] See J. Gijsel, 'Het *Protevangelium Iacobi* in het Latijn', *Antiquité Classique* 50 (1981), 351–66, for an overview of the Latin versions. Unfortunately, J.-D. Kaestli, 'Le Protévangile de Jacques en latin. Etat de la question et perspectives nouvelles', *Revue d'histoire des textes* 26 (1996), 41–102, appeared too late to be taken into account here.

[30] See de Strycker, *La forme*, pp. 39–40; the work is edited by A. Schoene, *Eusebii Chronicorum liber prior* (Berlin, 1875), Appendix, pp. 177–239.

16

translated in the Carolingian period.[31] Paris, Bibliothèque Sainte-Geneviève, 2787 has an almost complete Latin *Proteuangelium*, covering chs. 1, 3 to 24, 2.[32] Montpellier, Bibliothèque Universitaire, Section de Médecine 55, a ninth-century legendary, contains parts of two separate translations of the *Proteuangelium*, one of chs. 1 to 8, 1, with some omissions, on fols. 94r–97v,[33] and the other of chs. 8, 2 to 25, 2, also with some omissions, on fols. 179r–82v.[34] While it is, of course, tempting to view them as two halves of the same translation, as Canal-Sánchez thought that they were, Gijsel argues that they are parts of two separate adaptations of an earlier translation.[35] Madrid, Real Academia de la Historia, 78 (eleventh century) has a very short fragment of a Latin translation and there is an even shorter one in the Fleury manuscript, Paris, Bibliothèque Nationale, nouv. acq. lat. 453 (tenth to eleventh century).[36] Fragments of a very free Latin *Proteuangelium* are also preserved in the fourteenth-century breviary from Soyons, Paris, Bibliothèque Nationale, nouv. acq. lat. 718, and of an even freer version in a fifteenth-century Mainz breviary, Paris, Bibliothèque Nationale, lat. 1062.[37] Vattioni has published a translation of chs. 1 to 7 of the *Proteuangelium* from the twelfth-century Vatican City, Biblioteca Apostolica Vaticana, Reginensis lat. 537[38] and this text is also found in Karlsruhe, Badische Landesbibliothek, K 506 (combined with *Pseudo-Matthew*)[39] and in the English manuscript, Cambridge, Pembroke College, 25, though this last

---

[31] M. R. James, *Latin Infancy Gospels: a New Text, with a Parallel Version from the Irish* (Cambridge, 1927); see also J. Gijsel, 'Les "Evangiles latins de l'Enfance" de M. R. James', *AB* 94 (1976), 289–302, who lists further manuscripts.

[32] This text, discovered by R. Beyers, has not yet been edited; see Beyers, *Libri de natiuitate sanctae Mariae*, pp. 132–3.

[33] J. M. Canal-Sánchez, 'Antiguas versiones latinas del Protoevangelio de Santiago', *Ephemerides Mariologicae* 18 (1968), 431–73.

[34] E. de Strycker and J. Gribomont, 'Une ancienne version latine du Protévangile de Jacques', *AB* 83 (1965), 365–410.

[35] See Gijsel's review of Canal-Sánchez's article in *AB* 87 (1969), 503–5, and his 'Het *Protevangelium Iacobi* in het Latijn'.

[36] Both edited by Canal-Sánchez in 'Antiguas versiones latinas', pp. 469–72.

[37] Both fragments are edited by J. de Aldama, 'Fragmentos de una versión latina del Protoevangelio de Santiago y una nueva adaptación de sus primeros capítulos', *Biblica* 43 (1962), 57–72.

[38] F. Vattioni, 'Frammento latino del Vangelo di Giacomo'.

[39] Signalled by Gijsel, 'Het *Protevangelium Iacobi* in het Latijn', p. 354, and in Geerard, *Clauis Apocryphorum*, p. 27.

is not signalled in the literature.[40] Gijsel constructs a stemma of all these different versions, which indicates two separate Latin translations of the *Proteuangelium*, both giving rise to different adaptations.[41]

THE GOSPEL OF PSEUDO-MATTHEW

More important than any of these versions, however, was a new text created by reworking the *Proteuangelium* and combining it with other sources, the Latin *Gospel of Pseudo-Matthew.*[42] This work is probably from the period 550 to 700[43] and seems to be the work of a monastic author.[44] The oldest manuscripts, already belonging to two separate families, A and P, are from the ninth century.[45] The *Gospel of Pseudo-Matthew* consists of (1) a prologue, which can be either a letter from the bishops Chromatius and Heliodorus to Jerome, asking him to translate a Hebrew Gospel by the apostle Matthew into Latin (hence the title *Pseudo-Matthew*), and Jerome's reply, promising them the text, or a translation of the epilogue to the *Proteuangelium;*[46] (2) a revised version of the *Proteuangelium* (*Pseudo-Matthew* chs. 1 to 17, 2);[47] (3) an account of the miracles performed by the child Jesus on the flight into Egypt, based on a different source; and

---

[40] See Clayton, *The Cult*, p. 4, n. 14.

[41] Gijsel, 'Het *Protevangelium Iacobi* in het Latijn', p. 366.

[42] A new edition of this work has recently appeared, too late to be taken fully into account here: *Libri de natiuitate Mariae: Pseudo-Matthaei Euangelium*, ed. J. Gijsel, Corpus Christianorum Series Apocryphorum 9 (Turnhout, 1997). I am grateful to Professor Gijsel for making his texts of the A and P families available to me in advance of publication. The standard edition of the text up to now has been that of Tischendorf, ed., *Evangelia Apocrypha*, pp. 51–111.

[43] Gijsel, *Die unmittelbare Textüberlieferung*, p. 12, but he says on p. 27 'um 600'. In Gijsel, ed., *Libri de natiuitate Mariae: Pseudo-Matthaei Euangelium*, p. 67, he dates to between the middle of the sixth century and the last decades of the eighth, and says that 'il est probable qu'il a vu le jour dans le premier quart du vii^e siècle'.

[44] Arguments for a monastic author were advanced by Amann, ed., *Le Protévangile de Jacques*, p. 106; Gijsel, *Die unmittelbare Textüberlieferung*, p. 13.

[45] All of the manuscripts are described and discussed by Gijsel, *Die unmittelbare Textüberlieferung*, but see the reservations expressed by G. Philippart, 'Le Pseudo-Matthieu au risque de la critique textuelle', *Scriptorium* 38 (1984), 121–31.

[46] The letters occur in the oldest manuscripts of the A family, while the *Proteuangelium* epilogue occurs in uncorrupted manuscripts of two of the four subgroups of the P family. For further discussion of the letters prologue, see below, pp. 85–6.

[47] The chapter numbers here are from Gijsel's edition.

(4) a fourth section, missing in most manuscripts, based on the *Infancy Gospel of Thomas* and recounting various exploits of Jesus as a child. The last part is clearly not part of the original text of *Pseudo-Matthew* and is not included in Gijsel's edition, but was included by Tischendorf in his very influential edition, with the label 'Pars Altera'. It was added to the text at the stage of the Q redaction, dated probably to the eleventh century, and is not found in the earlier manuscript families, A and P.[48] Gijsel argues that the flight into Egypt did not belong to the text originally either, even though it occurs in all of the complete manuscripts: there is no satisfactory transition to this section of the text; its lack of theological care and its sensationalism are alien to the first section; stylistically and structurally it is far clumsier than the preceding section; and one manuscript has a new title at the beginning of this section, *Narratio Elysiodorii de factis Iesu Christi*, which may well be a trace of the originally different origins of this section.[49] The oldest manuscripts of *Pseudo-Matthew* have a title *De natiuitate sanctae Mariae* or something very similar and this, Gijsel argues, is probably original, again suggesting that the section set in Egypt, which is about Jesus rather than Mary, is a later addition.[50] According to Gijsel, even the A family of manuscripts, the most primitive extant, does not give us the most ancient form of the text; we lack this, but his second family of manuscripts, the P group, goes back to this older form rather than to the A family. As a text *Pseudo-Matthew* was enormously successful: Gijsel lists 135 manuscripts and its success also seems to have been responsible for the lack of impact of the Latin translations of the *Proteuangelium*. As the Anglo-Saxon text edited here corresponds only to the first section of *Pseudo-Matthew*, that based on the *Proteuangelium*, I shall concentrate on that part of the Latin text in my discussion.

In reworking the *Proteuangelium*, the author of *Pseudo-Matthew* made changes which reflect a different purpose and a different age.[51] No longer is it necessary to combat pagan or Jewish polemic and the moral question of the best forms of the Christian life is instead much more dominant, with clear influences from hagiography. There is much more emphasis on Joachim in the Latin text: his piety and his pious use of his riches in the

---

[48] For the Q family of manuscripts, see Gijsel, *Die unmittelbare Textüberlieferung*, pp. 174–231.
[49] *Ibid.*, pp. 15–17.    [50] *Ibid.*, p. 17.    [51] *Ibid.*, pp. 12–15.

way in which he divides his possessions is stressed far more than was the case in the Greek source, and here the influence of the Book of Tobias is again to be felt. The monastic ideal is clearly crucial to Mary's vow of virginity, which is highlighted twice in the text (chs. 6, 2 and 12, 8) and which must be responsible for the introduction of the episode in which Abiathar offers bribes to have Mary marry his son. That Mary must have made such a vow was first suggested in the East by Gregory of Nyssa (*d. c.* 395) and in the West was deduced by Augustine (*d.* 430) from her response to Gabriel at the Annunciation.[52] This idea is not present in the earlier *Proteuangelium*, where there is no emphasis on a voluntary and resolute vow of virginity, though it is of course stressed that Mary remains a virgin. In *Pseudo-Matthew* it is crucial to that text's much more internalized view of Mary's purity: she discovers a new order of virginity for herself, as the high-priest says, 'A sola Maria nouus ordo tacendi inuentus est, quae promittit deo se uirginem permanere' (VIII, 1, A text), and she holds out against social pressure, correcting the priests and her relations by preaching that 'Deus in castitate primo omnium probatur et adoratur' (VII, 1, A text) rather than in the Jewish way of producing offspring. We can here see very clearly the cross-fertilization of apocrypha and church fathers: the earlier apocryphon had no doubt contributed to the climate of opinion which allowed the church fathers to go beyond the canonical gospels in this way and these patristic arguments then fed into the later apocryphon to idealize Mary even further.

Mary's cloistered and regular life in the temple, where she devotes herself to work and prayer, reflects this monastic background also. She in effect follows a monastic rule in her division of the day: 'Hanc autem sibi ipsa regulam statuerat ut a mane usque ad horam tertiam orationibus insisteret, a tertia uero usque ad nonam textrino se in opere occupabat. A nona uero hora iterum ab oratione non recedebat, usque dum illi dei angelus appareret de cuius manu escam acciperet, et ita melius atque melius in dei timore proficiebat' (VI, 2, A text). This is again not a feature of the *Proteuangelium*, which has almost no details about Mary's daily life in the temple, other than that she was fed by an angel. The fifteen steps of the temple which Mary climbs recall the fifteen gradual psalms, so prominent in monastic life.[53] Her inner dedication and moral

---

[52] De sancta uirginitate, IV.4 (PL 40, col. 398).
[53] Gijsel, *Die unmittelbare Textüberlieferung*, p. 30, n. 50.

worth are reflected also in her knowledge of divine law and in her outstanding virtue: 'Denique cum a maioribus suis uirginibus in dei laudibus agere docebatur, zelo nimio bonitatis satagebat ut in uigiliis inueniretur prior, in sapientia legis dei eruditior, in humilitate humilior, in carminibus dauiticis elegantior, in caritate gratiosior, in puritate purior, in omni uirtute perfectior' (VI, 2, A text). In this part of *Pseudo-Matthew*, she is clearly being presented as a model for dedicated virgins living according to a monastic life.

Increasing Marian piety is evident in the way in which Joseph's direct reproaches to Mary are omitted; he laments her pregnancy, but she is immediately defended by the five virgins who are her companions in his home. These five companions, who are not found in the *Proteuangelium*, also allow Mary to live a communal quasi-monastic life, dedicated to virginity, even when she moves from the temple to Joseph's home. The age-gap between Mary and Joseph is increased, too, by Joseph's already having grandchildren older than Mary when she is entrusted to him. Mary's own lineage is elaborated in *Pseudo-Matthew* also; in the *Proteuangelium* she is already considered of Davidic descent, but here Joachim belongs to the tribe of Judah and Anna to that of David. The author's desire to glorify Mary is evident as well in her title *regina uirginum*, a title confirmed by an angel after having been uttered in jest by the other virgins. The virgins ask Mary to pray for them (VIII, 5) and she has miraculous powers of healing, another new feature, reflecting a model of sanctity which had become conventional by the time of the composition of *Pseudo-Matthew*: 'Si quis autem de infirmantibus tetigisset eam, saluus ab ea eadem hora reuertebatur' (VI, 3, A text). Joseph is a far more humble figure in the Latin than in the Greek, a step further towards a saintly Joseph.

*Pseudo-Matthew* also smoothes out some inconsistencies between its source and the canonical infancy gospels: so, for example, it has Jesus born in a cave, from where Mary moves to a stable on the third day, and three days later the family settles in Bethlehem. Whereas in the *Proteuangelium* the adoration of the Magi immediately follows the birth, in *Pseudo-Matthew* it occurs two years later, in accordance with Matthew II.16. Some episodes from the canonical gospels, which had featured in the *Proteuangelium*, are omitted from the later text, such as the Visitation, but conversely *Pseudo-Matthew* adds to the *Proteuangelium* by including the Circumcision and the Purification. Altogether, *Pseudo-Matthew* is a much more smoothly flowing, consistent and detailed text, which witnesses to a significant growth in Marian devotion in the four or more centuries which separate it from its Greek source.

By implication, however, the nature of Mary's conception continues to cause problems. Joachim spends five months in the desert and takes another thirty days to return to Anna after the angel's announcement to him; Mary is born nine months after his return. However, the angel tells Joachim that he should know that Anna 'ex semine tuo concepisse filiam' (III, 2, A text, to which the P text adds 'quod tu nesciens reliquisti eam') and that he will find her 'habentem in utero' on his return and Anna greets Joachim with the news that she is pregnant, not that she will become so. The time-scale would seem again to rule out a normal conception, as in the case of the *Proteuangelium*. This is not commented upon in the text itself, which never announces a miraculous conception in the absence of Joachim, but it certainly goes beyond the Old Testament analogues of the simpler miracle of conception in a sterile couple.

As is evident already, the manuscripts of *Pseudo-Matthew* can be divided into groups, which are discussed in great detail by Gijsel. The two oldest families are A and P, while Q, which adds the section based on the *Infancy Gospel of Thomas*, as well as making numerous other changes, dates from around the eleventh century and R, which replaces parts of the text with parts of the *De natiuitate Mariae* and has a very idiosyncratic version of the miracles of the child Jesus, dates perhaps from the twelfth century.[54] Self-evidently, A and P are the branches important in a discussion of the Anglo-Saxon translation. A, which must go back to about, or before, 750,[55] seems to be closest to the original, but is not itself the original, and offers the most primitive extant form of *Pseudo-Matthew*, although brief passages are missing from all the manuscripts of this group. The oldest versions are often found in legendaries; this is no longer true of the more recent manuscripts, presumably because the apocryphal gospel was no longer considered suitable for liturgical use. The P form of the text, which also antedates 800 according to Gijsel, is a revision, not of A but of the original text, which aimed to improve the text stylistically, to change the pre-Vulgate biblical readings to Vulgate forms and to alter some details in the interest of decorum or consistency. Anna's bitter complaint about her childlessness, for example, is softened by the addition of 'tibi

---

[54] For the R manuscripts, see *ibid.*, pp. 232–53.    [55] *Ibid.*, p. 123.

gratias ago soli quia ut uoluisti ita ordinasti' (2, 5) and the other virgins' address to Mary in 8, 8 'cum sis ultima et humilis' becomes 'cum tu iunior sis omnibus'. Altogether, there are about 150 changes noted by Gijsel. None of the uncontaminated manuscripts of this group has the epistolary exchange between the bishops and Jerome and two of the four subgroups have a prologue based on the epilogue to the *Proteuangelium*. Gijsel considers this prologue to be the original prologue to *Pseudo-Matthew*, which was probably replaced by the apocryphal exchange between the bishops and Jerome at the A stage of the text.

The early chapters of *Pseudo-Matthew* were reworked and sanitized even further in the tenth or very early eleventh century to give the even more theologically acceptable *De natiuitate Mariae*, which in its turn ousted its source to a considerable degree.[56] The apocryphal exchange between the bishops and Jerome is also found prefacing this text, transferred from *Pseudo-Matthew*. Joseph is not a widower in this text but has never been married, so making it more agreeable to orthodox views. St Jerome had already objected to the view that Jesus's brothers in the gospels were sons of Joseph, arguing instead that they were cousins, and here Pseudo-Jerome is brought into line with Jerome himself.

---

[56] *Ibid.*, p. 13; see also Beyers, ed., *De natiuitate Mariae*, and 'De natiuitate Mariae: problèmes d'origines', *Revue de théologie et de philosophie* 122 (1990), 171–88.

# 2

# The death and assumption of Mary: the Syriac and Greek traditions

In contrast to the relatively straightforward and linear development of the textual tradition concerning the birth and childhood of Mary, the apocryphal texts on her death and assumption are manifold and their textual connections confused and often obscure, with significant differences among apocrypha in different languages and even within the same language. Different terms are used in connection with Mary's death (*dormitio*, *transitus* and *assumptio*) and it is difficult to be certain of the exact implications of the early uses of these terms and whether there are important differences in meaning among them. Some modern scholars use them indiscriminately, others wish to distinguish between dormition and assumption: by dormition meaning simply the death of Mary and separation of her body and soul, with her soul being taken to heaven and her body somewhere else, known or unknown; by assumption generally, though not always, meaning the resurrection of Mary's body, its lasting reunion with her soul and the transfer of both together.[1] When the dogma of the assumption was proclaimed in 1950 soul and body were said to have been transferred to heavenly glory after the Virgin had completed the course of her earthly life, but in the apocryphal texts they are generally transferred to a paradise separate from heaven; the term assumption will be used for both destinations here. A distinction can also be made, as it is by Mimouni, between assumption without resurrection, underlying which is the concept of immortality, and assumption with resurrection, which of course implies the concept of Mary's death. The 1950 definition does not commit itself on this point. The dormition is held by Mimouni to be the prior tradition, which then developed into

[1] See the discussion by Mimouni, *Dormition*, pp. 7–21.

24

that of the assumption, but that is by no means self-evident from the texts, unless we take assumption to mean only assumption of body and soul into heaven. That is certainly a later development within the tradition.

The recent *Clauis Apocryphorum* counts sixty-four different apocrypha of the death and assumption, some of them fragments, in Syriac, Greek, Coptic (both Sahidic and Bohairic dialects), Arabic, Ethiopic, Latin, Georgian, Armenian and Irish.[2] As this chapter concerns the development of the tradition, especially in relation to the Old English texts, I shall focus on texts in those languages crucial to that development: Syriac, Greek, Coptic and Latin.

The apocrypha concerning Mary's death seem to be significantly later than those of her birth and attempts to date them to the second century have failed to win any general acceptance. The earliest manuscripts are Syriac and date from the end of the fifth or the beginning of the sixth century, which means that the tradition concerning the Virgin's death must have developed by the second half of the fifth century and that the Marian feast of 15 August, attested in Jerusalem from the fifth century on as a feast dedicated to the memory of Mary and centring on her divine maternity, must have developed into a feast commemorating her death during this period. As feasts in memory of saints were generally celebrated on the day of their death – the *dies natalis* of the saint – the existence of a feast in memory of Mary would naturally have given rise to conjecture about her death and this may well have led to the development of accounts of the death and the fate of Mary's body and soul.[3] Mimouni conjectures, convincingly, that the coincidence of this transition to an interest in Mary's death with the aftermath of the Council of Chalcedon must be significant and that the growth of interest in Mary's death took place in Monophysite circles, always favourable to Mary.[4] Van

---

[2] Geerard, *Clauis Apocryphorum*, pp. 74–95.

[3] R. Laurentin, *Court traité sur la Vierge Marie*, 5th edn (Paris, 1968), pp. 59–61, and Mimouni, *Dormition*, pp. 662–3.

[4] *Dormition*, p. 665. The Council of Chalcedon, held in 451, was called to deal with the heresy of Eutyches, who denied that Christ's manhood was consubstantial with that of other people and argued that there were two natures before, but only one after, the union of both in the incarnate Christ. The statement of faith drawn up by the council was not accepted by the Monophysites, who came into being as a distinct group immediately after Chalcedon and who argued that Christ had only one, divine, nature.

Esbroeck, too, connects the Monophysites of Gethsemane with the feast of Mary's death and regards the apocrypha as texts composed to justify the developing interest in the death.[5] The earliest Syriac manuscripts seem to be of Monophysite origin, lending further support to this theory.[6]

All the apocrypha have some details in common (Mary is told in advance of her death, which takes place in Jerusalem; all or some of the apostles arrive, almost always miraculously, to be present; the Jews attempt to sabotage the funeral) but other details differ greatly (the interval between Jesus's and Mary's death varies from two to fifteen to twenty-two years; Mary's house is variously localized in Bethlehem and Jerusalem, while she is buried at what is described as the Mount of Olives or the valley of Jehoshaphat or at Gethsemane;[7] her body is preserved incorrupt in paradise, with or without the soul, or it decays in the tomb for three or for 206 days before being resurrected and assumed).[8] The *transitus* texts are very much intermeshed in debates concerning belief in the death, resurrection and assumption of Mary, which were formulated at a very early stage, whereas what was to become the doctrine of the immaculate conception, which could be regarded as implicit in the birth stories, was not formulated until the twelfth century and accordingly did not play the same role in the details of those narratives. As the development of belief and doctrine is implicit in the *transitus* narratives and as so many of the elements in the two Old English apocrypha edited here appear in other versions, some of these stories will be summarized in the course of the chapter.

There have been many attempts to classify these texts and to arrive at a chronology which would enable the establishment of an *Ur*-text, but agreement has been hard to reach. The *Clauis Apocryphorum* summarizes six of these different attempts at classification according to chronological development, and they differ widely.[9] Two recent studies, those of Van

If Christ has no human nature, then this has obvious repercussions for views on his mother. On the Monophysite position with regard to the Virgin, see below, pp. 43–5.

[5] Van Esbroeck, 'Les textes littéraires', p. 279, but see Mimouni, *Dormition*, pp. 637–40.

[6] Mimouni, *Dormition*, pp. 665–6.

[7] All three places are in fact in close proximity to each other: the Mount of Olives is the highest hill in the east of Jerusalem, separated from the city by the valley of Jehoshaphat, and the Garden of Gethsemane is near its foot.

[8] Mimouni, *Dormition*, pp. 69–71.    [9] Geerard, *Clauis Apocryphorum*, pp. 74–7.

Esbroeck and Mimouni, seem to me particularly useful, however, even though they are incompatible in their conclusions, and I shall use elements of both of them extensively here.[10]

Van Esbroeck divides the apocrypha into two families on the basis of similarities among texts: the 'Palm from the tree of life' and 'Bethlehem and the burning of Incense'.[11] The first group is characterized by the presence of the palm from the beginning of the story: it is brought to Mary from paradise when she is told of her forthcoming death and it plays a major role in the narrative. The apostles debate on who is to carry the palm and it is used to heal the hands of the Jew who attacks Mary's bier and who subsequently heals his fellow-Jews from blindness by means of it. In the early versions of this family, Mary's body is placed under the tree of life, from which the palm was taken (the Syriac *Obsequies* and the Greek *R*, for example).[12] The Coptic accounts form a separate group within this family. In the other family, characteristic features are Mary's journey to Bethlehem from Jerusalem, the arrival of the apostles in Bethlehem and their journey back to Jerusalem with Mary, where she dies, and the constant incense burning which punctuates the text. Mary's body is preserved in paradise at the end of these texts, but without mention of the tree of life. Key texts in this family are the Greek *Pseudo-John* and the Syriac *Six Books*.

The second, more recent work, by Mimouni, builds on earlier research, particularly the work of Baldi and Mosconi and of Cothenet.[13] Mimouni is, however, often unreliable in details, especially textual details, and this adversely affects his alternative scheme of grouping the texts and, his main concern, of tracing the development of the tradition. In a series of articles and in his book, *Dormition et Assomption de Marie*, he classifies the dormition and assumption apocrypha into three groups according to two

---

[10] Several different approaches, including that of Van Esbroeck, are critically discussed by Mimouni, *Dormition*, pp. 44–54.

[11] Van Esbroeck, 'Les textes littéraires'.

[12] See Manns, *Le récit*, pp. 122–4, on the tree of life as a palm.

[13] *Dormition* is Mimouni's major work; see also 'La tradition littéraire syriaque de l'histoire de la dormition et de l'assomption de Marie: Préliminaire à une nouvelle édition critique', *Parole de l'Orient* 15 (1988–9), 143–68; '"Histoire de la Dormition et de l'Assomption de Marie": Une nouvelle hypothèse de recherche', *Studia Patristica* 19 (Louvain, 1989), 372–80; 'Genèse et évolution'; and 'Les Transitus Mariae sont-ils vraiment des apocryphes?'

main criteria, one topographical,[14] the other doctrinal, but he draws also on liturgical developments and on archaeological discoveries, particularly in Jerusalem. The strength of his book is in the range of evidence used, but he does not take much account of literary similarities among different texts and this is a major weakness in his study. Mimouni's three groups are (A) all of the Syriac texts and the Greek *Pseudo-John*, as well as texts dependent on them, which, he says, localize the house of Mary in Bethlehem and which attest to belief in the dormition only; (B) the Coptic texts and texts dependent on them, which form a transitional group and which localize Mary's house in Jerusalem and attest to belief in the dormition or the dormition and assumption, without any fusion of these separate beliefs; and (C) the other Greek and the Latin texts, as well as texts dependent on them, which all localize Mary's house in Jerusalem and all attest to belief in the assumption, either with or without a resurrection. Mimouni's groups, therefore, cut across those of Van Esbroeck, who focuses on textual families rather than on the beliefs encapsulated in each text. They differ crucially in the group to which they assign a key text, the Syriac *Obsequies*, thought by both to be the earliest surviving text in the entire tradition, and this is fundamental to how they view the tradition and its development. As will become evident, Van Esbroeck seems to me to offer by far the better analysis of the texts.

In this chapter I shall follow Van Esbroeck's division of the texts into two families, while drawing on much of the extra-textual material available in Mimouni's study. For convenience I shall take what for the purposes of this study is the less important group first, the Bethlehem and the burning of incense group, as this is more limited, has almost no influence in the Latin West and is therefore not the family to which the Old English texts belong.

## BETHLEHEM AND THE BURNING OF INCENSE

To this family belong a group of Syriac texts and the Greek *Pseudo-John*, extant also in Latin, Arabic and Georgian translations. While in the Syriac texts the story of Mary's death is part of a longer narrative to do

---

[14] For which he prefers the term topological, on the grounds that it does not evoke the geographical realities of the places mentioned: see *Dormition*, p. 5, n. 7.

with the Jews and the finding of the true cross, the Greek text lacks all these extraneous elements and concentrates on the Marian narrative.[15] For this reason it will be convenient to summarize it here, as it can serve to characterize the entire textual family.

The text begins with Mary, who lives in Bethlehem, going frequently to her son's sepulchre in Jerusalem to pray, invisible to the watchmen. On a Friday the angel Gabriel comes to her at the sepulchre and announces her imminent death, according to her own request. She returns to Bethlehem, where three virgins minister to her, and prays that John and the other apostles be sent to her. John, the intermittent first-person narrator, is caught up by a cloud in Ephesus and brought to Bethlehem. Mary tells him that she has heard the Jews say that they will burn her body when she is dead, but John assures her that her body will not see corruption. All of the apostles, including Paul, are then likewise brought on clouds to Mary, those apostles already dead having been told by the Holy Spirit that this is not the resurrection but the day of Mary's death. At Mary's request, they tell her how they came to her. Celestial voices and 'a voice as of the Son of Man' are heard and the saints come to Mary's house, where many miracles occur, so that multitudes come also from Jerusalem seeking a cure. Having been healed, 'all Jerusalem returned from Bethlehem'.[16] The Jewish priests and people are so enraged by this that they decide to send men against Mary and the apostles, but a mile from Bethlehem the Jews see a terrible vision and cannot proceed. The chief priests then inform the governor and demand that Mary be driven out of Bethlehem and, compelled, he sends a thousand men. The apostles and Mary are warned by the Holy Spirit and are brought on a cloud to Jerusalem, where they sing praises for five days. It is then made known to the governor that Mary is in her house in Jerusalem (she has two houses, then, one in Bethlehem and one in Jerusalem) and the Jews come, desiring to burn the house, but are prevented by an angel who causes fire to issue from the house and burn them. The governor believes as a result,

[15] There are numerous manuscripts of the Greek *Pseudo-John* and no modern critical edition. The text was edited by Tischendorf, *Apocalypses Apocryphae*, pp. 95–112, using only five manuscripts. See Mimouni, *Dormition*, pp. 118–20 on the manuscripts. The text is translated by Elliott, *Apocryphal New Testament*, pp. 701–8, under the title 'The Discourse of St John the Divine concerning the Falling Asleep of the Holy Mother of God'.

[16] Elliott, *Apocryphal New Testament*, p. 704.

as do some of the Jews. The Holy Spirit then tells the apostles that the Annunciation, the Nativity of Christ, Christ's entrance into Jerusalem and the resurrection all happened on Sunday and that the Last Judgement and the death of Mary will likewise fall on this day. On the same Sunday Christ appears with multitudes of angels and calls upon Mary to rejoice. He tells her that her body will be translated to paradise and her soul will be 'in the heavens in the treasuries of my Father in surpassing brightness'.[17] Mary prays that the Lord grant help to all who entreat in her name and again that he sanctify every place where there is a memorial of her name and accept the offerings and prayers of those who glorify him through her name; her wishes are granted. The apostles then begin to sing, whereupon Mary's face shines and she blesses each one of the apostles, and then 'the Lord spread forth his unstained hands and received her holy and spotless soul'.[18]

As the apostles carry out her body a Jew named Jephonias attacks the bed on which Mary is laid, but his hands are cut off by an angel and are left hanging in the air. The Jews and Jephonias himself then recognize that Mary is the mother of God and Jephonias is healed when he begs her for mercy. The apostles carry Mary and lay her in a new tomb in Gethsemane. A sweet odour comes from the tomb and the voices of invisible angels are heard glorifying Christ for three days. After three days the voices were heard no more and 'we all perceived that her spotless and precious body was translated into paradise'.[19] After it is translated the apostles see Elizabeth, Anna (Mary's mother), Abraham, Isaac, Jacob and David singing and all of the choirs of saints worshipping Mary. Such is the ending in Tischendorf, who followed one manuscript (his C) only. The other manuscripts he collated, however, apart from one, all have the apostles transported on clouds to paradise, along with Mary, where they take part in the ceremony of worshipping Mary's body. This accords with the Syriac texts in this group, in which the apostles are also brought to paradise, and as a result is likely to be original. As Cothenet points out, there is a logical evolution from the apostles' visit to the next world in the Syriac, to their participation in the paradisal ceremony in most of the *Pseudo-John* manuscripts, to the last vestige of the apostles' journey, the mere vision of such a ceremony in Tischendorf's C, 'dernier terme de

---

[17] *Ibid.*, p. 706.     [18] *Ibid.*, p. 707.     [19] *Ibid.*, p. 708.

[20] Cothenet, 'Marie dans les apocryphes', p. 122.

l'évolution'.[20] What we have here, therefore, is a text which affirms only the dormition of Mary: while her soul is in heaven, her body is preserved incorrupt in paradise, without a reunification of the two. As in the Syriac texts in this group, Mary shows no fear of death in *Pseudo-John*.[21]

Tischendorf thought that this text dated from the fourth century, or perhaps even earlier,[22] while Jugie placed it in the second half of the sixth century, between 550 and 580, pointing out that it does not mention a feast of the death of Mary, but insists on her death on a Sunday rather than the specific date of 15 August.[23] As 15 August was fixed as the date of the feast throughout the Byzantine empire by the Emperor Maurice (582–602), the apocryphon must predate this decree. The feast of the death was already celebrated in Jerusalem on 15 August (superseding the feast of the memory of Mary on the same date) from the end of the fifth or the beginning of the sixth century, however, and this text seems to have originated in Jerusalem, where it was probably used liturgically.[24] This means that the text must have been composed by the beginning of the sixth century at the latest, not after 550 as Jugie thought, while the feast of the memory of Mary, to which the text alludes, provides us with a date after which it must have been composed.[25] This feast is found in Jerusalem from the fifth century onwards, so that the text could be from the fifth or early sixth century; Mimouni inclines towards the latter date.[26]

This Greek text is clearly related to the fragmentary Syriac text edited by Wright from London, British Library, syr. add. 14484, fols. 9r–11r, a ninth- or tenth-century manuscript,[27] to the almost complete account in London, British Library, syr. add. 12174, fols. 449r–452r,[28] a manuscript of the end of the twelfth century, and to the Syriac *Six Books*[29] and *Five*

---

[21] See Rivière, 'Rôle du démon', pp. 99–100.

[22] *Apocalypses Apocryphae*, pp. xxix–xlvi.     [23] Jugie, *La mort*, p. 117.

[24] See Mimouni, *Dormition*, p. 124, and 'La lecture liturgique et les apocryphes du Nouveau Testament. Le cas de la Dormitio grecque de Pseudo-Jean', *Orientalia Christiana Periodica* 59 (1993), 403–25.

[25] See Cothenet, 'Marie dans les apocryphes', pp. 118–19; Mimouni, *Dormition*, p. 124.

[26] Mimouni, *Dormition*, p. 124.

[27] Wright, ed., *Contributions*, pp. 18–24 (English translation).

[28] *Ibid.*, pp. 24–41 (English translation).

[29] Wright, 'Departure of my Lady Mary', 6, 417–48 (first part of Syriac text), 7, 108–28 (second part of Syriac text) and 129–60 (English translation). Other manuscripts are signalled by Mimouni, *Dormition*, pp. 91–2, n. 64.

*Books*.[30] All present essentially the same story of the death, but there are many other elements in the Syriac.

The most important of these texts is the Syriac narrative known as the *Six Books* or *Pseudo-James*, which is preserved in numerous manuscripts, of which the oldest dates from the second half of the sixth century, though palimpsest fragments attributed to the fifth century are extant.[31] Liturgical indications in the text also support a date before the end of the sixth century.[32] It is a long narrative, divided into six books: the first relates the origin of the work and contains elements from the story of the finding of the true cross; the second contains the correspondence between Abgar and the emperor Tiberius demanding that the emperor punish the Jews for crucifying Jesus and it describes the gathering of the apostles; the third book tells of miracles performed by the Virgin; the fourth of the death; the fifth of the Virgin's visit to paradise; and the sixth of her visit to hell. Although known as *Pseudo-James*, the prologue attributes the work to the twelve apostles (two to each book) and explains that it was discovered by means of the appearance of John the Evangelist in a vision at Ephesus.[33] John is central to this work too, then, and the prologue also contains a letter from James, Bishop of Jerusalem (and supposed author of the *Proteuangelium*), testifying to the writing of this book by the apostles. In this way the narrative furnishes itself with impeccable credentials. The prologue also says that the work was translated from Greek into Syriac at Ephesus.[34] In the story, which is largely similar to the Greek just summarized, a noteworthy feature is the way in which Mary is laid in the tomb (a bench in the third of three caves in the Mount of Olives) while still alive and in which the attack by the Jew on the bier also takes place while she is alive. In placing Mary's death next to her tomb at the Mount of Olives, this text connects to a tradition, attested from the middle of the fifth until the middle of the sixth century, placing Mary's death (as distinct from her burial) in the valley of the Mount of Olives.[35] Her

---

[30] A. Smith-Lewis, ed., *Apocrypha Syriaca*, pp. 12–69 (English translation). Van Esbroeck, 'Les textes littéraires', p. 266, regards the *Six Books* and the *Five Books* as one text, while Mimouni, *Dormition*, pp. 102–3, is more cautious and prefers separate sigla.

[31] The fragments attributed to the fifth century were published, without translation, by Smith-Lewis, ed., *Apocrypha Syriaca*.

[32] Mimouni, *Dormition*, p. 99.

[33] Wright, 'Departure of my Lady Mary', pp. 131–3.     [34] *Ibid.*, p. 133.

[35] Mimouni, *Dormition*, p. 97, n. 76.

death happens here only in the fourth book, when Eve, Anna, Elizabeth, Adam and other patriarchs come to greet her, followed by a procession of heavenly chariots and Christ. Mary's soul goes from her and Christ sends it to 'the mansions of the Father's house'. The apostles close her eyes and are then commanded to place Mary on a chariot of light which they bear to the 'paradise of Eden', where the just await future bliss.[36] There is a contradiction between the Holy Spirit's command to the apostles to place Mary in the tomb (the cave) and the lack of any description of this later in the text, as the body of Mary is taken to the 'paradise of Eden' immediately after her death. Christ then comes to Mary in paradise and restores her to life in order to see paradise, heaven and hell, before bringing her back to the 'paradise of Eden'; it is not clear whether body and soul remain in paradise or body only. Her soul may in fact have been in paradise from the moment of her death, as the text does not specify whether its destination is paradise or heaven: the 'mansions of the Father's house' described later in the text are in the 'paradise of Eden', suggesting that her soul and body had been brought separately to paradise to be reunited there.[37] The description of Mary's fate after death is not at all as clear as in the Greek *Pseudo-John*, therefore, which unambiguously separates body and soul, and casts doubt on Mimouni's classification of both together as dormition, not assumption, texts. Following Cothenet, he argues that Mary's resurrection is merely a provisional one, but this is far from being obvious from the text.[38] Many of the texts themselves resist clear doctrinal categories and Van Esbroeck's literary divisions, which allow for the fluidity of beliefs demonstrated in the endings of the texts, are far more helpful.

The resuscitation of the Virgin's body in order to participate in the visit to hell was necessary according to Semitic ideas of the relationship between body and soul, according to Cothenet: 'Pour eux l'âme séparée ne peut acquérir aucune nouvelle connaissance et ne conserve qu'une existence fort diminuée'.[39] On seeing the torments awaiting the evil, the Virgin begs Christ to have mercy on them at the Day of Judgement. The work is notable also for its emphasis on Sunday, as in the Greek text – this insistence seems to have a polemical purpose, but it is not entirely

---

[36] Wright, 'Departure of my Lady Mary', p. 152.   [37] *Ibid.*, p. 156.

[38] Mimouni, *Dormition*, pp. 81–4; Cothenet, 'Marie dans les apocryphes', pp. 124–5.

[39] 'Marie dans les apocryphes', p. 128.

clear against whom the polemic is directed.[40] This work gave rise to the Syriac *Transitus* called the *Five Books* (of which only palimpsest fragments dated to the end of the fifth or the beginning of the sixth century have been preserved), the Ethiopic *Six Books* and the Arabic *Six Books*.

A poetic homily in Syriac on Mary's death, attributed to the Monophysite Jacob of Sarug (449–521) and probably genuine, describes the death of Mary on top of the Mount of Olives and her burial in an unknown place.[41] The homily dates itself in the *incipit* by reference to a council in 489, so that it provides us with another late fifth-century Monophysite witness to interest in Mary's death.

These Syriac and Greek narratives, therefore, form a group which is characterized by the way in which Mary's house is placed in Bethlehem (though with a doublet in Jerusalem where the texts cover the whole story) and by a very serene account of her death, in the face of which she shows only longing and no fear.[42] Her body is preserved incorrupt in paradise, awaiting the Last Day, while her soul is in heaven in the Greek text and its fate is unclear in the Syriac *Six Books*, but it seems to be in paradise. Underlying this narrative are Jewish ideas concerning the necessity to undergo the Last Judgement before experiencing the fullness of joy awaiting the elect,[43] which meant that Mary could not yet participate fully in heaven, coupled with a reluctance to submit the body of the mother of God to decay. Characteristic of many of the texts in this group also is the journey Mary and the apostles make to paradise after Mary's death and her journey to hell and heaven, a theme characteristic of Judaism, in which it is applied to the prophets, and of early Christianity, as in the *Apocalypses* of Peter and Paul, from the second half of the second and the first half of the third centuries respectively.[44] These texts can be divided into two groups, one centred on the Syriac *Pseudo-James* (the *Six Books* and translations of them, the *Five Books* and the fragmentary texts published by Wright) and the second on the Greek *Pseudo-John* (*Pseudo-John* and the texts dependent on it), but it is not yet possible to be certain

---

[40] See Mimouni, *Dormition*, pp. 99–100, and Van Esbroeck, 'Le culte de la Vierge de Jérusalem à Constantinople aux vi$^e$ et vii$^e$ siècles', *Revue des études byzantines* 46 (1988), 181–90.

[41] Mimouni, *Dormition*, pp. 105–9.  [42] See Rivière, 'Rôle du démon', pp. 101–2.

[43] F. Manns, 'La mort de Marie dans le texte de la *Dormition de Marie*', *Augustinianum* 19 (1979), 507–15, and Mimouni, *Dormition*, p. 60.

[44] Mimouni, *Dormition*, p. 60, and Cothenet, 'Marie dans les apocryphes', pp. 127–8.

which developed first and what the links between the texts are, though they are clearly close.[45] The strong probability is that the Syriac texts are prior: Van Esbroeck points out that *Pseudo-John* is the end result of a process of development, not a starting point, and that the attribution to John the Evangelist must postdate the explanation of this attribution in the Syriac *Six Books*.[46] As against this, the prologue of the *Six Books* says that they were translated from Greek into Syriac at Ephesus.

## THE PALM FROM THE TREE OF LIFE

### THE SYRIAC *OBSEQUIES*

The second family of texts, the palm from the tree of life family, contains what is thought to be the earliest of all the *transitus* texts, the fragmentary Syriac *Obsequies*, and to this family belong also most of the Greek texts, almost all of the Latin, the Old Irish text, the Coptic texts (which hold a place slightly apart from the others) and the Ethiopic *Liber Requiei*, an immensely important text as it agrees almost word for word with the Syriac *Obsequies* where both texts overlap and can be used, to some extent, to supply the missing parts of the Syriac. The *Obsequies of the Holy Virgin*, as Wright entitled it, was published by him from fragments, some of them palimpsests, in the British Library, which date from the end of the fifth or the sixth century (Wright dated them first to the second half of the fifth century, subsequently to the fifth or sixth century).[47] Some of

---

[45] *Ibid.*, p. 59. Jugie, *La mort*, pp. 120–1, argued that the Syriac *Six Books*, which is about ten times the length of the Greek, is dependent on the Greek, while van Esbroeck, 'Les textes littéraires', pp. 269–70, argues that the dependence is possibly in the other direction and Mimouni that the differences between the two texts are such that, despite their links, it is preferable to consider them independently, though he seems to incline towards viewing the Greek as an abbreviated version of a lost text from which stem the Syriac *Six Books* and *Five Books* (Mimouni, *Dormition*, pp. 103–4).

[46] Van Esbroeck, 'Les textes littéraires', pp. 270 and 275.

[47] Wright, ed., *Contributions*, pp. 42–51; other, briefer, fragments are transcribed in the introduction to the same volume, pp. 10–16, some with an English summary, others without. Parts of the text not translated by Wright are translated and discussed by Wenger, *L'assomption*, pp. 63–4, n. 1. Wright dated the fragments to the second half of the fifth century in *Contributions*, p. 11, and to the fifth or sixth century in *Catalogue of the Syriac Manuscripts in the British Museum Acquired since the Year 1838* (London, 1870), I, 369. See Mimouni, *Dormition*, p. 79.

these fragments are very difficult to decipher, but British Library add. 14665, fols. 21r–24r, which are not translated by Wright, contain parts of the story of the death of Mary. The beginning is missing so we do not know where this narrative located the house of Mary or how her imminent death was announced to her. What survives begins with the apostles gathered around Mary; Jesus arrives and greets both them and Mary, while Mary salutes him, calling herself the anointed of the Lord. Mary's soul then leaves her body, her face suffused with happiness, and Christ takes it and gives it to Michael, who wraps it in precious material of indescribable brightness. Peter then begins to speak to Christ. The next folio has a description of the funeral procession, with the Jewish high-priests hearing the singing and learning of the death of Mary; then of the blinding of the Jews by the angels; of the Jew who tries to overthrow the bier touching it where the palm is and having his arms fixed to the bier and then cut off; the healing of the Jew's arms; and his receiving part of the palm from Peter, by means of which he heals five thousand blinded people.

The first of the longer fragments (translated by Wright) of this text contains a story told by Paul about Solomon and about vain attempts to buy off death. At the end, the other apostles ask Paul to go on speaking, saying that the Lord has sent him to gladden them during 'these three days' (which they are spending watching before the entrance to Mary's tomb) but in fact because they are reluctant to reveal the Lord's 'glorious secrets' to him.[48] Paul asks them instead to tell him what they preach and is answered in turn by Peter, who preaches constant fasting, by John, who preaches the necessity for strict virginity in order to see God, and by Andrew, who preaches total separation from the world.[49] When Paul criticizes all three teachings as too severe for those new in the faith the other apostles are angry, but Jesus appears and supports Paul's policy of leading people gently to the faith, telling him also not to be upset that the apostles have not revealed the mysteries to him, because what is on earth has been revealed to them, but what is in the heavens will be taught to him (a clear allusion to the *Apocalypse of Paul*). The terms in which Christ supports Paul are surprisingly strong and notable especially for the anti-Petrine attitude: 'And hail to thee, Paul, thou adviser of good things!

[48] Wright, ed., *Contributions*, pp. 43–4.
[49] On this discussion, see Gribomont, 'Le plus ancien Transitus'.

Verily I say unto thee, Peter, that thy counsels were at all times detrimental, thine and Andrew's and John's. But I say unto you that ye should receive those of Paul.'[50] Gribomont has discussed this passage in the light of debates about encratism and has suggested that it fits the conditions of the Syriac church in the period when it was in the process of adopting a Mediterranean ecclesiastical system, with tensions resulting between proponents of ancient local traditions and the new.[51] Such a discussion seems to have had an independent existence also, as is testified by the Ethiopic *Book of the Mysteries of Heaven and Earth*.[52]

Jesus then summons Michael and orders him to have the angels take the body of Mary into the clouds, followed by the apostles, and he orders the clouds to go to the entrance to paradise: 'And when they had entered Paradise, the body of Mary went to the tree of life; and they brought her soul and made it enter into her body'.[53] The angels are then sent back to their places and the apostles ask Christ to show them the place of torment, as he had previously promised. They are all, including Mary, taken on a cloud to the west; the Lord speaks to the angels of the pit and the earth springs upwards, revealing the torments. The tormented souls appeal to Michael for respite, and Mary and the apostles fall down 'because of the distress of those who were in the pit'.[54] Michael tells them that the angels constantly intercede for all creation. Unfortunately, the rest of this episode has not survived. The next fragment consists of a story told by Michael to Mary about the bones of Joseph and the last fragment consists of a conversation between Jesus and the apostles about trees which threw down stinking worms at the apostles. The story of Joseph comes from a well-attested Jewish midrash[55] and that of the trees and the worms also has many Jewish analogues.[56] These fragments can be put in their proper order by comparison with the Ethiopic *Liber Requiei*, which contains all of these elements as part of a full apocryphon, in a form strikingly close to the Syriac fragments: it is in fact the opposite of Wright's order.[57]

---

[50] Wright, ed., *Contributions*, p. 46.

[51] Gribomont, 'Le plus ancien Transitus', p. 246.

[52] 'Le livre des mystères du ciel et de la terre', ed. J. Perruchon, *Patrologia Orientalis* 1 (1907), 1–97, at 86–7; see Manns, *Le récit*, p. 79.

[53] Wright, ed., *Contributions*, pp. 46–7.      [54] *Ibid.*, p. 47.

[55] Cothenet, 'Marie dans les apocryphes', p. 129; Manns, *Le récit*, pp. 76–7.

[56] Manns, *Le récit*, pp. 75–6.

[57] See Arras, ed., *De transitu*, II, vii. The manuscripts are fifteenth and eighteenth century.

The *Obsequies*, the oldest extant apocryphon, has generally been cited as a witness to the resurrection of Mary's body,[58] as it describes the placing of her soul back into her body under the tree of life in paradise (where the soul has been in the interim is not specified, neither here nor in the closest parallels). Both Cothenet and Mimouni, however, argue that this is not the case.[59] By comparing this Syriac text with the other Syriac witnesses, they deduce that the reuniting of body and soul is merely a temporary one, to allow Mary to witness the torments of hell with the apostles.[60] According to them, the other Syriac versions of the story, without the breaks which the fragmentary nature of this text impose, show that, once the tour of hell is over, Mary's body is placed back under the tree of life in paradise, to await the general resurrection on the Last Day, while her soul is taken to dwell with God. Her resurrection is, then, according to Cothenet and Mimouni, a provisional one, not the permanent resurrection of a reunited body and soul. Their main witness to this is the Syriac *Six Books*, as the other two Syriac texts in question are also fragmentary, and it is questionable whether this is actually what the *Six Books* contain: they never specify a separate fate for Mary's soul when she is returned to paradise.[61] As well as misrepresenting the *Six Books* somewhat, Cothenet and Mimouni also do not give sufficient weight, I believe, to the important differences between the *Obsequies* and the other Syriac texts and to the similarities between the *Obsequies* and the Ethiopic and Old Irish texts. By separating the *Obsequies* and placing them in a different textual tradition to all the other surviving Syriac texts, Van Esbroeck's discussion is radically different to that of Mimouni. Mimouni includes the *Obsequies* in the *Pseudo-James* group of his A family, but in textual terms there are very significant differences between this and all the A family and Van Esbroeck's division is, I believe, justified. Unfortunately, the *Obsequies* text is fragmentary, but some of the gaps in its narrative can be supplied by a comparison with texts which are closely related to it, especially by the Ethiopic *Liber Requiei*[62] and the Old Irish

---

[58] See Wenger, *L'assomption*, pp. 62–3.

[59] Cothenet, 'Marie dans les apocryphes', pp. 124–6; Mimouni, *Dormition*, pp. 81–6.

[60] This is the case in the Syriac life of the Virgin, not considered here; see Mimouni, 'Les Vies de la Vierge: Etat de la question', *Apocrypha* 5 (1994), 211–48, at 244.

[61] See above, p. 33.

[62] Arras, ed., *De transitu*, II, vi, says that the *Obsequies* 'uerbum ad uerbum, saluis quibusdam uariantibus, textui nostro consonant'.

*transitus*,[63] which clearly also belongs to the same textual tradition, although it is shorter than the Ethiopic and does not have parallels to the bones of Joseph or the trees of worms episodes. Clearly, this is a procedure to be undertaken with caution, as texts develop and change, and the Ethiopic has episodes not found in the Old Irish, so all three texts were by no means identical. Unlike all of Mimouni's A group, however, the *Obsequies* has the dispute among the apostles, almost exactly as in the Ethiopic and the Old Irish, as well as the stories about the bones of Joseph and the trees dropping worms, both also in the Ethiopic. The apostolic dispute is particularly important because traces of it survive in Greek and Latin texts and this, together with other similarities to the *Obsequies*, enables us to establish important textual connections between this text and Mimouni's C family (which corresponds to most of Van Esbroeck's palm family), though Mimouni is very unwilling to accept such a connection. The *Obsequies* is also the only one of the Syriac narratives to have the palm, as in the source of the Ethiopic[64] and in the Old Irish, again aligning it with the Greek and Latin texts of the supposed C family. It is probable that the *Obsequies* was unique among the Syriac narratives also because it emphasized Mary's fear of death: this is not a feature of the extant fragments, but it is of passages in the Ethiopic and Old Irish which are not paralleled in what remains of the Syriac text. The passage on the bones of Joseph, extant in Syriac, in the Ethiopic text is part of a reassurance to Mary that she need not fear death[65] and this is more than likely its original context in Syriac too. The palm itself, indeed, is proof of the presence of this fear in the text, as it functions in all the *transitus* apocrypha in which it features as a symbol of victory, reassuring Mary that the evil spirits which she fears will be vanquished; Cothenet's explanation of its role in the *Transitus of Pseudo-Melito* holds true for the other texts also: 'gage de victoire, il garantit à Marie

---

[63] The Old Irish text is extant in two manuscripts, both from the fifteenth century, but preserving a much older text. The version in Oxford, Bodleian Library, Laud Misc. 610 is edited by Donahue, ed., *The Testament of Mary*, and Herbert and McNamara, *Irish Biblical Apocrypha*, pp. 119–31, translate the Irish text based on the 'Liber Flauus Fergusiorum', Dublin, Royal Irish Academy, 23 O 48. The text is discussed by StJ. D. Seymour, 'Irish Versions of the Transitus Mariae', *Journal of Theological Studies* 23 (1921–2), 36–43, and Willard, 'The Testament of Mary'. See Donahue, *The Testament of Mary*, p. 55, for the appeal of the damned.

[64] See below, p. 50.     [65] Manns, *Le récit*, p. 77.

l'assistance des armées angéliques lors de la rencontre avec Satan, et joue un rôle prophylactique contre les mauvais esprits'.[66] The *Obsequies*, therefore, was probably unique among the surviving Syriac texts in not sharing their view of the serene nature of the Virgin's attitude towards death. In Mimouni's scheme all texts in the A family locate a house of Mary in Bethlehem: there is no localization of the house in the *Obsequies*, as the beginning of the text is missing, but in the Ethiopic and Old Irish texts Mary's house seems to be located in Jerusalem as she ascends the Mount of Olives after the first announcement of her imminent death and all the trees adore the palm (Ethiopic: book) she holds, and in the Ethiopic the Christ-angel who appears to Mary at the beginning tells her that his name cannot be uttered in the middle of Jerusalem. It seems probable that the *Obsequies* was set apart from the other Syriac texts in this respect also, then.

The *Obsequies* is fundamentally different to the texts in the A group and does not belong with them, therefore, and its ending presumably had more in common with the Ethiopic and Old Irish parallels. The Ethiopic *Liber Requiei* describes Mary's body being placed under the tree of life in paradise, where her soul is reunited with it, in terms almost identical to the Syriac: 'Et cum peruenissent simul in paradisum, posuerunt corpus Mariae apud arborem uitae. Et attulerunt animam eius et posuerunt super corpus eius.'[67] This is followed by the visit to hell and heaven with the apostles, after which: 'Et attulerunt alium thronum pro Maria et erant circa illam decem millia angelorum et tres uirgines. Et sedit illa et iuit in paradisum et in tertio coelo steterunt ibi dum cantabant.'[68] It is clear from this that the third heaven is paradise (cf. II Cor. XII.2–4), not identical with the seventh heaven, of which Mary and the apostles are given a foretaste earlier in the narrative.[69] In the Old Irish *transitus*, Mary's soul is again put back into her body under the tree of life in paradise and she visits hell (only) with the apostles, but, once hell is closed: 'The Virgin Mary was then brought under the tree of life in paradise and the Saviour and Michael rose to heaven after raising Mary nobly under the tree of life with the host of God about her praising the

---

[66] 'Marie dans les apocryphes', p. 139.     [67] Arras, ed., *De transitu*, II, 35.
[68] *Ibid.*, 53–4.
[69] See Cothenet, 'Marie dans les apocryphes', p. 126, where it is clear that Adam and Abel are also in the third heaven.

Saviour . . .'; or, in the *Liber Flauus* version: 'The body of Mary was placed under the tree of life in paradise and there was a host of God about her praising the Lord for ever'.[70] The two Old Irish manuscripts do not separate Mary's body and soul again, just as the Ethiopic does not, but body and soul seem to be returned together to a paradise which is not identical to heaven. Both Ethiopic and Old Irish texts, then, suggest that the missing end of the Syriac *Obsequies* would have described Mary's body and soul being placed back under the tree of life, and that it was an assumption text, that assumption being to paradise or the third heaven.

Cothenet has suggested that the way in which Mary and the apostles play a role which is very much secondary to Michael in that part of Wright's text where they view hell indicates that the Virgin was introduced by the author into a text where she had previously had no place.[71] He points out that she does not even intercede here, whereas in the later, fully developed *Apocalypse of the Virgin* texts she intercedes successfully for the sinners.[72] It is possible, however, that the fragmentary state of the text may be misleading here, as in the related Ethiopic *Liber Requiei* the tormented appeal to her explicitly later on in the narrative,[73] as they do in the Old Irish *transitus*.[74]

The *terminus ante quem* for this text is established by the date of the manuscript fragments (though we should be cautious about relying too much on dates suggested at the end of the last century and not examined since then), but it is difficult to place the text more precisely than this. Cothenet suggests that this text forms the link between the apocalypses of the apostles, which are dependent on the Jewish apocalypses, and the apocalypses of the Virgin, which are found in Greek as independent texts and in Syriac, as here, as part of dormition texts, as well as in other languages.[75] The connections between this Syriac text and the *Apocalypse of Paul*, he suggests, enable us to place this Syriac apocryphon, or at least its source, in Judaeo-Christian circles at the beginning of the third century, at least two centuries before the date of the manuscripts.[76] The similarity between the apocalypse part of this text and the *Apocalypse of*

---

[70] Donahue, ed., *The Testament of Mary*, p. 55.

[71] 'Marie dans les apocryphes', p. 127.

[72] On the apocalypses of the Virgin, see Mimouni, 'Les *Apocalypses de la Vierge*: état de la question', *Apocrypha* 4 (1993), 101–12.

[73] Arras, ed., *De transitu*, II, 38.     [74] Donahue, ed., *The Testament of Mary*, p. 55.

[75] 'Marie dans les apocryphes', p. 129.     [76] *Ibid.*

*Paul* is undeniable and the link between the two texts is underlined within the Syriac text when Jesus tells Paul that he will reveal the mysteries of the heavens to him. Such a very early date is, however, difficult to accept in the absence of any supporting evidence and it is much more in keeping with other evidence for the development of belief in Mary's dormition or assumption to date the text to the end of the fifth century.[77] It is, of course, equally possible that a fifth-century redactor could have made use of the sources suggested by Cothenet. While the text cannot, therefore, be dated as early as the third century, it is indisputably early in terms of the development of the tradition, as is proved by the date of the surviving fragments and especially also by the importance accorded to the apostles: this is generally considered a sign of an early stage in the textual tradition which, as it develops, focuses more on the Virgin herself and less on the apostles.[78] Relations among the apostles are notable here, moreover, for their lack of Christian charity and their dispute seems to be a particularly early feature, later texts correcting this to a stress instead on concord and unity among the apostles.

### THE COPTIC TEXTS

In Van Esbroeck's scheme the Coptic texts form a separate group, though within the palm family, while they, along with some Ethiopic and Arabic texts which are dependent on Coptic, form Mimouni's second group of texts, B, and demonstrate a transitional stage between the other two groups, witnessing to a development in liturgical and doctrinal concerns.[79] The Coptic tradition was most probably influenced by the Syriac, but it developed in a distinctive fashion,[80] and it is of special importance because some of the texts witness to the development of belief in the full resurrection and corporal assumption of the Virgin to heaven. These texts localize Mary's house in Jerusalem and attest to belief either in the dormition only or in the death and resurrection/assumption as two separate events, which are not compounded, as is often the case with the

---

[77] Mimouni, *Dormition*, p. 86.

[78] Cothenet, 'Marie dans les apocryphes', p. 129; Lausberg, 'Zur literarischen Gestaltung des Transitus Beatae Mariae', p. 30; and Mimouni, *Dormition*, p. 85, n. 44.

[79] For a discussion of the Coptic texts, see Van Lantschoot, 'L'assomption'; Mimouni, 'Genèse et évolution'; and Mimouni, *Dormition*, pp. 173–210.

[80] See Mimouni, *Dormition*, pp. 181–2.

Greek and Latin texts, according to Mimouni. Those Coptic texts which distinguish dormition and assumption conform to Coptic liturgy, which has two feasts of Mary, one on 21 Tobi (16 January) and the second on 16 Mesore (9 August), 206 days apart. The first of these feasts may well have been originally the date on which the first Egyptian church was dedicated to Mary; this then became a feast in memory of Mary, focusing particularly on the flight into Egypt, always of great importance for the Egyptian church, and later, probably around the end of the fifth or the beginning of the sixth century, developed into the feast of her death, the same type of development as gave rise to the feast of 15 August elsewhere in the church.[81] Whereas in most other places the death and assumption of Mary were celebrated together on 15 August, the Egyptian church instead added a second feast, under the influence of the feast of 15 August and approximating to it in date, to celebrate the assumption. This new feast of the assumption seems to have been introduced in Egypt under the influence of Jerusalem.[82]

The feast of the assumption on 9 August was probably introduced after the middle of the sixth century, possibly as a result of the conflict between the followers of Severus of Antioch (*d.* 538) and Julian of Halicarnassus (*d.* after 518), the two factions in the Monophysite church of Alexandria.[83] The followers of Julian, termed *phantasiastae* or *incorrupticolae*, held that the body of Christ, from the very moment of his conception, was incorruptible, immortal and impassible, as it was after the resurrection, and held that the suffering and death on the cross was a miracle contrary to the normal conditions of Christ's humanity. Certain of them even believed that the body of Mary had undergone a transformation before the incarnation which made it incorruptible, as a preparation for the incarnation.[84] It is logical to suppose that this group would also have wished to preserve Mary's dead body from corruption, though explicit statements on this have not survived, and this may have led them to the belief that Mary had not died; this theory is supported by the polemic against such a position which is contained in several of the extant Coptic texts. The followers of Severus, termed the *corrupticolae*, believed in

---

[81] See Jugie, *La mort*, pp. 179–80; Mimouni, 'Genèse et évolution', pp. 124–33, and *Dormition*, pp. 413–28 and 447–8.

[82] Mimouni, 'Genèse et évolution', pp. 81 and 132, and *Dormition*, pp. 448–50.

[83] Jugie, *La mort*, pp. 132–3, and Mimouni, *Dormition*, pp. 426–8 and 448–50.

[84] Mimouni, *Dormition*, p. 667.

Christ's voluntary subjection of his body to death and decay according to the normal human condition and accordingly held that the body of Mary too had been subjected to decay in death. This is a most unusual view in terms of depictions of Mary's body after death, as, even in apocrypha which do not contain a resurrection, her body is usually preserved from decay, fragrant and perfect. One Coptic homily, by Theodosius of Alexandria, an adherent of Severus, has Christ tell his mother that he would have liked to exempt her from death but that this would have led people to think her a sort of angelic power descended from heaven: Jesus says to Mary, as she prays to be delivered from the terrors of the next world, 'wicked men will think concerning thee, that thou art a power which came down from heaven; and that this dispensation [the Incarnation] took place in appearance'.[85] It is possible that this conflict within the Monophysite church about the corruptibility of the body of Christ was in fact at the origin of not only the adoption of the feast but also belief in the assumption of the Virgin to heaven in Egypt (and possibly throughout the East).[86] Churches with one feast, including in it both death and assumption, would not have experienced the same need to distinguish so clearly between the two. While some of Julian's followers seem to have held that Mary could not have died but had to have been assumed directly into heaven, the followers of Severus (who were very close to the orthodox Catholic position on the nature of Christ) declared that Christ must have subjected his mother to the fate of decay in the tomb according to the common law of mankind, because otherwise she would have been considered a celestial being, not a human. If Mary were not human, then neither could Christ be incarnate. Coptic homilies for the feasts stress again and again Mary's mortal body. A compromise between the two factions seems to have been reached by means of accepting the new, Julianist, belief in Mary's assumption, not in the 'immortalist' sense of the followers of Julian, but by maintaining Severus's emphasis on death and decay. The new belief replicated the stages of Christ's death, resurrection and ascension, with assumption replacing ascension.[87] As a simple transformation of the feast of Mary's death in January into a feast of the assumption would have seemed like an

---

[85] Robinson, ed., *Coptic Apocryphal Gospels*, p. 109. Quoted by Jugie, *La mort*, p. 132, and Mimouni, 'Genèse et évolution', p. 120. See also below, p. 46.

[86] Mimouni, 'Genèse et évolution', pp. 119–22.     [87] *Ibid.*, p. 121.

acceptance of the Julianist arguments, the new feast of the assumption was celebrated in Egypt instead on a date, 9 August, approximating to that of the feast in Jerusalem (15 August), while retaining the older Egyptian feast of Mary's death in January. This new feast seems to have been introduced at the end of the sixth or the beginning of the seventh century.[88]

Homilies for the older feast of the death were adapted for the new feast of the assumption by adding on to the description of Mary's death an account of her resurrection and assumption, and the gap of 206 days between the new feast of the assumption and the older feast of the death became the number of days Mary spent in the tomb, underlining her subjection to the common human fate of death. These liturgical and theological developments are reflected in the extant Coptic texts. Most of these are not apocryphal *transitus* texts in the strict sense, but are homilies for the feasts of the death and assumption which draw freely on apocryphal narratives. As a group, the Coptic texts, which will not be treated individually here,[89] affirm belief in Mary's death and some of them testify also to the new belief in her resurrection and assumption. The *Gospel of Bartholomew*, the homily attributed to Cyril of Jerusalem and the sermon on the dormition attributed to Evodius of Rome all contain Mary's dormition only, and her body is preserved until the resurrection on the Last Day, either under the tree of life in paradise, or hidden in some secret place, while her soul is in heaven. In the other texts, the Sahidic and Bohairic *transitus* narratives and the assumption text attributed to Evodius of Rome, the sermon of Theodosius of Alexandria and the homily attributed to Theophilus of Alexandria, Mary is resurrected and assumed into heaven, body and soul, on 16 Mesore. In this way the Coptic texts form an intermediate group, witnessing – but not seamlessly – to the transition from an earlier to a more advanced state of belief. In several of the texts it is even possible to discern the process by which new beliefs were grafted on to older texts, with interpolations which are at odds with other parts of the texts.[90] In this way the Coptic texts, as one might

---

[88] *Ibid.*, p. 133.    [89] For detailed discussions, see n. 79.

[90] As, for example, in Recension A of the Sahidic homily on the dormition falsely attributed to Cyril of Jerusalem (Recension A was edited by E. A. Wallis Budge, 'The Discourse on Mary Theotokos by Cyril, Archbishop of Jerusalem', in *Miscellaneous Coptic Texts in the Dialect of Upper Egypt* (London, 1915), pp. 49–73 (English translation pp. 626–51) and Recension B by Robinson, ed., *Coptic Apocryphal Gospels*,

expect from sermons rather than straight apocrypha, directly bear the inscription of doctrinal concerns. Theodosius of Alexandria's sermon on the assumption, written probably in 566 or 567, seems to have been written as part of his efforts to make the new feast of the assumption acceptable in Egypt, and it shows very clearly how Mary's corruptible body is resurrected: after she has spent 206 days in the tomb, Jesus arrives with the soul of his mother seated in his bosom and calls to her body: 'Arise, o thou body, that dies according to its nature, wear thy deathless soul, that thou mayest be altogether deathless, and that I may take thee to the land of the living. Arise, o thou body, which dissolves and becomes corrupt according to nature, wear thy incorruptible soul.'[91]

The Coptic accounts all place the house of Mary in Jerusalem and her tomb in the valley of Jehoshaphat. Peter is of great importance,[92] whereas in other traditions (Greek, for example) the emphasis is more on John. Unlike the Greek and Syriac texts, it is not essential in the Coptic texts that all the apostles should be present at Mary's death,[93] and in some of these texts the apostles flee from the Jews, abandoning the body of Mary. Jesus himself announces to Mary her forthcoming death and Mary's fear is stressed in most of the texts, the terrors of the next world being described in detail in several of them, showing the influence of native Egyptian ideas of the other world. There is, however, no journey to the next world in the Coptic narratives, which end with the dormition or the assumption, as is appropriate to their nature as homily for the feast. Several of the Coptic texts describe Mary's soul leaping into the bosom of her son at her death. The palm-branch features in the Sahidic fragment as the means by which the blind Jews are healed, just as in the *Obsequies*.

Cothenet and Mimouni both suggest that, because the Copts composed

---

pp. 24–41; the text is summarized by Elliott, *Apocryphal New Testament*, pp. 697–8), in a sermon on the dormition attributed to Evodius of Rome (W. Spielberg, 'Eine sahidische Version der Dormitio Mariae', *Receuil de travaux relatifs à la philologie et à l'archéologie égyptiennes et assyriennes* 25 (1903), 2–4; discussed by Van Lantschoot, 'L'assomption', pp. 502–4) and in a sermon on the assumption attributed to the same author (Robinson, ed., *Coptic Apocryphal Gospels*, pp. 64–5; see Mimouni, 'Genèse et évolution', pp. 104–5 and 116, and *Dormition*, pp. 200–1).

[91] Robinson, ed., *Coptic Apocryphal Gospels*, p. 109. See also M. Chaine, 'Sermon de Théodose, patriarche d'Alexandrie, sur la dormition et l'Assomption de la Vierge', *Revue de l'Orient Chrétien* 29 (1933–4), 272–314, at 275; Jugie, *La mort*, p. 132.

[92] Mimouni, 'Genèse et évolution', p. 112.

[93] Jugie, *La mort*, p. 138; Mimouni, 'Genèse et évolution', p. 79.

few original texts, there may have been a Greek text at the origin of the Coptic tradition, and that this may have been the lost (if, that is, there ever was such a text) apocryphon attributed to the heretic Leucius.[94] Mimouni supports this theory by reference to the Latin *Pseudo-Melito* apocryphon, which purports to be an orthodox revision of Leucius's account and which has some features in common with the Coptic texts. It seems to me, however, that this theory may be true in a different sense to that intended by Mimouni and that the Greek text at the origin of the Coptic texts (assuming, of course, this hypothesis to be correct in the first place) may well have been a Greek text related to the Syriac *Obsequies*[95] and that the Copts then developed this narrative in distinctive ways, influenced partly by those liturgical developments relating to the feasts of the death and assumption which were peculiar to the Egyptian church, and partly by native Egyptian concepts of the afterlife. This would explain the tree of life and the palm-branch, as well as the fear of death which is so characteristic of the Coptic texts, as such a fear is also part of the *Obsequies* textual tradition. This hypothetical Greek source would then be, not the immediate ancestor of *Pseudo-Melito*, as Cothenet and Mimouni suggest, but an ancestor several degrees back from the Latin *transitus*.

## THE GREEK TEXTS

Mention of the Greek and Latin brings us to the other relevant texts in Van Esbroeck's palm family; these correspond to Mimouni's third group, C, to which he assigns the Greek *transitus* known as *R*, the Latin *Transitus A*, which seems to be an abridged translation of a text closely related to *R*,[96] the two versions of John of Thessalonica's assumption narrative, the Latin *Transitus W*,[97] the Latin *transitus* edited by Capelle and sometimes known as *Transitus C* or the *Colbert transitus*, the Pseudo-Joseph of

---

[94] Cothenet, 'Marie dans les apocryphes', pp. 143–4; Mimouni, *Dormition*, p. 63. On Leucius, see below, pp. 84–5.

[95] On such Greek texts, see below, p. 50.

[96] Some of these titles are confusing. Two Latin texts are known as *Transitus A*: that edited by Wenger, for which the title will be reserved here, and the apocryphon attributed to Joseph of Arimathaea, to which Tischendorf gave the title *Transitus A*, under the (mistaken) impression that it was the oldest of the extant Latin texts.

[97] Called *Transitus W* after its editor Wilmart, but often known also as *Transitus C*. To

Arimathea *transitus* (or Tischendorf's *Transitus A*), the Ethiopic *transitus* known as the *Liber Requiei*, the Georgian *transitus* of Pseudo-Basil of Caesarea and the Armenian *transitus*.[98] Mimouni also assigns the two versions of the Latin *Pseudo-Melito* (*Transitus B*), indisputably 'palm' texts, to his C group, despite some features which he thinks they share with the B (Coptic) group of apocrypha. The Latin texts will be discussed individually in the next chapter. All of these texts localize the house of Mary in Jerusalem and in their original state Mimouni thinks that they all affirmed belief in the assumption, with or without a preceding resurrection of Mary, although in many manuscripts we find revised endings. From the middle of the sixth century we have evidence for belief in what was thought to be the tomb of Mary in Gethsemane, which is in the valley of Cedron in Jerusalem, at the foot of the Mount of Olives,[99] and this accords with what is suggested in these texts about Mary's burial-place. Mimouni suggests that, because tradition situated the house of Mary in Jerusalem, this led to her tomb being localized there also.[100] Because it unequivocally affirms belief in the assumption, Mimouni assigns the origins of this group of texts to around the second half of the sixth century, at about the time when the feast of the death and assumption was instituted at the Marian church in Gethsemane by the decree of the Byzantine emperor, Maurice (582–602). Mimouni does not assign the *Obsequies* to his C group, having already included it in his A group, and he discounts the obvious similarities between it and the Greek and Latin texts, largely because such a connection does not fit his theory. In doing so, however, he distorts the clear textual relations linking the Syriac and the Greek and Latin texts of the palm family. Textually there can be no doubt that they descend from the *Obsequies* or a closely related text and, as we have seen, that text was already an assumption text. The manuscript of the *Obsequies* predates Maurice's decree, so Mimouni's hypothesis cannot be correct. As the supposed C group is, for the most part, doctrinally identical and textually related to the *Obsequies*, there is no justification for three groups and Van Esbroeck's two groups are sufficient. The remaining texts relevant here can be divided into Eastern

---

avoid confusion with the Colbert *transitus* edited by Capelle and sometimes known as *Transitus C*, I shall refer to Wilmart's text as *Transitus W*.

[98] All of these texts are part of Van Esbroeck's palm family, except Tischendorf's Pseudo-Joseph of Arimathaea.

[99] Mimouni, *Dormition*, p. 67.     [100] *Ibid.*, pp. 577–8.

and Western subgroups, the Eastern represented by the Greek texts, and texts directly dependent on them, including Wenger's Latin *Transitus A*, the Western group by the other Latin texts.

## THE GREEK *R*

The first of the Eastern subgroup is the text edited by Wenger and named *R* by him, because he discovered the manuscript in Rome (Biblioteca Apostolica Vaticana, grec. 1982, fols. 181r–189v, from the eleventh century or perhaps a little earlier).[101] Wenger argues, convincingly, that *R* is a sixth-century text.[102] The title in the sole manuscript attributes the text to John the Evangelist, but it has little in common with the most popular Greek text, the *Pseudo-John*, and it appears that this attribution is not part of the original text.[103] Wenger considers that the original title of *R* is that found in some manuscripts of John of Thessalonica's assumption homily, a text which draws on the same source as *R*: 'This is the book about the repose of Mary, the holy mother of God, along with that which was revealed to her, in five chapters'.[104] It seems more likely, however, that this was the title of *R*'s source, as *R* itself has no trace of a five-book structure and has no proper section devoted to what was revealed to Mary. 'What was revealed to her' presumably refers to a visit to hell and/or heaven, whereas *R* ends with the assumption of Mary. Those manuscripts of what we know as John of Thessalonica's homily with this title also attribute the work to James, the brother of Jesus and Bishop of Jerusalem (and supposed author of the *Proteuangelium*). Wenger and Mimouni both connect this title to the Syriac *Five Books*, though *R* (and John of Thessalonica's narrative) has little in common with the *Five Books*. Instead I believe that it should be connected with the Ethiopic *Liber Requiei*, whose title in one of the two manuscripts reads, in Latin translation, 'In nomine Patris et Filii et Spiritus Sancti. *Liber Requiei* Mariae qui de ea reuelatus est in quinque libris et in quinque coelis.'[105] This text is, as pointed out already, very close to what is extant of the Syriac *Obsequies* (which may, of course, also have been in five books, as it certainly deals with Mary's 'repose' and with what was revealed

---

[101] Wenger, *L'assomption*, p. 22. This edition includes a French translation. The text is also edited by Manns in *Le récit*.

[102] Wenger, *L'assomption*, pp. 61–7.

[103] *Ibid.* p. 32; Mimouni, *Dormition*, pp. 128–9.     [104] Wenger, *L'assomption*, p. 33.

[105] Arras, ed., *De transitu*, II, 1.

to her) and *R* clearly belongs also to the same textual family, as will become evident. In the Ethiopic the five books deal with (1) the announcement to Mary by the angel of her death in three days' time and the bringing of a book (the Ethiopic translator, who was probably translating from Greek, may have confused Greek *biblion*, book, and *brabeion*, the sign of victory or palm);[106] Mary goes to the Mount of Olives; there is a long excursus on the palm (which seems out of place, as the angel has brought a book, not a palm – an indication that the source had the angel bring a *brabeion* or palm) and the flight into Egypt; (2) Mary's prayer; the arrival of John; the arrival of the other apostles; death of Mary; burial of Mary, with the episode of the Jew who wished to overturn the bier; (3) the apostolic controversy at the tomb of Mary; (4) the body of Mary is brought to paradise, placed under the tree of life and the soul is replaced; Mary and the apostles visit hell and heaven with Jesus; Paul is taken by Jesus to show him the glorious mysteries, but he has first to fight the devil in Rome with the aid of Peter; (5) the conclusion to the Paul and Peter story; their return to paradise; the apostles and Mary visit the seventh heaven; a throne is brought for Mary and placed in the third heaven; Michael returns the apostles to the Mount of Olives. *R* corresponds closely to the first two of these books and then has an allusion which suggests that its source contained the equivalent of the third book, though it has omitted the apostolic controversy;[107] its account of the bringing of the body to paradise and the replacing of the soul is almost identical to the same episode in the Ethiopic fourth book. *R* has nothing corresponding to the visit to hell and heaven or the Paul and Peter story, but if the title of *R*'s source was that which Wenger suggests, then it seems probable that that source had a visit to the Otherworld also (otherwise why the 'that which was revealed to her'?). *R*, therefore, may well be an abbreviated version of a Greek text in five books, translated from Syriac (the *Obsequies* or a text close to it) into Greek or written in Greek originally and then translated into Syriac to give us the *Obsequies* (the attribution to James seems perhaps more likely to be of Syriac origin, as in the Syriac *Six Books*, than Greek, as the more common Greek attribution is to John the Evangelist).[108]

---

[106] See Erbetta, ed., *Gli Apocrifi del Nuovo Testamento*, I, 2, 423, n. 2. The word *brabeion* is always used of the palm in the Greek *R*.

[107] On which see below, pp. 56–7.

[108] Wenger, *L'assomption*, p. 58, says: 'D'après le contenu, nous pencherions volontiers pour l'antériorité de Syr sur le grec, du moins sous la forme de *R*'.

In his discussion Mimouni adverts to, but in effect refuses to realize the significance of, the textual relationship between *R*, the key text in his C group, and the Syriac *Obsequies*: he quotes Wenger on the undeniable links between these two texts but says that, as the *Obsequies* had a provisional resurrection of Mary, it should be classed as a dormition text, whereas *R* is an assumption text, without a resurrection.[109] As already argued, there is nothing in the *Obsequies* or its closest parallel, the Ethiopic *Liber Requiei*, to indicate a provisional resurrection, so this is not a valid argument. Precisely this Ethiopic text is also clearly closely connected to *R*[110] but Mimouni questions, too, the relationship between the *Obsequies*, *R* and the Ethiopic *Liber Requiei*, on the same doctrinal grounds that the Syriac text is a dormition text and the Ethiopic and Greek are assumption texts. He admits the literary affinities among all three texts, saying that 'ils véhiculent la même tradition littéraire sur le sort final de Marie et ils décrivent, en termes presque identiques, le transfert de Marie au paradis sous l'arbre de vie avec la réunion de l'âme et du corps . . .' but concludes merely: 'Si ces rapprochements littéraires correspondaient à des rapprochements doctrinaux, S1 [the *Obsequies*] affirmerait clairement l'assomption sans résurrection mais avec passage au tombeau. Auquel cas, S1 serait l'un des témoins les plus anciens (fin du v^e siècle ou début du vi^e siècle) de la croyance à l'assomption.'[111] The implications of accepting the relationship between these three texts go far beyond merely transferring the *Obsequies* to a different group, however, but Mimouni never explores the repercussions for his theory of the origins of the C group or the implications of the possibility that *R* is an abbreviated version of a *transitus* with apocalypse attached. It is not difficult to imagine one text descending from another but being altered in such a way as to witness implicitly to a different theological position: such alterations can be traced within some of the surviving Coptic texts. This is in fact what one would expect to happen, and Mimouni's resistance to such a process seems inexplicable.

As *R* is so important for most of the Latin texts, including the sources of the Old English texts, it is worth giving its narrative at some length,

---

[109] Mimouni, *Dormition*, p. 133.

[110] Arras, ed., *De transitu*, II, vii. See also the table showing the corresponding passages in *R*, the *Liber Requiei* and the *Obsequies* in Manns, *Le récit*, p. 255.

[111] Mimouni, *Dormition*, p. 83, n. 37.

while indicating its kinship with the Ethiopic and the Syriac, even though this narrative of course overlaps with the Syriac fragments already described.[112] After Mary had learned from the Lord that she was to die, an angel appears to her, bringing her a palm and announcing that in three days she will leave her body.[113] She is instructed to give the palm to the apostles, who will be sent to her by the angel. Mary is uneasy about the single palm, fearing that the apostles will quarrel about it. The angel tells her that the palm will perform many miracles and, in reply to Mary's request to know his name, he says that it is too powerful to be uttered in Jerusalem, but that he will tell it to her on the Mount of Olives. Mary then goes to the Mount of Olives, bearing the palm and accompanied by the angel, and all the trees on the mountain bow and adore the palm. When Mary sees this she thinks that Jesus is present and the angel tells her that only the Lord of glory could perform these miracles and that he, the angel, is responsible for bringing souls to the place of the just when they leave their bodies, and that he will raise Mary on the fourth day, just as the Lord was resurrected on the third day. The angel seems to be partly Michael, the psychopomp, partly Christ as angel, a concept found in other early texts: the angel speaks of his father who has sent him and calls Mary his mother.[114] Mary then asks whether there is a special prayer or sacrifice which she should perform in order to ensure that the angel come to her at her death, but he tells her that not only he, but all the celestial armies, will sing hymns at her death and he communicates his name and a special

[112] I have included the Old Irish in this comparison only occasionally, even though it agrees with these texts in so much, partly because it is much briefer than the Ethiopic, partly because the translating style of the Old Irish was clearly much freer and the text has also been subjected to scribal editing, including the misplacing of the section on Paul.

[113] 'tu déposeras ton corps' in Wenger's French translation, *L'assomption*, p. 211: the work is full of euphemisms for death. The beginning of the work may seem odd in that it says nothing of how Mary's death was first communicated to her and seems to imply a prior narrative, but it agrees precisely with the *Liber Requiei*: 'Et quando audiuit Maria a Domino quia requiesceret corpus suum . . .'. It is tempting to suppose that a prior recension had a scene like that in the Greek *Pseudo-John*, in which Mary prays for death and Gabriel is sent to tell her that her wish will be granted, but this is probably not the case, as such a scene is recapitulated in *R* in Mary's prayer of thanks when she returns to her house and quotes both her appeal to Christ and his reply.

[114] See Manns, *Le récit*, pp. 155–62.

prayer from the Father (neither of which the reader learns),[115] which she is to utter at the moment of her death and is also to teach to the apostles. When the angel leaves, Mary returns to her house, which trembles because of the palm, washes, dresses in fresh garments and prays to the Lord, reminding him of his promise to give her a garment which will distinguish her from all her race (the garment of incorruption) and to bring her to the seventh heaven and requesting also that no power (of darkness) come to her at the hour when she leaves her body. She also reminds her son of his promise to come himself for her soul. Mary's request in *R* to be brought to the seventh heaven is significant: in the *Liber Requiei* Mary is brought to the seventh heaven towards the end of the fifth book. This, along with what Wenger thinks was *R*'s original title, is a further indication that the source of *R* contained the visit to hell and heaven and that *R* is an abbreviated text which cut out these sections of its source, leaving some elements, such as this, hanging. Mary then orders her servant to summon her relations and friends, to whom she announces that she will leave her body the next day, asking that they stay with her for two days and nights (the Ethiopic and *R* agree on having Mary say that she will leave her body the next day, though this is only the first of the three days covered by the narrative of her death; the time scheme is not absolutely consistent). All of this is almost exactly as in the Ethiopic, except that the Ethiopic has the story of the palm on the flight into Egypt and the episodes of the trees dropping worms, of Rachel and Eleazar and of the bones of Joseph, while it has a longer version than *R* of the encounters between Mary and her neighbours.[116] The Syriac *Obsequies*, as mentioned already, has the episodes of the trees and the bones of Joseph. In the dialogue between Mary and her neighbours the *Liber Requiei* gives a passage virtually unknown elsewhere, however, which furnishes an explanation of why Mary was afraid of death. This refers back to an episode on the flight into Egypt when Mary lacked faith and regarded herself as having sinned.[117] This must surely be a very early episode, dating from before

---

[115] In the *Liber Requiei* the angel does give his name as Misericors, so presumably it has been edited out in *R*: Arras, ed., *De transitu*, II, 13, para. 35.

[116] This is clearly original, as it is also found in John of Thessalonica, who drew on the same source as *R*; see Wenger, *L'assomption*, p. 60.

[117] Arras, ed., *De transitu*, II, 16. The only other reference to this is in a Georgian apocryphon which contains only the beginning of an allusion to it: see M. Van

the period when Mary's sinlessness could be taken for granted, and later versions, including *R*, presumably omitted it because it offended the sensibilities of their redactors.

While Mary and her companions pray, John arrives on a cloud and enters Mary's house; she weeps on seeing him, reminding him of how Jesus entrusted her to him at the Crucifixion and saying that they are the only two to know the secret uttered to John at the Last Supper, as he lay on Jesus's breast. John is disturbed, apparently taking Mary's speech as an accusation, and tells her that he had to obey the Lord's command to preach throughout the world but that he had left a servant to care for her. Mary then tells him that she is to leave her body after the next day and asks him to protect it, because she has heard the high-priests say that they will burn it. John weeps and Mary takes him aside, teaching him the prayer which the angel has taught her and showing him a casket in which is a book containing revelations made by the five-year-old Jesus to her, concerning all of creation as well as the apostles. Mary then shows her funeral garments to John and the palm which he is to carry in front of her and, again, John is uneasy, saying that this could lead to disputes among the apostles and that there is one among them greater than he is. A great clap of thunder resounds and all of the apostles are suddenly brought by a cloud to Mary's house, including Paul, second after Peter and counted among the apostles. The apostles greet each other in amazement, then, after a courteous exchange between Peter and Paul, Peter prays, his hands in the form of a cross, and when John arrives they all embrace according to their rank among the apostles.

John explains how he had been preaching in Sardes with twenty-eight disciples when he was lifted away by the cloud and brought to Mary. Again, all of this is as in the Ethiopic, except that it does not have Sardes: the *Liber Requiei* instead reads: 'quando uos eratis in Nerdo regione', with second person plural  instead of first singular.[118] John tells the apostles

---

Esbroeck, 'Apocryphes géorgiens de la Dormition', *AB* 91 (1973), 55–75, at 58 and 65.

[118] Arras, ed., *De transitu*, II, 20. The mention of Sardes is surprising and Wenger, *L'assomption*, p. 45, n. 1, asks whether 'Le transitus grec aurait-il été fabriqué par un chrétien de Sardes qui aurait profité du récit pour attribuer à sa ville une origine apostolique?' Arras, ed., *De transitu*, II, 91, says, à propos of Sardes, 'In narratione aethiopica facile esset substituere locutioni *nedor regio* locutionem *nakir regio* (*aliena regio*), sed aenigmaticum maneret quomodo apud graecos et latinos auctores uoca-

not to weep when they enter Mary's house, lest the people doubt, thinking that even the apostles are afraid of death, and he explains that this is the secret the Lord confided to him as he leaned on his breast. The apostles then enter Mary's house, explaining how they were all gathered together. Mary blesses the Lord, thanking him for fulfilling his promise that all the apostles should be present when she had to leave her body. The apostles then watch with Mary and on the night before the third day Peter preaches to all. This part of the text is much shorter in *R* than in the *Liber Requiei*, but again John of Thessalonica (and, in part, the Latin *Transitus W*) witnesses to the primitive character of the Ethiopic, while *R* has clearly abbreviated its source here.[119] At dawn on the morning of the third day Mary rises, says the prayer taught to her by the angel and lies down on her bed. At the third hour there is thunder and an odour of perfume which puts all except the three virgins, who are caring for Mary, and the apostles to sleep. Jesus then arrives with his angels and Mary gives thanks once again, before 'completing her economy', her smiling face turned towards the Lord. He takes Mary's soul and gives it to Michael: it has a perfect human appearance, but without sexual organs, and is seven times brighter than the sun. The destination of the soul is not given. Jesus then orders Peter to take the body of Mary, to go out by the left of the city and to place it in a new tomb which they will find there. On hearing this the body of Mary calls out, saying to remember it, and Jesus assures it that he will not abandon it, calling it his pearl, his inviolate treasure, his sealed treasure. He then leaves, and the apostles and the three virgins place the body of Mary on a bier.

Peter gives the palm (still the book in the *Liber Requiei*) to John, telling him to carry it in front of the bier, while John in turn wishes Peter to precede the bier; Peter resolves the difficulty by placing the palm on the bier and the apostles set out, singing. The Lord and his angels sing also, invisible among the clouds above, so that the Jews hear the hymns and learn of the death of Mary. Satan enters into them, inciting them to kill the apostles and to burn the body, but the Jews are struck blind by the angels, all except the high-priest. He approaches the bier in order to

---

bulum "aliena" in Sardes nomen mutatum sit'. It seems probable that the redactor of *R*'s source (John of Thessalonica also has Sardes, so it must have been in the source he shares with *R*) deliberately replaces *aliena regio* with a particular place, Sardes, perhaps for the reason suggested by Wenger.

[119] Wenger, *L'assomption*, p. 60.

overturn it, touching the place where the palm lies, and immediately his hands cling to the bier and are cut off at the elbow. The high-priest begs the apostles not to abandon him, reminding Peter that his father had helped him when he was challenged by the female doorkeeper.[120] Peter tells him that only belief in the Lord can help him, and Jephonias[121] explains that the Jews had always known that Jesus was the son of God, but that love of money had blinded them. Peter then stops the bier and Jephonias praises Mary for three hours. His hands are rejoined to his arms and, following Peter's orders, he takes a leaf of the palm (Ethiopic: a leaf of the book) and with it cures the blind who are willing to believe.

The apostles then bring Mary to her tomb and while they wait there for three days Paul asks Peter to tell him the mysteries revealed to Peter on the Mount of Olives, as he, Paul, is new to the faith. Peter refuses, saying that Paul should not hear them unless the Saviour should give his permission in three days' time, when he comes to raise the body of Mary. This exchange between Peter and Paul is almost exactly as in the Syriac *Obsequies*, which, however, has a longer account, as has the Ethiopic in chs. 79 to 89; both give first the story about Solomon and death, told by Paul, then they both have the controversy among the apostles about what they should teach to those new in the faith.[122] The Old Irish text has the apostolic controversy, though not the Solomon story. The connections among the texts suggest that *R*'s source was very similar to the Syriac and the Ethiopic[123] but that *R*, an abbreviated version for liturgical reading,[124] has shortened this section. In doing so, it has of course deprived the previous intimations of conflict among the apostles of their rationale, as they clearly prepare for this omitted episode. In *R*, the apostles then discuss teaching and the faith (this is a clear allusion to the longer episode in the Syriac and Ethiopic, which *R* has omitted in

---

[120] Although the text has Peter's father, in the next clause it mentions the high-priest himself and the father reading seems to be a corruption arising from the address 'father Peter': see Wenger, *L'assomption*, pp. 48–9. This part of the text is slightly different in the Ethiopic, see Arras, ed., *De transitu*, II, 96–7.

[121] The name is given in *R* and in the long version of John of Thessalonica, but not in the Ethiopic, where he is simply the high-priest, or in any of the Latin versions except for *Pseudo-Melito*. It is also in the Greek *Pseudo-John* and the related Syriac texts.

[122] See above, pp. 36–7.

[123] Wenger, *L'assomption*, p. 54: 'R conaissait donc soit le récit syriaque soit plus probablement un récit grec qui détaillait les discussions des apôtres'.

[124] Wenger, *L'assomption*, p. 61.

abbreviating its source) until the Lord arrives and promises Paul to reveal the mysteries of heaven to him (this promise is made in exactly the same terms in the Syriac, Greek and Ethiopic).

While thousands of angels sing, the Lord tells Michael to take the body of Mary on a cloud and to place it in paradise; the apostles are also taken on clouds to paradise where they place Mary's body under the tree of life. Wenger points out that here the relationship between Syriac and Greek is so close that the Syriac allows corrupt readings in the Greek to be corrected.[125] Michael then brings Mary's soul, which is placed in her body, and the apostles are sent back to the places where they were preaching. The only difference here between the Greek, on the one hand, and the Syriac and the Ethiopic, on the other, is that in the Greek it is the apostles who are sent away, while in the other two texts, where an apocalypse follows, it is the angels who are dismissed, while the apostles and Mary set out towards the West on clouds.

It is probable that the source of *R* also included such a visit to the Otherworld. One unedited Latin text, in Paris, Bibliothèque Nationale, lat. 3550 (thirteenth century), follows a narrative of the death of Mary with a short apocalypse, very like the Syriac;[126] Wenger assigns the text to the family of the Latin *Transitus W*, but says that it has so many variants that it is probably an independent, more faithful, translation from Greek.[127] Presumably the Old Irish *transitus*, which also has a similar apocalypse, was translated from Latin, so this provides us with another Latin witness for this part of the text.[128] The 'Irish' Latin version

---

[125] *Ibid.*, p. 56.

[126] Though unedited in its entirety, Wenger, *L'assomption*, pp. 258–9, gives the apocalypse section.

[127] *Ibid.*, p. 30.

[128] Arras, ed., *De transitu*, II, vii, says of the Old Irish text: 'Quod ille solus narrationem retinuit de itinere in Aegyptum, quod solus probationem Pauli retulit et quod de itinere per transmundana testimonium seruauit, satis est argumenti eius adhuc tempore codices graecos uel latinos exstitisse multo integriores codicibus nobis hodie notis'. The tenth- or eleventh-century Old Irish *Vision of Adamnan* also has a reference to the apocalypse of Mary: 'Moreover, on the day of the death of Mary, all the apostles were brought to see the pains and pitiable tortures of the wretched, when the Lord ordered the angels of sunset to open the earth before the apostles, so that they might see and contemplate hell with its many torments, as he himself had promised them long before his crucifixion'. (Herbert and McNamara, eds., *Irish Biblical Apocrypha*, p. 137).

in Dublin, Trinity College Library, MS F. 5. 3 (fifteenth century), totally neglected by critics, is a very much abbreviated text, similar to but not identical with the source of the Old Irish version and superior to it in some details, which also has a very brief account of Mary's and the apostles' journey to hell, of the struggle of Paul and Peter against the devil and of the celestial mysteries being revealed to Paul.[129] Greek versions including the apocalypse must have existed, therefore, as the Latin texts with apocalypse are much more likely to have been translated from Greek than from Syriac. The presence of the apocalypse in these texts related to *R* and in the related Syriac *Obsequies*, coupled with what Wenger regards as the title of *R*'s source, makes it very probable that an apocalypse was also part of that source. Arras and Manns point to a series of readings in the *Liber Requiei* which seem to depend on a confusion on the part of the Ethiopic translator of different but similar Greek words:[130] the *Liber Requiei* therefore seems to have been translated from Greek, again proving the existence of a long Greek text including the apocalypse. *R*'s omission of the apocalypse is understandable as *R* seems to have been intended for liturgical reading on 15 August and appropriately ends with Mary's assumption. The *R* adaptor presumably, then, voluntarily limited himself to the story of the death of Mary, omitting its aftermath.

Mimouni, who considers this text to be possibly the oldest witness to the belief in the assumption of Mary, points out that it is somewhat hesitant about this belief, implying rather than stating it clearly.[131] He points out too that it rigorously avoids mention of Mary's death; though this is implicit in the narrative, the vocabulary has been carefully chosen to avoid mentioning death.[132] In keeping with this avoidance, it also does not have a proper resurrection of Mary's body: it is placed under the tree of life in paradise, where Michael replaces her soul in the body, but the reunited body and soul seem to just remain beneath the tree of

---

[129] Donahue, eds., *The Testament of Mary*, pp. 67–70.

[130] Arras, ed., *De transitu*, II, 75–105, and Manns, *Le récit*, pp. 80–1. Manns, pp. 81–2, points to other readings which, he says, imply a Semitic original behind the Greek text. This is not unlikely, given that the most probable scenario for the origin and development of belief in the dormition and assumption of Mary is that this took place in Monophysite circles in Jerusalem (see Mimouni, *Dormition*, p. 674), where both Syriac and Greek were spoken. The text behind the *Liber Requiei* could, therefore, have been a Syriac text translated into Greek and from there into Ethiopic.

[131] *Dormition*, p. 135.      [132] *Ibid.*, p. 130; see also p. 132.

life.[133] There is, as he points out, no description of a clear resurrection, which of course would imply a death. Because of these features of *R*, Mimouni suggests that it may have been written, perhaps in Constantinople, after the conflicts between the followers of Julian and Severus, that is, in the second half of the sixth century, at around the time when the feast of the death of Mary was instituted throughout the Byzantine empire by the Emperor Maurice.[134] He argues that, given the text's discretion about death, the redactor may have been concerned to find a way around ideas offensive to some.[135] It seems to me, however, that the process of arriving at this particular ending may have been far more accidental than this.

The conclusion of *R* is identical to the corresponding passages in the Syriac and the Ethiopic, and very similar to the Old Irish and the Irish Latin text: in all of the related texts, however, this is not the conclusion proper and their conclusions, insofar as they have been preserved, place Mary's body back in paradise after the apocalypse sections of the texts. In the Ethiopic, as in the two Irish texts, Mary is clearly resurrected in the apocalypse section and both Mary's body and soul seem to be in paradise at the conclusion. *R*'s ultimate source, therefore, almost certainly had a resurrection of Mary. *R*'s lack of a resurrection may well be the inadvertent consequence of dropping the following apocalypse, rather than of a fully thought out theological position. This suggestion of an inadvertent lack of resurrection is supported by the almost literal agreement between *R*, the Syriac and the Ethiopic in their descriptions of Mary's body being taken to paradise and having its soul replaced: if the adaptor of *R* were carefully negotiating conflicting theological positions with regard to Mary's death, he would presumably have had a more individual description. The avoidance of the vocabulary of death is a feature of the Ethiopic text too and presumably also of *R*'s source.

It appears to me that what we have in *R* is essentially an abbreviation

---

[133] *Ibid.*, p. 131.

[134] *Ibid.*, pp. 134–5. His argument for Constantinople as place of origin of the text is not very convincing, however: he suggests that the insistence in the text on Mary's funeral garments may be connected to the veneration in Constantinople, from the end of the fifth or the beginning of the sixth century, of a relic of these garments. The *Liber Requiei*, however, has the same stress on the funeral garments and this must have been translated from *R*'s source, not *R* itself.

[135] Mimouni, *Dormition*, p. 132, n. 54.

of a text very similar to the Syriac *Obsequies* and the Ethiopic *Liber Requiei*. We cannot reproduce the source of *R* in every detail, but the process of adaptation can be deduced from a comparison with these two texts, with the two versions of John of Thessalonica's narrative, which draw on the same source as *R*, with the Latin text which Wenger calls *A* and with the Latin text in the M manuscript of *Transitus W*.[136] There must, therefore, have been a longer Greek apocryphon, the source of the *Liber Requiei*, which has not survived. Traces of it can also be seen in other texts: the discourses of Cosmas Vestitor (who probably lived between 750 and 850) on the assumption, for example, which have not survived in Greek but in a Latin translation.[137] It seems that *R*, or possibly the source of which *R* is an abbreviated version, is in some respects an orthodox revision of its source. We cannot, of course, know which revisions are the work of the *R* redactor in the sixth century and which are later editorial alterations: the text has come down to us in only one manuscript, of the eleventh century, and it is possible that some alterations were made even at this stage or at some earlier point after the sixth century. Wenger, for example, seems to suggest that some of the omissions in *R* can be explained 'par une censure théologique: au xi^e siècle, les craintes de Marie en face de la mort, la déclaration du Seigneur sur les âmes qui naissent dans l'état d'innocence,

---

[136] On which see below, p. 69.

[137] The third discourse says that 121 virgins kept watch with Mary and the apostles (Wenger, *L'assomption*, p. 325), while the *Liber Requiei* has twenty-one virgins: these numbers are clearly related, though one of them has presumably been altered in the course of transmission. Wenger argues that Cosmas Vestitor is following both *R* and John of Thessalonica for many of his details, but that for the number of virgins he must have been following 'une source apocryphe qui nous est inconnue' (*ibid.*, p. 164). Cosmas's number must be related to that given in the *Liber Requiei*, however, and this suggests that Cosmas's source was not *R*, but a fuller Greek apocryphon, the source of *R* and even closer than it is to the *Liber Requiei*. We need not, therefore, assume that Cosmas Vesitor drew on three apocrypha (*R*, John of Thessalonica and a third) but instead he must have been using the common source of *R* and John, which was fuller than either of these witnesses. In his fourth discourse on the assumption, Cosmas again has a passage which puzzled Wenger (*ibid.*, p. 168) but which again draws on a source similar, if not identical, to the end of book five of the *Liber Requiei*: 'Traditio autem refert quemadmodum exitum anime, ita et transmigrationem corporis uirginis matris Christi, apostolos tanquam dignos operum semper Dei conspectores uidisse. Si enim Moyses et quidam prophetarum una cum Stephano primomartyre gloriam Dei reuelata facie et sicut poterant capere conspexerunt, quomodo non et apostoli tunc magnalia Dei perspexerunt . . .' (*ibid.*, p. 330).

choquaient gravement la piété chrétienne'.[138] Short of discovering new manuscripts, we are unlikely to arrive at certainty on this point. Most of *R*'s omissions can be explained by the necessity to abbreviate for liturgical reading but such changes as the elimination of the unedifying controversy among the apostles, its replacement with a stress on the unity and accord of the apostles, and the dropping of the apocalyptic component of the text, ending instead with what now became the assumption of Mary without a full resurrection, are likely to have been made with more than simply brevity in mind. The Greek text has a marked pro-Petrine emphasis, upholding Peter's supremacy at every opportunity, which is clearly very different to the apostolic controversy in the Syriac text, in which it is only Paul who is supported by Christ.

JOHN OF THESSALONICA'S HOMILY FOR THE ASSUMPTION

John of Thessalonica's (*d. c.* 630) homily for the assumption of Mary, which exists in two forms, the short and the long or the interpolated (which has by far the better text, though full of minor additions),[139] is essentially similar to *R*, with some passages not found in *R* but attested by Latin texts dependent on *R*'s source (Wenger's *Transitus A* and Wilmart's *Transitus W*) and by the Ethiopic *Liber Requiei*. *R* and John therefore seem to have been drawing on the same or very closely related sources, but in some cases selecting different details.[140] John of Thessalonica (or, possibly, a previous redactor) went further than *R* in censoring

---

[138] *Ibid.*, p. 61.

[139] Both forms of the text were edited by M. Jugie, *Saint Jean, Archévêque de Thessalonique (mort vers 630), Discours sur la Dormition de la Sainte Vierge, Patrologia Orientalis* 19 (1925), 375–436. See Capelle, 'Les anciens récits', pp. 225–8, on the superiority of the longer text.

[140] Several of what are considered the best manuscripts of John of Thessalonica's narrative lack his prologue and incipit and attribute the text, not to John, but to James of Jerusalem, with the title already quoted in the discussion of *R* (see above p. 49). It is possible, therefore, that these manuscripts preserve the text of John of Thessalonica's direct source, a Greek text in five books attributed to James of Jerusalem, to which John merely added a prologue (see Mimouni, *Dormition*, pp. 143–4, and A. Wenger, 'Les homélies inédites de Cosmas Vestitor sur la Dormition', *Revue des études byzantines* 11 (1953), 284–300, at 289). John's input may have been minimal, therefore, restricted essentially to copying this text. All that this means in terms of discussing the text is that those changes and omissions now attributed to John of Thessalonica

their common source: as Wenger points out, John suppresses the prayer taught to Mary by the angel and recited by her at sunrise of the day on which she dies, the secret book, the angel of light, the garment of incorruption, the seventh heaven and the three servants for the three paths.[141] Whereas *R*, in spite of its revisions, kept many hermeneutic and esoteric details John of Thessalonica (or a predecessor) eliminated these. The ending of the text varies widely in the manuscripts: in editing fifteen manuscripts, Jugie found eleven different endings, representative of the different currents of thought in Byzantine Marian thinking, and there has been much disagreement about what the original ending was.[142] Jugie summarizes these endings: five manuscripts are completely silent on the fate of Mary's body after her burial; two lack the ending altogether; one has the body translated to the terrestrial paradise under the tree of life; four have the same transfer to paradise with the addition of a vague phrase suggesting a resurrection (they add 'and now she is living forever'); and three have a clear resurrection.[143] Mimouni seems to be the only one to argue that John of Thessalonica originally affirmed his belief in the assumption of Mary and that those manuscripts which contain only her dormition contain later revisions, reflecting a reaction against belief in the assumption.[144] That *R* and John draw on the same source, which seems to have affirmed the assumption, supports Mimouni's argument.

There has been disagreement too on John of Thessalonica's sources, even since the appearance of Wenger's work, which seems to prove conclusively that John drew on a source related to *R*. Jugie argued that one of John's main sources was the Latin *Transitus of Pseudo-Melito* and thought that the reason that John of Thessalonica had John the Evangelist come from Sardes, rather than the more common Ephesus, to Mary's house was because he had Sardes in mind from the prologue to *Pseudo-Melito*:[145] this argument does not carry any weight, however, as we now

would have to be attributed instead to a previous redactor, whose work John incorporated wholesale.

[141] *L'assomption*, p. 62.

[142] See Jugie, *La mort*, p. 140 and n. 6; Capelle, 'Les anciens récits', pp. 232–3; and J. M. Bover, *La asunción de Maria* (Madrid, 1947), p. 192.

[143] Jugie, *La mort*, p. 140.

[144] *Dormition*, pp. 146–7.

[145] Jugie, *La mort*, p. 145, n. 2; see also D. Baldi and A. Mosconi, 'L'Assunzione di Maria SS. negli apocrifi', in *Atti del congresso nazionale mariano dei frati minori d'Italia, Roma*

know that the Greek text *R* and the Latin *A* share this detail and that John simply took this over from his source. John is much closer to *R* than to *Pseudo-Melito*, which itself seems to descend from a Latin text descended in turn from a Latin translation of *R*'s source; that both John of Thessalonica and *Pseudo-Melito* both go back to the same ultimate source sufficiently explains the undeniable similarities between them.[146] Jugie's arguments can safely be discounted then. Mimouni's, the most recent account of the sources, is most peculiar in ignoring the work of Wenger, other than his suggestion that the title in some manuscripts is to be connected with the Syriac *Five Books* and to suggest that John of Thessalonica's work stems from these.[147] He never compares the contents of the two works, however, and they in fact have little in common: as suggested above, the *Five Books* of the title probably points rather to a connection with the related Greek/Syriac sources of the Ethiopic *Liber Requiei*.[148]

## OTHER GREEK TEXTS

The homily on the assumption attributed to Theoteknos of Livias, belonging probably to the seventh century, the homily on the assumption attributed to Modestus of Jerusalem, but probably by someone of the end of the seventh or beginning of the eighth century not living in Jerusalem, the three homilies on the assumption by Andrew of Crete (*c.* 660–740), the three homilies on the assumption by John of Damascus, from the mid-seventh to mid-eighth centuries, and the three homilies of the assumption attributed to Germanus of Constantinople, patriarch between 715 and 729, all form a fairly homogeneous group, all localizing Mary's house in Jerusalem, at Mount Sion, and all witnessing to a belief in

---

*29, aprile-3 maggio 1947*, Studia Mariana 1 (Rome, 1948), pp. 73–125 at pp. 100–6, who present a summary of *Pseudo-Melito* and John of Thessalonica in parallel, designed to prove the dependence of one on the other. What this table of parallels proves is the dependence of both texts on a common source.

[146] Mimouni, *Dormition*, p. 142, n. 88, is not correct in saying that John of Thessalonica and *Pseudo-Melito* are the only two texts to place John's ministry in Sardes: *Pseudo-Melito* in fact places it in Ephesus, while John shares Sardes with *R* and *A* and probably with the original Old Irish text.

[147] Mimouni, *Dormition*, pp. 143–4.    [148] See above, p. 49.

Mary's assumption after three days in the tomb (apart from Germanus of Constantinople, who has an immediate resurrection).[149]

## THE GREEK AND THE SYRIAC TRADITIONS

It is striking how, within the two textual families discussed here, the same differences can be observed between the Greek and Syriac texts: whereas the Greek are shorter and more focused on the death of the Virgin, the Syriac texts tend to be much more diffuse and intermeshed with other themes, such as the finding of the true cross, debates on the apostolic ministry, motifs from Jewish midrash. The Greek texts, with their exclusively Marian focus, are clearly liturgical and were intended for reading on the feast of Mary's death or assumption. It is much more difficult to imagine a context for the wordy, digressive Syriac texts, other than to see them as issuing from a desire to provide 'proof' of the final fate of the Virgin. It is as if all the other themes dealt with have the function of in some way bolstering the central theme of Mary's assumption: the presence of all of these familiar themes serves to authenticate the entire text, including the Marian enterprise. At least one Greek text, that of the source of the *Liber Requiei*, must have been very similar to the long Syriac accounts, however, and this suggests that the surviving Greek texts may give a misleading impression.

It is difficult to decide on which of the traditions discussed is prior and within each tradition, whether the Greek versions stem from the Syriac or the Syriac from the Greek. Critics generally regard the *Obsequies* as the oldest extant text but this naturally does not prove that the 'palm from the tree of life' textual family is the earliest one. The 'Bethlehem and the burning of incense' shares certain themes with the *Obsequies* family, in particular the coming of the apostles and the story of the Jews' attempt to sabotage the funeral procession, indicating that the two are not unconnected. It is possible that the Bethlehem family stems from a desire to correct the *Obsequies* tradition in two main respects: by removing the emphasis on Mary's fear of death and replacing it with a desire to be reunited with her son, and by introducing Bethlehem and giving it a place in the story of Mary's death, even at the expense of introducing a note of absurdity with Mary having to go from Jerusalem to Bethlehem

---

[149] See Mimouni, *Dormition*, pp. 152–70, on these texts.

and from Bethlehem back to Jerusalem. The emphasis on Mary's fear in the 'tree of life' tradition seems more primitive than that on her mystical desire for death, and the introduction of Bethlehem, with the subsequent clumsiness of the journey to and fro, smacks also of a later attempt to gain a place for that city, although the tradition of death in Jerusalem seems to have been already too strong to override. Van Esbroeck points out, too, that the Bethlehem family has had virtually no influence on the Latin texts and he considers this to be a sign of its 'efflorescence tardive'.[150] It seems probable, therefore, that the *Obsequies* tradition is prior.

That both textual traditions have at their beginning Mary's assumption into paradise is important: this is common to the *Obsequies* family and the Syriac *Six Books*. Only in some of the Coptic texts is Mary assumed into heaven rather than paradise. The dormition appears, then, to be a secondary belief, not, as Mimouni thinks, the original one. All the earliest texts in both families contain an account of Mary's otherworldly tour to heaven and/or hell and this must also be an original feature, with the intercessory motif perhaps explaining some of the function of these texts.

On the question of the priority of the Syriac and Greek texts it can be said that, in general, the tendency is for Syriac texts to be translated from Greek in this period. If these texts follow that general rule, then the origin of the *Obsequies* family would have to be a Greek text corresponding to the *Obsequies*, the source, presumably, of the Ethiopic *Liber Requiei*, in which the story of the death was followed by an apocalypse of Mary. Such a Greek text has not, of course, survived, but its existence is beyond doubt, attested also by the Old Irish text, which must have been translated from a Latin version of that lost text. A desire for shorter texts dealing only with the death, suitable for reading on 15 August, seems to have resulted in the Greek tradition preferring abbreviated accounts without an apocalypse from an early date; hence the loss of the earlier, more copious, texts.

[150] 'Les textes littéraires', p. 270.

# 3

# The death and assumption of Mary: the Latin tradition

The Latin apocryphal texts, apart from the Latin translation of *Pseudo-John* already discussed,[1] which exists in a single fourteenth-century manuscript, seem to have been uniformly in favour of the assumption when first composed, although the endings of many of the texts have been altered in the manuscripts, as happened also with the Greek manuscripts. There was a current of opinion against the apocrypha in the West, best represented by the so-called Gelasian Decree and the Pseudo-Jerome *Epistula Beati Hieronymi ad Paulam et Eustochium de assumptione Sanctae Mariae Virginis*, written in all probability by Paschasius Radbertus in the ninth century,[2] and this doubtless contributed to the tinkering with texts which is evident in so many of the manuscripts. Apart from the *Pseudo-John* translation and the *transitus* attributed to Joseph of Arimathaea (Tischendorf's *Transitus A*), all of the Latin *transitus* texts are in the tradition of the *R* family: Wenger's *Transitus A*, *Transitus W*, *Transitus B¹* and *B²* and Capelle's composite *transitus* text (the Colbert *transitus*).

## TRANSITUS A

The Latin *Transitus A* in Karlsruhe, Landesbibliothek, Codex Augiensis CCXXIX, fols. 184v–190v, is a very literal translation of a Greek text corresponding closely to *R*, but in part preserving more complete and apparently more archaic readings, even though it also abbreviates,

---

[1] Ed. Wilmart, 'L'ancien récit', pp. 357–62. See above, pp. 28–35.

[2] Von Dobschütz, ed., *Das Decretum Gelasianum*; *Paschasii Radberti: De assumptione sanctae Marie Virginis*, ed. A. Ripberger, CC Continuatio Mediaeualis 56 C (Turnhout, 1985), pp. 97–172.

particularly where there are long prayers.[3] In many of its departures from
*R* it is supported by the readings of John of Thessalonica and Wilmart's
manuscript M (Paris, Bibliothèque Nationale, lat. 13781, fols. 20r–24r)[4]
proving that it goes back to a source behind *R*. At the very beginning *A*
has Christ himself appear to Mary, before the appearance of the angel: this
detail is shared by the Old Irish *transitus*. Both redactors (the Old Irish
text cannot go back to *Transitus A*, as it has scenes, such as the apostolic
controversy, not paralleled in *A*) were probably puzzled by the ambiva-
lence of the presentation of the Christ-angel in their sources and
simplified by specifying that Christ himself appeared. *A*'s alteration also
eliminates the clumsy doubling in *R*, where the Christ-angel appears
twice and gives Mary the palm twice, once in her house and once on the
Mount of Olives; in *A* Christ appears first and tells Mary to go to the
Mount of Olives, where she receives the palm from the angel.

*A* preserves two scenes, found also in John of Thessalonica and the
*Liber Requiei* but missing from *R*, in which Mary preaches to her
neighbours about the two angels, *unus iusticie et alius malitie*, which attend
every death, followed by a dialogue with the women, who ask: 'Et si
pastor timuerit lupum, ubi fugient oues?'[5] It does not keep the detail of
the secret communicated to John when he leant on Christ's breast, known
only to John and Mary, or the passage about the book containing the
revelations made to Mary, presumably because they smacked too much of
the esoteric. It omits also the pious debate between Peter and Paul about
who is to pray, when the apostles find themselves reunited outside Mary's
house. *A* preserves, however, a very important passage which was omitted
in *R* and altered by John of Thessalonica but which is preserved also in
the Ethiopic, in a fuller form. In it Peter is preaching to the other apostles
and to the three virgins who are watching with Mary and he tells them:
'Viri fratres, nolite suspicare mortem esse mortem marie. Non est mors
sed uita aeterna . . .'; a light then illuminates the house and a voice says:
'Petre uide ne reuelaris hoc, quia uobis solis datum est hec cognoscere et
loqui scientiam'.[6] This injunction about Mary's death not being death is
in keeping with the avoidance of the direct vocabulary of death

---

[3] Ed. Wenger, *L'assomption*, pp. 245–56.

[4] On the distinctive version in this manuscript, see below, pp. 69 and 71.

[5] Wenger, *L'assomption*, p. 247.

[6] *Ibid.*, p. 251. The strong vein of elitism is a primitive feature.

throughout *R* and *A*, which was obviously a feature of their common source.[7] Following this injunction to say no more about Mary's death, *A* preserves an episode omitted by *R* but present in John of Thessalonica and the *Liber Requiei*, in which the virgins beg Peter to preach to them and in which he tells a parable in celebration of virginity.

At the scene of Mary's death, *A* omits the description of Mary's soul as being without sex but then, like John of Thessalonica but unlike *R*, preserves Peter's question about who has a soul as white as Mary's and Christ's reply: 'Si quis custodit a multis peccatis, anima eius inuenietur candida sicut marie'.[8] As Wenger points out, this reply takes no account of the doctrine of original sin and it is implied in the narrative that the souls of those who avoid sin are completely pure.[9] *A*, like *R*, fails to mention the destination of Mary's soul. *A* is the only Latin *transitus* text to place Mary's tomb to the left of Jerusalem, in accordance with *R*: Christ instructs Peter: 'exi de sinistra parte ciuitatis et inuenies monumentum nouum'.[10] The Old Irish text in the *Liber Flauus Fergusiorum* has the left side also, but the Irish Latin version has the right side. *A* is also the only Latin text to place John's mission in Sardes, as in *R* and in John of Thessalonica. There is a unique reading at the very end of the narrative, where Mary's body is taken to paradise, along with the apostles, and the Lord replaces her soul in her body and a very clear resurrection follows: 'Dominus autem accepit animam eius de manu michaelis archangeli et restituit eam in corpus marie. Exsurgens autem beata maria a pedibus suis, ambulauit et angeli ymnum psallebant.'[11] This seems to be an independent addition of *A*, as there is no other witness to such a scene. Again, body and soul seem to remain in paradise, as the narrative ends at this point, after the return to earth of the apostles. Mimouni points out that the text is not explicit on the three days Mary spends in the tomb, never posing the question of whether or not her body experienced normal human decay.[12] Such questions tend to be posed only in the obviously polemical Coptic texts, however, and are not a feature of other traditions.

It is difficult to know when *A* was composed; style is of no help as *A* is

---

[7] *A* uses terms like *deponebis corpus* (Wenger, *L'assomption*, p. 245); *egredior de corpore* (*ibid.*, p. 246); *exeo de hoc mundo* (*ibid.*, p. 248); *exeo de corpore* (*ibid.*, p. 250); *compleuit statum suum* (*ibid.*, p. 253). Compare also *R*, see above p. 58.

[8] Wenger, *L'assomption*, p. 254.  [9] *Ibid.*, p. 84.  [10] *Ibid.*, p. 254.

[11] *Ibid.*, p. 256.

[12] *Dormition*, p. 280.

a very literal translation, 'un décalque'.[13] Wenger suggests that the sixth century is probable, while not excluding that it could be as late as the end of the eighth,[14] though in his tabular presentation of the *R* family he places *A* in the seventh to ninth centuries.[15] Mimouni dates it to the seventh or eighth centuries, on the grounds that its developed assumption scene suggests that it belongs to a period when the feast of the assumption was well established in the West, and this seems plausible.[16] *Transitus A* seems to be a translation made for liturgical use[17] and the sole surviving manuscript was copied at Reichenau at the beginning of the ninth century. We do not know whether the abbreviation was made by the same person who translated the text from Greek into Latin or whether the translator worked from a Greek text which had already been abbreviated. In Wenger's table of texts he shows *Transitus A* as descending from a prior Latin translation, which has not survived in its entirety but parts of which have been entered into manuscript M of *Transitus W*, the thirteenth-century Paris, Bibliothèque Nationale, lat. 13781, supplementing the text of *Transitus W* in this manuscript.[18] The additions in M come from a text which is fuller than that of *Transitus A* and they are closely related to the Greek *R*, often translating *R* literally but with some elements not paralleled in *R* that are clearly primitive. They do not, however, agree word for word with *Transitus A*, where these two texts overlap; instead they have the same substance in different words. This means that *A* probably descends either from a separate translation of a Greek source, the same Greek source as the full text from which M's additions were translated or a different, shorter text, or that it was translated directly from Greek.

## TRANSITUS W AND TRANSITUS B

Either another Greek text of the same family or a Latin translation, whether the complete text which lies behind M or a different, lost, text (or texts), seems to have been the source for two further Latin apocrypha, *Transitus W* and *Transitus B* or the *Transitus of Pseudo-Melito*,[19] the sources

---

[13] Wenger, *L'assomption*, p. 88.   [14] *Ibid.*, p. 91.   [15] *Ibid.*, p. 66.

[16] *Dormition*, pp. 279–80.   [17] Wenger, *L'assomption*, pp. 69 and 92.

[18] *Ibid.*, p. 66.

[19] *Transitus W* is edited by Wilmart, 'L'ancien récit', pp. 323–57; there are two versions of *Transitus B*, $B^1$ and $B^2$. There is no critical edition of $B^1$, but it has been edited by

for the two Old English homilies. They do not depend on *Transitus A*, as they are sometimes fuller than it and preserve some different, primitive details. Capelle, even before Wenger's discovery and publication of *R* and *A*, argued that John of Thessalonica, *Transitus W* and *Pseudo-Melito* all went back to a common Greek source and that *Transitus W* was a translation, abridged for liturgical use, of this source, while the most probable hypothesis to explain the origins of *Pseudo-Melito* was that it is derived from the complete Latin text of which *Transitus W* is an abbreviation.[20] Wilmart, without going into the question of sources, had already suggested that *Transitus W* was the source behind *Pseudo-Melito*.[21]

Capelle demonstrates his theory by taking three representative scenes and comparing their treatment in John of Thessalonica, *Transitus W* and *Pseudo-Melito*, showing how what he calls a law of progressive devaluation operates.[22] In all three scenes, which are representative of the treatment of the same basic narrative in all three works, the procedure is that primitive elements are progressively edited out, leaving behind vestiges which fail to make complete sense in the absence of their full, original context. In the three treatments of John's response to Mary's giving him the single palm, this can be seen clearly: in John of Thessalonica, Mary gives John the Evangelist the palm, asking that he carry it in front of her bier, and he replies that he cannot take it without his fellow-apostles being present, lest there be grumbling and jealousy among them, and he says that there is one among them greater than he is. This is obviously original and has been prepared for earlier in the text where Mary tells the angel of her misgivings about the single palm (and, of course, its original nature has been verified since the appearance of Capelle's article by the presence of this scene in *R* and in the Ethiopic *Liber Requiei*). In *Transitus W*, Mary asks John to see that the palm is carried in front of her bier and here

---

Tischendorf, *Apocalypses Apocryphae*, pp. 124–36, from a single fourteenth-century manuscript, and there is another edition in Migne, PG 5, cols. 1231–50. There is a critical edition of *Transitus B²* by Haibach-Reinisch, *Ein neuer 'Transitus'*, drawing on eighteen manuscripts. Two further manuscripts of *B²* are noted by Mimouni, *Dormition*, p. 266, n. 32. Haibach-Reinisch lists twenty-six manuscripts of *Transitus B¹*, *Ein neuer 'Transitus'*, pp. 31–2, and a critical edition of this version is badly needed. See Wenger's table, *L'assomption*, pp. 66 and 90–1, on relations between these versions.

[20] Capelle, 'Vestiges', p. 29.      [21] 'L'ancien récit', p. 323.
[22] Capelle, 'Vestiges', pp. 24–8.

John's reply has become innocuous, consisting only of: 'Hoc enim non possum facere solus, nisi aduenerint fratres et coapostoli mei'.[23] All mention of jealousy among the apostles has disappeared. In *Pseudo-Melito* this becomes a question: as Capelle says: '*Mel.* va la dénaturer tout à fait en en élargissant brusquement l'objet: "Quomodo ego solus tibi parabo exsequias, nisi uenerint fratres et coapostoli . . .?" L'idée de préparer les obsèques a été intentionnellement substituée à celle de porter la palme, et il semble que le scrupule de delicatesse ait fait place à un simple aveu d'impuissance, sous forme de question.'[24] Capelle's thesis with regard to John of Thessalonica and *Transitus W* has been confirmed with Wenger's publication of *R*, which is an abbreviated version of the longer text drawn upon by John of Thessalonica and the source of *Transitus W*.

Capelle suggests further that the source of *W* was probably the full Latin text which lies behind the additions to *W* in the M manuscript,[25] arguing that parts of this common source text must have been transcribed into the margins of a manuscript of *W* as glosses augmenting *Transitus W* and that these glosses were later incorporated in the text of the *transitus* itself, giving us the form of the text in the M manuscript. The faulty translations found in both texts are for him proof that *W* and M stem from the same translation: this translation was slavishly literal and its translator understood Greek badly. Differences between M and *W* are to be explained by the *Transitus W* redactor's freer adaptation and more drastic summarizing, while the interpolations in M seem not always to have been inserted in the correct place.[26] We cannot be certain of this common source, as by their very nature the additions in M do not overlap with the text of *W*, but it seems probable. The M manuscript of *Transitus W*, therefore, if this is correct, gives us a text very close to the source of *Transitus W*, combining as it does those parts of the source omitted by *W* with the text of *W*.

Capelle is supported by Wenger, who also argues for the relationship between *W* and *Pseudo-Melito* on the basis of similarities between these two texts. Wenger is somewhat more cautious than Capelle about the origins of *Pseudo-Melito* and its precise relation with *W*, while accepting

---

[23] Wilmart, 'L'ancien recit', p. 331.

[24] Capelle, 'Vestiges', p. 27; see also the discussion in the notes to the Old English text of *exceptis omnibus membris* in *Transitus W* for a similar case, pp. 293–4.

[25] The text of these additions is included in the apparatus to Wilmart's edition.

[26] Capelle, 'Vestiges', pp. 32–3.

that there are literary affinities between *W* and *Pseudo-Melito* not explicable by the extant Greek texts and not paralleled in *Transitus A*.[27] He explains this caution by pointing out that *Pseudo-Melito* is generally thought to be a very old, probably fifth-century, text and that an early date for *Pseudo-Melito* would naturally have consequences for the dating of all the other texts, both Latin and Greek.[28] This uncertainty is evident in Wenger's discussion of the Latin texts related to *Transitus A*, where several times he appears to say that the author of *Transitus W* was drawing on *Pseudo-Melito*; see, for example: '*Domini mei* de W est une glose manifeste qui peut provenir du Pseudo-Méliton'[29] and 'La formule par laquelle Marie rapporte les propos des Juifs s'inspire dans W du Pseudo-Méliton'.[30] Despite these comments, Wenger, in his table of textual relationships, shows *W* and *Pseudo-Melito* as both descending from a common lost intermediary, itself descended from the full translation which is the source of the additions in M.[31] This seems to me a more convincing explanation than that *W* is drawing on *Pseudo-Melito*: *Pseudo-Melito* is a much more maverick text, which one would expect to have left more traces on *Transitus W*, had it been a source for the latter text. On the question of date, Wenger's problems can of course be solved by placing *Pseudo-Melito* considerably later than the fifth century: there is little justification for such an early date[32] and therefore no obstacle of date to the theory that *Pseudo-Melito* and *Transitus W* are both descended from a common source.

Haibach-Reinisch, whose knowledge of Wenger's work was belated, includes only a five-page epilogue taking it into account.[33] She too acknowledges that *Pseudo-Melito* is descended from a member of the *R* family, that it is closely related to *Transitus W* and that there are elements which only these two texts share, but she is still reluctant to accept that *Pseudo-Melito* and *W* have a source common to them only, on the grounds that 'die Bearbeitungsmotive in *Transitus B* zu offensichtlich und die Priorität dieses Textes gesichert erscheint'.[34] Like Wenger, she is therefore influenced by her belief in an implausibly early date for *Transitus B*; her other reason is also not convincing, as the *Transitus B* redactor's reworking of his source is not called into question by Capelle's theory. Her own

---

[27] Wenger, *L'assomption*, p. 90.   [28] *Ibid.*, pp. 90–1.   [29] *Ibid.*, p. 74.
[30] *Ibid.*, p. 75.   [31] *Ibid.*, p. 66.   [32] See below, p. 85, on the date.
[33] *Ein neuer 'Transitus'*, pp. 315–19.   [34] *Ibid.*, p. 317.

suggestion, that *Transitus W* is a translation of a Greek text made with the help of *Pseudo-Melito* or a combination of a text of the *R* family already translated into Latin and *Pseudo-Melito*, seems unlikely. As suggested above, *Pseudo-Melito* is so individual a text that one would expect it to have left more trace on *Transitus W*, had this been the case. The most likely argument, therefore, is still that *Pseudo-Melito* and *Transitus W* share a common source, which *W* adapted comparatively little and which *Pseudo-Melito* reworked much more radically.

Capelle's argument is that both *Transitus W* and *Pseudo-Melito* are descended from the complete Latin text of which *W* is an abbreviation; this complete text he identifies as that represented by the additions in M. This text, however, as he himself points out,[35] is a very literal translation of a Greek source and one would not expect such a text to introduce independently the points common to *Transitus W* and *Pseudo-Melito* which are not paralleled in any other Greek or Latin source. In addition, *Pseudo-Melito* shares nothing with the additions in M, as one would expect had it descended directly from the complete text behind M. In fact Capelle himself, although he explicitly says that *Pseudo-Melito* 'se montre par endroits si proche du *Transitus* de Wilmart que l'hypothèse la plus probable est qu'il procède de lui – ou, plus exactement, du texte latin complet dont *Wil* n'est qu'un résumé',[36] speaks of the relationship between the two texts as if *Pseudo-Melito* were descended from *W* (the law of progressive devaluation that he formulates suggests that *Pseudo-Melito* descends from *W* rather than that both it and *W* descend from the same source). One passage in particular presents a difficulty to Capelle's theory, however: that concerning the high-priest and his appeal to Peter to have mercy on him. This passage was evidently corrupt from a very early stage in the *R* tradition: it does not survive in the Syriac *Obsequies*, but there are difficulties with it in the Greek *R* and in the Ethiopic *Liber Requiei*. The fragmentary Sahidic *transitus*[37] is probably the nearest non-Latin text to what must have been the original reading of this passage, in whatever language that was: there the high-priest says, in French translation: 'Souviens-toi du moment où la portière discuta avec toi en disant: "Tu es un disciple de Jésus." Moi je l'ai réprimandée. Maintenant donc, mon père Pierre, ne me laisse pas mourir dans ce tourment.'[38] This is close to

---

[35] 'Vestiges', p. 33.    [36] *Ibid.*, p. 29.    [37] See above, pp. 45–6.
[38] Quoted by Capelle, 'Les anciens récits', p. 222.

the biblical account, John XVIII.15–17, where John and Peter follow Jesus after his arrest and John, because he is known to the high-priest, gains access to the high-priest's palace, while Peter stands outside: 'Exiuit ergo discipulus alius, qui erat notus pontifici, et dixit ostiariae: et introduxit Petrum.' The accounts of Matthew, Mark and Luke of the doorkeeper's accusation are also drawn upon. The apocryphon has, of course, gone beyond the bible, in having the high-priest himself responsible for defending Peter, but this is nearer to the biblical accounts than later renditions of the scene. In the Greek *R*, the high-priest has become the high-priest's father, probably, as Capelle suggests,[39] because of confusion with the vocative 'father Peter', and it reads, again in French translation: 'Souviens-toi, Pierre, de mon père lorsque la portière, la servante, te questionne et te dit: "Toi aussi, tu es un disciple de cet homme." Rappelle-toi comment et de quelle manière je t'ai interrogé.'[40] As Wenger points out, this is a troubled passage, especially because of the first-person verb in the last clause,[41] as is the Ethiopic, where the high-priest's father has even become Peter's disciple, leading Arras to state: 'Verba excusationis hominis castigati iam ab antiquo uitiata censenda sunt'.[42] *Transitus A* and *Transitus W* perpetuate the father, *W* reading: 'Rogo te praecipue, sancte Petre, ut memor sis quid tibi praestiterit pater meus, quando ostiaria illa interrogauit te et dicebat: "Vere tu cum illo eras, quomodo te excusauit, ne conprehendereris."[43] *Pseudo-Melito*, on the other hand, reads: 'Memento quando ancilla ostiaria calumniabatur tibi, ego locutus sum pro te bona. Sed nunc quaeso te, ut miserearis mei per Dominum.'[44] Here the source is handled with the freedom usual in *Pseudo-Melito*, but, as in the Sahidic, it is the high-priest himself who has defended Peter. A further Latin text, the Colbert *transitus*, Paris, Bibliothèque Nationale, lat. 2672, fols. 7v–12r, the bulk of which is not dependent on *Pseudo-Melito*, also has what seems to be the correct reading here: 'Presertim tu, beatissime Petre, memor est qualiter te excusauerim, cum te ostiaria illa accusabat et dicebat quod ex illis esses.'[45] *Colbert* combines the beginning and end of *Pseudo-Melito* with another version of the same story, similar to *Transitus W* but shorter and preserving some

---

[39] 'L'ancien récit', p. 222, n. 11. See also Wenger, *L'assomption*, p. 49.

[40] Wenger, *L'assomption*, p. 235.     [41] *Ibid.*, p. 235, n. 3.

[42] *De transitu*, II, 96–7.     [43] Wilmart, 'L'ancien récit', p. 351.

[44] Haibach-Reinisch, ed., *Ein neuer 'Transitus'*, p. 81.

[45] Capelle, 'Vestiges', p. 47. This article includes an edition of all of the Colbert text.

original details lacking in the latter text. Capelle suggests that, while *Colbert* could not be dependent on *W*, *W* could be derived from the same text from which *Colbert* stems, each of them keeping some original details which the other chose to omit.[46] Where *Colbert* parallels manuscript M of *Transitus W* which, Capelle argues, is very close to the source of *W*, it does not have the same wording, however.[47] In addition, *W* and *Colbert* do not agree on the high-priest's appeal. If it were not for this second, apparently independent, Latin witness, one would think that *Pseudo-Melito* had corrected its source here and this would fit with the evident familiarity with the bible demonstrated throughout this text, but the correct reading in *Colbert* suggests that both of these witnesses could stem from a text which had not been corrupted in the manner of the other witnesses. The matter is complicated by the evident closeness of *W* and *Pseudo-Melito* in other respects, where *Colbert* differs in having a text closer to the Greek: to take just one example, *Colbert* describes the punishment of the same high-priest, in terms very close to John of Thessalonica, *R* and the Syriac *Obsequies*: 'Et statim manus eius heserunt in lectum, et excesserunt a cubitis eius.'[48] Reversing the order of clauses, *W* reads: 'Statim uero manus eius ambae aruerunt ab ipsis cubitis et adhaeserunt ad lectum',[49] while *Pseudo-Melito* has: 'Et statim aruerunt ambae manus eius ab ipsis cubitis et adhaeserunt feretro (*B¹*: lecto)'.[50] The agreement of *W* and *Pseudo-Melito* cannot be coincidental and makes it difficult to argue that *Pseudo-Melito* is descended from another strand of the tradition. Since the scribe of *Colbert* was clearly familiar with *Pseudo-Melito*, it may be the case that *Pseudo-Melito* independently corrected the detail of the father of the high-priest, and that this correction was then incorporated into his text by the *Colbert* scribe. It is difficult to be certain, in short, of the exact relation of *Pseudo-Melito* to *W* and *Colbert*, but the most likely theory is that *Pseudo-Melito* and *W* do share a common source, possibly a lost intermediary text which itself descends from M, as Wenger suggests;[51] this intermediary must have been an abbreviated text which introduced

---

[46] *Ibid.*, p. 39.

[47] See *ibid.*, pp. 37 and 38: where M has *affines et notos meos*, *Colbert* has *omnes affines et amicos suos* and where M has *ardentibus lucernis*, *Colbert* has *Erant enim omnium lampades et lucerne accense*, suggesting that they stem from different translations from the Greek.

[48] *Ibid.*, p. 47. See also pp. 39–40.    [49] Wilmart, 'L'ancien récit', p. 350.

[50] Haibach-Reinisch, ed., *Ein neuer 'Transitus'*, pp. 80 and 102, for texts of *B1* and *B2*.

[51] Wenger, *L'assomption*, p. 66.

some fairly minor original phrases and ideas. It was presumably copied fairly faithfully by *W* and transformed stylistically by *Pseudo-Melito*.

### TRANSITUS W

Although in a simple style, *Transitus W* is a less literal text than *A*, 'un arrangement à partir d'une traduction',[52] 'un récit retouché', as Wenger terms it,[53] intended again for liturgical use.[54] While the first parts of *Transitus W* seem to treat its source quite freely, as the text goes on it becomes more faithful, as can be seen from some passages which agree with the more literal *Transitus A*. It appears to be meant especially for religious, as it has a unique expansion of Peter's address to the virgins at Mary's bedside, in which he tells them that bodily integrity alone is not enough and that they need, too, to be vigilant in what they say and to spend their time in vigils and prayers.[55] This seems to be the only *transitus* apocryphon to caution in this way against an overvaluation of virginity and it would seem, therefore, that the *W* adaptor had a specifically religious audience in mind here.

The *W* adaptor (or his immediate source, as throughout this discussion) makes a series of relatively minor alterations to his source, often in the interests of decorum and meticulousness. The coyness about the assumption which is a feature of the *R* tradition texts up to this point disappears in *Transitus W*, where the angel tells Mary at the very beginning of the text that 'post tres dies adsumenda es. Et ecce ego mittam omnes apostolos ad te sepeliendam, ut uideant gloriam tuam quam acceptura es.'[56] The corresponding passage in *Transitus A* reads much more non-committedly, even though assumption does not necessarily imply a corporal assumption: 'dic omnibus quod post triduum deponebis corpus. Et mittam ad te omnes apostolos meos; et ipsi te fouebunt et gloriam tuam uidebunt.'[57] (Only in its title does *A* mention the assumption, *adsumptio*, never in the text itself.) In keeping with this, the assumption is mentioned several times in the course of *W*. The *Transitus W* adaptor seems also not to have been comfortable with his source's depiction of Mary's fear of death and he toned it down somewhat, omitting any

---

[52] *Ibid.*, p. 74.     [53] *Ibid.*, p. 68.     [54] *Ibid.*, p. 71.

[55] Wilmart, 'L'ancien récit', pp. 339–41; see also Capelle, 'Les anciens récits', p. 221.

[56] Wilmart, 'L'ancien récit', p. 326.     [57] Wenger, *L'assomption*, p. 245.

mention of her weeping.[58] Neither did he like the scene where John does not understand that Mary is about to die and becomes defensive about his own actions in leaving her, with a servant to care for her, in order to fulfil Christ's command to preach; this scene is omitted altogether.

Another instance of the author of *W* leaving his own imprint on the text is evident in his treatment of Peter and the heavenly voice. This scene comes just after all the apostles have arrived at Mary's house, when they have settled down to watch with her for three days. All of the other apostles urge Peter to teach both them and the people watching with them and Peter begins to preach; *A* gives a very good idea of the source's version of this passage:

Tunc petrus cepit dicere: 'Viri fratres, nolite suspicare mortem esse mortem marie. Non est mors sed uita aeterna. Quoniam mors iustorum conlaudabitur apud deum. Haec enim gloria est et secunda mors non potest illi molesta esse.' Haec cum adhuc loquerentur, lumen refulsit in domo ita ut superaretur lumen lucernarum et facta est uox dicens: 'Petre uide ne reuelaris hoc, quia uobis solis datum est hec cognoscere et loqui scientiam'. Conuersus autem petrus dixit: 'Fratres, manifeste est quod potestatem non habemus que uolumus dicere. Sed qui gubernat corda nostra, ipse nos custodiat.'[59]

The author of *Transitus W* was evidently uneasy about this whole passage and changed it to:

dixit beatus Petrus . . . 'Fratres karissimi, nolite suspicari hanc uocationem beatae Mariae esse mortem. Non est enim illi mors, sed uita aeterna, quoniam mors iustorum laudatur apud deum, quia haec est gloria magna.' Et cum haec diceret, subito lumen magnum refulsit in domo illa, ita ut uix aliquis aut conspicere posset aut enarrare prae magnitudine luminis. Et facta est uox, dicens: 'Petre, ecce ego uobiscum sum omnibus diebus usque ad consummationem saeculi'. Petrus uero eleuauit uocem suam, dicens: 'Benedicimus te, guberna-culum animarum nostrarum, et petimus ut a nobis non discedas. Benedicimus te, inluminator saeculi, qui omnibus misereris.'[60]

A powerless Peter admonished by the divine voice not to preach evidently did not suit the didactic interests of the *W* adaptor, who has made the whole passage much more bland, eliminating also the contradiction of death not being death.[61] The new intervention by the divine voice has

---

[58] *Ibid.*, p. 71.    [59] *Ibid.*, p. 251.    [60] Wilmart, 'L'ancien récit', pp. 338–9.
[61] Wenger, *L'assomption*, pp. 79–80.

nothing to do with the immediate context, the *W* adaptor supplying instead a familiar biblical quotation. Another small indication of *W*'s punctiliousness is the alteration of the description of Mary's soul being placed in Michael's hands, where *A*'s 'posuit in manus michaheli archangeli'[62] becomes *W*'s 'tradidit eam sancto angelo Michahel',[63] eliminating the soul in Michael's hands. In Christ's reply to Peter's question about who has a soul as white as Mary's, *A*'s passage implying that souls are born totally pure is made theologically acceptable by specifying that the souls are pure 'cum de sancto lauacro lotae processerint'.[64]

*Transitus W* was edited by Wilmart using nine manuscripts dating from the eighth to the fourteenth century, among which there is much variation.[65] They divide into two main families, one consisting of the manuscripts F, G, M, P, T and V, the other of B, R and S.[66] Wilmart gives preference to the first family in producing what he terms a neutral text, rather than attempting to work back to an original form.

The ending of the work differs considerably in these two families: both relate the apostles' arrival at the sepulchre, the coming of Jesus, his command to Michael to receive the body of Mary into the clouds and the apostles being received into the clouds also. Jesus then commands the clouds 'ut irent in paradiso', with two manuscripts (R and S) specifying 'sub arbore uitae'.[67] The manuscripts of the first family, represented here by G, M and P, read 'Et sic deposuerunt nubes corpus beatae Mariae in paradiso, et est ibi glorificans deum cum omnibus electis eius'.[68] Wilmart considers this reading superior.[69] According to the second family, R and S

---

[62] *Ibid.*, p. 253.    [63] Wilmart, 'L'ancien récit', p. 344.

[64] *Ibid.*, p. 345. See also above, p. 68, for *A*.

[65] Three more manuscripts are listed by Mimouni, *Dormition*, p. 281, n. 85, to which should be added Cambridge, Pembroke College, 25 (see Appendix I). The text had already been edited, from a single manuscript, by D. M. Férotin, *Le Liber Mozarabicus Sacramentorum* (Paris, 1912), pp. 786–95; Marocco has published two fragmentary versions in 'Nuovi documenti'.

[66] Paris, Bibliothèque Nationale, nouv. acq. lat. 1605, fols. 22v, 27r–30v (F); Saint Gall, Stiftsbibliothek 732, fols. 115r–42r (G); Paris Bibliothèque Nationale, lat. 13781, fols. 20r–24r (M); Vatican City, Biblioteca Apostolica Vaticana, Palat. lat. 430, fols. 109r–111r (P); Troyes, Bibliothèque municipale 1396, fols. 45v–48r (T); Silos, fonds reconstitué 2, fols. 188r–205r (V); Paris, Bibliothèque Nationale, Baluze 270, fols. 167r–174r (B); Vatican City, Biblioteca Apostolica Vaticana, Reginensis lat. 119, fols. 132r–135v (R); and Rome, Biblioteca Nazionale, Sessoriano 121, fols. 83v–93r (S).

[67] Wilmart, 'L'ancien récit', pp. 356–7.    [68] *Ibid.*, p. 357.    [69] *Ibid.*

(B lacks the end), the body of Mary is placed in paradise[70] and her soul is replaced in her body; S reads: 'Et adtulerunt angeli animam sanctae Mariae et posuerunt eam in corpore ipsius, iubente domino nostro Iesu Christo, et habebit gloriam ibi in sempiterna saecula saeculorum amen';[71] and R: 'Tulerunt igitur angeli animam beate marie et posuit eam dominus in corpore ipsius'.[72]

Comparing these variant forms of the ending with the Syriac *Obsequies* and with R is interesting and suggests that Wilmart was incorrect in seeing in G, M and P the original ending. Both the *Obsequies* and the Greek R have Mary's body being placed under the tree of life, her soul being brought (by the angels in the *Obsequies*, by Michael in the Greek R) and replaced in her body. This proves that the tree of life in Wilmart's R and S manuscripts is original, as is their account of the angels replacing Mary's soul in her body. Wilmart seems to be wrong about the superiority of the ending of his G, M and P manuscripts, then, as his R and S manuscripts are undoubtedly closer to the original ending of this textual family.[73] The Latin text in origin must have been an assumption text testifying to Mary's body and soul being reunited in paradise, but the G, M and P manuscripts have omitted the reunification of body and soul, concluding with the placing of Mary's body in paradise. The phrases 'et est ibi glorificans deum cum omnibus electis eius' in G, M and P and 'et habebit gloriam ibi in sempiterna saecula saeculorum amen' in R and S were probably both added in order to provide suitable endings.[74]

Two manuscripts, one from each family, add a further sentence to the endings given above; R adds 'Tunc praecepit dominus restituere apostolos unumquemque unde assumpti fuerant',[75] followed by a further passage which does not belong to the apocryphon, while M, the expanded version of *W*, adds 'Et iterum precepit dominus angelis ut irent unusquisque in locum, ubi sunt cotidie cum magno gaudio letantes et benedicentes deum'.[76] Both sentences are paralleled elsewhere in the tradition, as in the Syriac *Obsequies* the angels are returned to their places, in R the apostles. M's account of the angels being returned to their places is primitive therefore, as it agrees with the Syriac, and earlier than the

---

[70] Where the other manuscripts read *irent* in the clause quoted above, R reads *deponerent illud*, giving 'ut deponerent illud in paradiso sub arbore uitis [*sic*]' (Wilmart, 'L'ancien récit', p. 356).

[71] *Ibid.*, p. 357.     [72] *Ibid.*     [73] See also Wenger, *L'assomption*, pp. 87–8.

[74] Wilmart, 'L'ancien récit', p. 357.     [75] *Ibid.*     [76] *Ibid.*

apostles being returned to theirs, as we find in the Greek *R* and the Latin *Transitus W* manuscript R. In the Syriac the angels' departure forms the beginning of the transition to the apocalypse part of the text. The agreement of M and the Syriac is striking and suggests that the fuller account from which M's additions were taken may have been a version with apocalypse, as in Paris, Bibliothèque Nationale, lat. 3550, from the thirteenth century, which contains a text which seems to be an independent translation of a Greek source similar to that which lies behind *Transitus W.*[77] The part paralleling *W* ends: 'Et sic corpus beate marie posuerunt in paradiso, sub arbore uite. Et attulerunt animam beate marie angeli domini et posuerunt eam in corpore eius. Et dominus precepit angelis ut irent in locum suum';[78] it is followed by a short apocalypse, very similar to that in the Syriac *Obsequies.*[79]

Unlike *R* and *A*, *Transitus W* (like *Pseudo-Melito*) places the tomb of Mary on the right-hand side of Jerusalem. In *A*, as in *R*, Christ directs Peter 'exi de sinistra parte ciuitatis et inuenies monumentum nouum',[80] whereas in *W* Christ says 'egredere in dexteram partem ciuitatis, et inuenies ibi monumentum nouum'.[81] In the previously unedited version of *W* in Cambridge, Pembroke College, 25, the body of Mary is buried in the valley of Jehoshaphat, named near the end of the text when she is committed to the tomb.[82] The Old Irish version also has the left side, as have John of Thessalonica[83] and the *Liber Requiei*, which suggests that this was also the reading in the Syriac *Obsequies*. This reading is undoubtedly primitive and it is strange that no critic has attempted to explain the subsequent alteration to the right in the Latin texts other than *A*. All of the named sites of Mary's tomb in other texts place it on the Mount of Olives or in Jehoshaphat or in Gethsemane, all three in close proximity to each other, to the right of Jerusalem when viewed on a map, and the tradition in Jerusalem is unanimous from the sixth century onwards in placing it in Gethsemane, in the church dedicated to Mary there.[84] The tomb is never localized in any other area around Jerusalem

---

[77] Wenger, *L'assomption*, p. 30.  [78] *Ibid.*, p. 258.  [79] *Ibid.*, pp. 258–9.
[80] *Ibid.*, p. 254.  [81] Wilmart, 'L'ancien récit', p. 345.
[82] See Appendix I, p. 333.
[83] See Wenger, *L'assomption*, p. 85, n. 1, who points out that Jugie, in his Latin translation of John of Thessalonica's Greek text, inadvertently translated left as right, giving the mistaken impression that the Greek text had the right-hand side.
[84] Mimouni, *Dormition*, pp. 549–79.

and all the important sites outside the walls of Jerusalem are to the east of the city (the right, viewed aerially or on a map). Either *R* and the texts related to it witness to a different tradition, unattested elsewhere, then, or their directions, despite the difference between left and right, point also to the area around the Mount of Olives. In these texts Christ directs Peter to go out by the left of the city and it is probable that the author is thinking here in terms of being in Jerusalem and leaving it by a southern gate, in which case one would have to turn left to go towards the Mount of Olives. This is certainly the route one would follow leaving from the church of Mary on Sion (where the tradition in Jerusalem, from the seventh century onwards, placed Mary's house and death)[85] and heading for the area of the Mount of Olives, and this may well have been what was intended. Before Mary's house was localized in Sion, it had been localized in Gethsemane (from the fifth century), which then developed into the site of Mary's tomb, and in the church of the Kathisma in Bethlehem (middle of the fifth century onwards).[86] In the *R* texts Bethlehem or Gethsemane clearly do not come into question as the site of Mary's house, and hence her death, as they place Mary's house within Jerusalem (the Christ-angel tells her that he cannot say his name in the middle of Jerusalem, lest it be destroyed, and that he will reveal it to her on the Mount of Olives). Either these texts are an early witness to Mary's house in Sion, as the *Obsequies* are generally dated to the end of the fifth century, or the localization in Jerusalem is here a vague one, not specific to any particular site in the city.

Two points in the *Liber Requiei* also offer support for the view that this textual family placed the burial place of Mary to the east of the city: the first is where the apostles are waiting at Mary's tomb and Paul asks Peter to reveal to him what was revealed to Peter on the Mount of Olives. When Peter refuses and they are deliberating among themselves, two men pass by 'ex Ierusalem in Cedron':[87] this shows that the apostles are waiting in the valley of Cedron (identical to the valley of Jehoshaphat), to the right of the city. The second point is when the apostles are returned to the Mount of Olives, having viewed hell and heaven with the Virgin.[88] It seems natural that they should be returned to their starting point near Mary's tomb, although the Mount of Olives is not named in connection

---

[85] *Ibid.*, pp. 533–47.   [86] *Ibid.*, pp. 489–532.
[87] Arras, ed., *De transitu*, II, 30.   [88] *Ibid.*, p. 54.

with the tomb itself. If the *Liber Requiei* is a reliable guide to the *R* family, therefore, it placed the tomb of Mary in the valley of Cedron (or Jehoshaphat), near the Mount of Olives, to the right of the city. That no place is named in explicit connection with Mary's tomb may well be because the origins of the text predate the firm establishment of a tradition associated with a definite place, Gethsemane, but the tomb was localized there because it was the natural place to think of in the vicinity of Jerusalem. It would seem, then, that the directions to go by the left side of the city reflect a tomb in or around Jehoshaphat.

The same area is clearly intended as the site of Mary's tomb in *Pseudo-Melito* in which, like *Transitus W*, Peter is directed: 'serua corpus Mariae et deferentes illud in dexteram partem ciuitatis', but with the additional direction 'ad orientem'.[89] When they reach the tomb, *Transitus B²* has 'uenerunt ad locum monumenti',[90] but *B¹* reads 'peruenerunt ad locum uallis Iosaphat'.[91] Presumably all of these directions refer to the same localization of the tomb in Jehoshaphat. The 'right' is probably the result, then, of thinking of the right and left side of the city viewed as on a map, rather than in terms of directions to follow on the ground, as in those texts which specify the left. The difference is probably one of perspective, rather than one between two different traditions. The change may also have been influenced by the happier Christian associations with the right.[92]

There has been almost no discussion of the date of *Transitus W*. Wilmart does not give a date, but he regards *Transitus B* as dating from the sixth century and says that *Transitus W* is the text behind *Transitus B*.[93] This would mean that it dates from the sixth century at the latest; Wenger considers that it probably dates from the seventh or eighth century,[94] while Mimouni does not suggest a date. In this connection Gregory of Tours' (*d*. 593 or 594) account of Mary's death and assumption is interesting: in his *Septem libri miraculorum* he includes the following summary of a *transitus* text:

Posthaec, dispersi sunt per regiones diuersas ad praedicandum uerbum Dei. Denique impleto a beata Maria huius uitae cursu, cum iam uocaretur a saeculo,

---

[89] Haibach-Reinisch, ed., *Ein neuer 'Transitus'*, p. 76.   [90] *Ibid.*, p. 83.

[91] Tischendorf, ed., *Apocalypses Apocryphae*, p. 134.

[92] Haibach-Reinisch, ed., *Ein neuer 'Transitus'*, pp. 147–9.

[93] Wilmart, 'L'ancien récit', p. 323.   [94] Wenger, *L'assomption*, p. 66.

congregati sunt omnes apostoli de singulis regionibus ad domum eius. Cumque audiissent quia esset assumenda de mundo, uigilabant cum ea simul, et ecce Dominus Jesus aduenit cum angelis suis, et accipiens animam eius, tradidit Michaeli archangelo, et recessit. Diluculo autem leuauerunt apostoli cum lectulo corpus eius, posueruntque illud in monumento, et custodiebant ipsum, aduentum Domini praestolantes. Et ecce iterum adstitit eis Dominus, susceptumque corpus sanctum in nube deferri iussit in paradisum: ubi nunc, resumpta anima, cum electis eius exsultans, aeternitatis bonis, nullo occasuris fine perfruitur.[95]

In Gregory, Mary's body is taken to paradise and reunited with her soul, where it still (*nunc*) remains. *Transitus W* seems to be the nearest Latin *transitus* to Gregory's account[96] (despite Mimouni's arguments for *Pseudo-Melito*)[97] and this would mean that it, its source or a closely related version had to be circulating by the end of the sixth century at the latest.

### THE TRANSITUS OF PSEUDO-MELITO

*Transitus B*, or the *Transitus of Pseudo-Melito*, has been transmitted in two forms, termed *B¹* and *B²* by the editor of the latter.[98] There are at least forty-six known manuscripts of this text, ranging in date from the eighth to the fifteenth century.[99] The earliest of the *B²* manuscripts is from the eleventh century, but Bede already quotes from this version and Haibach-Reinisch says that Anglo-Saxon missionaries brought the text to southern Germany, from where it gradually spread.[100] This means that both versions must have been circulating by the eighth century.

Both versions contain a prologue attributing the text to Melito, Bishop of Sardes in the second century and disciple of John the Evangelist, purporting to have heard the story from John himself and saying that this narrative has been written in reaction against the version of Mary's death

---

[95] *De gloria beatorum martyrum*, PL 71, col. 708.

[96] See Capelle, 'Vestiges', pp. 31–2.

[97] Mimouni, *Dormition*, p. 269, n. 43. Mimouni says that Gregory's summary contains a version of Mary's corporal assumption next to the tomb and in response to a request by the apostles, with Christ kissing Mary. Mimouni has confused the texts here and his argument is totally invalid.

[98] See n. 19 for editions. Tischendorf's text of *B¹* is translated by Elliott, *Apocryphal New Testament*, pp. 708–14.

[99] They are listed by Mimouni, *Dormition*, pp. 264–6.

[100] Haibach-Reinisch, ed., *Ein neuer 'Transitus'*, p. 53.

composed by the heretic Leucius, who 'transitum beatae semper uirginis Mariae ita deprauauit stilo, ut in Ecclesia Dei non solum legi, sed etiam ridiculum sit audiri'.[101] Leucius was particularly dangerous because he transmitted much that was true about the apostles, but lied concerning their teaching.[102] Pseudo-Melito purports instead to give only those things which he heard from John and as proof of his orthodoxy adduces his belief in the Trinity and in one nature in man, created by God and corrupted by the serpent.[103] This prologue is clearly modelled on that of the *Passio Iohannis* of Pseudo-Melito, in which Melito, here presented as bishop of Laodicea, speaks of the unease caused by the acts of John supposedly written by Leucius: 'Volo sollicitam esse fraternitatem uestram de Leutio quodam, qui scripsit apostolorum Actus Ioannis euangelistae et apostoli sancti Andreae et Thomae apostoli; qui de uirtutibus quidem quas per eos Dominus fecit uera dixit, de doctrina uero eorum plurimum mentitus est.'[104] As with the Marian *Pseudo-Melito*, the John prologue goes on to speak of the heretical doctrine of two natures, good and evil. The information given here about Leucius seems to be drawn from Turibius (*c.* 440), and the *Passio Iohannis*, with its prologue, probably dates from the end of the fifth or the beginning of the sixth century and is perhaps from Rome.[105] The prologue to the Marian *transitus* adds a *transitus* text to the list of works by Leucius and corrects the error in the John prologue by making Melito Bishop of Sardes, retaining the Laodicea of the *Passio Iohannis* by making the church of Laodicea the addressee of the prologue. This correction is probably drawn from Eusebius's *Historia ecclesiastica*, the same source as the original error.[106] It is, therefore, unlikely that the two prologues are by the same hand. That almost all of the prologue of the Pseudo-Melito *transitus* is indebted to the *Passio Iohannis* makes it very unlikely that the Marian source from which Pseudo-Melito was working was ever attributed to Leucius: the name was almost certainly for the author a convenient one on which to hang his accusations of heresy, adopted from the *Passio Iohannis*. Opinion is divided on whether this Leucius was ever a real individual or merely a pseudonym adopted by various heretics at

---

[101] *Ibid.*, p. 64.   [102] *Ibid.*   [103] *Ibid.*, p. 65.

[104] PG 5, col. 1239; see Junod and Kaestli, eds., *Acta Iohannis*, I, 766–9, and Haibach-Reinisch, ed., *Ein neuer 'Transitus'*, pp. 41–4.

[105] Junod and Kaestli, *L'histoire*, p. 104; Junod and Kaestli, eds., *Acta Iohannis*, I, 768–9.

[106] Haibach-Reinisch, ed., *Ein neuer 'Transitus'*, p. 43.

different times,[107] but at any rate it is clear that here, as in the Gelasian decree, Leucius is merely a name, that of an author of apocryphal and, consequently, heretical works, to whom further suspect works can be attributed.

This prologue is, as has been pointed out, in many ways also very similar to the prologue to the Latin *Gospel of Pseudo-Matthew*, to such an extent that one probably depends on the other: both take the form of a letter; both propose to refute a heretical account already circulating; both attribute this heretical account to Leucius.[108] A further prologue, based on that of *Pseudo-Matthew*, is found prefacing the later *Liber de natiuitate Mariae* and this adds two further points of agreement with the *Pseudo-Melito* prologue, in that it distinguishes the true narratives of Leucius from his heretical teaching and describes Leucius's heresy as a belief in two human natures, one good and one bad (*Pseudo-Melito*) or, giving it its theological label, Manichaeism (*De natiuitate*). Of the two earlier Marian apocryphal prologues, it seems more likely that the *Pseudo-Melito* is prior and that the *Pseudo-Matthew* prologue depends on it, though the dates of both texts are still somewhat uncertain. There has been much debate about the date of *Pseudo-Melito*, many arguing for the fifth century,[109] or even earlier, but Mimouni, taking into account the advanced character of the text in doctrinal terms, suggests instead the seventh century or, at the earliest, the end of the sixth and this seems likely to be correct, being supported also by the eighth-century date of the earliest manuscripts.[110] This fits also with the date of the related *Transitus W*. *Pseudo-Matthew* probably dates from the period 550 to 700, so the two apocrypha date from the same period. The text of the Marian *Pseudo-Melito* shows evidence of knowledge of the text of the Pseudo-Melito *Passio Iohannis*, however, and this suggests that whoever wrote the *Pseudo-Melito transitus* prologue knew the entire text, whereas the *Pseudo-Matthew* prologue could have been based simply on the *Pseudo-Melito* Marian prologue. This suggests that *Pseudo-Matthew* has copied the *Pseudo-Melito* prologue rather than the other way round. In addition, the prologue, though longer in

---

[107] See Mimouni, *Dormition*, p. 270, n. 47, and Junod and Kaestli, *L'histoire*, pp. 137–43.

[108] See A. Dufourcq, *Etude sur les Gesta Martyrum romains. IV: Le Néo-Manichéisme et la légende chrétienne* (Paris, 1910), pp. 285–90, and Mimouni, *Dormition*, p. 271, n. 49 and n. 50.

[109] Haibach-Reinisch, ed., *Ein neuer 'Transitus'*, pp. 44–7.

[110] Mimouni, *Dormition*, p. 272.

*Pseudo-Melito B²*, is found in both versions of *Pseudo-Melito* and was therefore presumably part of the original, whereas it is absent from the P family of *Pseudo-Matthew* texts, which instead have a prologue based on the prologue to the Greek source, the *Proteuangelium*. The epistolary prologue similar to that of *Pseudo-Melito* seems to have been introduced by the redactor of the A family of *Pseudo-Matthew* and to be later than the P family prologue.[111] The author of the *De natiuitate* would then seem to have been familiar with both the *Pseudo-Matthew* and *Pseudo-Melito* prologues, drawing on both to compose the last in this series of epistolary prologues to Marian apocrypha.

The prologue to *Pseudo-Melito* is very important, testifying as it does, despite its dependence on a prior text, to a self-conscious author professing to evaluate critically a previous account and find it lacking. This self-consciousness is in many ways the defining characteristic of this version of the narrative of Mary's death: it is decidedly more than yet another abbreviation for liturgical use or another fairly straightforward though somewhat censored version of its source, as is the case with *Transitus W*. Stylistically, it is much more individual, 'literary' and syntactically complex, unlike the generally paratactic and more artless *Transitus W*, for example. In its treatment of the central issue, the assumption of Mary, the author of *Transitus B* reveals his awareness of the implications of the narrative by having the apostles declare clearly the basis for the assumption. *Pseudo-Melito*, indeed, gives more weight to the resurrection and assumption than any other apocryphal narrative does and in this it reads like a reflective development of the tradition, the work of someone meditating on a prior text. Only in *Pseudo-Melito* does Christ ask the apostles what should happen to Mary's body. Their reply sets forth a 'theological' reason for the necessity of such an assumption: Peter and the apostles say: 'Domine, tu elegisti uasculum istud in tabernaculum mundissimum tibi, omnia autem ante saecula praescisti. Si ergo potuisset fieri ante decretum tuae potentiae, uisum fuerat nobis famulis tuis, ut, sicut tu deuicta morte regnas in gloria, ita resuscitans matris corpusculum, tecum eam deduceres laetantem in caelum.'[112] Christ accedes to the apostles' logic and raises up Mary's body, saying to it: 'Surge, proxima mea, columba mea, tabernaculum gloriae, uasculum uitae, templum caeleste; et dum non sensisti labem delicti per coitum, non patiaris

---

[111] See above, p. 23.    [112] Haibach-Reinisch, ed., *Ein neuer 'Transitus'*, p. 85.

resolutionem corporis in sepulchro'.[113] Her perfect virginity and virginal motherhood are here made the basis for her corporal assumption.

In treating of the assumption the author of *Pseudo-Melito* seems to have known not only the prologue to the *Passio Iohannis*, but also, as might be expected, the text itself and it draws on features of the *Passio Iohannis* to supplement what it takes from its Marian source. Haibach-Reinisch has pointed to similarities between the texts, especially in the prayers, the trinitarian formulas and the stress on 'our lord, Jesus Christ'.[114] Drusiana in the *Passio Iohannis* says, for example: 'Si uideam apostolum Dei oculis meis, antequam moriar',[115] while Mary, in the *Pseudo-Melito transitus*, says 'Dominus . . . permisit me, uidere uos corporalibus oculis antequam moriar'.[116] The light surrounding Mary's body after her death may also owe something to the *Passio Iohannis*, where 'lux tanta apparuit super apostolum una fere hora, ut nullus hanc sufferre ualeret aspectus',[117] though it probably also draws on a description, like that in *W*, of Mary's soul being seven times brighter than snow. John prays in the *Passio* that 'principes tenebrarum non occurrant mihi et manus extranea non contingat me',[118] while Mary requests 'ut nulla potestas Satanae occurrat mihi et ne uideam tetros spiritus obuiantes mihi, neque conspiciam principem tenebrarum'.[119] The reason for John's assumption is his virginity, 'custodisti corpus meum ab omni pollutione',[120] the same justification as for Mary's. The *Passio Iohannis* seems, therefore, to have fed into the text of the *Pseudo-Melito transitus*, as well as being the main source for its prologue.

The importance of the bible is such that it can be considered a further source: Manns argues that the author wished to present his work as an explicit biblical midrash,[121] rereading the events of his source in the light of the bible. *Pseudo-Melito*, for example, reproduces the scene from John XIX.26, where Christ entrusts Mary to John, compares the transport of the apostles on the clouds to the biblical account of the transport of Habacuc (*B²* only), describes the apostles as the judges of Israel as in Matthew XIX.28 and draws on the account of the punishment of the citizens of Sodom in the section of the text recounting the Jewish attack

[113] *Ibid.*, pp. 85–6.    [114] *Ibid.*, pp. 42–3.    [115] PG 5, col. 1241.
[116] Haibach-Reinisch, ed., *Ein neuer 'Transitus'*, p. 73; see also p. 42.
[117] PG 5, col. 1250.    [118] *Ibid.*
[119] Haibach-Reinisch, ed., *Ein neuer 'Transitus'*, p. 74.    [120] PG 5, col. 1250.
[121] Manns, *Le récit*, p. 46.

on Mary's funeral procession. Manns justifiably regards this habit of allusion as a mark of the 'caractère tardif' of the text.[122]

The principal source for *Pseudo-Melito*, nevertheless, is unquestionably a text of the *R* family, as has already been argued.[123] *Pseudo-Melito*, however, has been adapted more freely and thoroughly than was the case with previous texts; Capelle justly terms it 'un témoin aberrant'.[124] This is evident from the very beginning: where *Transitus W*, like the Greek *R*, begins quite abruptly with the appearance of the angel, *Pseudo-Melito* instead starts by going back to the scene at the Crucifixion, alluded to later in *Transitus W* by Mary, where Christ entrusted Mary to John. This is typical of *Pseudo-Melito*'s preference for a step-by-step order, with events recounted in the sequence in which they occurred, whereas the previous texts in this tradition favoured recounting some events through dialogue at a later point. This can also be seen with the transport of John the Evangelist to Mary's house: in *R*, *Transitus W* and the other texts, the means by which John arrives is not explained until after the arrival of the other apostles, whereas in *Pseudo-Melito* it is brought forward to be narrated at the point in the narrative at which it occurs. Here in the opening chapter *Pseudo-Melito* quotes the bible and highlights the importance of John, as befits a supposed disciple of the Evangelist, and the heightening of Mary's desire for Christ is also notable, as can be seen by comparison with *W*:

In illo tempore, cum esset beata Maria diebus ac noctibus uigilans et orans post ascensionem domini, uenit ad eam angelus domini . . .[125]

Igitur cum Dominus et Saluator noster Jesus Christus pro totius saeculi uita affixus clauis crucis penderet in ligno, uidit iuxta crucem matrem suam stantem et Iohannem euangelistam, quem prae ceteris apostolis ideo peculiarius diligebat, eo quod ipse solus plus ex eis uirgo esset in corpore.

Tradidit igitur ei curam sanctae Mariae dicens ad eum: 'Ecce mater tua', et ad ipsam inquiens: 'Ecce filius tuus'.

Ex illa hora sancta Dei Genitrix in Iohannis cura permansit, quamdiu uitae istius incolatum transegit.

Et dum apostoli mundum suis sortibus in praedicatione sumpsissent, ipsa in domo parentum illius iuxta Montem Oliueti consedit.

Secundo igitur anno postquam Dominus caeli alta conscendit, die quadam

---

[122] *Ibid.*    [123] See above, pp. 69–76.    [124] 'Vestiges', p. 29.
[125] Wilmart, 'L'ancien récit', p. 325.

desiderio eius succensa, lacrimari sola in domus illius receptaculo coepit.
Et ecce angelus magni luminis habitu splendens ante eam astitit . . .[126]

It is significant that this passage specifies both the place in which Mary
lived and the year of her death: *Transitus W* says merely 'in illo tempore'
and that the angel 'uenit ad eam'. *Transitus B* is alone in specifying that
the house in which Mary lived (and consequently the place of her death)
was the house of John's parents beside the Mount of Olives. The place
references in *Pseudo-Melito* have been the subject of much debate, centring
on this placing of the house in which Mary lived after Christ's death next
to the Mount of Olives and the naming of Jehoshaphat in *B¹* as the place
of Mary's tomb. The text as a whole shows ignorance of the geography of
Jerusalem, as Haibach-Reinisch demonstrates:[127] the author appears to
think that the Mount of Olives is within, rather than outside, the city
and does not seem to realize that Jehoshaphat is right next to the Mount
of Olives. Mimouni, without giving an explanation, suggests that the
Mount of Olives as the place of Mary's house may be the oldest
localization of all,[128] while Haibach-Reinisch attributes this detail to the
apocryphal *Acta Iohannis* of Pseudo-Prochorus, a text which she sees as
determining much of the account of Mary's death in *Transitus B²* (this
belief is completely undermined by Capelle and Wenger's work,
however).[129] It is possible that the significance of this detail may have
been overestimated and that the *Pseudo-Melito* redactor understandably
got the impression from his source text, where Mary climbs the Mount of
Olives immediately after the angel's announcement, that the house in
which she lived was next to the Mount: *Transitus W*, for example, reads
'Cum haec audisset beata Maria, ascendit in montem Oliueti'.[130] The
*Pseudo-Melito* redactor seems to have been anxious to give precise names
and to specify also for how many years Mary lived after the Ascension,
whereas vagueness characterizes the *R* family up to now in these respects.
*Transitus B²* says that the assumption took place two years after the
Ascension, whereas *Transitus B¹* varies between twenty-two and two
years. *Transitus W* gives the impression of a short period, but does not
define it: 'In illo tempore, cum esset beata Maria diebus ac noctibus

[126] Haibach-Reinisch, ed., *Ein neuer 'Transitus'*, pp. 65–6.     [127] *Ibid.*, p. 13.
[128] Mimouni, *Dormition*, p. 275.
[129] Haibach-Reinisch, ed., *Ein neuer 'Transitus'*, pp. 36–7.
[130] Wilmart, 'L'ancien récit', p. 326.

uigilans et orans post ascensionem domini'.[131] Haibach-Reinisch again suggests that *Pseudo-Melito* derived the two-year time-span from the *Acta Iohannis* of Pseudo-Prochorus, but the reference there, in some manuscripts only, does not give a number of years but merely gives the impression of a short time.[132] Since no greater specificity is to be gained from the *Acta Iohannis*, it is safer to assume that the *Transitus B* redactor pinned down the number of years to two in the interest of appearing to have a very detailed knowledge of events and that his source here, as throughout, was a member of the *R* family similar to *Transitus W*. Bede knew of and objected to the two-year period and Haibach-Reinisch is probably correct in arguing that the time-span of twenty-two years in *B¹* was a later alteration, aimed at countering objections such as Bede's to a shorter length as being incompatible with the Acts of the Apostles.[133] *Pseudo-Melito* specifies also that John was preaching in Ephesus, the first text in the *R* tradition to do so; this detail is probably taken from the description of John's ministry in the Pseudo-Melito *Passio Iohannis*. There can be little doubt, then, that this appearance of definite, authoritative knowledge was part of the redactor's attempt to gain acceptance for his text: his self-presentation as a disciple of John the Evangelist would have been seriously undermined by the lack of precision of his source. It is highly likely, as a result, that little reliance can be placed on place and time references in *Pseudo-Melito*: apart from the Ephesus reference, they are likely to have been the contribution of the author himself and not of great antiquity.

The description of the angel in *Pseudo-Melito*, 'angelus magni luminis habitu splendens', is probably a development of *W*'s account in ch. 3 of the angel ascending into heaven 'cum magno lumine':[134] this is an example in miniature of Pseudo-Melito's propensity to retain elements of the source but to move them around. He has so thoroughly assimilated the source that he can handle it with a degree of freedom unusual among these texts. The mannered, self-conscious quality of *Pseudo-Melito*, with its love of biblical quotation, is apparent in the angel's salutation which follows; *W* reads: 'Maria, exsurge et accipe palmam quam nunc tibi detuli, quoniam post tres dies adsumenda es. Et ecce ego mittam omnes apostolos ad te sepeliendam, ut uideant gloriam tuam quam acceptura

---

131  *Ibid.*, p. 325.     132  Haibach-Reinisch, ed., *Ein neuer 'Transitus'*, pp. 37–8.
133  *Ibid.*, pp. 141–3.     134  Wilmart, 'L'ancien récit', p. 326.

es.'[135] *Transitus B²* (very similar to *B¹* here) reads instead: 'Aue, benedicta a Domino, suscipiens illius salutem qui mandauit salutem Iacob per prophetas suos. Ecce, inquit, ramum palmae de paradiso Dei attuli tibi; quem portare facies ante feretrum tuum, cum in die tertio fueris assumpta de corpore. Ecce enim expectat te Filius tuus cum thronis et angelis et uniuersis uirtutibus caeli.'[136] While in *W* the angel immediately pro-mises to send the apostles to Mary, in accordance with an extra-textual promise of Christ referred to later (in ch. 17) by Mary, in *Pseudo-Melito* she asks the angel for this and he promises that they will all come through the power of God: *Pseudo-Melito* is much more self-contained as a text, its author apparently not liking references to events not recounted within the text itself and preferring to make everything explicit.

Much has been made of Mary's fear of death in *Pseudo-Melito* and it is indeed quite marked,[137] but it is an exaggeration, I think, to argue that *Pseudo-Melito* is exceptional in accentuating this fear. Before the angel departs, Mary asks him: 'Peto ut mittas super me benedictionem tuam, ut nulla potestas Satanae uel inferni occurrat mihi, et ne uideam tetros spiritus obuiantes mihi'.[138] The angel reassures her that she will not see the prince of darkness and tells her that this is granted not by him, but by her son. Later in the text, when Christ comes to claim Mary's soul, she prostrates herself and again begs: 'Memor esto mei, rex gloriae, cuius nomen sanctum et laudabile cum Patre et Sancto Paraclito in una permanet dignitate. Deprecor te ut audias uocem ancillae tuae, ut nulla potestas Satanae occurrat mihi et ne uideam tetros spiritus obuiantes mihi, neque conspiciam principem tenebrarum.'[139] Even compared to *Transitus W*, which has toned down its source's account of Mary's fear, this is not out of the ordinary; in *W* Mary does not address a request to the angel, but returns to her house and prays: 'Peto domine ut mittas super me benedictionem tuam ut nulla potestas occurrat mihi inimici uel inferni, in illa hora cum me iusseris de hoc corpore recedere, siquidem ipse pollicitus es mihi, dicens: "Noli tristis esse Maria"'.[140] *Pseudo-Melito* has clearly remodelled a text like *W*, eliminating the reference back to an earlier conversation not reported in the text and probably drawing on the

---

[135] *Ibid.*   [136] Haibach-Reinisch, ed., *Ein neuer 'Transitus'*, pp. 66–7.

[137] See, for example, Rivière, 'Le plus vieux "Transitus"', p. 12.

[138] Haibach-Reinisch, ed., *Ein neuer 'Transitus'*, p. 67.   [139] *Ibid.*, p. 74.

[140] Wilmart, 'L'ancien récit', p. 327.

*Passio Iohannis* for the 'principem tenebrarum', but has not added any-thing of substance. *W* follows this with the conversation between Mary and the neighbours she summons, which *Pseudo-Melito* has dropped altogether, and in this Mary explains about the angel of good and the angel of evil present at every death, prompting her listeners to ask what their own fate will be if she, the mother of the Lord, is so sad. Again, this conversation has the effect of stressing fear of death. When Christ comes for Mary's soul in *W*, the dead body of Mary cries out to him to be remembered – this is at more or less the same point in the text as Mary's second speech of fear in *Pseudo-Melito*, also beginning 'memor': 'Memor esto mei, rex gloriae, quoniam opera manuum tuarum sum. Memor esto mei, quoniam custodiui commendatum tuum thesaurum.'[141] It is easy to see what *Pseudo-Melito* has done here: it has kept the beginning of its source's speech, though attributing it to a live rather than dead Mary, presumably to avoid the possibility of offence by having a soulless Mary speak (in *Pseudo-Melito* she speaks again only when body and soul have been reunited), and has then simply paraphrased the first speech again, making explicit the fear which is implicit in Mary's begging Christ to be mindful of her. What *Pseudo-Melito* has done, therefore, is to alter its source to some degree in its presentation of Mary's anxiety, but it does not constitute a new departure. Its excision of the scene with Mary's neighbours is typical of its concern to cut the overall number of episodes and to highlight the essentials of the story, assimilating anything regarded as necessary into other scenes.

The two scenes in *Pseudo-Melito* which Capelle points to as unparalleled are that describing the preparation of Mary's body (which probably owes something to the *Passio Iohannis* of Pseudo-Melito) and that in which the apostles, as a foretaste of their role at the Last Judgement (Matthew XIX.28), are allowed to decide on the fate of Mary's body.[142] The first of these is in keeping with the greater emphasis on Mary's body in *Pseudo-Melito*, the apocryphon which gives most weight to the corporal assump-tion. The second scene is designed to focus attention on the theological necessity for Mary's corporal assumption and it also, as Cothenet points out, presents the corporal assumption as part of the apostolic faith.[143] The fuzziness which one finds in many of the earlier apocryphal texts has

---

[141] *Ibid.*, p. 346    [142] Capelle, 'Vestiges', pp. 29–30, n. 2.
[143] 'Marie dans les apocryphes', p. 141.

disappeared here and the apostles present reasons which Christ accepts as compelling. Theirs is in essence the argument which the later, non-apocryphal Pseudo-Augustine tract was to present with great success.[144] Their argument had already been implicit in earlier texts, however; it is implied, for example, in the appeal of Mary's dead body and Christ's reply in *W*: ' "Memor esto mei, quoniam custodiui commendatum tuum thesaurum". Et dixit dominus ad corpus beatae Mariae: "Non te derelin-quam, margarita mea, quoniam inuenta es fidelis et seruasti creditam tibi commendationem. Non te derelinquam quia tu es templum dei." '[145] *Pseudo-Melito* has grasped clearly the implications of its source here and has made the argument more explicit by having Christ pose the problem to the apostles. It is alone in specifying that the reunion of body and soul took place on earth: Christ brings with him Mary's soul when he returns after the three days which the body spends in the tomb, and body and soul are then assumed together. Presumably this was guided by doctrinal considerations: the raised body could not be left without a soul, even for the space of time required to transport it to the next world.

The question of *paradisus* and *caelum* in *Pseudo-Melito* needs some elucidation. In *W* the only word used in connection with Mary's body is *paradisus*, with *caelum* being reserved for Christ, but both words are found in *Pseudo-Melito*, though distributed differently in each version of the text. Haibach-Reinisch argues that $B^1$ preserves an original distinction better than $B^2$, with Mary's body brought to paradise and Christ ascending to heaven, but it is difficult to be sure whether or not there was a real distinction in meaning for the author or redactors of this text.[146] In $B^2$ Christ, at Mary's deathbed, tells her (presumably her soul): 'intra in receptaculum uitae aeternae, expectant te enim caelestes militiae, ut introducant te in paradisi gaudia'.[147] Three days later, at the tomb, Peter asks Christ to bring Mary with him 'laetantem in caelum' and Mary is resurrected. Having taken leave of the apostles, 'Dominus, cum canen-tibus angelis et matre sua receptus est in paradiso'.[148] From this it would appear that Mary and Christ are together after her assumption, in a location which is called paradise or heaven, apparently without distinc-

---

[144] Lausberg, 'Zur literarischen Gestaltung des *Transitus Beatae Mariae*'.
[145] Wilmart, 'L'ancien récit', p. 346.
[146] Haibach-Reinisch, ed., *Ein neuer 'Transitus'*, pp. 162–4. I am most grateful to Ananya Kabir for discussing this problem with me.
[147] *Ibid.*, p. 75.     [148] *Ibid.*, p. 87.

tion. In *B¹*'s deathbed scene Christ first tells Mary 'intra receptaculum uitae aeternae', then later says: 'Veni secura, quia expectat te caelestis militia, ut te introducat ad paradisi gaudia'.[149] Peter makes the same request that Christ bring Mary to *caelum* and at the end: 'dominus . . . receptus est in caelum, et angeli cum eo, deferentes beatam Mariam in paradisum Dei'.[150] In *B¹* it is possible that the two locations are separate, as the conclusion may differentiate the destination of Christ from that of Mary, but the angels who are carrying Mary's body to paradise are with Christ as he goes to heaven and in this version Peter also asks that Mary be taken to heaven. Consequently it seems that in this version too heaven and paradise are probably synonymous. It is possible that the obscuring of an initially sharper distinction in fact contributed to the authoritative definitiveness with which *Pseudo-Melito* presents the corporal assumption: because for him his source, though it clearly demanded the clarification he felt it necessary to supply, presented Mary's assumption to full cohabitation with Christ, he felt able to give this aspect of the text greater prominence than ever before in the apocryphal tradition. This therefore seems to be the first Western apocryphal text to place Mary's body and soul together in heaven, rather than in a paradise separate from heaven, though the author might well not have considered this an innovation.

One point in *Pseudo-Melito* which is puzzling is that Mary is told by Christ that she, like him, will have to see Satan when she dies, despite her prayer to be spared this; Christ tells her: 'Dum ego a Patre missus pro totius saeculi uita acerbae mortis sustinerem supplicia, ad me princeps tenebrarum uenit; sed cum nullum sui operis uestigium in me inuenisset, uictus abscessit. Tu igitur uidebis eum quidem communi lege humani generis, per quam sortita es finem mortis; non autem nocere poterit tibi, quia ego tecum sum, ut adiuuem te.'[151] Despite this, Mary never sees Satan in the text. Rivière points this out, suggesting that it is possible that two different ways of imagining Mary's death have been juxtaposed here, without being brought into agreement: 'l'une qui la fait entrer directement au paradis, l'autre qui lui impose, au préalable, la visite de Satan'.[152] It is possible that at this relatively early stage in the text the *Pseudo-Melito* author was planning a more radical rewriting than he in fact

[149] Tischendorf, ed., *Apocalypses Apocryphae*, p. 129.    [150] *Ibid.*, pp. 135–6.

[151] Haibach-Reinisch, ed., *Ein neuer 'Transitus'*, p. 75.

[152] Rivière, 'Le plus vieux "Transitus"', p. 53.

ultimately carried out and that he simply silently dropped a plan to have Mary see Satan, without revising the early part of the text. This speech by Christ is unique in the *R* tradition and is not paralleled in the *Passio Iohannis*, so it may be indebted to a different source.

*Pseudo-Melito*, then, is an important text not because of any radical innovation, apart from heaven as the destination of Mary's reunited body and soul, but for the way in which it tightens the narrative, focusing on Mary and the apostles, and highlights the corporal assumption. Its form of the narrative became, to quote Wilmart, quasi-official in the Latin tradition[153] and its manuscripts outnumber those of any other Latin text. The claim in the preface to be revising a heretical text is overstated, like most selling-pitches, as its source was not very different in import: *Pseudo-Melito* in fact carries the implications of the source-narrative further, rather than modifying them in the interests of caution.

The two versions of *Pseudo-Melito*, both descended from a common original, differ in many details, most of them minor, and Haibach-Reinisch, who discovered and edited $B^2$, argues that $B^2$ in general better represents the lost original, while recognizing that some passages in it are the independent additions of its redactor, who seems to have been particularly interested in dogma and in adding what could be seen as supporting evidence for miracles.[154] Her case is based partly on stylistic grounds (she regards the $B^1$ redactor as being much more interested in style) but largely on the inclusion in $B^2$ of passages which seem likely to be original, but whose omission by $B^1$ is understandable given the particular interests of its redactor, who in her view was much more concerned with the logical progression of the narrative, and who liked to abbreviate and correct. She does not rule out the preservation in $B^1$ of original passages excised or altered in $B^2$, such as the mention of Mary's *secretarium* in ch. 3, which she, rightly, regards as unlikely to have been introduced by the $B^1$ redactor and whose original status is supported by the *R* tradition.

Haibach-Reinisch's views have been challenged, notably by Bagatti, on the grounds that $B^1$ better preserves Judeo-Christian ideas and that $B^2$ must therefore be the later text, though both versions may well preserve archaic features altered in the other.[155] He dates $B^1$ to the first half of the

---

[153]  Wilmart, 'L'ancien récit', p. 323.

[154]  Haibach-Reinisch, ed., *Ein neuer 'Transitus'*, pp. 109–72.

[155]  Bagatti, 'Le due redazioni'.

fourth century[156] and sees it as influenced by the fight against Arianism, but regards it as based on a document of the second century, such as *R*. Both dates are highly unlikely to be accurate, as is the argument that the mention of the valley of Jehoshaphat, in particular, which we find in *B¹* but not in *B²*, is primitive.[157] If, however, we accept that *W* and *Pseudo-Melito* are closely related texts and that *Pseudo-Melito* is an idiosyncratic member of the *R* family, then we have a control which allows us to decide, in very many cases, which is the primitive and which the altered reading. That *Transitus B¹*, manuscripts of which date from the eighth century onwards, is the earliest text in the *R* tradition to name Jehoshaphat suggests that *Transitus B²*'s lack of name is original. At the point in *B¹* in which this is mentioned, *B²* has instead 'ad locum monumenti',[158] though both versions earlier have 'in dexteram partem ciuitatis ad orientem',[159] which also fits Jehoshaphat. The eleventh-century Pembroke 25 version of *Transitus W* similarly names Jehoshaphat[160] but it seems to be the only manuscript of *W* to do so and the name may well have been added in both cases, *B¹* and *W*, because of a scribe's/redactor's prior knowledge of the supposed burial place. Jehoshaphat was generally acknowledged to be the site of Mary's tomb from the end of the sixth century onwards,[161] shown to pilgrims and described in itineraries, and knowledge of the name can hardly have been unusual. This seems to me much more plausible than the thesis that the name is an archaic feature, of crucial significance for the dating of *B¹* and *B²*. The result of comparing both versions of *Pseudo-Melito* with *Transitus W* and other texts of the *R* family suggests that both versions preserve some primitive details, but *B²* rather more than *B¹*. So, for example, *B²*'s speech by Mary in ch. 5, 'Benedictus Dominus qui impleuit desiderium meum, quin potius non me fraudauit a conspectu uestro, sed permisit me, uidere uos corporalibus oculis antequam moriar'[162] (of which *B²* has only 'Non me fraudauit Deus conspectu uestro')[163] is paralleled in *R*, the *Liber Requiei* and *Transitus W* and therefore has to belong to the original. *B¹*

---

[156] *Ibid.*, p. 284.    [157] *Ibid.*, p. 281, and Mimouni, *Dormition*, pp. 273–5.

[158] Haibach-Reinisch, ed., *Ein neuer 'Transitus'*, p. 83.

[159] *Ibid.*, p. 76; Tischendorf, ed., *Apocalypses Apocryphae*, p. 130; see Haibach-Reinisch, ed., *Ein neuer 'Transitus'*, pp. 144–51 for discussion.

[160] See Appendix I, p. 333.    [161] Mimouni, *Dormition*, pp. 548–79.

[162] Haibach-Reinisch, ed., *Ein neuer 'Transitus'*, p. 73.

[163] Tischendorf, ed., *Apocalypses Apocryphae*, p. 128.

preserves also the Jewish high-priest's application of the Old Testament to Mary: 'et coepit . . . de libris Veteris Testamenti Mariae testimonium reddere, quod ipsa sit templum Dei',[164] paralleled in *R*, the *Liber Requiei* and *W*, whereas *B¹* has replaced this with 'de libris Moysi testimonium reddere laudibus Christi',[165] presumably because its redactor was aware that the Old Testament does not contain such a reference to Mary.[166] *B²* preserves Christ's command to the apostles to get into the cloud with him at the end of the text: this is an original detail, paralleled in the Syriac *Obsequies* and going back to the stage of the text when the apostles accompanied Mary and Christ to view the next world. Even in *Transitus A* and *W*, the apostles accompany the body to paradise, returning immediately once Mary's soul has been replaced in her body. As there is no longer any reason for the apostles to come into the cloud with Christ (in *Pseudo-Melito* they are brought on different clouds back to their preaching stations), the *B¹* redactor, with the concern for narrative progression identified by Haibach-Reinisch, dropped 'in nube' from the command 'Accedite ad me in nube.'[167] Again, therefore, in *B²* as in all of these later texts, we find redundant features testifying to the rewriting of an earlier version. The role of the apostles is more marked in *B²* than *B¹*: whereas in *B²*, as in *R*, *Transitus A* and *W*, Christ, arriving at Mary's deathbed, addresses the apostles before he turns to Mary (which he does only in response to her plea), in *B¹* he addresses Mary first, saying as soon as he arrives 'Veni preciosissima margarita, intra receptaculum uitae aeternae'.[168] This again is undoubtedly one of the archaic features preserved by *B²*, as the impetus within the tradition as a whole seems to be towards increasing the importance of Mary rather than the apostles. This is not the place to go through the text discussing all the differences between the two versions, an undertaking handicapped also by the lack of a critical text for *B¹*, but it seems to me probable that such a systematic work would support Haibach-Reinisch's overall conclusion about *B²*'s greater

---

[164] Haibach-Reinisch, ed., *Ein neuer 'Transitus'*, p. 82.

[165] Tischendorf, ed., *Apocalypses Apocryphae*, p. 133.

[166] See Haibach-Reinisch, ed., *Ein neuer 'Transitus'*, p. 128. How complicated the matter is can be seen from the fact that *R*, the *Liber Requiei* and *Transitus W* all mention the books of Moses, as in *B¹*, but apply their testimony to Mary rather than Christ, as in *B²*.

[167] Tischendorf, ed., *Apocalypses Apocryphae*, p. 135.

[168] *Ibid.*, p. 128; see also Haibach-Reinisch, ed., *Ein neuer 'Transitus'*, pp. 121–2.

fidelity to the common archetype. $B^1$ undoubtedly also preserves some original details, but probably fewer than $B^2$. Mimouni, though not agreeing with his dating, supports Bagatti on the priority of $B^1$, mainly because of the mention of Jehoshaphat in $B^1$,[169] but he never compares *Pseudo-Melito* to the other texts in the R tradition and this undermines the validity of his views.

Mimouni also suggests, somewhat tentatively, that *Pseudo-Melito* is the link text between the three groups of dormition and assumption narratives that he distinguishes, A, B and C. He argues that it has archaic features which align it with the A and B groups (belief in the dormition, according to Mimouni, though he does not explain this) but that it also witnesses very emphatically to the resurrection and assumption, so belonging to the C group. He accordingly puts forward the hypothesis that *Pseudo-Melito* is 'un écrit attestant le lien entre le groupe ancien et le groupe récent, tout en ayant pu donner naissance au groupe intermédiaire'.[170] In other words if *Pseudo-Melito* is, as the prologue says, a revision of a heretical text, that prior text, which Mimouni identifies as the Pseudo-Leucius, belonged to the A group, affirming belief only in the dormition (this, according to Mimouni, being the heresy). The B group of texts, all Coptic, may well have been derived from a Greek source, and it is possible, Mimouni argues, that this hypothetical, lost Greek text was also the lost narrative attributed to Leucius. The Copts, as belief in Mary's assumption grew among them, added an account of Mary's assumption on to the dormition narrative and the extant texts witness to this doctrinal development. The Latin reworking of this lost text, the *Transitus of Pseudo-Melito*, would then be a further adaptation of this Greek source and, according to Mimouni, it is 'à l'origine du groupe récent'.[171] Mimouni stresses that the theme of Mary's fear of death, which is so prominent in the Coptic texts, is also developed in *Pseudo-Melito*,[172] but, as argued above, this is a general characteristic of the R tradition and *Pseudo-Melito*'s development of it is often exaggerated. Mimouni avoids ever adverting to the theory advanced by Rivière, Capelle and Wenger that *Pseudo-Melito* is dependent on the common source it shares with W because it does not fit with his views, but his neglect of their arguments seriously undermines his own case. In placing *Pseudo-Melito* at the beginning, rather than the

---

[169] Mimouni, *Dormition*, p. 275.     [170] *Ibid.*, p. 66.     [171] *Ibid.*, p. 67.
[172] *Ibid.*, p. 63, n. 80.

culmination, of the Latin tradition, Mimouni ignores the many features pointing to its being a development of previous texts, not a starting-point. He also places too much reliance on the Pseudo-Leucius, since we have no proof outside the Preface to *Pseudo-Melito* of the existence of this text, and it is very likely to be nothing but a device to gain credibility for *Pseudo-Melito*. The evidence, therefore, does not support his conjectures.

## THE *TRANSITUS* OF PSEUDO-JOSEPH OF ARIMATHAEA

The final text in the Latin tradition, which has left no mark on Anglo-Saxon England, is the *transitus* attributed to Joseph of Arimathaea, edited by Tischendorf from three Italian manuscripts of the thirteenth and fourteenth centuries.[173] This is the only Latin text to contain the episode of the apostle Thomas arriving too late for the assumption but receiving Mary's girdle as a compensation. It appears to draw on Eastern sources and must be later than the seventh century,[174] though M. R. James dated it to thirteenth-century Italy.[175] This text needs to be studied in more detail.

## CONCLUSION

The Latin tradition, therefore, apart from the translation of the Greek Pseudo-John and the Pseudo-Joseph of Arimathaea, is indebted to texts ultimately stemming from the Syriac *Obsequies* or a related Greek text. In origin this textual family affirms belief in the assumption of Mary's body and soul to paradise and contains an apocalypse as an integral part, but in the Latin texts, apart from isolated exceptions, the apocalypse element has become detached from the apocryphon. This belief in the assumption reaches its apex in the *transitus* of *Pseudo-Melito*, in which Mary's body and soul seem to be assumed to heaven rather than a separate paradise and which is also the furthest from the untidy early texts in its single-minded concentration on Mary's fate after death. Whereas the Syriac *Obsequies* and the related Ethiopic *Liber Requiei* pile on episodes only tangentially related to the central narrative, *Pseudo-Melito* is a focused, self-contained

---

[173] Tischendorf, ed., *Apocalypses Apocryphae*, pp. 113–23.
[174] Mimouni, *Dormition*, p. 291.
[175] *The Apocryphal New Testament* (Oxford, 1924), p. 218.

narrative, the work of someone who has reflected on the implications of its source and has taken them to their logical conclusion. To compare it with the beginning of this tradition is also to realize how so many theologically dubious elements have been suppressed or rendered harmless, as successive texts have been increasingly assimilated into mainstream Christianity. As with the apocryphal versions of Mary's birth and childhood, the trend is towards ever-increasing conformity and acceptability.

# 4

# The apocrypha of the Virgin in Anglo-Saxon England

Evidence for Anglo-Saxon knowledge of and interest in the apocryphal legends of the Virgin begins with Adamnan's (*d.* 704) account of Arculf's visit to Jerusalem in his *De locis sanctis*. In describing the church dedicated to Mary at Jehoshaphat, where the tomb of Mary had been thought to have been located since the end of the sixth century, he says:

in cuius orientali parte altarium habetur, ad dexteram uero eius partem Mariae saxeum inest uacuum sepulchrum, in quo aliquando sepulta pausauit. Sed de eodem sepulchro quo modo uel quo tempore aut a quibus personis sanctum corpusculum eius sit sublatum uel in quo loco resurrectionem exspectat nullus, ut refert, pro certo scire potest.[1]

This passage clearly states that Mary had died and that her body had been buried in the now empty sepulchre, but professes ignorance on its subsequent fate. Ignorance of course absolves Adamnan from taking up any position on the apocryphal narratives which were certainly circulating widely by this date and with which Arculf, at least, could not but have come into contact in Jerusalem. Adamnan's statement about where Mary's body awaits resurrection implies, however, that her body had not yet been resurrected: Mary's resurrection was, of course, a central tenet of all the Latin assumption stories and Adamnan therefore was either not familiar with these or he rejected them outright. It seems probable that he would have known of accounts of Mary's assumption from Arculf, if from no other source, but he was clearly uncomfortable with such stories and avoided committing himself on the question of their status by asserting the impossibility of certain knowledge.

[1] D. Meehan, ed., *Adamnan's de locis sanctis*, Scriptores Latini Hiberniae 3 (Dublin, 1958), p. 58.

101

The implied doubts of Adamnan become rejection of one of the apocryphal assumption narratives in Bede. In his *Liber de locis sanctis* he abridged Adamnan's account of the empty tomb: 'ad eius dexteram monumentum uacuum, in quo sancta Maria aliquando pausasse dicitur, sed a quo uel quando sit ablata, nescitur'.[2] Bede, then, omits Adamnan's implied denial that the resurrection of Mary could already have taken place, but again insists that no one knows by whom or when her body was removed from the tomb. In the case of Bede, however, we can be absolutely certain of his knowledge of at least one of the apocryphal assumption narratives, as he quotes the *Transitus of Pseudo-Melito* ($B^2$) at length and verbatim in his second commentary on the Acts of the Apostles, the *Retractatio in Actus Apostolorum*, written probably between 725 and 731, where he takes exception to the apocryphon's timing of Mary's death. $B^2$ places Mary's death in the second year after the Ascension, when the apostles, including Paul, were scattered and preaching all over the world, and Bede points out that this chronology is incompatible with the Acts of the Apostles, in which it is said that the apostles remained in Jerusalem for what Bede says must have been a considerable time and in which it is evident that Paul was not appointed an apostle within two years of Christ's death. Bede recognizes the inauthenticity of the attribution to Melito and argues, too, that John the Evangelist would not so quickly have abandoned the Virgin, committed to his care by Christ on the cross:

Si dispersa ecclesia apostoli *remanserunt in Hierusalem*, ut Lucas ait, constat quia mendacium scripsit ille qui ex persona Militonis episcopi Asiae, librum exponens de obitu beatae genetricis dei, dicit quod secundo post ascensionem domini anno apostoli fuerint omnes toto orbe ad praedicandum in suam quisque prouinciam diuisi. Qui uniuersi adpropinquante obitu sanctae Mariae *de locis in quibus praedicabant uerbum dei eleuati in nubibus rapti sunt Hierusolymam ac depositi ante ostium domus eius*, inter quos etiam Paulus nuper ex persecutore ad fidem Christi conuersus, qui adsumptus fuerat cum Barnaba in ministerium gentium. Quae scriptura etiam specialiter de Iohanne apostolo refert quod eo tempore Ephesi praedicauerit. Quae cuncta uerbis beati Lucae aperte contradicunt, quibus narrat apostolos ceteris fidelibus ab Hierosolyma propulsis remanisse ibidem et praedicasse per omnia, donec ecclesia per totam Iudaeam et Galilaeam et Samariam pacem haberet, quod in uno anno perfici non potuisse nulli dubium

---

[2] P. Geyer, ed., *Bedae liber de locis sanctis, Itinera Hierosolymitana saeculi iiii–viii*, Corpus Scriptorum Ecclesiasticorum Latinorum 39 (Vienna, 1898), pp. 301–24, at 309.

est; qui etiam manifeste insinuat Paulum non secundo post ascensionem domini anno, sed longo post tempore in ministerium gentium cum Barnaba ordinatum. Absit autem ut credamus beatum Iohannem apostolum, cui dominus in cruce matrem suam uirginem uirgini commendauit, post unum annum recessisse et eam reliquisse solam ac tanto tempore deiectam, ut etiam corpus suum defunctae timeret ab hostibus esse comburendum eumque, postquam raptus in nubibus ad se redisset, uelut oblitum siue incuriosum sui sollicita precaretur, dicens: *Rogo te, fili Iohannes, ut memor sis uerbi magistri tui, domini mei, Iesu Christi, qui me commendauit tibi. Ecce enim uocata ingrediar uiam uniuersae terrae. Audiui autem consilia Iudaeorum dicentium, expectemus diem quando moriatur quae portauit Iesum Nazarenum et corpus eius igne comburamus. Nunc ergo curam habeto obsequiarum mearum.* Haec ideo commemorare curaui quia noui nonnullos praefato uolumini contra auctoritatem beati Lucae incauta temeritate adsensum praebere.[3]

In terms of chronology, morality and authenticity Bede clearly suspects *Transitus B*[2] and he returns to his suspicions later in his commentary, concluding: 'ac per hoc praefatum de obitu beatae Mariae libellum, cum manifeste erret in tempore, in ceteris quoque suspectae fidei esse comperit'.[4] What is so striking about his comments, of course, is that they fail to take up a direct stand on the central issue of *Pseudo-Melito*, the corporal assumption, other than to imply that it must be as questionable as other aspects of the text.

The next account of the Virgin's fate after death is in another account of a pilgrimage to Jerusalem, this time that written by Hygeburg, an Anglo-Saxon nun writing *c.* 780 in the continental foundation of Heidenheim. Her narrative, included in her *Vita SS Willibaldi et Wynnebaldi*, is obviously dependent on apocryphal accounts, but differs in detail from all of them. In describing a monument she says that it was erected at the place:

ubi Iudei uolebant tollere corpus sanctae Mariae. Cumque illi .xi. apostoli tollentes corpus sanctae Mariae portauerunt illum de Hierusalem, et statim cumque ad portam uenerunt ciuitatis, Iudaei uoluerunt conprehendere illum. Statimque illi homines qui porrigebant ad feretra et eam tollere conabant, retentis brachiis quasi glutinati inherebant in feretro et non poterant se mouere, antequam Dei gratia et apostolorum petitione iterum resoluti fuerant, et tunc eos reliquerunt. Sancta Maria in illo loco in medio Hierusalem exiuit de seculo, qui nominatur Sancta Sion: et tunc apostoli .xi. portauerunt illum, sicut prius

---

[3] Laistner, ed., *Retractatio in Actus Apostolorum*, pp. 134–5.    [4] *Ibid.*, p. 145.

dixi, et tunc angeli uenientes tulerunt illum de manibus apostolorum et portauerunt in paradiso.[5]

What is striking here is that all the Jews seem to have become attached to the bier, instead of the usual one. Mary also seems to have been carried straight to paradise from the hands of the apostles by the angels, with no mention of the tomb, although Hygeburg later alludes to it. This cannot be derived from *Transitus A* or *W*, in which the apostles accompany Mary to paradise; the nearest Latin version would seem to be *Transitus B*, *Pseudo-Melito*, in which Christ and the angels take the resurrected Mary from the tomb to paradise. The parallel is still not very close, however, as in *Pseudo-Melito* Mary spends three days in the tomb and Christ and the apostles debate on her fate before her soul is replaced in her body. It is probable that Hygeburg was not using any written version of the apocryphon as source, but was basing her account on hearsay, presumably on what she had heard from Willibald. Her location of the place in which Mary died as Sion, in the centre of Jerusalem, is the usual location from the seventh century onwards, although it is not specified in the Latin apocrypha. Presumably she would have derived this detail from Willibald, if it was not common knowledge by this date. Hygeburg also mentions the tomb of Mary at Jehoshaphat: 'sepulcrum eius, non de eo quod corpus eius ibi requiescat, sed ad memoriam eius'.[6] Hygeburg, therefore, although her account of Mary's assumption is lacking in specificity, seems to have been a believer in the corporal assumption to paradise and shows a combination of apocryphal knowledge and knowledge of the sites in Jerusalem associated with the events recounted in the apocrypha.

The first artistic proof of acquaintance with the apocryphal legend of Mary's death and assumption is a scene on the Wirksworth slab in Derbyshire, a rectangular red sandstone slab which probably once formed part of a stone shrine or sarcophagus. The recent review article on the slab by Jane Hawkes suggests a date in the late eighth or early ninth century;[7] this is based both on the iconography (most of the scenes depicted have models originating in Eastern art, 'particularly the work of the Syro-

---

[5] Holder-Egger, ed., *Vita Willibaldi*, pp. 97–8.      [6] *Ibid.*, p. 98.

[7] Hawkes, 'The Wirksworth Slab'; see also B. Kurth, 'The Iconography of the Wirksworth Slab', *The Burlington Magazine* 86 (1945), 114–21, and R. W. P. Cockerton, 'The Wirksworth Slab', *Derbyshire Archaeological Journal* 82 (1962), 1–20.

Palestinian provinces of the sixth century'[8] and they lack any sign of the iconographic developments associated with the Carolingian period) and the figural style, which points to similar influences. The slab is in two registers and has been broken off on the left, while the upper right-hand corner has also been lost: the upper register depicts the washing of feet, a lamb on a Greek cross surrounded by the symbols of the four Evangelists (the *Agnus Victor*, according to Hawkes) and the death of the Virgin with an incomplete scene which may be an extension of the preceding one; the lower register has a puzzling scene which seems to be Christ's descent into hell, the *Anastasis*, but which has also been identified with the Nativity and the washing of the infant Christ,[9] the Ascension, the Annunciation and a further scene which is most probably the Presentation, but which Harbison identifies as the Adoration of the Magi.[10] The central scenes, therefore, are the *Agnus Victor* and the Ascension and on the left are grouped scenes from the life of Christ, while on the right of the slab are Marian scenes showing that Christ's 'supreme example is emulated by his mother, the Virgin Mary, who having dedicated her life to God, with the humble obedience of a handmaiden, is rewarded in death'.[11] Hawkes suggests that the person for whom the sarcophagus was made may have been a female patron or member of the community at Wirksworth.[12]

The depiction of the death and, possibly, the assumption of the soul of the Virgin shows a figure bearing a palm (John, according to the apocrypha) on the right of the scene, preceding a bier borne by two further figures (Peter and Paul). A body, presumably that of Mary, lies on the bier and underneath, parallel to the Virgin's body, is the figure of the Jew attached to the bier by his hands, while above are six heads in an oval glory or cloud, presumably the angels who sang as the bier was carried to the sepulchre. Hawkes has argued that the scene next to this, on the far right, for which no convincing interpretation had yet been suggested, is an extension of it, depicting, it seems, 'an angel reaching towards a swaddled infant held by a male figure'.[13] If this is what it is, then the scene corresponds to the apocryphal narratives at the moment when

---

[8] Hawkes, 'The Wirksworth Slab', p. 261.
[9] See Hawkes, 'The Wirksworth Slab', pp. 255–6, and Harbison, 'Two Panels', pp. 36–8.
[10] Hawkes, 'The Wirksworth Slab', pp. 260–1; Harbison, 'Two Panels', pp. 38–40.
[11] Hawkes, 'The Wirksworth Slab', p. 274.    [12] *Ibid*.    [13] *Ibid*., p. 255.

Christ hands over Mary's soul (depicted iconographically as an infant) to the archangel Michael.[14] Alternatively, it could also depict the moment when the angel returns with Mary's soul so that Christ can reunite it with her body.[15] Hawkes regards the former scene as the more likely, despite the chronological inconsistency of having the funeral procession before the moment of death.

The most startling aspect of this scene or pair of connected scenes is that they form the earliest extant depiction of the death, as the earliest Eastern treatments date from the tenth century or perhaps the second half of the ninth, and the only extant treatment of the burial procession until the twelfth century. This does not mean, however, that no iconography of Mary's death had been developed before this: this would in itself be highly unlikely, given that the other scenes on the slab draw on standard iconography, and many of the details on the slab resemble later treatments. Schiller suggests that the iconography of the legend would have been initiated in the East around 600, when celebration of the feast of the assumption began, and that the evidence must have been destroyed by the iconoclasts.[16] The *Liber pontificalis* records the donation of textiles depicting the assumption by a number of popes, beginning with Hadrian I (771–5).[17] Apart from the slab, the earliest surviving *transitus* images are three scenes remaining from a fresco cycle in the Roman church of Santa Maria Egyziaca, painted between 872 and 882, probably from Eastern exemplars.[18] They show Christ announcing her death to Mary, the raising up of three apostles on clouds and John greeting the apostles

---

[14] *Transitus A* reads: 'Dominus autem suscepit animam eius et posuit in manus michaheli archangeli' (Wenger, *L'assomption*, p. 253); *Transitus W*: 'Et sic suscepit animam eius dominus, et tradidit eam sancto angelo Michahel' (Wilmart, 'L'ancien récit', p. 344); and *B²*: 'Tunc Saluator commendauit animam sanctae Mariae Michaheli archangelo' (Haibach-Reinisch, ed., *Ein neuer 'Transitus'*, p. 76).

[15] In *Transitus A* this happens in paradise: 'Dominus autem accepit animam eius de manu michaelis archangeli et restituit eam in corpus marie' (Wenger, *L'assomption*, p. 256); in *W* it is also in paradise, though in this text it is angels rather than Michael alone who bring the soul; while in *Transitus B²* it happens on earth: 'Statimque iubente Domino accedens Michael archangelus, praesentauit animam sanctae Mariae coram Domino.' (Haibach-Reinisch, ed., *Ein neuer 'Transitus'*, p. 85).

[16] Schiller, *Ikonographie*, IV.2, 92.

[17] *Le 'Liber pontificalis'*, ed. L. Duchesne, 2nd edn, 3 vols. (Paris, 1957), I, 500; II, 14, 61 and 145.

[18] See Lafontaine, *Peintures médiévales*, pp. 29–35.

in front of Mary's house. The frescoes in the Cappadocean church of Agac Alti, dated *c.* 850–950, show Mary on her bed, with John holding the palm and Christ at her side.[19] Above this Christ is shown again, holding Mary's soul while Michael stands beside him ready to receive it. Presumably, therefore, the carvers of the slab had access to a model or models depicting the death, and probably also to an apocryphal narrative which dealt with the story, as the choice of scenes was clearly a planned and deliberate one, based on knowledge of the theological implications of the events included. As Deshman points out, the placing of the assumption directly above the Annunciation scene 'affirmed that her motherhood of God was the cause of her future resurrection, which is symbolized by the triumphal palm an apostle carries before the bier'.[20]

The *Old English Martyrology* is, like the slab, in some sense a Mercian work, the work of a learned author drawing on a variety of sources, probably written in Anglo-Saxon between *c.* 850 and the end of the ninth century, and providing entries for most days of the liturgical year.[21] We still do not know whether the text as we now have it is an original compilation in English or whether it was translated from an Anglo-Latin compilation, which could have been put together by a different person, at a different place and time. The entry for 15 August, the feast of the assumption, avoids all mention of the apocryphal narratives and uses instead responses for the feast, a note on Mary's age probably derived from an addition in Eusebius's *Chronicle* and Aldhelm: it is striking that there is no description of Mary's death, even though the *Martyrology* provides such a description for almost every other saint. Either the martyrologist was not acquainted with the legends of Mary's death, despite his wide reading, or he deliberately avoided them. Elsewhere Adamnan's *De locis sanctis*, with its profession of ignorance about the fate of Mary's body, is used in the *Martyrology*, so it is possible that the avoidance of any description of Mary's death was prompted by Adamnan's caution. Such avoidance of an apocryphal source is not, however, a feature of the entry for 8 September, the feast of Mary's nativity:

On ðone .viii.ᵃⁿ dæg þæs monþes byþ Sancta Maria acennednes. Hyre fæder wæs nemned Ioachim ond hire modor Anna, ond hi wæron .xx. geare somod ær þon

---

[19] See Hawkes, 'The Wirksworth Slab', p. 255.

[20] Deshman, *The Benedictional*, p. 131.

[21] Kotzor, ed., *Das altenglische Martyrologium*.

hi bearn hæfdon. Þa wæron swiþe unrote; þa oþywde Godes engel hiora ægðrum onsundrum hine, ond him sæde ðæt hi sceoldon habban swylc bearn swylce næfre ær in worold come, ne ær ne eft. Ða æfter .xx. gearum cende Anna dohtor, ond hieo nemde þa Maria. Ond þa hio wæs þreo geara eald, ða læddon hi fæder ond modor to Hierusalem, ond sealdon hi þær in þara fæmnena gemænesse þe ðær on Godes huse lofsang dydon dæges ond nihtes. Þa wæs þæt cild sona snotor ond anræde, ond swa fulfremed þæt nænig æþelicor ne sang þone Godes lofsang; ond hio wæs swa beorht on ansyne ond wliti þæt mon hyre meahte uneaþe onlocyan. Ond on hyre mægdenhade hio dyde fela wundra on webgeweorce ond oþrum cræftum ðæs þe þa yldran don ne meahton.[22]

This entry draws, as Herzfeld already recognized, on the first six chapters of the *Gospel of Pseudo-Matthew*, summarizing the main events leading to Mary's birth and her presentation in the temple, and it constitutes our first proof of knowledge of this apocryphon in Anglo-Saxon England. This very abbreviated paraphrase of *Pseudo-Matthew* chs. I–VI, 1 is too brief and lacking in detail for us to be able to say to which family, A or P, it belongs,[23] but it is a very important testimony to the circulation of the apocryphon in Mercia in the ninth century.

After the *Martyrology* we have no proof of the use of the apocrypha of the Virgin for over 150 years. The Benedictional of St Æþelwold, London, British Library, add. 49598, is a de luxe lavishly illustrated manuscript, probably dated to *c.* 973, which originally included illustrations for all the major feasts of Mary, but that accompanying the benediction for the feast of Mary's nativity has been lost.[24] It is possible, but, of course, impossible to prove, that it drew on apocryphal narratives of Mary's birth to depict the event, as the assumption miniature draws on apocryphal legends of her death.[25] Deshman suggests that 'it must have been the picture cycle of a Byzantine lectionary that gave Æþelwold, with his personal devotion to the Virgin, the novel idea of including feast pictures of her Birth and Death in his own manuscript'.[26] The miniature accompanying the benediction for the feast of the assumption, on fol. 102v, is in two registers: the lower shows nine apostles, those in front

---

[22] *Ibid.*, II, 201–3.   [23] See above, pp. 18–23.

[24] The authoritative study of this manuscript is Deshman, *The Benedictional*; see pp. 260–1 for the date of the manuscript. The facsimile edition is *The Benedictional of St Æthelwold*, ed. G. F. Warner and H. A. Wilson, The Roxburghe Club (Oxford, 1910).

[25] *Ibid.*, p. 163.   [26] *Ibid.*

making speaking gestures; in the top register a haloed Mary lies on a bed, her hands outstretched towards two weeping women, one of whom makes a speaking gesture, while a third woman behind her adjusts her pillow. The hand of God, flanked by four angels, lowers a crown in the middle of the top register; two of the angels make gestures of reverence, while the third has draped hands and the fourth holds a sceptre. The scene clearly illustrates passages from a *transitus* text, though it is debatable which one.[27] The three virgins occur in *Transitus A, B* and *W* and they remain awake with the apostles when everyone else sleeps during Mary's death; the apostles are gathered together in all three Latin apocryphal accounts also. The crown and sceptre do not feature in *transitus* accounts and this miniature is the earliest surviving depiction of the Coronation of the Virgin, though a crowned Virgin is common, especially in Roman iconography, from a much earlier period.[28] The scene draws also on other developments in Marian thought and Deshman sums up his discussion of it by describing it as 'a complex fusion of the interrelated iconographic traditions of *seruus Mariae genetricis Dei* and *Maria regina*, the symbolic narrative of the Transitus, and the liturgy'.[29]

The miniature is remarkable in that both registers feature scenes which are not found elsewhere, other than in the direct copy of the top register in a later English manuscript, the Benedictional of Robert of Jumièges. Surviving representations of the *transitus* texts depict other scenes, but not the reunion of the apostles or Mary with her servants. There is no doubt that the death of Mary was represented from a considerably earlier period, as the Wirksworth slab proves, but it is difficult to be sure whether the miniaturist was following a model or constructing these scenes from his knowledge of a text. Deshman argues that the Benedictional's inclusion of apocryphal scenes from Mary's life was influenced by a Byzantine lectionary, even though the scene bears no likeness to Byzantine iconography: 'Although stimulated by the lectionary's unusual subject matter, Æþelwold and his painters were independent enough to devise their own novel version of the theme'.[30] This independent procedure

---

[27] Reproduced *ibid.*, pl. 34, and in Clayton, *Cult*, pl. VI. See O. Sinding, *Mariae Tod und Himmelfahrt* (Oslo, 1903), p. 66; O. Homburger, *Die Anfänge der Malerschule von Winchester im X. Jahrhundert*, Studien über christliche Denkmäler, ns 13 (Leipzig, 1912), p. 52; Deshman, *The Benedictional*, p. 124 and n. 99.

[28] See Deshman, *The Benedictional*, pp. 126–7.    [29] *Ibid.*, p. 138.

[30] *Ibid.*, p. 163.

involved drawing on other scenes in the Benedictional and Alexander argues that the dormition miniature is 'an invention of the Winchester artist, put together from other scenes known to him'.[31] Almost all of the elements in it can be paralleled elsewhere in the manuscript; it 'appears undeniable that the miniature combines features from the manuscript's own pictures of the Nativity and the Baptism as well as from the iconography of the Ascension and perhaps also the Crucifixion'.[32] We cannot, therefore, be certain about the presence of an illustration of a *transitus* text in Winchester: it is possible that the sources for the content were textual, though it is also possible, but perhaps less likely, that an older tradition of *transitus* imagery was reworked by borrowing features of New Testament iconography already utilized in the manuscript.

While Æþelwold's Benedictional has to be interpreted as an endorsement of the *transitus* narratives, his most famous pupil, Ælfric, wished to prohibit rather than support those same narratives. In his two homilies for the feast of the assumption he explicitly referred to these texts: in *Catholic Homilies I*, he took over the warning against the *transitus* narratives contained in his source, Paschasius Radbertus's *Cogitis me*,[33] and in *Catholic Homilies II* he returned to the topic, referring to such books in both Latin and English, and declaring:

> Hwæt wille we eow swiðor secgan be ðisum symbeldæge. buton þæt maria cristes modor wearð on ðisum dæge of ðisum geswincfullum middanearde genumen up to heofenan rice. to hire leofan suna. ðe heo on life abær. mid ðam heo blissað on ecere myrhðe. a to worulde; Gif we mare secgað be ðisum symbeldæge þonne we on ðam halgum bocum rædað þe ðurh godes dihte gesette wæron. ðonne beo we ðam dwolmannum gelice. þe be heora agenum dihte oððe be swefnum fela lease gesetnyssa awriton. ac ða geleaffullan lareowas Augustinus. Hieronimus. Gregorius. and gehwilce oðre þurh heora wisdom hi towurpon; Sind swa ðeah gyt ða dwollican bec ægðer ge on leden. ge on englisc. and hi rædað ungerade menn . . .[34]

Ælfric does not specify what the heretical teaching of these *transitus* narratives is and much of his objection to them is undoubtedly based

---

[31] J. J. G. Alexander, 'The Benedictional of St Æthelwold and Anglo-Saxon Illumination of the Reform Period', in *Tenth-Century Studies*, ed. D. Parsons (Chichester, 1975), pp. 169–83, at 179.

[32] Deshman, *The Benedictional*, p. 127.    [33] See my discussion in *Cult*, p. 236.

[34] Godden, ed., *Ælfric's Catholic Homilies*, p. 259.

on their having been condemned by authorities whom he respected.[35] Ananya Kabir, however, argues that much of Ælfric's problem with these texts centred on their designation of paradise as the location of Mary's assumed body,[36] while Ælfric, as this quotation makes clear, believed her to have been assumed into heaven (though he does not specifically mention her body and never commits himself on its location).[37] Ælfric, as Kabir shows, subscribed to the Augustinian belief in heaven and paradise as equivalent terms, while most of the *transitus* narratives, apart from *Pseudo-Melito*, clearly differentiate them, describing the afterlife of Mary's body as taking place in a paradise distinct from heaven.[38] This may explain some of his objection to Latin *transitus* texts, but the two vernacular narratives edited here both use *Pseudo-Melito* and seem to follow that text's identification of paradise and heaven.[39] The CCCC 198 text is so confused, however, that it would not be surprising if Ælfric took exception to it and there may well have been other vernacular accounts of Mary's assumption, now lost, based on other *transitus* texts. Ælfric's own comment quoted above suggests, too, that he had difficulties with any pinning down of Mary's fate, preferring to leave it open, and this would have led him to oppose the CCCC 41 text also. Ælfric is our only vernacular witness to such opposition to the apocrypha and there is little evidence that his warnings had any effect.

The so-called Benedictional (properly a pontifical) of Robert of Jumièges, Rouen, Bibliotheque Municipale, 369 (Y. 7), usually dated *c.* 980 but now redated by Dumville to the second quarter of the eleventh century, is closely related to the Benedictional of Æþelwold.[40] Three pictures are still extant, for Easter, Pentecost and the assumption, and all three, Deshman argues, are 'simplified, direct copies of the miniatures in

---

[35] See Clayton, *Cult*, pp. 236–8 and 243.

[36] *The Interim Paradise*, dissertation in progress (Trinity College, Cambridge), ch. 2.

[37] See also *The Homilies of the Anglo-Saxon Church. The First Part, Containing the Sermones Catholici, or Homilies of Ælfric*, I, ed. B. Thorpe (London, 1843), p. 440: 'Ne wiðcweðe we be þære eadigan Marian þa ecan æriste, þeah, for wærscipe gehealdenum geleafan, us gedafenað þæt we hit wenon swiðor þonne we unrædlice hit geseþan þæt ðe is uncuð buton ælcere fræcednysse'.

[38] See above, pp. 93–4.      [39] See below, pp. 143–4 and pp. 146–7.

[40] See E. Temple, *Anglo-Saxon Manuscripts 900–1066* (London, 1976), pl. 87. D. Dumville redates the manuscript in *Liturgy and the Ecclesiastical History of Late Anglo-Saxon England*, Studies in Anglo-Saxon History 5 (Woodbridge, 1992), p. 87.

Æþelwold's book'.[41] In the later assumption miniature Mary lies on a bed, her hands in an orant position, attended by four grieving women, while above her is suspended a crown, attached by rays to the hand of God in a roundel above. The narrative elements have disappeared, therefore, and the close modelling on the *transitus* is disrupted by the introduction of a fourth virgin: it is difficult to know whether any particular significance should be attached to this.

At the very end of the Anglo-Saxon period we find the first artistic depictions of the apocryphal legends of the conception and birth of the Virgin. The Cotton Troper, London, British Library, Cotton Caligula A. xiv, a manuscript dated to the second half of the eleventh century, was written, probably in a Benedictine house, in England, possibly in Winchester or in Worcester from a Winchester exemplar.[42] The feast of the Nativity of the Virgin is marked by two miniatures. On fol. 26r a standing angel announces Mary's birth to Joachim, who is portrayed standing with his animals (two goats, a ram, sheep and what seems to be an ox).[43] Both Joachim and the angel hold blank scrolls, presumably originally intended to be inscribed. The titulus around the miniature reads:

> Credidit angelico Ioachim per nuntia uerbo
> Credens foecundam conceptu germinis Annam.
> Christum glorificat inopi qui semper habundat.

On the verso Joachim and Anna, holding the infant Mary, all three nimbed, sit within an architectural frame, while the hand of God emerges from the arc of heaven above, in blessing.[44] The hexameter inscription here reads:

> Ecce patet partus quem e[di]erat Anna per artus
> Aecclesie matrem genuit pregnando salutem
> Quam Domino uouit pater ad templumque dicauit.[45]

Once again, we are faced with the peculiarity that the troper's depiction

[41] Deshman, *The Benedictional*, p. 268.

[42] See Teviotdale, 'The Cotton Troper', pp. 279–80.

[43] Reproduced in Temple, *Anglo-Saxon Manuscripts*, pl. 294, and in Clayton, *Cult*, pl. VII.

[44] Reproduced in Clayton, *Cult*, pl. XIII.

[45] Letters in square brackets conjecturally restored by Teviotdale, 'The Cotton Troper', pp. 311–12.

of the Annunciation to Joachim is the earliest extant in the West, although we know that scenes from the Virgin's infancy had been introduced in Western art much earlier. According to the *Liber pontificalis*, Pope Leo III (*d.* 816) commissioned a cycle of paintings based on the story of Joachim and Anna for a Roman church and presented a tapestry depicting the story of Mary to the church of Santa Maria Maggiore.[46] Some scenes from a cycle of frescoes painted between 872 and 882 in the Roman church of Santa Maria Egyziaca survive: these show Joachim in the wilderness, the maid's reproaches to Anna and the arrival in Bethlehem.[47] The oldest Eastern cycle, that in the church at Kizil Cukur in Cappadocia, dates from the ninth century and probably relies on exempla from before the middle of the ninth century.[48] The Annunciation to Joachim is almost always presented within a cycle of the infancy of the Virgin and it is most probable that the Cotton troper illustration also goes back to such a cycle. As Teviotdale points out, there is a striking affinity between the troper scene and a depiction of the same event in the Psalter of Henry of Blois, sharing the same basic composition, the sorts of animals depicted and the feature that Joachim is without a halo.[49] It is possible, therefore, that the troper scene and the infancy of the Virgin cycle in the mid-twelfth-century Psalter of Henry of Blois 'reflect a picture cycle of the infancy of the Virgin that was available in England in the eleventh century'.[50] The animals depicted with Joachim point to this cycle having being derived from one designed to accompany the Greek *Proteuangelium*, as this text specifies that Joachim ordered the slaughter of ten lambs, twelve calves and a hundred kids when the angel announced Mary's conception to him. In the Latin *Gospel of Pseudo-Matthew*, on the other hand, Joachim's flocks are restricted to sheep. An unillustrated *Proteuangelium* has survived from Anglo-Saxon England and there were undoubtedly more versions of the apocryphon circulating. The hexameters accompanying the Annunciation illustration could be read as implying that Anna was already pregnant when the angel appeared to Joachim, a reading in accordance with both the *Proteuangelium* and the *Pseudo-Matthew*.[51]

---

[46] See Schiller, *Ikonographie*, IV.2, 34.

[47] See Lafontaine-Dosogne, *Peintures médiévales*, pp. 20–8.

[48] Schiller, *Ikonographie*, IV.2, 33–4.

[49] Teviotdale, 'The Cotton Troper', pp. 189–90.     [50] *Ibid.*, p. 190.

[51] See above, pp. 15–16 and 22.

The second illustration, of Mary and her parents, is likewise the earliest surviving such group and Teviotdale considers it 'most probable that the artist devised the iconography of this painting for this context'.[52] The inscription draws attention to Mary and then refers to her father's vowing her to the Lord and to her dedication to the temple. This inscription suggests knowledge of the *De natiuitate Mariae* rather than the *Proteuangelium* or the *Pseudo-Matthew*, in that in both of these earlier texts it is Anna, rather than Joachim, who vows the child to the Lord. In the *De natiuitate*, on the other hand, the couple have vowed together to dedicate any offspring to the Lord and when the angel announces the conception of Mary to Joachim he refers to this prior vow of Joachim's.[53]

There are also some traces of the infancy apocrypha in liturgical texts from Anglo-Saxon England. In the late Anglo-Saxon period two new feasts were introduced in England, the first country in the West to celebrate these feasts, whose adoption must be the result of Eastern influence.[54] The feast of the conception of the Virgin was introduced in Winchester *c.* 1030 and a mass for the feast is extant in the New Minster Missal, Le Havre, Bibliothèque Municipale 330, of the middle of the eleventh century, and in the Leofric Missal, Oxford, Bodleian Library, Bodley 579, where it was added about the time of the Conquest.[55] The first prayer reads:

Deus, qui beate Mariae uirginis conceptionem angelico uaticinio parentibus predixisti, presta huic presenti familiae tuae eius presidiis muniri, cuius conceptionis sacra sollempnia congrua frequentatione ueneratur.[56]

This alludes to the angel's announcement of Mary's birth to Joachim and Anna in terms too general to be able to tell with which of the infancy apocrypha the author was acquainted. The unique benedictions in the Exeter Benedictional, London, British Library, add. 28188, fol. 161r, also

---

[52] Teviotdale, 'The Cotton Troper', p. 199.

[53] Beyers, ed., *Libri de natiuitate Mariae*, III, 8 (p. 289).

[54] On the introduction of the two feasts, see my 'Feasts of the Virgin in the Liturgy of the Anglo-Saxon Church', *Anglo-Saxon England* 13 (1984), 209–33; *Cult*, pp. 42–7; and Bishop, 'On the Origins of the Feast of the Conception', in his *Liturgica Historica*, pp. 238–59.

[55] On the date of the addition in the Leofric Missal, see E. Drage, 'Bishop Leofric and the Exeter Cathedral Chapter (1050–1072): a Re-Assessment of the Manuscript Evidence' (unpubl. D.Phil. dissertation, Oxford University, 1978), p. 359.

[56] *The Missal of the New Minster*, ed. D. H. Turner, HBS 93 (London, 1962), p. 190.

probably composed in Winchester, similarly refer to the angel's announcement of the Virgin's birth:

Sempiterna[m] a Deo benedictionem uobis beate Marie uirginis pia deposcat supplicatio, quam concipiendam omnipotens, ex qua eius conciperetur unigenitus, angelico declarauit preconio, quam et uobis iugiter suffragari benigno, ut est benignissima, sentiatis auxilio.[57]

In the benedictions for the feasts of the presentation of Mary in the temple and for the feast of her conception in London, British Library, Harley 2892, a Canterbury manuscript whose texts were probably again composed in Winchester,[58] we again find allusions to the apocryphal narratives of Mary's birth and childhood. In the benedictions for the presentation of Mary there is another reference to the angelic prophecy of her conception and, naturally, to her presentation, a feature of the apocrypha only, while the benedictions for her conception allude again to the angelic prophecy and refer also to Mary's having been sanctified before birth by the dignity of her name: 'Et qui illam prius sanctificauit nominis dignitate . . .'.[59] This reference to the prior announcement of Mary's name is interesting, as this is not a feature of the *Gospel of Pseudo-Matthew*, but in some Latin versions of the *Proteuangelium*, including that in the English manuscript London, British Library, Cotton Nero E. i, Joachim holds a feast seven days after Mary's birth, during which there is a divine declaration of her name.[60] In the *De natiuitate*, the angel who announces Mary's conception to Joachim in the desert also tells him that she is to be called Mary.[61] If the *prius* means before Mary's birth, the natural interpretation of it, then the text being drawn on here has to be the *De natiuitate* and it is our earliest indication of knowledge of it. In all of these texts, then, there is some reference to events known only from the apocrypha: this is, of course, what we would expect as the feasts themselves are based on the apocryphal accounts of Mary's infancy.

---

[57] The Benedictional as a whole is unpublished, but this benediction is quoted by Bishop, *Liturgica Historica*, p. 240, and in *Corpus benedictionum pontificalium*, ed. Moeller, II, 811 (no. 1987). On the Winchester composition see also Prescott, 'The Structure', p. 130.

[58] Prescott, 'The Structure', pp. 132–3.

[59] *The Canterbury Benedictional*, ed. R. M. Woolley, HBS 51 (London, 1917), p. 119, and Moeller, ed., *Corpus benedictionum pontificalium*, I, 161 (no. 387).

[60] See below, p. 321.  [61] Beyers, ed., *Libri de natiuitate Mariae*, III, 8 (p. 289).

Manuscripts of texts of the Latin apocrypha survive from this period also: a Latin translation of part of the Greek *Proteuangelium* is contained in the Bury St Edmunds collection, Cambridge, Pembroke College, 25;[62] the *Gospel of Pseudo-Matthew* forms part of the collection of saints' lives in London, British Library, Cotton Nero E. i, a Worcester manuscript;[63] and the *De natiuitate Mariae* is included in the versions of the homiliary of Paul the Deacon in Durham, Cathedral Library, A. III. 29, and in Salisbury, Cathedral Library, 179. *Transitus W* is contained in Pembroke 25 also.[64]

From the beginning of the eighth century onwards, therefore, we have evidence of knowledge, not always favourable, of the apocrypha of the death and assumption, while evidence of the birth and infancy of Mary apocrypha is found from the ninth century onwards. This evidence, together with that of the three Old English texts to be considered in the next chapter, which prove that other Latin versions of the apocrypha must also have been circulating in Anglo-Saxon England, show that the apocryphal gospels were known and used throughout most of the Anglo-Saxon period. Evidence is from Northumbria and Mercia in the earlier part of this period, while from the later part it is largely from southern centres, especially Winchester.

---

[62] Edited in Appendix I, pp. 319–22.  [63] Edited in Appendix I, pp. 323–7.

[64] Edited in Appendix I, pp. 328–33.

# 5

# The manuscripts

The manuscripts are described here in the order in which the Marian
apocrypha which they contain are edited: first those with the Old English
*Gospel of Pseudo-Matthew*, then those containing the vernacular assumption
apocrypha and, finally, the Latin manuscripts from Anglo-Saxon England.

## OXFORD, BODLEIAN LIBRARY, HATTON 114 (O)

This manuscript originally formed a set with Oxford, Bodleian Library,
Junius 121 and Hatton 113, Junius 121 containing ecclesiastical in-
stitutes, confessional and penitential texts, many of them associated with
Archbishop Wulfstan, the two Hatton manuscripts containing homilies,
mostly by Wulfstan and Ælfric.[1] The three manuscripts are largely the
work of one scribe of the third quarter of the eleventh century. Hatton
113 and 114 contain first a set of homilies for any occasion, items 1–32,
mostly by Wulfstan or pseudo-Wulfstanian texts (Hatton 113, fols.
1r–115v); then homilies for festivals from Christmas to the Annunciation, items 33–40, all by Ælfric (Hatton 113, fols. 115v–144v and
Hatton 114, fols. 9r–36v; the break between the manuscripts comes in
the middle of item 36); then homilies for Sundays from Quinquagesima
to the first Sunday after Easter and for Rogationtide, Ascension Thursday
and Pentecost, items 41–58 (Hatton 114, fols. 36v–140r); and homilies
for the Sanctorale from Gregory (12 March) to All Saints (1 November),
items 59–75 (Hatton 114, fols. 140r–230r). The original table of
contents in Hatton 113 covers these articles. Additions in early hands

---

[1] Ker, *Catalogue*, no. 331; see also Pope, ed., *Homilies of Ælfric*, I, 70–7, and Godden, ed.,
*Ælfric's Catholic Homilies*, pp. li–liv.

were made at the beginning of Hatton 114, fols. 1r–8r, and at the end, fols. 230r–247r, some of them by the main scribe of the manuscript. The origins of the collection are diverse, as Godden has proved in relation to the Ælfric items.

The homily for the nativity of Mary, item 72, fols. 201r–212r, is headed V *De natiuitate sanctae mariae* in the manuscript, with 'LVIIII' inserted superscript and '.LIX. De Natiuitate' as running title across each verso and '.LIX. Sanctae Mariae' across each recto; presumably the V was copied from the exemplar, as it does not make sense in the context of this manuscript. It is the only non-Ælfrician item in the sequence for saints' days in which it occurs, apart from two short pieces on the duties of priests from the *Penitential of Pseudo-Egbert* which come immediately before it. Ker says that the 'appearance of the writing changes and there is perhaps a change of hand at the beginning of art. 72', whereas Godden, for example, speaks of a single scribe for the main part of the collection.[2] The appearance changes rather at the top of fol. 201r, at the end of the previous item, with the writing becoming larger. The source collection from which the texts for saints' days in the last part of Hatton 113 and 114 were selected was a revised issue of *Catholic Homilies I*, which would most probably have included Ælfric's later homily for the nativity of Mary, Assmann III: a similar group of texts in the twelfth-century manuscript, Oxford, Bodleian Library, Hatton 116 was derived either directly or indirectly from the same source as this part of Hatton 113 and 114, and the twelfth-century manuscript includes Assmann III.[3] It seems probable, then, that the compiler of Hatton 113 and 114 deliberately chose the *Pseudo-Matthew* text in preference to Ælfric's nativity of the Virgin homily, despite Ælfric's objections to such apocryphal texts.

Hatton 114 was written at Worcester and the collection was probably assembled there also.[4] It was glossed by the tremulous hand of Worcester in the first half of the thirteenth century.[5] His glosses to this homily, labelled *apocrifum* in the tremulous hand, have been included in a separate section of this edition, although no attempt has been made to categorize them according to the state of the glossing hand, as Franzen does in her

---

[2] Ker, *Catalogue*, pp. 398–9; Godden, ed., *Ælfric's Catholic Homilies*, p. lii.
[3] See Clemoes, *Angelsächsische Homilien und Heiligenleben*, ed. Assmann, pp. xx and xxix.
[4] Godden, ed., *Ælfric's Catholic Homilies*, p. liv.
[5] On this glossator see the study by C. Franzen, *The Tremulous Hand of Worcester* (Oxford, 1991).

study. Quite a few of the glosses are doublets: either the same word written twice at different times or different glosses to the same word, often with one superscript and the other in the margin. Most of the glosses are in Latin, but there is a number in Middle English. The same hand has added some word-divisions and superscript vowels (usually *e* for *y*), as well as superscript *i* over the verbal prefix *ge*-; these are not noted here. The *Pseudo-Matthew* homily has received several corrections and additions in a hand which may be different from that of the main scribe: the *gædere* of *ætgædere* (fol. 202r) has been added over an erasure in a smaller, finer hand with an *r* which does not seem to be the same as that of the main scribe; this hand also seems to have been responsible for *ðearft ðu þe* over an erasure on fol. 203r, possibly the inserted *is* on fol. 205r, superscript *and is* on fol. 211v and superscript *for hire bene* on fol. 212r. There are two instances of *þo* on fol. 209r, at the ends of lines 3 and 4, which seem to be by a different hand again.

CAMBRIDGE, CORPUS CHRISTI COLLEGE, 367,

PART II, FOLS. 3R–6R, 11R–29R (f^a)

This is a fragmentary manuscript, made up of parts of six quires, which now contains ten items, some of them imperfect.[6] It was written in the twelfth century, probably by one scribe. The fragments are now muddled together, but it is probable that they were originally in the order of the church year. Eight of the items are by Ælfric, seven from the *Catholic Homilies* and one from the *Lives of Saints*. The occasions covered are Easter Sunday and Monday, Rogation Tuesday, the assumption of Mary, the feast of St Bartholomew, the Exaltation of the Cross, the feast of St Matthew and the feast of St Michael. The other two items are the anonymous homily based on the *Gospel of Pseudo-Matthew* (fols. 11r–16r), entitled *Sexta idus septembris. natiuitas sancte marie uiginis* (*sic*) in the manuscript, which is incomplete, lacking the contents of the last leaf, and a fragmentary copy of Vercelli iv on a single leaf.

The manuscripts with which the Ælfric texts in this manuscript are connected are Cambridge, University Library, Ii. 4. 6 and London, British Library, Cotton Vespasian D xiv, a manuscript in turn linked to Bodleian Library MSS 340+342, CCCC 198 and CCCC 162; as these manuscripts

---

[6] Ker, *Catalogue*, no. 63; see also Godden, ed., *Ælfric's Catholic Homilies*, pp. lvi–lvii.

119

have south-eastern links, Godden suggests that 'the collection was originally compiled in the south-east'.[7]

### OXFORD, BODLEIAN LIBRARY, BODLEY 343 (I)

This is a large collection written in the second half of the twelfth century.[8] It contains homilies and other pieces: about three-quarters of them are by Ælfric, including texts from the *Catholic Homilies*, *Lives of Saints* and his pastoral letters; some are by Wulfstan; some are anonymous; and there is a group of sixty-seven short Latin sermons. All of the English items date from before the Conquest, at least a century before the manuscript was copied, and Irvine suggests that the most likely use of a manuscript like this 'would be devotional reading for English-speaking monks and nuns, and a reading book for secular clergy which could be assimilated and adapted for use in preaching'.[9] The manuscript is probably the work of two nearly contemporary scribes, one responsible for fols. vir–xxxixr, the second for fols. 1r–170r, and was written in seven sections, each of which begins with a fresh quire. The texts by Ælfric in particular are clearly derived from very different sources, reflecting different stages of the development of his texts, and the complex textual history suggests 'faithful copying, probably at various stages of transmission, of many small collections which were themselves drawn from larger collections'.[10]

The anonymous homily on the nativity of Mary, consisting of a translation of part of the *Gospel of Pseudo-Matthew*, entitled *Natiuitas sancte marie* in the manuscript, is item 16, on fols. 30r–33v, and forms part of the fourth section, section (d). The text forms part of the group of saints' texts from Laurence to Martin, a group whose chronological ordering, as Irvine points out, cuts 'across the groupings by textual origins',[11] showing that here, as elsewhere, the compiler must have been selecting from a manuscript or manuscripts already arranged chronologically. The Marian apocryphon, Irvine also suggests, may have come from the same collection as that from which the Martin, Chair of St Peter and Edmund

---

[7] Godden, ed., *Ælfric's Catholic Homilies*, p. lvii.

[8] Ker, *Catalogue*, no. 310. Also described by Pope, ed., *Homilies of Ælfric*, I, 14–18; Godden, ed., *Ælfric's Catholic Homilies*, pp. xxxvii–xl, and in detail by Irvine, ed., *Old English Homilies*, pp. xviii–liv.

[9] Irvine, ed., *Old English Homilies*, p. liii.     [10] *Ibid.*, p. l.     [11] *Ibid.*, p. xxxv.

texts (all three from Ælfric's *Lives of Saints*) were taken, as well as the Laurence, Bartholomew and Andrew texts from Ælfric's First Series of *Catholic Homilies*. The presence of the anonymous homily in this presumed source is puzzling because the First Series homilies in this section of Bodley 343 are related to those in CCCC 188, a manuscript which contains Ælfric's own homily for the nativity of Mary (Assmann III), but Irvine convincingly suggests the apocryphal gospel was chosen by the compiler of Bodley 343 because it offered pure narrative rather than exegesis.[12] If this was the case, then this manuscript must have contained exactly the mixture of his own works with anonymous homilies of which Ælfric disapproved and against which he sought in vain to protect himself.

A text for St Wulfhad added in the thirteenth century and an inscription mentioning 'Wolstane' suggest, Ker points out, that Bodley 343 is from the West Midlands[13] and Irvine concludes, on the basis of textual and other connections, that it was probably written somewhere near Worcester, though not at Worcester itself.[14] The scribe's dialect seems to have been a West Midlands one.[15] The language of the texts in the manuscript, 'despite the scribe's obvious aim for linguistic fidelity', has been modernized[16] and 'vocabulary and syntax were altered to conform to twelfth-century linguistic practice'.[17]

There are three glosses to the nativity text, all on the same third of a page: *comedit* for *burigde*, *yrre* for *wrað* and *chidon* for *tælan* (fol. 31v); they appear to be by the scribe of the main text. Occasional corrections appear to be largely in the text hand also.

## CAMBRIDGE, CORPUS CHRISTI COLLEGE, 41 (D)

Originally this manuscript contained a complete copy of the Old English translation of Bede's *Ecclesiastical History*, written in the first half of the eleventh century by two scribes.[18] Shortly afterwards, probably also in the first half or about the middle of the same century, a third

---

[12] *Ibid.*, pp. xxxiv–xxxv.    [13] Ker, *Catalogue*, pp. 374–5.
[14] Irvine, ed., *Old English Homilies*, p. lii.    [15] *Ibid.*, p. lv.    [16] *Ibid.*
[17] *Ibid.*, p. xvi.
[18] Ker, *Catalogue*, no. 32; the *Ecclesiastical History* is edited by T. Miller, *The Old English Version of Bede's Ecclesiastical History of the English People*, EETS o.s. 95, 96, 110, 111 (London, 1890–8).

scribe,[19] whose hand is difficult to date, added sixteen further items in blank spaces and on lines ruled in the margins of the Bede. These include masses and liturgical texts in Latin, some with Old English rubrics, part of the *Old English Martyrology*, charms, part of a verse dialogue between Solomon and Saturn and six Old English homilies, concluding with a record of the gift of the manuscript to Exeter by Bishop Leofric (*d.* 1072), in a fourth hand. The manuscript is not, however, mentioned in the list of Leofric's donations to Exeter. The Old English homilies are an eschatological text (Vercelli iv), a text for the assumption of Mary, an *Apocalypse of Thomas*, a *Gospel of Nicodemus*, a text on St Michael and a homily composed of a translation of Matthew chs. 26 and 27, with a homiletic beginning and ending.[20] The first four of the homilies occur as a group (Ker, items 9, 11,12 and 13: Ker, item 10 is a Latin charm already in the manuscript before the homilies were written) and the other two are written separately further on in the manuscript. The first and fourth homilies occur elsewhere (the Vercelli Book and CCCC 303 respectively), but the others are all unique and seem to represent a different anonymous tradition to the contents of other anonymous manuscripts.

The script in which the Old English texts is written is small and angular, on lines ruled very close together. Tristram quotes the opinion of T. A. M. Bishop that the hand of the marginal additions shows features of tenth-century insular script, seeming therefore earlier in appearance than the hands of the main text.[21] The assumption homily is written on the top, bottom and outer margins of the pages, pp. 280–7, in ink whose colour varies from dark to light brown. The letter *o* is particularly distinctive and is very angular and easily confused with *a*. Corrections appear to be by the scribe of the homily.

---

[19] Or, perhaps, scribes: Ker (*Catalogue*, p. 45) says 'probably all in one unusual angular hand'. See Kotzor, *Das altenglische Martyrologium*, I, 94 and 104.

[20] Three of the homilies are edited by Grant, *Three Homilies* (the assumption, St Michael and the Matthew homily) and Tristram, *Vier altenglische Predigten*, has also edited the assumption and Michael texts. The assumption homily is, of course, reedited here. The *Apocalypse of Thomas* has been edited by M. Förster, 'A New Version of the Apocalypse of Thomas in Old English'. The *Gospel of Nicodemus* is edited by W. H. Hulme, 'The Old English Gospel of Nicodemus', *Modern Philology* 1 (1903–4), 579–614. The parallel text to Vercelli iv is collated by Scragg, ed., *The Vercelli Homilies*, pp. 90–104.

[21] Tristram, ed., *Vier altenglische Predigten*, p. 32.

Although the manuscript was given to Exeter Cathedral Library by Leofric, it does not seem to have been written there and has none of the characteristics of the Exeter scriptorium.[22] Miller, the editor of the Old English Bede, argues on the basis of language that the version in this manuscript was written in Wessex, in the neighbourhood of Abingdon or Winchester.[23] Grant, drawing on Wormald's description of the drawings in the manuscript as of the Winchester school and on his own analysis of the liturgical texts, also suggests that the book might come from Winchester, pointing to its 'similarity to the Missal of Robert of Jumièges and Corpus 422, both products of the New Minster'.[24] Kotzor, too, quotes Collier's [Drage's] opinion that the manuscript could have originated in Winchester.[25] In his edition of three of the homilies Grant further points out that the manuscript, to judge by the way in which it was produced, 'is either the product of a poor house or a second-rate product of a larger institution intended for everyday use'.[26] Hohler, however, in his review of Grant's 1978 work, is scathing about the Winchester connection postulated by Grant for the liturgical texts and points out that they must have been added by a secular priest, as they follow secular use; he suggests that they were written by a secular priest working in the neighbourhood of Glastonbury: 'as four verses of St Sechnall's Hymn are among the things [the adding scribe] entered, it would be natural to suppose that he lived somewhere near the obvious centre of the cultus of St Patrick in England (namely Glastonbury) and that he was being told to bring his liturgical books up to date by a reforming bishop of Wells, probably then Dudoc (1033–61), less probably Giso (1061–88)'.[27] Förster assumed that the homilies (and therefore presumably the liturgica, as at least some are definitely in the same hand as the homilies) were added to the manuscript when it was already in Exeter,[28] but this seems unlikely as they do not have the

---

[22] See Kotzor, ed., *Das altenglische Martyrologium*, I, 104.

[23] T. Miller, *Place Names in the Old English Bede* (Strasburg, 1896), p. 5.

[24] R. J. S. Grant, *Cambridge, Corpus Christi College 41: the Loricas and the Missal*, Costerus n.s. 17 (Amsterdam, 1978), p. 50.

[25] Kotzor, ed., *Das altenglische Martyrologium*, I, 104, n. 287.

[26] Grant, ed., *Three Homilies*, p. 1.

[27] C. Hohler, review of R. J. S. Grant, *Cambridge, Corpus Christi College 41: the Loricas and the Missal*, *Medium Ævum* 49 (1980), 275–8, at 275.

[28] M. Förster, 'A New Version of the Apocalypse of Thomas in Old English', p. 11.

characteristics of the Exeter scriptorium. Kotzor again draws on Collier, who suggests that the marginal additions were also made in Winchester but does not adduce evidence for this.[29] On balance, therefore, it seems safer to leave the question of where the marginal texts were added open, but it seems unlikely to have been Exeter; probably only the donation inscription was added there.

## CAMBRIDGE, CORPUS CHRISTI COLLEGE, 198 (F)

This is a large collection of homilies, the first part of it written in the early eleventh century, which was added to shortly afterwards and again in the second half of the century.[30] Robinson refines earlier descriptions of the growth of the collection by showing how the manuscript developed by the addition of booklets:

In the early eleventh century the collection contained an ordered series of thirty-two homilies for the temporale and sanctorale from Christmas to the beginning of May (now fols. iii, 1–149 and 160–217). . . . [T]hese groups [of quires] were a little later treated as self-contained units when three further booklets (fols. 150–9, 218–47 and 248–87) were inserted into the series. The earliest of them (fols. 248–87) contains eleven homilies[31] copied by scribe 4, who left the last of these homilies [on St Paul] incomplete, and the other two booklets were added by scribe 5. He also provided the essential rubrics to convert the collection into a homiliary, assigning each of the original homilies as well as each of the additions by scribe 4 and himself to a specific occasion. Soon after, four more scribes (6, 7, 7a and 8) contributed to the growing collection. Scribe 6 copied three booklets (now fols. 328–59, 360–6 and 378–85), which were originally arranged consecutively to form a short orderly series of homilies for saints' days in August, September and November. He was assisted by scribe 7, who wrote the last homily in the first of these three booklets, and scribe 7a, who wrote the last twenty-one lines on 366v in the second booklet. Scribe 8 worked independently. He completed the homily which scribe 4 had left unfinished at the end of his booklet (fols. 248–87) and then supplemented the booklet with six further

---

[29] *Das altenglische Martyrologium*, I, 106, n. 298.

[30] Ker, *Catalogue*, no. 48; the manuscript has also been described by Sisam, *Studies*, pp. 154–6; Pope, ed., *Homilies of Ælfric*, I, 20–2; Godden, ed., *Ælfric's Catholic Homilies*, pp. xxviii–xxxi; Robinson, 'Self-contained Units', pp. 236–7; and Scragg, 'The Homilies of the Blickling Manuscript', pp. 309–15.

[31] Robinson follows Ker's numbering, but in Godden's numbering there are eight texts, three of them in two parts.

homilies in four extra quires. Scribe 8 also produced another booklet (fols. 386–94) which contains a homily on St Andrew. In the second half of the eleventh century a further booklet (fols. 367–77) was added by scribes 9 and 11 who each copied a homily in it. Scribe 9 also began to copy a homily on St Bartholomew on leaves (321v–7v) which scribe 8 had left blank at the end of his extension of scribe 4's booklet; this was completed by scribe 10.[32]

Such a method of compiling a collection, which may have been left unbound for quite a while, allowed booklets to be drawn upon for preaching or other uses and then to be reinserted in the whole. This procedure also explains the different textual origins of the items in the collection. The collection as first copied, with the addition of the items copied by scribe 4, corresponds, as Sisam pointed out, closely to the first part of the collection in Bodley 340+342, although it cannot have been copied from it: the two collections must share a common source.[33] Bodley 340+342 is a two-volume Kentish homiliary, from Rochester or Canterbury, composed of First and Second Series homilies by Ælfric, rearranged into a single set covering the liturgical year from Christmas to Advent, supplemented by eleven non-Ælfrician homilies. Very probably scribe 4's work had originally also included further items from the Canterbury homiliary, presumably covering the period after Pentecost to Advent, if Bodley 340+342 is a reliable guide, but, as Scragg suggests, these were discarded when the collection was rethought by later scribes.[34]

The items added by scribe 5 are textually different from the original collection and clearly come from a different source,[35] but the aim was to augment the original collection by inserting, in their proper place in the liturgical year, two further homilies for Lent and, somewhat out of place, three more homilies for Easter and three for the Common of Saints. These homilies all come from the Second Series of Ælfric's *Catholic Homilies* and seem to have had, as their immediate source, a copy of the Second Series itself or a selection from it, rather than the Bodley 340+342 type collection.[36] The later scribes, 6 to 8, seem, however, to have aimed to change, rather than simply to augment, the character of the homiliary and 'to end the Temporale sequence soon after Pentecost and then to

---

[32] Robinson, 'Self-contained Units', pp. 236–7; but see below on the homily which scribe 4 had left unfinished.

[33] Sisam, *Studies*, pp. 154–6.

[34] Scragg, 'The Homilies of the Blickling Manuscript', p. 310.

[35] See Godden, ed., *Ælfric's Catholic Homilies*, pp. xxix–xxxi.     [36] *Ibid.*, p. xxx.

concentrate in the latter part of the year on a Sanctorale', so producing what Scragg terms a unique and original arrangement.[37] As part of this rethinking scribe 8 seems to have recopied the conclusion of the homily on Paul, which had therefore probably not been left unfinished by scribe 4 but was the only part of a now to be discarded quire which was still required for the new arrangement. Item 54, the anonymous homily for the assumption of Mary on fols. 350r–359r, headed *In assumptione Sancte Marie uirginis*, was copied by scribe 7, who completed a booklet with it; it ends halfway down fol. 359r and the lower half of the page has been cut out. The verso is blank. Scragg says that 'the blank spaces between the blocks show that these items [the work of scribes 6, 7 and 7a] were assembled here for the first time':[38] these items are the *Lives of Saints* Maccabees text for 1 August, the *Catholic Homilies I* Laurence text, the assumption text, the *Catholic Homilies I* Michael text and the Life of Martin from *Catholic Homilies II*. The assumption text is therefore the only anonymous text in this section and it is one of relatively few non-Ælfrician texts in the manuscript.

The homiliary to result from all these alterations and additions has significant similarities in arrangement to the Blickling Homilies, which are 'a Temporale running from some point before Lent to Pentecost, followed by a Sanctorale'.[39] F in its finished state contains a *temporale* from Christmas to the third Sunday after Pentecost, followed, with interruptions, by a *sanctorale*.

The manuscript is glossed by the thirteenth-century tremulous hand of Worcester and Ker notes that spellings in arts. 65–67 (the items added in the second half of the eleventh century) suggest that these articles were written in the west of England in the second half of the eleventh century.[40] Pope thought that the 'one thing that seems probable about its early history is that it was not at Worcester itself in the eleventh century', on the grounds that the Worcester scribes of that period had access to a greater range of Ælfric's work than is attested in this manuscript and that 'even their known styles of writing do not seem to resemble those of the very numerous hands here', and he says that 'there is a chance that it originated in or near Kent'.[41] Godden, on the other hand, suggests that

---

[37] Scragg, 'The Homilies of the Blickling Manuscript', p. 312.    [38] *Ibid.*, p. 311.
[39] *Ibid.*, p. 316.    [40] Ker, *Catalogue*, p. 82.
[41] Pope, ed., *Homilies of Ælfric*, I, 22; see also Sisam, *Studies*, p. 155, n. 4.

the manuscript may have been written at Worcester, arguing that, although the collection from which the original part of the manuscript was copied must go back to a south-eastern source 'since a majority of the manuscripts belonging to the same textual tradition come from Canterbury or Rochester', F itself shows no sign of such an origin and the Second Series homilies in the part of the manuscript written by scribe 5 have no south-eastern connections.[42]

While the texts in the first part of the manuscript have close textual affiliations with Kentish manuscripts, those parts added by scribes 5 to 8 do not share these connections and the manuscript with which this part of F has links is B, with which it shares the assumption homily (Blickling XIII), the Andrew text (Blickling XVIII) and part of Blickling X, as well as the similarities in organization noted above. Scragg suggests that the 'dislocation between the work of scribes 1 to 4 and that of 5 to 8 is consonant with the movement of the manuscript from one centre to another, and the likelihood is that part II was not made in the centre which produced part I'.[43] The whereabouts of that centre in which Part II was produced remains unclear, but Scragg argues fairly convincingly that it may have been the same scriptorium in which B was written, as the textual connections between F and B in all three of the shared texts are very close: F is 'not dependent upon B but is so close to it that we must assume that they have a common ancestor lying no great distance behind them'.[44] The Mercian language of B suggests a Mercian origin and it is possible that the second part of F therefore shared this origin.[45] It is possible, then, that the manuscript had two moves: one from a south-eastern centre to the scriptorium in which scribes 5 to 8 wrote, and from there to Worcester where scribes 9 to 12 worked in the second half of the eleventh century.

The assumption text is the only work of scribe 7 in the manuscript and, like the other texts, it is glossed by the tremulous hand. A visually striking feature of the text is that in the *Magnificat* which concludes the homily the Latin quotations have all been underlined, marking them out from the Old English text. The tremulous hand glosses, like those in O, have been included in a separate section of this edition.

---

[42] Godden, ed., *Ælfric's Catholic Homilies*, p. xxxi.
[43] Scragg, 'The Homilies of the Blickling Manuscript', p. 313.   [44] *Ibid.*
[45] *Ibid.*, p. 316.

This is a collection of eighteen homilies, eight of them unique, for Sundays and saints' days, covering the feast of the Annunciation, the Temporale from Lent to Pentecost, the assumption, the nativity of John the Baptist and the feasts of Peter, Michael, Martin and Andrew.[46] It is arranged largely in the order of the church year, with the Annunciation coming before Quinquagesima, as happens occasionally elsewhere, and the assumption (15 August) coming before the nativity of John (24 June).

The beginning and end of the manuscript are missing, as are some leaves throughout. Nineteen quires survive and probably at least five more are missing. The manuscript was written by two scribes: the first wrote all of the first seven quires and is also the main scribe in quires 8 to 16, while the second was solely responsible for quires 17 to 19, wrote the *incipit* to homily vii at the beginning of quire 8, and wrote parts of quires 10, 12 and 15. Scragg divides the quires into three blocks: the first, quires 1–8, from homily i to vii (Annunciation to Easter); the second, quires 9–16, homily viii to xv, covering the post-Easter period to the feast of Peter; and the third, quires 17–19, homily xvi–xviii, continuing the Sanctorale. In the first block the collection seems to be an original compilation, 'at least three breaks in the copying of items being discernible', indicating that it 'must have been pieced together, perhaps over a period of time, from a number of sources'.[47] The items in the second block, on the other hand, appear to have been written consecutively, although the way in which scribe 2 intervenes at times to write openings and conclusions might have been, Scragg suggests, 'to ensure that scribe 1 followed a preconceived selection from a variety of sources'.[48] The third block is all in the hand of scribe 2, with no apparent breaks. It is clear from the way the collection was compiled that the individual texts are very unlikely to be by the same author and Clemoes

---

[46] Ker, *Catalogue*, no. 382; the manuscript is edited by Morris, *The Blickling Homilies*; the facsimile is edited by R. Willard, *The Blickling Homilies*, EEMF 10 (Copenhagen, 1960); and the manuscript is also described in Scragg, 'The Homilies of the Blickling Manuscript'.

[47] Scragg, 'The Homilies of the Blickling Manuscript', p. 303.   [48] *Ibid.*

has also said that 'single authorship can be ruled out from the start on stylistic grounds'.[49]

B has no clear link with other anonymous collections, although it shares some items with other manuscripts. The closest association is with F, a collection of mainly Ælfric texts, with some anonymous items, but all the items in B must be pre-Ælfrician.

Homily xiii, the assumption text, is on fols. 84v–98v, with a later title, *Sancta maria mater domini*, to which a still later hand has added *Nostri Iesu Cristi*. A page is missing after fol. 85v, but there is no gap after fol. 86v, although Morris notes one in his edition, oddly placing it four words from the end of the page. It is written mainly by scribe 1, but scribe 2 intervened at fols. 86r and 86v.

The manuscript probably dates from around the millennium. The hand of the second scribe is described by Ker as rather later in appearance than hand 1,[50] but it must be contemporary as the two hands occur together on some pages. The place of origin of the manuscript is unknown; it 'was at Lincoln and probably in the possession of the Corporation from s.xiii/ xiv until s. xvii in'.[51] It was used for more than three centuries 'as a register of municipal memoranda'[52] and the margins, including those of the assumption homily, contain many additions and notes.

## THE LATIN MANUSCRIPTS

### CAMBRIDGE, PEMBROKE COLLEGE, 25 (P)

This is a late eleventh-century manuscript containing a copy of what is known as the Saint-Père homiliary.[53] It was in Bury St Edmunds by 1154 and Dumville suggests that it is perfectly possible that it was written there, but there is no proof of this at present.[54] The homiliary covers the

---

[49] P. Clemoes, review of R. Willard, ed., *The Blickling Homilies*, *Medium Ævum* 31 (1962), 60–3, at 61.

[50] Ker, *Catalogue*, p. 454.    [51] *Ibid.*, p. 455.

[52] Willard, ed., *The Blickling Homilies*, p. 47.

[53] There is a study of this manuscript by Cross, *Cambridge Pembroke College MS 25*. See also H. Barré, *Les homéliaires carolingiens de l'école d'Auxerre*, Studi e Testi 225 (Rome, 1962), pp. 17–25. See also pp. 315–18.

[54] D. Dumville, 'On the Dating of some Late Anglo-Saxon Liturgical Manuscripts', *Transactions of the Cambridge Bibliographical Society* 10 (1991), 40–57, at 41.

church year from Advent to the feast of St Andrew, followed by a *commune sanctorum* and sermons on general topics. The most detailed list of contents and sources is given by Cross and he prints eleven of the homilies, all of which are sources for vernacular texts. The collection was compiled after 822 and must have been available in England from the tenth century, as Old English homilies in the Vercelli Book and other vernacular collections clearly draw on it.[55] A fragment of the same collection survives in the early eleventh-century manuscript Canterbury Cathedral MS Addit. 127/12, and there are later English manuscripts of the homiliary also.[56] The text for the feast of the assumption of Mary is on fols. 113v–117v and that for the nativity of Mary on fols. 119v–122r.

## LONDON, BRITISH LIBRARY, COTTON NERO E. I (N)

This is a part of a large collection, the so-called Cotton-Corpus legendary, written in the third quarter of the eleventh century in Worcester.[57] It was originally part of a two-volume passional arranged according to the calendar year and the original collection consisted of Nero E. i, part i, fols. 55r–208r and part ii, fols. 1r–155r, covering from January to September, and Cambridge, Corpus Christi College, 9, pp. 61–458 and Nero E. i, part ii, fols. 166r–80r, covering from October to December. The Cotton and Corpus manuscripts have been separate since the late eleventh century, but the two parts of Nero E. i were together until early modern times. There are later accretions at the beginning of the Corpus manuscript and at the beginning of Nero part i and at the end of Nero part ii. The Cotton-Corpus legendary is the earliest English copy of this collection, which seems to have been originally compiled in northern France or Flanders in the very late ninth or the early tenth century, even though all the manuscripts that preserve it are of English origin.[58] It contains 165 saints' *uitae* and was extensively used by Ælfric in his composition of the *Lives of Saints*. The *Sermo de natiuitate S. Mariae*, assigned to the feast of the nativity of Mary, is on fols. 116v–118r.

---

[55] Cross, *Cambridge Pembroke College MS 25*, pp. 88–90.    [56] See p. 315–16.

[57] On this collection, see P. H. Zettel, 'Saints Lives in Old English: Latin Manuscripts and Vernacular Accounts: Ælfric', *Peritia* 1 (1982), 17–37, and Jackson and Lapidge, 'The Contents of the Cotton-Corpus Legendary'.

[58] Jackson and Lapidge, 'The Contents of the Cotton-Corpus Legendary', p. 134.

# 6

## The Old English texts

This chapter deals principally with questions of the origins of the three Old English Marian apocryphal gospels edited here, their function and their treatment of their Latin sources. No attempt is made to give a detailed linguistic description of the texts: because of the nature of this volume, with editions of three texts all from different manuscripts, drawing altogether on six manuscripts, such linguistic descriptions would result only in a mass of details of little real benefit to anyone. Instead only features which could be of use in helping to determine questions of date and place of composition are alluded to. All three are anonymous texts for which we have no firm dates and no firm localizations. All three, however, have no trace of Winchester vocabulary[1] and have been considered Anglian on the basis of vocabulary studies.

As an Anglian origin has been suggested for all three homilies, principally on the basis of vocabulary, this will be discussed first, before going on to separate treatments of the three texts. Hardy, in his discussion of the language of Blickling, came to the conclusion that the texts were clearly Anglian, but with some Kentish traces.[2] Menner's examination of the vocabulary of the homilies led him to conclude that, with a few possible exceptions, they were composed in Anglian, and he favours Mercia rather than Northumbria.[3] Vleeskruyer similarly thought them

---

[1] Hofstetter, *Winchester*, p. 169 (Blickling Homilies), p. 237 (*Pseudo-Matthew*) and p. 238 (the assumption homily in D). The only trace of Winchester vocabulary is to be found in the I manuscript of *Pseudo-Matthew*, where *gearcian* has been substituted for *gearwian* (*ibid.*, p. 237).

[2] Hardy, *Die Sprache der Blickling Homilien*, p. 125.

[3] R. J. Menner, 'The Anglian Vocabulary of the *Blickling Homilies*', *Philologica: the Malone Anniversary Studies* (Baltimore, 1949), pp. 56–64, at 62.

Mercian.[4] Schabram, in his discussion of words for *superbia*, also concluded that the majority, if not all, of the Blickling Homilies were Anglian, or more precisely Mercian, and suggested a date roughly between 875 and 925, though not excluding an earlier or later dating for individual homilies.[5] Wenisch, too, says that they are West Saxon copies of Anglian, probably Mercian, originals, composed, for the most part, before 950 and after 875.[6] Words in Blickling XIII, the assumption homily edited here from F, which are considered Anglian and discussed by Wenisch, are *feon*, *frignan*, *leoran*, *nænig*, *to hwon*, *wæccan*, *winnan*, *ymbsellan* and *gierwan*. The homily has one instance each of Anglian *oferhygd* and of *oferhygdig*, but also one of West Saxon *ofermod*, which Schabram thinks must be a West Saxon substitution.[7]

The second Old English vernacular assumption homily, that in D, has also been judged Anglian. Tristram, in her edition, thought it late West Saxon in the broadest sense,[8] but also pointed to a range of features which are not characteristic of West Saxon, but could be Kentish (e.g., the frequency of *io* forms and forms like *speceð* and *specende*) or Anglian (e.g., *gefea*, *cwomon*, *cigan*, as well as the consistent use of the unsyncopated forms of the second- and third-person present indicative forms).[9] She warns against taking these forms as proof of a northern English origin because late West Saxon includes many Anglianisms, but Wenisch nevertheless considers that the frequency of Anglianisms puts a southern English origin in doubt.[10] He points to the presence of Anglian *samnunga*, *geornes*, *nymðe*, *in*, *nænig*, *gymnesse* and *gierwan* and thinks that this is certainly an Anglian text preserved in a West Saxon copy.[11]

*Pseudo-Matthew*, too, has long been considered Anglian: Klaeber in 1904 pointed to Anglian vocabulary features, as did Vleeskruyer and Wenisch, who both consider it Mercian.[12] The situation in this text is, of course, different in that the three manuscripts all show differing degrees

---

[4] Vleeskruyer, ed., *The Life of St Chad*, pp. 56–7.     [5] Schabram, *Superbia*, pp. 73–7.

[6] Wenisch, *Spezifisch anglisches Wortgut*, p. 30.

[7] Schabram, *Superbia*, p. 76: 'ursprünglich dialektal einheitliches Wortgut anglischer Originale in späteren ws. Abschriften teilweise beibehalten und teilweise substituiert worden ist'.

[8] Tristram, ed., *Vier altenglische Predigten*, pp. 49–50.     [9] *Ibid.*, pp. 50–2.

[10] Wenisch, *Spezifisch anglisches Wortgut*, p. 51.     [11] *Ibid.*, pp. 148 and 166.

[12] Klaeber, 'Zur altenglischen Bedaübersetzung', p. 399; Vleeskruyer, ed., *The Life of St Chad*, p. 59; Wenisch, *Spezifisch anglisches Wortgut*, p. 44.

of lexical substitution and so enable us, to some extent, to be aware of how Anglian words have been edited out. With the other two texts, one extant in only one manuscript, the other in two almost identical copies, we have no such control allowing us to spot substitutions. Anglian vocabulary in this homily is listed and discussed in the editorial introduction to the text.[13]

Arguments have been advanced, therefore, for considering all three texts as Anglian or, in the case of two of them, Mercian. What these terms actually mean, however, is not entirely clear. Vleeskruyer himself was frank about the difficulties of what he was attempting in arguing for a Mercian literary dialect predating the work of Alfred, pointing out that 'it will often remain impossible to distinguish between genuine dialectal differences of vocabulary and varying usages at different times in one and the same dialect'[14] and that 'the danger of confusing chronological and regional variety may not always be escaped'.[15] He points out, too, that: 'Going further, doubt may be cast on the dialectological reality of "Anglian" and "West Saxon" vocabulary; such differences of usages as are met with may often prove to reflect not local speech, but rather the highly artificial idioms of various schools of translation. . . . West Mercian could be written at Canterbury, and late West Saxon in the North of England. The usage of literary "standard" dialect may help us in establishing provenance, but the distribution of centres of writing that could move with their leaders is a thing wholly apart from the frontiers mapped out in linguistic geography.'[16] Later Vleeskruyer suggests that the 'West Mercian written language . . . could during the ninth century be employed even in West Saxon and Kentish centres. Hence it would seem to be virtually impossible to establish the provenance of any text without factual, non-linguistic evidence. . . . "early Mercian" and "early Old English" often appear interchangeable.'[17] What this seems to amount to, in practice, is that the term Mercian means early rather than having a specifically regional application. Vleeskruyer's list of 'Mercian' texts consequently becomes essentially a list of early texts, although this has not prevented later scholars drawing on Vleeskruyer's work from understanding the term in a geographical sense: Wenisch, for example, says Anglian means 'im Süden ungebraüch-

---

[13] See below, pp. 157–61.    [14] Vleeskruyer, ed., *The Life of St Chad*, p. 23.
[15] *Ibid.*, p. 24.    [16] *Ibid.*, pp. 24–5.    [17] *Ibid.*, p. 61.

lich',[18] though he also says that what is in question is not dialects whose boundaries can be geographically defined but the language of texts whose shared features justify the use of the term 'dialect' as a working hypothesis.[19]

If Mercian implicitly means early rather than written in the Midlands then this leaves Vleeskruyer's arguments open to objection on the grounds that the words he considers characteristic of Mercian are by no means uniformly early. Bately shows that Vleeskruyer's list of so-called Mercian or archaic words in the *Life of St Chad* is very unreliable in dating and suggests that ' "absence from late West Saxon" . . . means little more than absence from the work of three or four authors – perhaps even "not approved by the school of Æthelwold" '.[20] She does not, however, question Wenisch's more authoritative list of Anglian words, though she does query his acceptance of Vleeskruyer's chronology of texts, and is undoubtedly right to do so, as no proof is presented for these datings.[21] Despite this, there is no doubt that Wenisch's list is a much more reliable set of words which were in some way restricted in use in Anglo-Saxon England. This is evident from the way in which we find substitutes for many of these words in a range of Old English manuscripts, including those of the *Pseudo-Matthew*. Scribes from a different tradition found such words alien to their own written usage and replaced them with more familiar terms. Whether this was because those words were not current in a particular area or had come to be considered archaic or were simply not part of the scriptorium tradition is still not clear. Bately raises the pertinent case of Ælfric's attribution of the Old English Bede to Alfred and asks: 'Did Ælfric read this work in a late manuscript with its most prominent Anglian features removed, or did he simply not associate with a specific geographical area what we today take to be distinctive Anglian fea-

---

[18] Wenisch, *Spezifisch anglisches Wortgut*, p. 12.     [19] *Ibid.*, p. 18.

[20] Bately, 'Old English Prose', pp. 109–10. She is also 'not convinced that all the so-called Mercian words must originally have been peculiar to the territory called Mercia, or even to territory controlled by Mercians. They could have been current also in a large area of Wessex and used by writers of West Saxon origin. We simply do not know, any more than we can determine the extent to which scribes of works preserved only in post-ninth-century copies have removed archaic or dialectal terminology which they found in their exemplars' (*ibid.*, p. 109). In a sense, though, this is unjust as Vleeskruyer himself leaves open the possibility of these words being used by writers of West Saxon origin too.

[21] *Ibid.*, p. 104 and n. 75.

tures?'[22] That two of the *Pseudo-Matthew* manuscripts come from Worcester and the area around Worcester, part of the old Mercian kingdom, and show partial linguistic replacement even of words like *nænig*, which survived into Middle English in the Midlands,[23] raises questions about why such a word should be replaced: it can hardly have been alien to the local vernacular or archaic. The remaining explanation is that the scriptorium tradition, following West Saxon practice, disapproved of such forms, regardless of whether or not they were current in the area in which the scriptorium was located. Such a conclusion also fits with Scragg's conclusions in his edition of the Vercelli homilies: although he confidently assigned groups of the Vercelli homilies to Mercia on the basis of linguistic studies in his 1973 article on the Vercelli Book, he had become much more reticent on the topic by the time the edition appeared in 1992, and he there questions the usefulness of the terms early West Saxon, late West Saxon, Kentish and Mercian, saying that they 'relate more to scriptorium traditions than to spoken dialects or to geographical areas'.[24] Even though he is criticized by Torkar for his 'leichtfertige Umgang mit den Ergebnissen wortgeographischer Studien',[25] Scragg's caution seems justified in the light of our very limited knowledge of the significance of these linguistic features. He points out elsewhere that the items in B and D 'look archaic linguistically, but this might simply be because they are not written in the Winchester language that characterizes the majority of surviving late Old English texts.'[26] Until we know more,

---

[22] *Ibid.*, p. 98, n. 39.

[23] See *ibid.*, p. 110, n. 106, on words recorded in Middle English texts from the Midlands but which Vleeskruyer considered characteristically Mercian and therefore early.

[24] Scragg, ed., *The Vercelli Homilies*, p. lxxi.

[25] Torkar, 'Die Ohnmacht der Textkritik', p. 240.

[26] Scragg, 'The Corpus of Anonymous Lives', p. 224. See also A. Amos, *Linguistic Means of Determining the Dates of Old English Literary Texts* (Cambridge, MA, 1980), pp. 171–7, on the difficulties of dating Old English prose; analysing a passage of the Alfredian *Pastoral Care* in the late eleventh-century copy in Cambridge, University Library, Ii. 2. 4, she says: 'I can find no phonological nor syntactical or lexical constructions . . . which would date its original to Alfred's time rather than Ælfric's. This failure in part represents an inability to date the late prose in any manner: phonological developments cannot be closely dated, since the orthography was increasingly conservative; the syntactic and grammatical tests apply in general to early changes in Old English and are not sufficiently limited in time to be of much use (Ælfric and the late Chronicle writers both use the instrumental just as Alfred does);

we cannot use language as proof of the date or the place of origin of a text. We can say with certainty that the texts did not originate under the influence of the Winchester school, but very little more.

None of the three texts edited here is accepted as indisputably from the ninth century in Bately's discussion of ninth-century prose, though she points out that 'homilies and saints' lives may have been composed in this period [the last thirty years of the ninth century]'.[27] The earliest manuscript of any of the Marian apocrypha is B, from the late tenth century. We can say with confidence, then, that the assumption apocryphon in B and F is from the tenth-century at the latest, but we do not know how long before the copying of the earliest manuscript it was composed. We know that Latin texts were being translated into Old English by Bede in the eighth century[28] (although we do not know whether Bede translated into verse or prose) and poetic texts extant in manuscripts contemporary with the earliest homiletic manuscripts are regularly assigned dates as early as the eighth century. Would we know that a version of the *Dream of the Rood* was circulating in Northumbria in the eighth century if we had only the text preserved in the Vercelli Book? The need for vernacular preaching texts must have been felt from an early date: Cubitt argues that the canon of the Council of Clofesho in 747 relating to sermons refers to sermons preached during the mass.[29] All that we can conclude is that there was a long tradition of translations and preaching and we do not yet have linguistic evidence which allows us to place the Marian apocrypha or other anonymous texts within this tradition with any degree of certainty.

## THE OLD ENGLISH *GOSPEL OF PSEUDO-MATTHEW*

This translation of chs. I to XII of *Pseudo-Matthew*, provided with a prologue and an epilogue, is found as a homily for the feast of the nativity of Mary, although the extent of the text is clearly not determined by what

and our knowledge of the chronological characteristics of the Old English vocabulary is uncertain' (pp. 176–7).

[27] Bately, 'Old English Prose', p. 118.

[28] See *Venerabilis Bedae Opera historica*, ed. C. Plummer (Oxford, 1896, repr. 1975), pp. lxxv–lxxvi and clxii.

[29] C. Cubitt, *Anglo-Saxon Church Councils c. 650–c. 850* (Leicester, 1995), p. 100 and n. 3.

would have been appropriate to the feast, as it continues the story of Mary's life beyond the Annunciation to her pregnancy. The Old English text belongs to the P family of manuscripts, already in existence by about 800. This can be seen in, for example, the inclusion of 'ic þe nu þanc secge þæt þu me ane ute atyndest fram þinre gyfe þære fremsumnysse', translating the very odd addition in P, 'tibi gratias ago soli, quia ut uoluisti, ita ordinasti, ut me solam a benignitatis tuae donis excludere' (II, 2); in 'niwe endebyrdnysse ongunnon Gode mid to gecwemanne', translating P's 'nouus ordo placendi deo' rather than A's 'nouus ordo tacendi' (VIII, 1); in the 'Þu eart ure gingast' of the virgins' speech, translating P's 'Cum tu iunior sis omnibus' rather than A's 'Cum sis ultima et humilis' (VIII, 5); and in 'Godes englas', translating P's 'angeli dei' rather than A's 'angelus dei' (XII, 1).[30] It is more difficult to see exactly where the Old English text fits within the P family. Gijsel distinguishes P[1], P[2] and the contaminated group P[3], all of which are further subdivided, of which P[1] is the most primitive. Of these, the Old English seems to be closest to P[1]: it has, for example, a translation of P[1]'s *triginta annorum* in VI, 1 rather than P[2]'s *plena annorum*,[31] and the reading *in conspectu populi* in II, 1, which is omitted in the P[1]b family but preserved in P[1]a.[32] All the extant manuscripts of the subgroup P[1]a finish at XII, 9, very close to the ending of the vernacular text, and this may well have determined the extent of the translation.[33] They also seem to lack a prologue, insofar as one can tell from Gijsel's catalogue of manuscripts, having neither the *Ego Iacobus* prologue found in some P manuscripts nor the apocryphal exchange of letters between Cromatius and Heliodorus.[34] This suggests that the manuscript from which the Old English text was translated may also have lacked a prologue and there is, of course, no trace of either of the Latin prologues in the Old English. The completely independent Old English prologue ends: 'Nu wille we eow secgan be ðære gebyrde þære eadigan fæmnan Sancta Marian, hu seo geworden wæs . . .'; and the *Pseudo-Matthew* proper begins: 'We habbað geræd on bocum . . .', without any indication of knowledge of the assumed author of the Latin. The Old English, as with the other two texts edited here, is doubly anonymous, therefore, both in the sense that we do

---

[30] See Gijsel, *Die unmittelbare Textüberlieferung*, p. 19.   [31] *Ibid.*, p. 129.
[32] *Ibid.*, p. 134.   [33] *Ibid.*   [34] See above, p. 18.

not know the identity of the translator and the translator shows no awareness of having known an identity for the author of the Latin.

The P family of texts, of which the P¹a family is the most primitive, was already in existence before 800, so it does not offer much help in dating the Old English. A Latin text, though the brevity of the vernacular adaptation does not allow us to decide which one, A or P, was used in the composition of the *Old English Martyrology*, almost certainly a ninth-century text.[35] This proves that *Pseudo-Matthew* was circulating in England by the end of the ninth century at the latest. The date of the Old English *Pseudo-Matthew* is very hard to establish, however. Scragg suggests that: 'Despite the lateness of all three extant copies of this item, there is reason to suspect that it derives from an early, perhaps pre-Ælfrician, translation. . . . Again it is possible that it stems from Canterbury.'[36] His footnote says that 'some linguistic features point to earlier composition',[37] but in support of this he cites only Hofstetter, who does not mention date in his brief treatment of the *Pseudo-Matthew*, and the shortcomings of such linguistic criteria have been discussed above. No evidence is cited in support of a Canterbury origin. Scragg also alludes to my own suggestion of a late (i.e. eleventh-century) date for the text, which was made partly on the basis of the type of Marian imagery in the prologue to the vernacular text.[38] The concentration on Mary in the elaboration of the star of the sea image still seems to me more likely to be from the eleventh century than, say, the ninth, but certainly does not exclude the tenth century, and there are early parallels for the epithets used of the Virgin here.[39] The conclusion of the epilogue echoes a Latin prayer to the Virgin which was current in English manuscripts from the ninth century onwards and which consequently does not help with dating, as it is found in eleventh-century English manuscripts also.[40] Prayer 56 in the Book of Cerne ends: 'Confidimus enim et pro certo scimus quia omne quod uis potes impetrare a filio tuo Domino nostro Iesu Christo';[41] this is recalled in: 'Nu we geare witan þæt heo mæg æt hire þam deoran sunu biddan, swa hwæt swa heo wile, and beon ðingere to urum Drihtne . . .'. In favour of a later rather than earlier date is the

---

[35] See above, pp. 107–8.   [36] 'The Corpus of Anonymous Lives', pp. 214–15.
[37] *Ibid.*, p. 228, n. 23.   [38] Clayton, *Cult*, p. 253.   [39] *Ibid.*, pp. 252–3.
[40] See *ibid*, pp. 99–121.
[41] Quoted from H. Barré, *Prières anciennes à la mère du Sauveur* (Paris, 1963), p. 68.

fact that Ælfric does not seem to know of a vernacular apocryphon dealing with Mary's birth and childhood. In a note in *Catholic Homilies II* explaining his refusal to write a homily for the feast of the nativity of the Virgin he said that he did not wish to retell the apocryphal story, with which he was clearly familiar, because of the danger of *gedwyld*, heresy or foolishness:

Hwæt wylle we secgan ymbe Marian gebyrdtide. buton þæt heo wæs gestryned þurh fæder. and ðurh moder. swa swa oðre men. and wæs on ðam dæge acenned þe we cweðað Sexta Idus Septembris; Hire fæder hatte Ioachim. and hire moder Anna. eawfæste men on ðære ealdan æ. ac we nellað be ðam na swiðor awritan þy læs ðe we on ænigum gedwylde befeallon.[42]

Ælfric knows the names of Mary's parents, therefore, and that they were *eawfæste*, righteous, but clearly feels that their story should be avoided, though he is not at all clear about the reasons for this.[43] In the similar case of the assumption apocrypha, however, Ælfric explicitly mentions vernacular as well as Latin texts; he again mentions here the danger of heresy and says: 'Sind swa ðeah gyt ða dwollican bec ægðer ge on leden. ge on englisc. and hi rædað ungerade menn'.[44] The Old English text is also missing from some earlier manuscripts where one might expect it, had it been available (F, for example, which has an apocryphal text for Mary's assumption). The word *sæsteorra* is used only in the prologue to the *Pseudo-Matthew* and in the late Trinity Homilies and is possibly a late introduction in Old English, though equally the non-occurrence of the word elsewhere could be just the result of a lack of a need to use it, and the compound is a standard Old English formation. None of this is conclusive, but it seems to point to a later rather than an earlier date and, as the earliest manuscript dates from the third quarter of the eleventh century, even a date of composition as late as the early eleventh century would allow time for the divergent manuscript readings to develop.

Vleeskruyer argued that the translation of *Pseudo-Matthew* edited here and Vercelli VI are connected on the grounds that the latter text also translates part of *Pseudo-Matthew* and that both are Mercian texts: 'it is probable that the two sermons are adaptations from the same translation or that they are renderings of two Latin sermons, companion-pieces

[42] Godden, ed., *Ælfric's Catholic Homilies*, p. 271.  [43] See Clayton, *Cult*, p. 245.
[44] Godden, ed., *Ælfric's Catholic Homilies*, p. 259.

compiled from the Pseudo-Matthew'.[45] Vercelli VI, assigned to Christmas Day in the manuscript, begins with praise of the Incarnation and portents anticipating the birth of Christ (these go back ultimately to Orosius but here are derived either from a lost source or composed freely from memory), then continues with one sentence from ch. XIII of *Pseudo-Matthew* and with what was originally probably most of chs. XVII, 2 to XXIV. This section of the text has been affected by the loss of a leaf of the manuscript so that the text now skips from XVIII, 1 to XXII, 1. The text ends with 'a blend of two verses from Luke and the last sentence of the *Euangelium* [Pseudo-Matthew] and . . . an exhortation to mark his words'.[46] Scragg, the editor of the Vercelli Homilies, thinks that the two homilies are independent: 'The fragmentary Vercelli VI is based in part on chs. 13–25 of the same apocryphal work, but none of the distinctive Anglian or archaic vocabulary of Vercelli VI appears in Assmann X, and the use of two halves of the same source in the two homilies is probably coincidental'.[47] While it is true that there is little overlap in the 'distinctive Anglian or archaic' vocabulary used, both homilies use such vocabulary (Wenisch lists *acweðan, carcern, gefeon, hwilchwugu, nænig* and *snytero* for Vercelli VI),[48] and both are similar in that they provide an extract of the *Pseudo-Matthew* with a homiletic beginning and ending. The scantiness of the overlap may be partly due to lack of opportunity (*carcern* and *snytero*, for example, are not needed in the *Pseudo-Matthew*). The two homilies begin very differently, however, Vercelli VI with the *Her sagað* formula 'popular with tenth-century homilists',[49] *Pseudo-Matthew* with the equally conventional 'Men ða leofestan', and *Pseudo-Matthew* does not share the Vercelli VI homilist's predilection for beginning sentences with *mitte*. Although we cannot be certain, I would agree with Scragg that the use of the Latin *Pseudo-Matthew* in both texts is probably coincidental and that we have two independently composed texts.

The Old English *Pseudo-Matthew* is an abbreviated version of the Latin, though not drastically so, except in the very last chapter, XII, which

[45] Vleeskruyer, ed., *The Life of St Chad*, p. 58.
[46] Scragg, ed., *The Vercelli Homilies*, p. 126.
[47] Scragg, ed., 'The Corpus of Vernacular Homilies', p. 244; what I say in *Cult*, p. 204, about the flight into Egypt not being part of *Pseudo-Matthew* at this date is not correct.
[48] Wenisch, *Spezifisch anglisches Wortgut*, pp. 100, 115, 138, 173, 192 and 218.
[49] Scragg, *The Vercelli Homilies*, p. 127.

describes how Joseph and Mary were forced to undergo the test of the water of the Lord and were proved clean, and how Mary then proclaimed her innocence. In shortening this chapter the translator was probably motivated by a desire to avoid having to explain the rather obscure Old Testament test, as well, presumably, as the wish to end the narrative. Otherwise, there are only minor abbreviations and some expansions, usually to spell out connections. So, for example, in III, 5 the explanation for the length of time it took Joachim to return to Anna is unique to the Old English, though it is merely making explicit what is implicit in the Latin. Similarly, in VI, 1 a connecting sentence is added again in the Old English, linking Anna's speech in the temple with the account of Mary's upbringing there. This may well be due to a desire to facilitate listeners, as the text was presumably read aloud to a congregation. There seems to be some avoidance of the notion of sacrifices to God: the translator omits mention of the lamb offered by Joachim in III, 3, referring only to *unwemme lac*, and Abiathar's sacrifice in VIII, 2 is omitted. Some of the more extraordinary features of Mary's life are dropped from the Old English: it does not, for example, describe her face shining like snow (VI, 1 of the Latin) and leaves out the detail that she was frequently seen conversing with angels, who obeyed her (VI, 3). On the other hand, what seems to be a mistranslation results in Mary's teaching the older virgins, rather than merely being taught with them (VI, 2). In the Old English Mary is younger than Joseph's children, whereas in the Latin she is younger than his grandchildren; it is hard to say whether this is a deliberate alteration or not. Other minor departures from the source are discussed in the notes, as well as the rare occasions when the translator seems to have had difficulty in understanding and rendering the Latin. In general, the translation is a faithful and accurate one.

## THE D ASSUMPTION TEXT

D's assumption text, like the Old English *Pseudo-Matthew*, has no trace of the Latin prologue (found in all but one of the extant manuscripts of its source, *Transitus B*[2]) and instead begins 'Her sagað ymbe þa halgan Marian, usses Dryhtnes modor'. Again, then, we find the *her sagað* formula which Scragg notes as characteristic of tenth-century homilies, though he adds that the same *incipit* is found in eleventh-century pieces 'but perhaps only in those which derive from lost tenth-century

141

items'.[50] Dating even such a short *incipit* is naturally open to the same difficulties as any other dating but at least we know that the formula is found in texts in tenth-century manuscripts, such as Vercelli and Blickling (*c.* 1000). Scragg suggests that this text and the St Michael text in D 'have items of vocabulary (e.g. *nimðe*), which suggest tenth-century composition', but this raises once again the question of the reliability of such linguistic dating.[51] The safest conclusion is probably to say that we have no reliable indications of date for this text.

The beginning of the text lacks any congregational address, as does the conclusion, which has no exhortation to prayer such as we find in the *Pseudo-Matthew* and the F assumption text. It is not unique in this: the Blickling text on St Andrew, for example, begins similarly with 'Her segð . . .'[52] and ends without any concluding address to a congregation. In this the Old English assumption text follows the Latin, where a similar lack of congregational address did not hinder use as a reading for the feast of the assumption. Here, however, there is also no rubric and nothing to suggest any connection with the feast. Given the format of the text, written in a small hand at the top, bottom and outer margin of the *Old English Bede*, it would also have been exceedingly difficult to use it in a preaching context from this manuscript, as it often requires very close attention to decipher it. The manuscript layout suggests rather that it was used for private reading, though presumably, once familiar with it, a reader could have used the text from memory to preach on the feast of the assumption.

The source of this text is clearly *Transitus B²*, but it is not easy to specify which version is closest to the Old English, partly because the vernacular abbreviates the Latin, partly because many of the differences among the Latin manuscripts are differences in word-order or different choices among words which are more or less synonymous. Such variations are virtually impossible to detect in a translation. Where the differences are more substantial, however, D's text seems to reflect a version like that in $O^1$, $O^2$ and V, closely related manuscripts of which two are English (the eleventh- to twelfth-century Oxford, Bodleian Library, Laud lat. 86, and the fourteenth-century Oxford, Bodleian Library, Rawlinson D. 1236). Though the vernacular does not reflect these manuscripts in all details, they seem to offer the closest parallel, as can be seen from the notes to the text.

---

[50] *Ibid.*, p. 127, n. 1.     [51] 'The Corpus of Anonymous Lives', p. 211.

[52] Morris, ed., *The Blickling Homilies*, p. 229.

The Old English text is an abbreviated version of the source, *Transitus B²*, typically omitting or shortening passages of the Latin, especially speeches, which are not strictly necessary to understanding the narrative. So, for example, the angel's speech to Mary in ch. 2, promising that the apostles would come, entirely cuts his lengthy explanation of the Lord's ability to gather the apostles together. The last part of Mary's speech at the end of the same chapter is also omitted, presumably because it is a general prayer with no specific reference to the story. Ch. 4 is much shortened in the Old English, which concentrates on what is directly relevant to Mary, rather than the apostles. The Latin text is concerned to emphasize Peter's supremacy among the apostles at this point, but this is of no concern to the translator. The translator's ability to adjust the vernacular text to take such cuts into account is evident at the beginning of ch. 5, where the Latin refers to what has been omitted from the Old English: 'Tunc omnes apostoli gaudentes super humilitate Pauli unanimiter consummauerunt orationem'. In the Old English we find instead: 'Mid þy þe hi þæt spræcon and hi to Drihtne gebædon . . .'. Such minor adjustments would not be worth commenting on were it not for the fact that the second Old English assumption homily is so singularly lacking in ability to make them. The exchange between Peter and the Jewish high-priest is also much abbreviated in the Old English, in keeping with its focus on Mary rather than less central characters. Some of the more emotional passages are also missing in the Old English: Christ's address to Mary's soul as she is about to die, for example, 'pretiosissima margarita mea, . . . proxima mea', is omitted, but this is also missing from three Latin manuscripts, including the oldest extant, Munich, Bayerische Staatsbibliothek, Clm 6264a (eleventh century).[53] It is possible that here the Old English was merely following its source, therefore. The similar address in ch. 16 is translated in the Old English. References to the Old Testament are in general omitted from the Old English, perhaps because the translator felt that his readers might not recognize them. In describing Mary's end, the text seems to follow its source's identification of paradise and heaven. It says that Mary will be led into *neorxnawonges gefean* (ch. 7), but Peter and the apostles ask that Mary be led into heaven (ch. 15) and at the end of the narrative Christ 'mid þam singendum englum and mid his meder he wæs onfangen on neorxnawonge' (ch. 17).

---

[53] Haibach-Reinisch, ed., *Ein neuer 'Transitus Mariae'*, p. 75.

As both he and Mary are received into the same place, paradise here is presumably identical to heaven.

Minor details seem to be added independently in the Old English: it is alone in specifying, for instance, that the scent which emanated from Mary's dead body was from her mouth (end of ch. 9), and when Peter says to John that Christ had commended Mary to him, the Old English has 'his þy arfæstan muðe þe þas ætfæste', whereas the Latin, in the extant manuscripts at any rate, has merely 'hanc tibi ore proprio commendauit' (ch. 10). In general, this text, even more than the *Pseudo-Matthew*, is a highly competent translation of its source.

### THE F ASSUMPTION TEXT

This text draws on two main sources, as well as the *Magnificat* and part of the Beatitudes: on all of *Transitus W* for its account of Mary's death and assumption, followed by a further account of the assumption which is drawn from *Transitus B²*.[54] Of all the manuscripts collated by Wilmart, the Old English text seems closest to his G, St Gall, Stiftsbibliothek, 732, from the ninth century, although clearly not identical in all details. Of the manuscripts of *Transitus B²* collated by Haibach-Reinisch, her T, F, O¹, O² and V share the detail of Gabriel pushing back the stone from the tomb at the point where this occurs in the Old English: O¹ and O² are English manuscripts and all five of these manuscripts are related, going back, according to Haibach-Reinisch's stemma, to a common original.[55] The part of the text dependent on *Transitus B²* is too short and agreement among the Latin manuscripts too common to offer many more significant details, but the Old English text can probably be counted among this family of *B²* manuscripts, as can the D assumption homily.

The two texts have been combined in a clumsy manner, in that the translator (if it was he who was responsible) has continued the story of Mary's death up to the very end of *Transitus W* and has then added on the final sections of *B²*, even though they overlap with what has already been recounted. Willard argued that the motive for the combination was a desire to give a fuller account of the assumption than was contained in

---

[54] See Willard, 'On Blickling Homily XIII' and 'The Two Accounts', and my 'Blickling Homily XIII Reconsidered'.

[55] Haibach-Reinisch, ed., *Ein neuer 'Transitus'*, p. 61.

*Transitus W*,[56] but it seems that the version of *Transitus W* from which the translator was working had been modified to eliminate the resurrection of Mary and this may also have been a factor. The ending of the part of the text translated from *W* reads: 'Ond Drihten bebead ðæm wolcnum þæt hie eodan on neorxnawange ond ðær asetton ðære eadigan Marian saule. Ond on neorxnawange bið a wuldor mid Gode ond mid eallum his gecorenum soðlice.' This is clearly based on the ending in Wilmart's manuscripts G, M and P, but the Old English, because of the addition of the end of *Transitus B²*, has changed body to soul: 'Et praecepit dominus nubibus ut irent in paradiso. Et sic deposuerunt nubes corpus beatae Mariae in paradiso, et est ibi glorificans deum cum omnibus electis eius.'[57] This family of manuscripts does not have a resurrection of Mary's body, merely placing it in paradise. Other details of the Old English translation, too, suggest a source which had been altered.[58] The Old English translator, therefore, was working with a version of *Transitus W* in which Mary's body and soul were not reunited, and this does not seem to have suited his own evident attachment to the idea of the corporal assumption of a resurrected Mary. He accordingly added on to *Transitus W* the end of *Transitus B²*, that version of the story which has the fullest account of the resurrection and corporal assumption of Mary. This attachment to the idea of the corporal assumption is manifest throughout the text, in which a series of mistranslations seems to have been motivated by a desire to recount this event.[59] While we obviously cannot be absolutely certain that it was the translator who combined the two apocrypha here, the clumsiness with which the transition is managed is very much in keeping with the numerous other faults which can be attributed to him, producing what Torkar calls the worst translated homily in Old English.[60]

The translator's incompetence in Latin is evident almost everywhere in the notes on the text, resulting in a vernacular version which often seems to bear very little resemblance to its source: sentences are confused, biblical allusions go largely unrecognized, dialogues are converted into narrative and vice versa and the basic narrative is constantly confused.

---

[56] 'The Two Accounts', p. 5.  [57] Wilmart, 'L'ancien récit', pp. 356–7.
[58] See notes 1, 2 and 15 to the F text.
[59] See, for example, notes 18 and 48 to the F text.
[60] 'Die Ohnmacht der Textkritik', p. 246, n. 103.

This, at least, is the verdict one would have to come to when comparing the Latin with the Old English. Reading the Old English without a knowledge of what it 'should' say is, of course, a different experience, though even students to whom I have given the text cold have realized that there is something radically wrong with it. At first sight it appears lucid, but that lucidity is often strictly local and attempting to construct an overall notion of the progress of the narrative is a frustrating affair, in which one is constantly thwarted in the attempt to follow what one feels should be a consequential narrative. One instance of this is in ch. 10 of the Old English, where a revealing mistranslation results in: 'Ond ða semninga ealle ða apostolas tugon hie upp mid wolcnum, ond sume hie wæron gesette beforan þæs huses dura ðære halgan Marian. Ond hie gesawon be him tweonum þæt heo wæs gewuldrod . . .' It is natural to read this as an assumption of sorts, but the narrative then continues without any further mention of this event. Similar and equally contextless is 'Ond ða apostolas togon hie up ond hie gesetton on ðæm fægran neorxnawange' in ch. 15 of the Old English. Immediately after this Mary prays and then summons the apostles into her room. Likewise 'Ond ða sæmninga ða embsealdon ealle ða apostolas ða halgan Marian ond hie gegripan on hire middel' in ch. 13 of the Old English is left hanging, with a reader bound to wonder what the apostles did while or after seizing Mary's waist. The enemies or fiends that are so unexpectedly present in Mary's house in ch. 19 of the Old English, 'ða ascan samninga mycel leoht on hire huse þæt ealle ða fynd wæron oferswiðede', never appear before or after, and such inconsistencies and discontinuities do not seem to have bothered the translator. The almost identical texts in both Old English manuscripts testify to a high degree of tolerance of such features on the part of the scribes of the two extant manuscripts and those responsible for the previous transmission of the text.

The text is very confusing in its account of where Mary's soul is in the interim between death and resurrection. Mary dies and her soul is given to Michael (ch. 25), but we are never told to where it is brought and where it is while Mary is being prepared for burial, while the funeral procession is attacked by the Jews, while the chief priest is attached to the bier and then healed and while the apostles bury Mary.[61] What are we to

---

[61] This interval is three days long in *Transitus B*[2] (ch. 15), but the Old English omits the specification of length.

make of its whereabouts? *Transitus W* does not specify either where Michael takes the soul, but this is less of a problem because it does not have a second taking of the soul. When the apostles are sitting around the tomb in the Old English text, Christ then arrives and Michael is directed to receive Mary's soul (body, of course, in the source, *Transitus W*) into the clouds, which he does (chs. 47–8); the translator takes no account of the fact that Michael had already received it. The clouds are then ordered to bear Mary's soul to paradise, where 'bið a wuldor mid Gode and mid his gecorenum soðlice', a mistranslation of 'est ibi glorificans deum cum omnibus electis eius' resulting in a seeming identification of paradise and heaven. This equation of the two is in keeping with the *Pseudo-Melito* text, to which the translator soon turns, but not with the *Transitus W* text which he was still following at this point. The careful separation of paradise and heaven in that text, which associates Christ with heaven and Mary with paradise, has already been disrupted near the beginning of the Old English, however, when Mary asks the apostles to reveal to her who told them that she was to go to heaven the next day (ch. 15). The Latin reads here, without any mention of heaven: 'quis uobis adnunciauit quod ego exitura sum de corpore?'[62] It would seem, therefore, that for the translator both terms could be used indiscriminately and that he did not appreciate *W*'s punctilious distinctions. When it comes to translating the conclusion of *Transitus B²*, the text has Michael present Mary's soul before Christ and Mary is received into paradise. A mistranslation again results in a double reception of Mary's resurrected body into the clouds: at the beginning of ch. 52 (17) Michael 'hie ða ahof up on wolcnum beforan Drihtnes gesyhðe'. A little further on in the same chapter 'ða apostolas on heora mægene hofon Marian lichoman up mid wolcnum ond hine ða asetton on neorxnawanges gefean'.[63] Any reader attempting to follow the exact course of events could not but be baffled.

The translator, presumably a cleric or monk of some sort, also shows an astonishing degree of ignorance of what one would expect to be basic religious teaching. He appears to think that the date of Mary's death was identical with that of Christ's death (chs. 6 and 7), not realizing that Easter and the feast of the assumption on 15 August were widely separated. The Old English also has John address Peter as a virgin (ch. 31). The sinlessness of Mary, firmly established by the date of the Latin

[62] Wilmart, 'L'ancien recit', pp. 336–7.   [63] See note 124 to the F text.

source, is called into doubt by the self-contradictory ch. 26 of the Old English, 'forðon hie lufode ma ðeostru for hire synnum ond heo wæs a ðeh gehealden fram hire synnum'. In the speech translated from *Transitus B²*, where Christ gives his reasons for Mary's corporal assumption, another mistranslation seems to result in a second, non-biblical incarnation, when 'ut sumerem carnem ex ea'[64] is rendered 'ic wearð eft on lichoman geseted'.

Ironically, in view of the shortcomings of the translator's Latin, this text is the only one of the three edited here to be liberally sprinkled with Latin tags: they come at fairly frequent intervals throughout the homily, and are especially frequent in the concluding rendition of the *Magnificat*. A similar use is found in, for example, Blickling XI and the text for the feast of St Martin, Blickling XVIII. Most of the Latin is clearly quoting significant passages, which would have been familiar to a religious audience, such as the beginning of the psalm 'In exitu Israel . . .' or John's greeting to Mary, 'Aue Maria, gratia plena . . .', suggesting either that such passages are aimed at this type of audience, or this section of an audience, or else that the translator was using such passages to give his text extra prestige, whether or not his audience could have been expected to understand Latin. Gatch has written of the unknowable audience of the Blickling Homilies, suggesting that 'little sense of a specific congregation or reading audience prevails in this collection of ancient and common-place materials for the instruction of Christian folk',[65] but it seems to me likely that the collection would have been used to provide English preaching materials to a possibly mixed congregation.[66]

The milieu in which such a text could be produced and transmitted can only be guessed at. It is, of course, tempting to situate the text in the pre-reform period and Ælfric, of course, was aware of the existence of such vernacular texts and preached against them.[67] Gatch, for example, tends to place both the Blickling and Vercelli collections 'at least a generation earlier than Ælfric's earliest publication of his work around 990'[68] and sees these collections as pre-reform: 'The monastic revival of the tenth century is, I believe, the theological watershed which lies between the

---

[64] Haibach-Reinisch, ed., *Ein neuer 'Transitus'*, p. 84.
[65] 'The Unknowable Audience of the Blickling Homilies', *ASE* 18 (1989), 99–115, at 115.
[66] See my discussion in 'Homiliaries and Preaching', pp. 221–6.
[67] See above, pp. 110–11.    [68] Gatch, *Preaching and Theology*, p. 8.

work of the earlier, anonymous Old English homilists and that of Ælfric and Wulfstan'.[69] There is no proof, however, that the vernacular apocrypha which Ælfric criticized were pre-reform: Ælfric's predecessors and contemporaries in the reform period were clearly interested in and well acquainted with apocryphal gospels on Mary's death and assumption and on her nativity. Evidence for the circulation of such texts in tenth- and eleventh-century England is almost entirely from reformed centres and in Winchester the apocrypha were drawn on in composing benedictions and other texts for the feasts of Mary.[70] F contains Ælfric texts mixed with its anonymous texts, as do several manuscripts dating from Ælfric's own lifetime. Any kind of distinction between pre- or non-reform and Ælfric on the grounds of milieu fails to explain the mixture of these works in the manuscripts of the period. Clearly, they were all circulating in the same orbit and we cannot confine the anonymous works to a separate sphere. While it is tempting, too, to argue that the poor Latinity and intellectual failures of all sorts in the text could only have arisen in a document composed before the monastic revival raised levels of education, this also cannot simply be taken for granted. Hohler is scathing about levels of Latin in reformed circles and the widespread use of English suggests, among other things, that many of the monks needed translations.[71] We cannot simply assume uniformly high levels of education throughout the reform movement. It seems to me, then, that we cannot rule out the reform period as the milieu of origin of a text like the B/F assumption homily, as we do not know enough about all aspects of the reform to do so. The earliest manuscript, Blickling, dates from about the time of Ælfric and we have no means of knowing how much earlier the text itself was translated. This observation about not ruling out a reform origin of some sort holds, in fact, for all three texts: we should not take for granted that because they are translations of apocryphal works, they must have come from a different, non-reform, milieu.

---

[69] *Ibid.*
[70] See above, pp. 114–15. See also my *Cult*, pp. 261–5.
[71] C. Hohler, 'Some Service Books of the Later Saxon Church', in *Tenth-Century Studies*, ed. D. Parsons (London and Chichester, 1975), pp. 60–83 and 217–27; see also my 'Homiliaries and Preaching', pp. 235–42.

# The Old English
*Gospel of Pseudo-Matthew*

# Editorial introduction

The Old English translation of *Pseudo-Matthew* is extant in three manuscripts, Hatton 114 (O: third quarter of the eleventh century), CCCC
367, Part II (f[a]: twelfth century), and Bodley 343 (I: second half of the
twelfth century). Of these, O and I (with the sigla J and N respectively)
were printed in parallel by Assmann, while f[a] has not previously been
printed.[1] Assmann's text of O is minimally edited, with no detailed
comparison with the source, and he made no attempt to correct what he
termed the 'öfters vorkommenden sinnlosen wortformen' in I.[2] The
present edition aims to produce a critical edition based on all three
manuscripts. Its transmission history makes this text an interesting
instance of some of the problems of editing Old English, especially when
the Old English is a translation.

The majority of textual readings show a close connection between f[a]
and I and suggest that they shared a common exemplar at some stage in
the transmission of the text. So, for example, where f[a] and I have 'Ða
ongan Anna hyre gemæccan bewepan and hire to drihtene gebiddan' (II,
2), O reads 'Ða ongann Anna, his gemæcca, wepende hi to drihtne
gebiddan', translating more accurately the Latin 'Quae dum fleret in
oratione sua. . .' . Where f[a] and I read 'forþam þe ic Godes willan to þam
ne ongeate' (III, 3), O has 'forðam gyf ic Godes willan to þan on þe ne
ongeate', translating the Latin 'nisi uoluntatem domini cognouissem'.[3] O
has the correct *on his ansyn* (Latin *in faciem suam*) in III, 4, where f[a] and I

---

[1] Assmann, ed., *Angelsächsische Homilien und Heiligenleben*, pp. 117–37; Donald Scragg
informs me that the text in f[a] is about to be published by Maria Butcher in the Bulletin
of the John Rylands Library.

[2] *Ibid.*, p. 260, n. 1.    [3] See note to the commentary 25 for a discussion of *forðam*.

have *on eorþan*, and at the beginning of IV O reads 'Hwæt, þa æfter þan wæron gefylde nigan monað hire geeacnunge' while, presumably due to homoeoteleuton, the other two manuscripts omit these words. In VII, 2 O has the probably correct *his broðor* where the other two manuscripts have *unwis*. Similarly, O has *gehyrsume to ælicum gyftum* where fᵃ and I have *æwfæston* (VIII, 1) and O has *heannysse* where the other two manuscripts have *hwæmmas* (VIII, 3). Where O more or less correctly reads 'Ac syle þam clænan fæmnan fultum þæt heo wunigen mid hig oðþæt ælice yldo' (Latin: 'Dentur aliquae ex sodalibus eius uirgines cum quibus interim degat'), fᵃ and I have 'ac ic onfo þære clænan fæmnan þæt heo wunige mid me oððæt heo hæbbe ælite [*sic* fᵃ; ælycre I] ylde' (VIII, 4).

In each of these cases, O appears to preserve the correct reading, as comparison with the Latin shows, but there are also cases where fᵃ and I preserve correct readings where O's reading is corrupt: for example, where O has the probably unoriginal *þonne ne gegearwie* (II, 2), fᵃ and I have *þonne ne gegearwode* (though I omits the negative particle). Where fᵃ correctly reads *unbeorþrum* (I *unbeoðrum*), translating *sterilis*, O has *mundbyrdum* (V: see note 41 to the commentary). Where O has the corrupt *her ætforan*, fᵃ and I preserve the correct reading *in eaforen* (VII, 1). In the case of the passage on Elias, it is clear from a comparison with the Latin source that the sentence has been rewritten in O, altering an original reading 'Helias wæs of þissere worulde alæded on lichaman' (Latin: 'Helias cum esset in carne assumptus est') to O's 'Helias wæs on þissere worulde ac he wearð alæded mid lichaman and mid sawle to heofonum' (VII, 2). The O scribe (or an exemplar at an earlier stage) seems to have had a propensity to make small additions to his exemplar: such additions, unparalleled in the Latin or in the other manuscripts, are *and acenned* (Prologue); *and smeade* (III, 4); *on þissum dæge* (IV); *Sancta Marian modor* (V); *and wisra* (VI, 2); *nu þonne* (VIII, 1); *and swyðe bliðe* (VIII, 4); *on gleo* (VIII, 5); *on his mode* (X, 1); *and swyðe bliðe* (XI). The O scribe also seems to have had a problem with the verbs *gecigde* and *gecydde*, reading *gecigde* where the other manuscripts read *gecydde* and *cydde him þæt* where the other manuscripts, probably correctly, read *hine cigde* (see III, 5, and VIII, 3).

fᵃ is the only manuscript to preserve a correct reading at one point. It has *tuddor for gefean* where O reads *tuddor forgeafon* and I *ðe þar i gefæn* (V).[4] Comparison with the Latin shows fᵃ must be original here, though it is

---

[4] See note to the commentary 41.

clear that an important element in the sentence as a whole, the verb, was lost at an early stage, before or at the stage of the archetype of all the surviving manuscripts. O's erroneous reading can be explained as an attempt to supply this loss. In ch. XI, where the $f^a$ text has already finished, I has the correct reading *mid gemynde þæs facnes* where O has the faulty *and gemunde þe facnes*.

While it is clear that $f^a$ and I are closely related, I cannot have been copied from $f^a$; a very telling detail is $f^a$'s version of the last virgin's name in VIII, 5, *Ansehel*, where I has the correct *Sehel*. Both $f^a$ and I must descend, then, from a common original which differed from the textual tradition behind O.

At the beginning of the text, however, this relationship among the manuscripts does not hold: in the Prologue and up to ch. II, 1, $f^a$ is aligned not with I, but with O, but in the course of this chapter the connection between $f^a$ and I becomes evident and continues for the remainder of the text, as can be seen from the textual apparatus. In the Prologue, for example, $f^a$ and O have 'nu wille we eow secgan', where I has 'þeonne magen we nu hwylcen seogum wordum sæcgan'.[5] O and $f^a$ have 'habbað geræd on bocum', where I has 'leorniæð'. O and $f^a$ both have the information about the birthplaces of Joachim and Anna in chs. I, 1 and I, 2, derived from the *De natiuitate Mariae*, whereas I does not. It would seem, then, that the exemplar of $f^a$ must have changed, from a manuscript with a text like that of O to one with a text like that of I. We do not, of course, know whether this switch occurred in $f^a$ or at an earlier stage in transmission. This first part of $f^a$ was not derived directly from O, however, as it does not share some readings which are probably due to the O scribe: '*and acenned*' at the end of the Prologue in O is unique to that manuscript, for example, but would presumably have been copied in $f^a$ had it been derived from O. Occasional agreements between O and $f^a$ as against I later in the text are probably to be explained by the scribe of I rewriting some passages, as in, for example, I's 'ne nan word yfeles of hire muðe ne com' instead of O and $f^a$'s 'ne nan man ne gehyrde yfel word of hyre muðe gan' in VI, 3, and there are many more lexical substitutions in I than in the other two manuscripts, undoubtedly because of its later date. It is clear from the diversity of manuscript readings that the text has been extensively altered by scribes at various stages in its transmission:

---

[5] See note to the commentary 6.

the difference between this and the assumption homily extant in B and F, where there are almost no differences between the two texts, is astonishing.

All of the manuscripts, as has been shown, have errors where one or both of the other manuscripts preserve the correct reading. But there are also points where all three manuscripts share readings which are demonstrably incorrect and which must derive from misreadings of an English text. These show that all three manuscripts descend from an archetype which was not the original translation; at least one copy must separate this archetype from the original. Such errors are *ane* (O), *ana* (f$^a$) and *anæ* (I) for the name *anna* (II, 4); *seo seleste* for *seo læste* (VIII, 3); *bearn* for, perhaps, *yldran* (VI, 1); and the omission of *ne* in *wunian ne sceolde* (VIII, 1). There also seems to have been some corruption in the archetype in the angel's speech to Joachim in III, 4, and the verb in *tuddor . . . for gefean* must have been lost at or before this stage also (V). The original translation itself, moreover, did not offer a perfect version of the Latin. Apart from some abbreviations and omissions and some probably deliberate alterations (e.g. *þrowung* instead of Latin *germen* (II, 3)), Anna's speech of thanksgiving in the temple in ch. V appears to have been somewhat confused from the beginning and in VI, 2 the translator did not understand the passive in the Latin.

We have, therefore, a not always accurate translation of the Latin, which has been transmitted to us in manuscripts which all descend from a faulty archetype. All three manuscripts, in addition, have introduced other errors and alterations into their texts, as all of the scribes clearly felt free to adapt the text and rewrite it in minor ways. One text, f$^a$, seems to be a composite one in terms of its textual history: at the beginning it is closely related to one of the other manuscripts, but then switches its alignment to agree with the other.

When it comes to choosing the base manuscript, I can be excluded on the grounds of its late date and the numerous lexical substitutions and other alterations it contains. Of the other two manuscripts O probably has the superior text as it offers more readings which, from a comparison with the Latin, seem to be correct. Another factor is, of course, that f$^a$ is incomplete and lacks the text from the middle of XI to the end, so that one would have to switch to another manuscript here and, as well, f$^a$ appears to be composite textually. I have, accordingly, chosen O as base manuscript. O is also the earliest manuscript although, in some points of orthography, f^a preserves features which seem to belong to an earlier state of the language, for example invariable *-um* in the dative plural of weak nouns, though the *-an* of O is a feature of the earliest Ælfric manuscripts and occurs sporadically even in Alfredian prose.

Although O is the base manuscript I have not always followed its readings, as I have aimed to produce a critical text. Where the Latin text and the Old English agree on a reading, this has normally been taken as an indication of the originality of that reading. This has been followed through even in such small details as the decision whether or not to include names present in f^a and I, but not in O or vice versa: thus, in chs. V and VIII, 3 *Sancta Marian modor* (in O only) and *Abiathar* (in f^a and I) have not been inserted in the edited text, as they are not in the Latin, but in ch. VIII, 5, f^a and I's *Marian* has been included, as it is also in the Latin. In cases where f^a and I differ from the base manuscript, but where the Latin does not correspond closely enough to either reading to be of use in determining the original reading, the base manuscript has been followed in the edited text, as in, for example, the choice of 'þæs þe hi þæs unrihtes hy oncuðan' in XII, 5. In the Prologue, where there is no Latin source to guide a choice, I have retained O's *Sancta Marian* even where it is not paralleled in the other two manuscripts and, similarly, in the Epilogue I have retained in the edited text those phrases found only in O (apart from the superscript *'and is'* and *'for hire bene'*). In the case of chs. I, 1 and I, 2, where only I agrees with the *Gospel of Pseudo-Matthew* in having no information on the birthplaces of Joachim and Anna, this information has been excluded from the edited text; the details are derived from the *De natiutiate Mariae* and were presumably added to the text at a stage after the common archetype. At this point f^a is derived from a manuscript closely connected with O, so it cannot be considered a separate witness in a real sense.

In places where all three Old English manuscripts do not agree with the Latin and have readings which a comparison with the Latin shows to have been incorrect, the Old English has not been emended to conform to what it ought, according to the Latin, to say. My aim has not been to correct the translator and as a result I have attempted only to correct errors which were manifestly introduced after the text left the translator's hands. So, for example, in the particularly corrupt speech of thanksgiving by Anna, the sense of the edited text differs from that of the Latin.

Producing a critical edition of this text is complicated by a further factor, that is, by the fact that the original Old English translation appears to have been an Anglian or archaic work, but that all three manuscripts have been 'entanglisiert' in slightly differing degrees.[6] In this discussion I use the term Anglian for convenience, but bearing in mind the difficulties of knowing what this term means, as outlined in Chapter 6. This gives rise to editorial problems in cases where the base manuscript O appears to have an altered reading, but where the presumably original Anglian reading has been preserved in one or both of the other manuscripts. Thus, in the case of the Anglian expression *gefeonde*, O seems to have altered one instance to *fægniende and swyðe bliðe* (VIII, 4) and to have supplemented the second with *swyðe bliðe* (XI), whereas f[a] and I preserve *gefeonde* in each case. O preserves *gefeoð* in II, 2. In the case of the Anglian *birigde*, O seems to have altered to *onbirigde*, while I has *burigde* with one of its rare glosses, *comedit*, and f[a] has the faulty *byrigene* (VI, 2). f[a] and I have the Mercian word *gemung* for marriage (VIII, 4 and XII, 1), where O has *gemænung*. Where O and f[a] read *buton* in I, 1, I has the Anglian *nymðe* (probably not even understood by the scribe, who has attached the *n* to the previous word and has written *ymðe* on its own). All three manuscripts preserve Anglian *scua* in the Prologue, Anglian *forhwon* (f[a] *forhwam*, I *forhwan*) in III, 1, and Anglian *ricene* in III, 4. O and f[a] have the Anglian *gegyrede* in VIII, 3, while I has *gescrydde* here. *To hwan*, again Anglian, is found in O and I in XII, 1, where f[a]'s text has already finished. f[a] and I have *in* in the phrase *in eaforen* (VII, 1), where O has the faulty *her ætforan* and I has two other instances of *in* (*in israel*, I, 1 and *in fremsumnesse* I, 1). O has three examples of Anglian *nænig* (I, 1; II, 1; and III, 4), while I has only one (*nænigne oðre gemæne* I, 1) and f[a] has eight (*nænig ærendraca* II, 1; *nænigum haligran* III, 4; *nænig man* VI, 3; *nænig gebyrde* VI, 3; *nænig heora stefne* VI, 3; *nænig yfel word* VI, 3; *nænig oþer wer* VIII, 4; and *nænig wer ne onhran* X, 1). Otherwise the three texts read *nan*. f[a] and I have Anglian *sæmninga* in VIII, 3, where O has *sona*.[7] According to Klaeber and Vleeskruyer, *leorniæð* (*habbað geræd on bocum* in O and f[a]) in I I, 1 is

[6] Wenisch, *Spezifisch anglisches Wortgut*, p. 109.

[7] See Wenisch, *Spezifisch anglisches Wortgut*, pp. 137–43 for *gefeon*; pp. 108–12 for *birigde*; p. 261 for *gemung* (see also Klaeber, 'Zur altenglischen Bedaübersetzung', p. 399); pp. 99, 107, 117, 118 etc. for *nymðe*; pp. 215–16 for *scua*; pp. 150–6 for *forhwon*; pp. 208–11 for *ricene*; pp. 289–92 for *gegyrede*; pp. 235–9 for *to hwon*; pp. 189–205 for *nænig*; and pp. 148, 166 etc. for *sæmninga*.

an archaic, non-West Saxon word for 'read',[8] and Vleeskruyer also argues that O's *herenyssa* in the Epilogue is Anglian, whereas I's *herunge* is not.[9]

Wenisch assumes that, in each case which he discusses, what he regards as the Anglian word is the original and the West Saxon a later substitute. If we accept this, it means that, wherever the base manuscript O has a non-Anglian word where one or both of the other manuscripts has an Anglian, the O scribe has replaced the Anglian word with one more familiar to him. The question then naturally arises of whether or not an editor should reverse this process and reinstate the Anglian word, on the grounds that this is almost certainly what the original translation had. Should a critical text, then, include all known Anglian words found in any of the three manuscripts, on the grounds that this takes us closer to the original than any other procedure, short of rewriting the text in Anglian dialect, could? Although superficially attractive, such a procedure is hard to defend. In the first place, our knowledge of dialect vocabulary is by no means so sound as to enable us to state with confidence in all cases which reading is Anglian and which not. Reinstating all known Anglian words (only those, for example, discussed in Wenisch's authoritative survey) would result in a text with a very interim status, which would need to be corrected if and when further words in one of the manuscripts are identified as Anglian. Secondly, it would be very difficult to decide where one would draw the line in tampering with the base manuscript's text. If, for example, every instance of *nænig* from all of the manuscripts is included, why not then change all other instances of *nan* to *nænig*, on the grounds that the original translation, if not the archetype, would always have read *nænig*? Should all instances of *on* be changed to *in* on the same grounds? And if any feature of Anglian vocabulary that has survived is to be admitted to the critical text, why not other Anglian features (e.g. phonological) as well? There seems to be little theoretical justification for giving priority to vocabulary over other linguistic features of the text. It seems to me, therefore, that the choice would have to be between an attempt at a thorough-going reconstruction of the presumed Anglian original, or inclusion in the critical text of only those instances of Anglian vocabulary

---

[8] Klaeber, 'Zur altenglischen Bedaübersetzung', p. 268, and Vleeskruyer, ed., *The Life of St Chad*, p. 31 and p. 59, n. 4.

[9] Vleeskruyer, ed., *The Life of St Chad*, p. 59, n. 4.

found in the base manuscript. Given that the former would produce a reconstructed *Ur*-text which is unverifiable, I have chosen the latter and have followed O in its retention or replacement of Anglian vocabulary. As the meaning remains more or less identical whether one chooses the Anglian word or its replacement, our understanding of the text itself is not greatly affected by this decision. It has the advantage, too, that the text we read has manuscript authority, which a reconstructed text would, of course, lack. This means that, for example, only the three examples of *nænig* found in O are included in the critical text and *gefeonde* is included only when O preserves it, with the replacement word *fægniende* where that is O's reading. I have, however, not included in the edited text the two instances of *blíðe* which O adds as a sort of gloss to both *gefeonde* and *fægniende*, as they seem to me to have the same status as an addition such as *and smeade*, which is likewise not included in the critical text (see note 28 to the commentary). In other words, O's substitutions, but not its additions, are accepted in the edited text.

This procedure is also, I think, more in keeping with what medieval scribes themselves regarded as important and in this regard Machan's work on late Middle English texts is illuminating. He demonstrates how a humanist idealist and lexical concept of a literary work has dominated textual criticism and how problematic this is for the discourse of late Middle English manuscripts.[10] Many of his conclusions are equally valid for Old English texts: that words are not integral to a text and that the conception of a work is of a 'nonlexical, not self-contained *res* inseparable from the supplements of others'.[11] Whereas for traditional textual criticism the aim is the recovery of the authoritative authorial work, equated in practice with the 'correct' text, for a medieval scribe or reader the actual words had no such authority and could be altered or supplemented if necessary, as the *Pseudo-Matthew* manuscripts make amply clear. Lexical substitution does not affect the meaning as there is nothing binding about the specific words and textual criticism's traditional view of alterations of authorial words as corruptions or degenerations is not in accordance with either medieval theory or practice. If there

[10] Machan, *Textual Criticism.*

[11] *Ibid.*, p. 165. The *res* is a mental concept lying behind the words, the intended meaning or absolute truth which is prior to the words, which are not seen as fixed in the same way.

is no compelling reason to valorize an individual's text, then any attempt to re-create that individual's lexical choices is hard to justify: what was important was the sense and O preserves the sense of the work in different words.

This text is, accordingly, a hybrid. O's linguistic forms have been followed in the edition, even where, in all probability, they are not the original forms, but where its readings differ from those of the other manuscripts each case has been decided on its own merits. The choice between different readings has, unlike that between different linguistic forms, been guided by what is likely to have been the original reading and here the Latin source is available as a control. In most cases one or other of the readings corresponds closely to those of the Latin textual family to which the source of this translation clearly belonged and so we can, with some confidence, declare it likely to have been the original reading. In a few cases the Latin, together with a reconstruction of the process of error, enables us to reject the readings of all of the manuscripts as corrupt because of an error in the archetype and to reach back beyond the corrupt archetype to what must have been the original reading. The aim, therefore, has been to rescue the work from error, but not to rescue it from its history in the world.

Because of its transmission history, therefore, this text seems to me to illuminate in interesting ways some of the problems involved in editing Old English texts. It emphasizes once again, if such emphasis were needed, how any edited text is simply an edition, one of many possible. It would be easy to quibble with the procedure adopted here, on the grounds that it combines two different stages of the text's history, in effect: it accepts all the linguistic adaptations of one textual witness, rejecting the synonyms in other manuscripts even where they are probably the actual words of the original, while at the same time accepting the reading of those same manuscripts when it comes to reconstructing what the original version contained. It has, nevertheless, appeared to me to be the best procedure to adopt, in view of the way in which the text has been transmitted to us.

As in the other texts in this volume, punctuation, word-division and capitalization are all modern and abbreviations have been silently expanded in the text. Variant readings exclude spellings and inflectional endings unless they have significance beyond their linguistic interest: the texts of all three manuscripts are available, so full manuscript variants seem superfluous. Inflectional endings have not been emended to accord with 'correct' Old English grammar; so, for example, where the base manuscript has *e* rather than *a* for genitive plural or *as* rather than *es* for masculine or neuter genitive singular, its spelling has been followed. Where the apparatus criticus has f ª, I, the spelling is that of the earlier manuscript f ª. Section numbers are from the Corpus Christianorum Series Apocryphorum edition of the Latin *Pseudo-Matthew* by Jan Gijsel; the Prologue and Epilogue, which are unique to the Old English, are not included in this numbering and are referred to as Prologue and Epilogue in the notes. The numerous tremulous hand glosses to the text in O are given separately; the few glosses in I are included in the apparatus.

# The text

DE NATIUITATE SANCTAE MARIAE[a]

Men ða leofestan,[1] weorþian[b] we nu on andweardnysse þa gebyrdtide þære eadigan fæmnan Sancta Marian, seo wæs cennystre[c2] ures Drihtnes Hælendes Cristes. Nu is[d] hyre nama gereht hlæfdige oððe cwen oððe sæsteorra.[3] Heo is hlæfdige gecweden[e] forðan þe heo cende þone hlaford heofonas and eorðan.[f] And heo is cwen gecweden[g] forðan þe heo com of ðam æðelan cynne and of ðam cynelican sæde Dauides cynnes. Sæsteorra / heo[h] is gecweden forðan þe se sæsteorra[i4] on niht gecyþeð scypliðendum mannum hwyder bið east and west, hwyder[j] suð and norð. Swa þonne wearð þurh ða halgan fæmnan Sancta Marian[k] gecyþed se rihte siðfæt[l5] to ðam ecan life þam ðe lange ær[m] sæton on þeostrum and on deaþes scuan and on þam unstillum yðum þære sæ þises middaneardes; and a syððan wyston ealle halige þone fruman middaneardes and ende and heofona rices wuldor and helle wite. Nu wille we eow[n] secgan be ðære gebyrde[o] þære eadigan fæmnan Sancta Marian, hu seo geworden wæs.[p6]

---

Text from O, fols. 201r–212r

[a] De natiuitate Sanctae Mariae] V `LVIII´ De natiuitate Sanctae Mariae O; Sexta idus septembris. Natiuitas Sancte Marie uiginis [*sic*] f[a]; Natiuitas Sancte Marie I  [b] Men ða leofestan weor] *in capital letters* O   [c] cennystre] godes kenninge I   [d] nu is] and I   [e] gecweden] inemned I   [f] *followed by* And heo is cwen gecweden forðan þe heo cende þone hlaford heofonas and eorðan *marked for deletion* O   [g] gecweden] inemned I; *om.* f[a]  [h] heo] sche *inserted in different hand* I   [i] se sæsteorra] se steorra O; sæsteorra f[a]; þeo sæsteorra I   [j] hwyder] and I   [k] Sancta Marian] *om.* f[a] *and* I   [l] se rihte siðfæt] se rihtes pæt f[a]  [m] lange ær] ær lange f[a], I   [n] Nu wille we eow] Þeonne magen we nu hwylcen seogum wordum I   [o] gebyrde] burdtide I   [p] seo geworden wæs] f[a]; seo geworden wæs and acenned O; heo iboren wæs I

164

# The translation

Most beloved people, let us honour now at the present time the nativity of the blessed virgin St Mary, who was the mother of our Lord, the Saviour Christ. Now her name is explained as lady or queen or star of the sea. She is called lady because she gave birth to the lord of heaven and earth. And she is called queen because she came from the noble family and from the royal seed of the people of David. She is called star of the sea because the star of the sea shows where east and west, where south and north are to seafaring people at night. In the same way, therefore, the right way to eternal life was shown by the holy virgin St Mary to those who sat in darkness for a long time and in the shadow of death and upon the restless waves of the sea of this middle-earth; and ever since all the saints have known the origin and end of middle-earth and the glory of the kingdom of the heavens and the torment of hell. Now we are going tell you about the birth of the blessed virgin St Mary, how it came to pass.

I, 1    We habbað geræd on bocum[a7] þæt wære sum swiðe[b] æþele wer on Israheliscum folce,[c] þæs[d] nama wæs Ioachim, of Iudan cynne.[e8] Se[f] wæs heorda his sceapa and[g] he wæs godfyrht man on bylewitnysse and on fremsumnysse,[h] and he næfde[i] nænige oðre gymene buton[j9] his eowde. Of þam eowde he fedde ealle þa ðe him Drihten ondredon[k] and of ðam wæstmum[l] he Gode þry/fealde[m] lac gebrohte and ealle his æhta on þreo todælde. Ænne dæl he sealde þearfan and wydewan and steopcildum and ælþeodigum mannum, and oðerne dæl he sealde[n] þam þe Gode ane þeowodon.[o10] Done[p] þriddan dæl he heold himsylfum and his hirede big to lifigenne.

I, 2    Ða mid þam[a] þe he þas ðing wæs donde þus, þa micclode God his woruldæhta þæt[b] on þa tid næs nan wer[c] him gelic on Israhelum.[d] Ðas þing he ongan don þa þe[e] he wæs fiftyne wintra, and mid þam þe he hæfde twentig wintra þa onfeng[f] he wif him to gemæccan. Seo[g] wæs gehaten Anna.[h11] Seo[i] wæs Achares dohtor of his agenum cynne, þæt is þonne of ðam æþelan cynne Dauides þæs cynincges. Hi ða wæron samod drohtniende[j] ætgædere[k] twentig wintra, swa hi nan bearn[l] ne begeaton.

II, 1    Ða gelamp hit sume dæge þæt he eode[a] to ðam Drihtnes temple and he ða Ioachim gestod betwyx þam mannum þe to Gode onseged-nysse[b12] brohton, and he gearwode his gyfe on Godes / gesihðe. Him ða togenealæhte þara bocera sum, þæs[c] nama wæs Ruben, and cwæð him to:[d] 'Nis þe alyfed[e] þæt ðu stande betwyx þam mannum[f] þe Gode onseged-nysse bringað, forðan þe Godes bletsung ofer ðe ne com þæt he þe ænig

I, 1    [a] habbað geræd on bocum] leorniæð I    [b] swiðe] *om.* f[a], I    [c] on Israheliscum folce] in israel I    [d] þæs] his I    [e] of Iudan cynne] I; se wæs of Iudan cynne and he wearð geboren on Galileiscre scire, on þære byrig þe is gehaten Nazareth O; se wæs of iudan mægþe and he wearþ geboren on Galileiscere scire on þære byrig þe is gehaten Nazareth f[a]    [f] se] he I    [g] and] *om.* f[a], I    [h] on fremsumnysse] on fremfulnysse f[a]; in fremsum-nesse I    [i] he næfde] næfde he I    [j] gymene buton] gemænen ymðe [*sic*] I    [k] ondredon] ondredæþ I    [l] wæstmum] wæstme I    [m] þryfealde] þreo *inserted in margin* f[a]    [n] he sealde] *om.* I    [o] þeowodon] seruedæn I    [p] ðone] *om.* I
I, 2    [a] ða mid þam] forþan I    [b] þæt] *om.* I    [c] wer] mon I    [d] Israhelum] israe-læ I    [e] þa þe] þa ða f[a]; þa I    [f] onfeng] nom I    [g] seo] heo I    [h] Anna] I; Anna and hyre cynn wæs on þære byrig bethleem O, f[a]    [i] seo] seo anna f[a]; heo I    [j] drohtniende] *om.* I    [k] ætgædere] -gædere *written in thinner, different hand over erasure;* ætsomne f[a]; togedere I    [l] bearn] bearn on worulde f[a]
II, 1    [a] he eode] heo eoden I    [b] onsegednysse] heoræ lac onsægednesse I    [c] þæs] his I    [d] him to] to him I    [e] alyfed] ilyfed I    [f] mannum] *om.* f[a], I

I, 1    We have read in books that there was a certain very noble man among the people of Israel, whose name was Joachim, from the tribe of Judah. He was the shepherd of his sheep and he was a godfearing man in innocence and in kindness, and he had no other care apart from his flock. By means of the flock he fed all those who feared the Lord and he brought God a threefold offering from the fruits [of his work] and he divided all his possessions in three. He gave one part to those in need and widows and stepchildren and strangers, and he gave the second part to those who served God alone. He kept the third part for himself and his household to live on.

I, 2    Then while he was doing these things in this way, God increased his worldly possessions, so that there was no man like him at that time among the Israelites. He began doing these things when he was fifteen years old, and when he was twenty he took a woman as his wife. She was called Anna. She was Achar's daughter from his own people, that is from the noble people of King David. They then lived together for twenty years, yet they begot no child.

II, 1    Then it happened on a certain day that he went to the temple of the Lord and Joachim then stood among the people who brought a sacrifice to God, and he prepared his gift in the sight of God. Then one of the scribes, whose name was Ruben, approached him and said to him: 'It is not permitted to you that you should stand among the people who bring a sacrifice to God, because God's blessing did not come upon you

bearn asende'.[g] He ða þæs[h] wæs myccle scame þrowiende beforan þam folce for þisum wordum and[i] he ða swa scamiende ut of ðam temple wepende gewat;[j] and he nolde þa[k] eft to his agenum hame hweorfan,[l] ac he gewat on westenum to his sceapum,[m] and ða hyrdas nam mid him, and ðær wunode fif monþa fæcc,[n] swa þæt[o] ðær nænig[p] ærendraca betweonan ne ferde[q] him and his gemæccan.

II, 2  Ða ongann Anna, his gemæcca, wepende hi[a] to Drihtne gebiddan[13] and ðus cwæð: 'Min Drihten, Israhela[b] God, þu ðe eart strang and mihtig ofer ealle gesceafta, and ðu me noldest næfre bearn ofer eorðan syllan and ðu minne wer me æt[c] gename, and ic nat hwæþer his lif is ofer eorðan, and, gif he forðgewiten is, þonne ne gegearwode[d] ic him byrgene.'[14] Ða heo þas word gecweden hæfde, þa eode heo eft / on hire cauertun[e] and hire eadmodlice to Drihtne gebæd. And æfter ðam þe heo hire gebed[15] gefylled hæfde,[f] þa ahof heo hire eagan up to Drihtne. Þa[g] geseah heo[h] spearwan nest on anum lawertreowe. Heo ða wependre[i] stefne clypode to Drihtne and cwæð: 'Drihten, þu ælmihtiga God, þu[j] sealdest eallum gesceaftum byrðor and hi on þan gefeoð, and ic[k] þe nu þanc secge[l] þæt þu me ane ute atyndest fram þinre gyfe þære fremsumnysse.[16] Hwæt, þu min Drihten canst and wast mine heortan. Hwæt, ic þe fram fruman[m] mines gesinscipes gehet,[n] gyf þu me sealdest sunu oððe dohtor, þæt ic hi wolde þe gebringan to þinum temple.'

II, 3  Ða heo þas word gecweden hæfde, hwæt[a] þa hyre ætywde[b] Drihtnes[c] encgel and ðus[d] cwæð: 'Ne ðearft[e] ðu þe ondrædan,[17] Anna, forðan þe[f] þin þrowung[18] is on Godes geþeahte.[g] Þæt[h] of ðe acenned bið, þæt bið on wundra eallum folcum[i] oðþæt woruldes ende.' Ða mid þam þe

[g] asende] sende I   [h] þæs] þær I   [i] and] *om.* I   [j] gewat] eode I   [k] he nolde þa] nolde þa f[a]; he þa nolde I   [l] to his agenum hame hweorfan] hweorfan to his agenum hame f[a], I   [m] sceapum] f[a], I; sceape O   [n] fæcc] f[a], I; fæce O   [o] þæt] *om.* f[a], I   [p] nænig] nan I   [q] betweonan ne ferde] ne ferde betweonan I

II, 2   [a] his gemæcca wepende hi] hyre gemæccan bewepan and hire f[a], I   [b] israhela] israele I   [c] me æt] æt me f[a], I   [d] þonne ne gegearwode] f[a]; þonne ne gegearwie O; þonne gearwode I   [e] cauertun] f[a], I; cauertune O   [f] hire gebed gefylled hæfde] hæfde hire gebeden gefyllede f[a]; hæfde hire bone ifylled I   [g] þa] and þa f[a], I   [h] heo] heo an I   [i] wependre] mid wependre I   [j] þu] ðu þe I   [k] and ic] ic f[a], I   [l] secge] sette f[a]   [m] fruman] frimþe I   [n] gehet] bihæt I

II, 3   [a] hwæt] *om.* I   [b] hyre ætywde] æteowde hire I   [c] Drihtnes] godes f[a], I   [d] ðus] *om.* I   [e] ne ðearft] nelt f[a]; nylt I. *O's* ðearft ðu þe *seems to be over an erasure in a smaller different hand*   [f] þe] *om.* f[a], I; *followed by a blank third of a line in O, underneath the erasure on previous line*   [g] geþeahte] þohte I   [h] þæt] þæt þæt f[a]   [i] folcum] mannum f[a], I

that he would send you a child'. Then on account of that he suffered great shame in front of the people because of these words and he departed weeping from the temple, feeling shamed like this; and he did not wish to return again to his own home, but he departed into the desert to his sheep, and took his shepherds with him, and remained there for a period of five months, so that no messenger went between him and his wife.

II, 2    Then Anna, his wife, weeping, prayed to the Lord and said as follows: 'My Lord, God of Israel, you who are strong and mighty over all creatures, and you never wished to give me a child on earth and you took my husband from me, and I do not know whether he is alive on earth, and, if he is dead, then I have not prepared a burial for him'. When she had spoken these words, then she went into her forecourt and humbly prayed to the Lord. And after she had completed her prayer, then she raised her eyes up to the Lord. Then she saw a sparrow's nest in a laurel tree. With a weeping voice she then called to the Lord and said: 'Lord, you almighty God, you have given all creatures offspring and they rejoice in that, and I now give thanks to you that you have excluded me only from your gift of liberality. Truly, you, my Lord, know and understand my heart. Truly, I promised you from the beginning of my marriage that if you gave me a son or daughter I would bring them to you to your temple.'

II, 3    When she had spoken these words, then an angel of the Lord appeared to her and spoke as follows: 'You need not be afraid, Anna, because your suffering is in God's plan. That which is born of you will be a source of wonder to all peoples until the end of the world.' When he

he þas word gecweden hæfde, þa wæs he fram hyre eagum ahafen. Þa wæs heo / swyðe forht geworden for ðæs engles gesihðe. Heo hire þa gewat[j] into hyre clyfan and ðær awunode[k] þone dæg and ða niht on hire gebede.[l]

II, 4   Ða þæs on mergen[a19] þa gelaþode heo hyre þinene hire to and hire to[b] cwæð: 'Hwæt, þu me gesawe on[c] wydewanhade beswicene and on mycelre nearonysse gesette and noldest me to frofre[d] cuman'.[20] Ða andswarode heo hire ungeþwærlice and hire cwæð to:[e] 'Ðeah þe[f] God þinne wer æt þe gename and ðinne innoð beluce, hwæt sceal ic þe þæs[g] don?' Ða þa[h] heo Anna[i] þas word gehyrde þa ongan heo biterlice wepan.[j21]

III, 1   Hwæt þa on þære ylcan tide[a22] ætywde him[b] sum swyðe wlitig wer on þam westene, þær þær he wæs mid his hyrdum, and him cwæð to:[c] 'Forhwan nelt ðu ham gehweorfan to þinum gemæccan?' Ða cwæð he[d] Ioachim: 'Twentig wintra ic wunode mid hyre and me God nan bearn of hyre ne sealde, ac ic swyðe geæswicod eode[e] ut of ðam Drihtnes[f] temple; forðan ic nylle eft ham gehweorfan, ac ic wylle her wunian þa hwile þe Drihten wile and ða Godes gyfe for / Drihtnes naman dælan, swa ic ær dyde'.

III, 2   Ða andswarode him se iunga[a] and cwæð:[b] 'Ic eom Drihtnes encgel and nu todæg ic me æteowde þinum gemæccan and hi gefrefrode, þa þa heo hi wepende and geomriende to Drihtne gebæd. And wite þu[c] þæt heo is of ðinum sæde geeacnod,[d] swa swa þu nystest[e] þa þa þu hi[f] ana forlæte, and[g] heo þe cenneð dohtor. And seo[h] bið on Godes temple fulfremed and se Halga Gast resteþ on hyre, and hire eadignyss astigeð ofer[i] ealle wifa cynn and hire ne bið gelic ænig þara þe ær wæs oððe æfter cymð.[j] Cyr nu to þinum gemæccan and ðu gemetest hi geeacnode and ðu þæs Gode þanc sege,[k] forðan þe[l] hyre sæd bið gebletsod and heo bið modor þære ecan bletsunge geseted.'

---

[j] heo hire þa gewat] and heo hire gewat f[a]; and heo þa eode I   [k] awunode] wunede I   [l] gebede] gebedum f[a]; bedum I

II, 4   [a] þæs on mergen] wæs on morgen geworden f[a]; wæs morgen iworden I   [b] hire to and hire to cwæð] hire to and cwæð O; to hire `and hire´ to cwæð f[a]; to hire and to hire cwæð I   [c] on] on minum f[a], I   [d] to frofre] to foren I   [e] cwæð to] to cwæð I   [f] þe] om. f[a], I   [g] þe þæs] þæs O   [h] þa] þe I   [i] Anna] ane O; ana f[a]; anæ I   [j] biterlice wepan] wepan biterlice f[a], I

III, 1   [a] tide] nihte f[a], I   [b] ætywde him] him æteowde f[a], I   [c] him cwæð to] him to cwæð I   [d] he] om. I   [e] geæswicod eode] geæswicode f[a]   [f] Drihtnes] godes I

III, 2   [a] iunga] ængel I   [b] cwæð] þus cwæð f[a], I   [c] þu] þu nu I   [d] is of ðinum sæde geeacnod] of ðine sæde ieacnod is I   [e] þu nystest] þu na ne wistest f[a]; þ[[a]]`u´ na hit ne wistest I   [f] þa þa þu hi] ða þe ðu I   [g] and] om. I   [h] seo] heo I   [i] astigeð ofer] oferstigeð f[a], I   [j] cymð] f[a], I; om. O   [k] ðu þæs Gode þanc sege] þas ðonce gode I   [l] þe] om. f[a]

had spoken these words, then he was lifted up away from her eyes. Then she was very frightened because of the sight of the angel. She went into her chamber then and remained there in prayer for the day and the night.

II, 4   Then the next morning she summoned her maid-servant to her and said to her: 'Behold, you saw me deceived in widowhood and placed in great distress and would not console me'. Then she answered her crossly and said to her: 'If God has taken your husband from you and locked your womb, what am I to do about it for you?' When Anna heard these words then she began to weep bitterly.

III, 1   Then at the same time a very beautiful man appeared to him in the desert, where he was with his shepherds, and said to him: 'Why will you not return home to your wife?' Then Joachim said: 'I lived with her for twenty years and God gave me no child by her, but I left the temple of the Lord greatly offended; therefore I do not wish to go home again, but I will live here for as long as the Lord may wish and I will distribute God's gifts in the Lord's name, as I previously did'.

III, 2   Then the young man answered him and said: 'I am the angel of the Lord and now today I appeared to your wife and comforted her, when she was praying to the Lord, weeping and mourning. And you should know that she has become pregnant by your seed, which you did not know when you left her alone, and she will give birth to a daughter for you. And she will be perfect in the temple of God and the Holy Spirit will rest on her, and her blessedness will surpass that of all womankind and nobody who existed before or who will come after will be like her. Return now to your wife and you will find her pregnant and give thanks to God for that, because her seed will be blessed and she will be made the mother of eternal blessing.'

III, 3    Ða wurþode hine Ioachim and him cwæþ to:[a] 'Gyf hit þus gewurðan scule swa þu cwyst, site mid me on minum huse and gebletsa þinne þeowa'.[b23] Ða cwæð se encgel to him: 'Hwi wylt þu la[c] cweðan þæt ðu sy min þeowa, ac þu eart min efenþeowa, forðan þe[d] wit syndon anes Godes þeow. And ic þe secge þæt min mete ne[e] min drenc ne mæg beon fram / mannum gesewen. Ac swa hwæt swa þu me to gyfe tihhie, bring þæt Gode to onsægednysse.' He þa Ioachim Gode[f] brohte unwemme lac and to ðam engle cwæð: 'Næs ic na gedyrstig þæt ic Gode sacerdlice onsægednysse brohte, þær[g] þu me ne hete'.[24] Ða cwæþ se encgel: 'Na ic ðe ne hete[h] Gode sacerdlice onsægednysse bringan, gyf[i] ic Godes willan to þan[j] ne ongeate'.[25] Ða gewat[k] se encgel samod mid þam stence þære onsægednysse into heofonum.

III, 4    He ða Ioachim wearð to þam forht þæt he feoll on his ansyn[a] and læg swilce he dead wære[26] fram þære sixtan tide þæs dæges oðþæt[b] æfen wæs. Him þa togenealæhton his hyrdas and hi hine þa gesawon licgan and nyston þone intingan on him ac ahofen hine up, and hi wendon[c] þæt he wolde hine sylfne acwellan. Ða ahof he his heafod up and he him asæde þa[d] his gesihðe þe he geseah. Ða wurdon hi sona afyrhte and eac wundrodon oðþæt he heom[e] eall asæd hæfde, and hi ða ealle[f] hine trymedon and lærdon þæt he gehyrsum wære þæs engles wordum and þæt he hraþe / gehwyrfde ham to his gemæccan. He ða Ioachim þreodode[g27] on his mode hwæt he embe þæt dyde. Þa wearð he færinga on slæpe gehwyrfed. Him þa eft[h] ætywde se ylca Godes encgel[i] on slæpe and him to cwæð: 'Ic eom Godes encgel and fram Drihtne ic eom þe to hyrde geset. Ac gewit[j] nu ham orsorh to ðinum gemæccan, and ingcer[k] mildheortnyss þe gyt[l] worhten[m] and ingcer[n] nama wæs gerædd beforan Godes[o] gesihðe on his þrymsetle.[28] And he ingc[p] syleð swa myccle grownysse on ingcran[q] beorðre swa he næfre nænigan halgan ær ne sealde, ne nu[r] eft ne syllað.' He þa Ioachim of þam

---

III, 3    [a] him cwæþ to] him to cwæþ f[a], I    [b] þeowa] þeow f[a], I    [c] la] *om.* f[a]    [d] þe] *om.* f[a], I    [e] ne] and f[a], I    [f] Gode] *om.* I    [g] þær] gyf f[a], I    [h] na ic ðe ne hete] [[na]] ic ðe ne het[[e]] O; na ic þe ne hete f[a]; na ic þe ne hate I    [i] gyf] forðam gyf O; forþam þe f[a], I    [j] þan] þan on þe O    [k] gewat] ferde I

III, 4    [a] on his ansyn] on eorþan f[a], I    [b] oðþæt] oððet hit I    [c] wendon] cwædon f[a], I    [d] he him asæde þa] sæde heom I    [e] he heom] he hit him man f[a]; he hit heom I    [f] hi ða ealle] heo alle þa I    [g] þreodode] þreodode and smeade O    [h] eft] *om.* f[a], I    [i] Godes encgel] engel eft f[a], I    [j] gewit] fare I    [k] ingcer] eower f[a], I    [l] gyt] ge f[a], I    [m] worhten] worhten is beforan godes gesihðe O, *where the* is *seems to have been inserted later*; worhton beforan godes gesihðe f[a]; worhton I    [n] ingcer] eower f[a], I    [o] Godes] drihtenes f[a], I    [p] he ingc] he Drihten ingc O; he eow f[a], I    [q] ingcran] eowran f[a], I    [r] nu] nu næfre f[a], I

III, 3 Then Joachim worshipped him and said to him: 'If it is to be as you say, sit with me in my house and bless your servant'. Then the angel said to him: 'Why are you saying that you are my servant, for you are my fellow-servant, because we are both servants of the one God. And I say to you that neither my food nor my drink can be seen by people. But whatever you intend as a gift for me, bring that as a sacrifice to God.' Then Joachim brought a pure offering to God and said to the angel: 'I was not so presumptuous to bring God a priestly offering, if you had not commanded me'. Then the angel said: 'I would not have commanded you to bring a priestly sacrifice to God if I did not know God's will concerning that'. Then the angel departed with the scent of the offering into heaven.

III, 4 Then Joachim was so afraid that he fell on his face and lay as if he were dead from the sixth hour of the day until it was evening. Then his shepherds approached him and they saw him lying and did not know the cause, but they raised him up and they thought that he wished to kill himself. Then he raised up his head and he described to them his vision which he had seen. Then they were immediately afraid and were also astonished until he had told them everything, and then they all exhorted him and urged him that he should be obedient to the words of the angel and that he should quickly return home to his wife. Joachim deliberated in his mind what he should do about this. Then he was suddenly returned to sleep. The same angel of God appeared to him again then in his sleep and said to him: 'I am the angel of God and I have been appointed by God as your guardian. But go home now without anxiety to your wife, and the works of mercy, which you both performed, and your name were read in the sight of God on his throne. And the Lord will give you both such prosperity in your offspring as he never before gave any saint, nor

slæpe aras and his swefen sæde his hyrdum. Hi ða ealle hine bædon and halsedon þæt he gehyrsumode þæs engles wordum and ricene ham gecyrde.[29]

III, 5    Ða wæs he ær gegan for his unrotnysse on þam westene to ðam[a] feor þæt he for xxx daga fæc ne mihte ham to his gemæccan gehweorfan. Heo þa Anna wæs æt hyre gebede, þa ætywde hyre Drihtnes encgel and hyre gecydde[b] þone hamsið / hyre gemæccan.[30] And heo ða mid hyre hyrede[c][31] him ongean ferde[d] mid mycclum gefean; swylce eac hyre mægðe[e][32] and eall Israhela bearn mycelne gefean[f] hæfdon be his hamcyme and be ðam hlisan hire geeacnunge.

IV    Hwæt þa æfter þan wæron gefylde nigan monað hire geeacnunge,[a][33] þa cende Anna hyre dohtor[b][34] and hyre naman gecigde[c] Maria,[d] and heo hi ða fedde þreo winter æt hire breostum. Ioachim þa[e] and Anna[f] læddon þæt cild mid heom to þære halgan ceastre and ða lac brohton mid heom to ðam[g][35] Drihtnes temple, þe Iudea gewuna wæs, and hi ða sealdon þæt cild on gemanan þære fæmnena, þe dæges and nihtes on Godes lofe wunodon. Heo þa[h] up eode mid þam oðrum fæmnum on þa fiftyne stæpas on þam temple, swa heo[i] on bæc ne beseah[j][36] ne æfter hyre yldrum ne murnde,[k][37] swa swa cildra gewuna is.[l] Ac heo wæs on gange and on worde and on eallum gebærum gelic wynsuman men, þe hæfde xxx wintra, and heo geornlice and eadmodlice þurhwunode on hyre gebede oðþæt þa biscopas and eall þæt folc / wundrodon[m] on hire gebære.[n][38]

V    Heo Anna þa[a][39] wæs gefylled mid[b] Halige Gaste and[c] witegode þa beforan þam folce and ðus cwæþ: 'Drihten, ælmihtig God, wæs gemyndig his worda, þe he sylfa cwæð, ðæt he wolde his folc gesecan mid[d] haligre geneosunge and ða þeode, þe wið[e] us arisan, he wolde geeadmedigan þæt hi gecyrdon to heora sylfra heortan and heora earan ontynon[f] to urum benum and ða bysmernyssa ura feonda[g] fram us acerron.[h][40] On þam

<hr />

III, 5    [a] to ðam] swa I    [b] gecydde] gecigde O; gekydde f[a]; cydde I    [c] hyrede] hærenne f[a]; hinene I    [d] ferde] eode f[a], I    [e] mægðe] magas f[a], I    [f] gefean] blisse I

IV    [a] hwæt . . . geeacnunge] *om.* f[a], I    [b] dohtor] dohtor on þissum dæge O    [c] gecigde] nemnode I    [d] Maria] *in capitals* O    [e] þa] *om.* I    [f] Anna] anna þa I    [g] to ðam] to ðære O; to þam f[a]; into þam I    [h] þa] *om.* f[a], I    [i] heo] heo ne f[a], I    [j] beseah] beseah ne heo na ne taltrade f[a], I    [k] murnde] myrde f[a]; rymde I    [l] cildra gewuna is] cilda gewuna wæs f[a]; childes gewunæ wæs I    [m] wundrodon] wundrade f[a], I    [n] gebære] gebærum f[a], I

V    [a] þa] þa SCA MARIAN modor O    [b] mid] mid þam f[a], I    [c] and] and heo I    [d] mid] *om.* f[a], I    [e] wið] mid I    [f] ontynon] ontyndon f[a], I    [g] feonda] feondum O, I    [h] acerron] acyrran f[a]; acyrdon I

will now give again.' Then Joachim arose out of his sleep and told his dream to his shepherds. Then they all entreated and implored him to obey the words of the angel and to go home quickly.

III, 5    Then because of his sadness he had gone so far into the desert that for a period of thirty days he could not return home to his wife. When Anna was at her prayer, then the angel of the Lord appeared to her and made known to her the homecoming of her husband. And then with her household she travelled towards him with great rejoicing; likewise her kinsfolk and all the children of Israel had great joy at his homecoming and at the report of her pregnancy.

IV    When after that the nine months of her pregnancy were completed, then Anna gave birth to a daughter and called her name Mary, and she fed her for three years at her breasts. Then Joachim and Anna took the child with them to the holy city and brought offerings with them to the temple of the Lord, as was the custom of the Jews, and they then gave the child into the company of those virgins, who remained day and night in praise of God. Then she went up the fifteen steps in the temple with the other virgins, in such a way that she did not look back nor did she long for her parents, as is the custom of children. But she was in her walk and in her words and in all her behaviour like a pleasant person who was thirty years old, and she eagerly and humbly persevered in her prayers until the bishops and all the people were amazed at her behaviour.

V    Then Anna was filled with the Holy Spirit and prophesied there in front of the people and said as follows: 'Lord, Almighty God, has been mindful of his words, which he himself spoke, that he would visit his people with his holy visitation and he would humiliate the peoples who rose up against us, so that they would turn to their own hearts, and he would open their ears to our prayers and would turn away the insults of our enemies from us. Through the sterile ones an offspring of eternal bliss

unbeorþrum^i ecre blisse tuddor wæs acenned^j for gefean^k on Israhelum,^141 swa me min Drihten forgeaf,^m þæt ic mot Gode gecweme lac bringan. Ær me mine fynd ascufon fram þære halgan onsegednysse for minre unwæstmberendnysse;^n Drihten min acerde hi fram me and me forgeaf ecne gefean.'^o

VI, 1 Ða heo þas word gecweden hæfde, þa cyrdon hi ham mid þam and þæt cild forleton æt ðam halgan^a temple mid oðrum^b fæmnum.^42 Heo^c ða weox and wearð fulfremed on godra mægna heanyssum / and heo ða sona godum towcræftum onfeng,^d swyðor þonne ænig þara þe heora yldran^e wæron, wifa and fæmnena.^43

VI, 2 And heo gesette hyre sylfre haligne regol, swa þæt heo wolde beon fram þære ærestan tide þæs dæges on hyre halgum gebedum wuniende oðþæt ða þriddan tid, and fram þære þriddan tide oðða^a nigoþan tid^b ymbe hyre webbgeweorc. And eft fram þære nigoðan tide heo þurhwunode standende on hyre gebedum oðþæt Godes encgel hyre ætywde and hyre brohte heofonlice swetnysse, and heo onbirgde þære^c of his handa. And heo syðþan wæs betere and swyðre on Godes lufan and on gastlicra mægna heannyssum.^d And heo yldran fæmnan lærde to Godes willan^44 and heo wæs getyddre and snotere on þære Godes æ^e þonne ænig þæra þe hyre beforan wæs. Heo wæs eadmodre and on Godes lufan glæddre and on hyre^f geþohtum clænre and on ðam dauidiscum sangum wrætlicre^g þonne heora ænig ær wære.^h45 Heo^i wæs þolemod and gestæðþig^j46 / on hire gebæran.

VI, 3 And ne geseah hi nan man yrre ne tælan^a ne wyrigean ne nan man ne gehyrde yfel word of hyre muðe gan.^b Ac hyre word wæron Godes

---

^i þam unbeorþrum] f^a; ða mundbyrdum O; þam unbeoðrum I ^j wæs acenned] *not in any manuscript* ^k tuddor for gefean] f^a; tuddor forgeafon O; ðe þar i gefæn is I ^l israhelum] israele I ^m forgeaf] geaf I ^n unwæstmberendnysse] unberednysse f^a; unberendnysse I ^o forgeaf ecne gefean] geaf ecce blisse I

VI, 1 ^a halgan] *om.* f^a, I ^b oðrum] oþrum þam f^a; þam oðre I ^c heo] and heo f^a, I ^d onfeng] onfeng and f^a, I ^e yldran] bearn O, f^a, I

VI, 2 ^a and fram þære þriddan tide oðða] on þa I ^b tid] *om.* f^a ^c onbirgde þære] þære byrigene f^a; þaræ burigde `comedit´ I ^d heannyssum] heahnysse f^a, I ^e æ] lage I ^f hyre] *om.* f^a, I ^g dauidiscum sangum wrætlicre] dauidtidiscum sangum wrætlicre and wisra O; dauitidiscum sangum wærlicre f^a; dauidisce sange wræsclicre I ^h þonne heora ænig ær] þone ænig f^a, I ^i heo] and heo f^a, I ^j gestæðþig] sceaðig I

VI, 3 ^a ne geseah hi nan man yrre ne tælan] ne geseah hi nænig man yrre ne tælan f^a; nan mon ne seah hire wrað `yrre´ ne tælan `chidon´ I ^b ne nan man ne gehyrde yfel word of hyre muðe gan] ne nænig gehyrde yfel word of hyre muðe gan f^a; ne nan word yfeles of hire muðe ne com I

was born as a joy among the Israelites, just as my Lord granted me that I may bring a suitable offering to God. Previously my enemies expelled me from the holy sacrifice because of my infertility; my Lord has turned them away from me and has granted me eternal joy.'

VI, 1   When she had spoken these words, they went home straight-away and left the child at the holy temple with the other virgins. She grew up and was perfected in the excellence of good virtues, and she at once engaged in good weaving, more than any of those, women and virgins, who were older.

VI, 2   And she set herself a holy rule, so that she used to remain at her holy prayers from the first hour of the day until the third hour, and from the third hour until the ninth hour at her weaving. And again from the ninth hour she remained standing at her prayers until the angel of God appeared to her and brought her heavenly sweet food, and she ate that from his hand. And then she was better and stronger in the love of God and in the excellence of spiritual virtues. And she instructed older virgins according to the will of God and she was more skilled and more clever in God's law than any of those who had been before her. She was humbler and more joyous in praise of God and purer in her thoughts and more excellent in the songs of David than any of them had been before. She was patient and grave in her behaviour.

VI, 3   And no one saw her angry or speaking ill or cursing nor did anyone hear an evil word come from her mouth. But her words were full

gyfe full, and heo wæs on hyre heortan smeagende þone wisdom[c] Godes
boca. And ða fæmnan, þe mid hyre wæron, heo getrymde[d] þæt hi on heora
gebedum þurhwunedon and on Godes lofa and þæt heora nan[e] stefne up ne
ahofe on idlum leahtre,[f] ne hy on heora tungan teonan ne cwæden, ne nan[g]
yfel word of heora muþe ut ne eode. And of hire[h47] aras ærest se gewuna,
þæt se man, se[i] ðe oþerne mid lufan gegrete,[j] þæt he him godcunde
bletsunge ongean sende.[k] And dæghwamlice heo onfeng[l] mete of ðæs
engles hande and mid þam gereordod[m] wæs; and ðone mete þe heo æt þam
bisceope onfeng[n] æt[o] ðam temple heo[p] gedælde þearfendum mannum.
And swa hwilc man swa hi untrum gesohte, eft he eode hal fram hire.

VII, 1 Ða gelamp hit þæt Abiathar, se sacerd, brohte myccle gyfe þam
bisceope and bæd hine þæt he gesealde Marian his sunu / to gemæccan. Ða
styrde Maria him and cwæð anrædlice:[a] 'Ne gewurð þæt næfre swa þæt ic
wer grete oððe wer me'. Ða andwyrdan þa biscopas hyre[b] and hyre mægðe[c]
ealle þe on þam temple wæron[d48] and cwædon: 'God wæs on bearnum
begangan and in eaforan weorþað[e] swa þæt a[f] gewunelic wæs on Godes
folce Israhelum'.[g49] Ða andwyrde[h] Maria and him cwæð to:[i]

VII, 2 'Næs nan rihtwis man ne nan[a] halig ær Abel, and hine arleaslice
his broðor[b] ofsloh.[50] He brohte twyfealde gyfe Drihtne, hluttre onseged-
nysse and his lichaman clænnysse. Swylce eac[c] Helias wæs of[d] þissere
worulde alæded[e] on lichaman,[f] forðan þe he his clænnysse geheold.'[51]

VIII, 1 Ða[a] wæs heo swylce heo wære xiiii wintra, ða gedemdon þa[b]
Phariseas þæt heo syððan wunian ne[c] sceolde on þam Godes temple.[52] Hy
ða geþeahtodon þæt hi Israhela folc gelaðodon to ðam Godes temple[d] þy

---

[c] wisdom] wisdom on I  [d] getrymde] ty`u´mede I  [e] þæt heora nan] nænig heora f[a];
nan heoræ I  [f] up ne ahofe on idlum leahtre] up ahofe on idelum leahtre f[a]; on ydele
læhtre up ahufe I  [g] nan] nænig f[a]  [h] hire] f[a], I; heom O  [i] se] *om.* I  [j] mid lufan
gegrete] grette mid lufan wordum f[a], I  [k] sende] sette f[a], I  [l] onfeng]
underfeng I  [m] mid þam gereordod] mid þig gereordod f[a]; mid þan heo ireordod I
[n] onfeng] underfeng I  [o] æt] on f[a], I  [p] heo] heo þone f[a]; þone heo I
VII, 1  [a] anrædlice] andredlice I  [b] andwyrdan þa biscopas hyre] andswaradon hyre þa
biscopas f[a], I  [c] mægðe] O; magas f[a], I  [d] ealle þe on þam temple wæron] f[a], I; on þam
temple O  [e] in eaforan weorþað] her ætforan weorþað O; in eaforen weorðeð f[a]; in
eaforen weorðaþ I  [f] a] an O; *om.* f[a], I  [g] israhelum] israele I  [h] andwyrde] andswarode
f[a]  [i] cwæð to] to cwæð f[a]
VII, 2  [a] nan] *om.* f[a], I  [b] his broðor] unwis f[a], I  [c] swylce eac] eac swilce f[a], I  [d] of]
f[a], I; on O  [e] alæded] f[a]; ilæd I; ac he wearð alæded O  [f] on lichaman] f[a], I; mid
lichaman and mid sawle to heofonum O
VIII, 1  [a] ða] *om.* f[a], I  [b] þa] *om.* f[a], I  [c] ne] *om.* O, f[a], I  [d] hy ða . . .temple] *om.* I

of the grace of God, and in her heart she contemplated the wisdom of God's books. And she exhorted the virgins who were with her that they should persevere at their prayers and at praise of God and that none of them should raise her voice in idle laughter, nor should they speak injury with their tongues nor should any evil word come from their mouths. And from her arose first the custom that the person who would greet another with love should utter a divine blessing to him. And daily she received food from the hand of the angel and was fed by that; and she distributed the food which she received from the bishop in the temple to poor people. And whatever person came to her sick, went from her healthy.

VII, 1   Then it happened that Abiathar, the priest, brought great gifts to the bishop and asked him to give Mary to his son as a wife. Then Mary prohibited him and said resolutely: 'That will never happen that I should know a man or a man me'. Then the bishops answered her and all her kinsfolk who were in the temple and said: 'God was worshipped by means of children and honoured in successors, as was always customary among the people of God, the Israelites'. Then Mary answered and said to them:

VII, 2   'There was no righteous man or holy man before Abel, and his brother cruelly killed him. He brought a twofold gift to the Lord, a pure offering and the purity of his body. Likewise also Elias was carried off in the body from this world, because he preserved his purity.'

VIII, 1   Then she was fourteen years old when the Pharisees decided that she should no longer live in the temple of God. They then agreed that they should summon the people of Israel to the temple of God on the

þriddan dæge.[53] Ða þa hy[e] þider gesamnod wæron, þa astah se heahbiscop
Isachar up on þone ytemestan stæpe,[f] clypode þa hluddre / stefne and ðus
cwæð: 'Gehyrað nu, Israhela[g] bearn, mine[h] word! Hwæt,[i] ge witon þæt
Salomon þis tempel getimbrode, and her wæron syðþan inne cyninga
bearn and witegena and heahsacerda, oðþæt hi becomon to ælicre[j] yldo,
and hi gelimplice heora yldran wæron gehyrsume to ælicum gyftum,[k]
and heora bearn eft Gode lac brohton swyðe gecweme[l] to þam Godes
temple and on[m] heora yldrena endebyrdnysse Gode gecwemdon.[54] Nu is
þonne gemeted þæt Maria hæfð niwe endebyrdnysse ongunnon Gode mid
to gecwemanne, cweð,[n] þæt heo wile Gode[o] hire mægðhad bringan.
Uton[p][55] secan þa andsware to Gode[q] ure axunge, þæt God us gecyðe
hwilcum wære we hi befæstan sculon to healdenne.'

VIII, 2   Ða gelicode þæt word ealre[a][56] þære gesamnunge and hy[b] ða
asenden[c] hlota ofer þa xii cyn Israhela.[d] Ða gefeoll þæt hlot ofer Iudan
cyn, Iacobes sunu. Ða bebead[e] se sacerd þæt þæt[f] Iudan cynn come eall[g]
þæs on mergen[h] to ðam halgan[i] temple, ælc þæra þe wif næfde, and
hæfde him[j] gyrda on handa.[57] Ða wæs þonon geworden / þæt Ioseph
wæs gehaten sum gewintrod man; eode[k] þyder mid iungum mannum
and his gyrde[l] bær. Þa genam se sacerd ealle þa[m] gyrde and bær into
þam[n] Sancta Sanctorum and bebead[o] þæt hi comon þæs[p] on mergen and
name ælc his gyrde, and ðonne sceolde culfre[q] fleogan of þære gyrde
foreweardre up oð þone[r] heofon. Þonne sceolde se wer beon hyrde þære
fæmnan.

VIII, 3   Ða wæs geworden on mergen þæs æfteran dæges þæt[a] hi
comon[b] ealle on þa tid þære onsægednysse, and he[c] ða inn eode se
biscop[d][58] into þam[e] Sancta Sanctorum, wæs þæt þæra[f] Haligra Halignys

---

[e] ða þa hy] þa hi þa f[a], I   [f] stæpe] stæpe and f[a], I   [g] israhela] israele I   [h] mine] min
f[a], I   [i] hwæt] *om.* I   [j] ælicre] ælcere f[a]   [k] gehyrsume to ælicum gyftum] æwfæston f[a];
eawfestæ I   [l] lac brohton swyðe gecweme] gecweme lac brohton f[a], I   [m] on] *om.* f[a],
I   [n] cweð] sægð I   [o] Gode] f[a], I; *om.* O   [p] uton] nu þonne uton O; ute f[a]; uton
I   [q] to Gode] to gode sylfum f[a]; æt gode sylfum I

VIII, 2   [a] word ealre] f[a], I; word O   [b] hy] *om.* f[a], I   [c] asenden] sendon f[a], I
[d] israhela] israhela bearnum f[a]; israele bearnum I   [e] bebead] bead I   [f] þæt] *om.* I   [g] eall]
*om.* f[a], I   [h] on mergen] mærgennes f[a]   [i] halgan] godes I   [j] næfde and hæfde him] næfde
and hæfde heora ælc f[a]; hæfde and næfde heoræ ælc I   [k] eode] and eode f[a], I   [l] gyrde] gyrd
þider f[a], I   [m] þa] *om.* I   [n] into þam] þa into f[a], I   [o] bebead] bead I   [p] þæs] *om.* f[a],
I   [q] culfre] an culfre I   [r] up oð þone] up inn on þone f[a]; up into I

VIII, 3   [a] þæt] ða f[a], I   [b] hi comon] comon hi f[a], I   [c] he] *om.* f[a], I   [d] biscop] bisceop
abiathar f[a], I   [e] into þam] inn to f[a]; into I   [f] þæra] *om.* f[a]

third day. When they were gathered there the archbishop Isachar climbed up to the top step, called out in a loud voice and spoke as follows: 'Listen now to my words, children of Israel! Truly, you know that Solomon built this temple, and since then there were children of kings and prophets and high priests in here, until they reached the legal age, and befitting their ancestors were obedient to lawful marriages, and afterwards their children brought very pleasing offerings to the temple of God and pleased God according to the order of their ancestors. Now it is found that Mary has started a new order with which to please God; she says that she wishes to offer her virginity to God. Let us seek an answer to our question from God, so that God may make known to us to what man we should entrust her to keep her.'

VIII, 2   Then this speech pleased all the assembly and they cast lots over the twelve tribes of the Israelites. Then the lot fell upon the tribe of Judah, the son of Jacob. Then the priest commanded that the tribe of Judah should all come the next morning to the holy temple, everyone who did not have a wife, and everyone was to have a staff in his hand. Then it happened that a very old man was called Joseph; he went there with the young men and carried his staff. Then the priest took all the staffs and carried them into the Sancta Sanctorum and commanded that they should come the next morning and each should take his staff, and then a dove would fly from the top of the staff up to heaven. Then that man would have to be the guardian of the virgin.

VIII, 3   Then it happened on the morning of the next day that they all came at the time of the sacrifice, and then the bishop went into the Sancta Sanctorum, that was the Holy of all Holies, and he took the staffs

ealra, and he[g] ða genam þa gyrde and sealde heora æghwilcum his gyrd[h] onsundran. Þa[i] wæs þæra manna þreo þusenda, ac[j] ða of nan[59] þara gyrda seo culfre ne[k] eode. Ða gegyrede[l] hine Abiathar se biscop mid þare heahsacerda gegyrlan and eode into ðam[m] Sancta Sanctorum and onbærnde þa onsegednysse and his bene to Drihtne sende. Ða ætywde him Drihtnes encgel and him cwæð to:[n] 'Seo læste[o60] gyrd is gyt unseald,[p] seo þe[q] þu / for naht ne telest. Nim þa and syle, þonne cymð þæt tacen of hyre þe[r] þu þær secest.'[s61] Wæs[t] þæt Iosepes gyrd. Ða næs he na gesoht[u] forðan þe he[v] wæs eald and ytemest[w] stod. Ða clypode se biscop mid mycelre stefne hine[x] and hine cigde,[y] and he ða sona onfeng þæra gyrda of ðæs bisceopes handum.[z62] Hwæt, þær of sona fleah culfre[a] swyðe hwit and geondfleah þa heannysse[b63] þæs temples, and heo[c] ða gewat into heofonum.[d]

VIII, 4    Ða wæs þæt folc swyðe fægniende[a64] and cwædon to Iosepe:[b] 'Eadig eart ðu on þinre ylde, nu þe God swa gewurðode þæt ðu scealt beon hyrde þære clænan fæmnan'. Eac swylce þa biscopas cwædon: 'Onfoh hyre nu,[c] forðan þe þu eart ana gecoren on þinum cynne hyre to hyrde fram Gode'. He ða Ioseph cwæð mid[d] bifiendre stefne: 'Nis min gemet swilcum cilde to onfonne, forðan þe[e] ic hæbbe fela bearna and ða synd ealle yldran þonne heo'. Ða cwæð se biscop to him: 'Gemune[f65] þu hu hit gelamp be[g] Dathan, hu[h] he forwearð, and manega eac[i] þa ðe Godes willan / forhogodon'.[66] Ða cwæð he Ioseph: 'Ne forhycge[j] ic na Godes willan, ac ic hy gehealde oðþæt ic ongyte Godes willan[k] on hyre;[67] and

---

[g] he] om. f[a]    [h] heora æghwilcum his gyrd] anra gehwylcum him f[a], I    [i] þa] om. f[a], I    [j] ac] and f[a], I    [k] ne] ut ne f[a], I    [l] gegyrede] gescrydde I    [m] eode into ðam] inn eode on þa f[a], I    [n] him cwæð to] him to cwæþ f[a], I    [o] seo læste] seo seleste O, f[a], I    [p] unseald] æfter f[a], I    [q] seo þe] seo f[a]; þe I    [r] þe] þæt f[a], I    [s] secest] secgst I    [t] wæs] *preceded by* þo *in a different hand* O    [u] gesoht] *followed by* þo *in a different hand* O    [v] he] ioseph f[a], I    [w] ytemest] on utemeste I    [x] mid mycelre stefne hine] mycelre stemne hine f[a]; hine mycle stefne I    [y] hine cigde] f[a]; cydde him þæt O; hine nemnode I    [z] he ða sona onfeng þæra gyrda of ðæs bisceopes handum] him his gyrde sealde f[a], I    [a] hwæt þær of sona fleah culfre] and þa sæmninga fleah þær culfre ut f[a]; and þa on sæmningæ fleah þær culfre ut I    [b] geondfleah þa heannysse] geondfleah þa hwæmmas f[a]; fleah geond þa hwæmmes I    [c] heo] om. f[a], I    [d] into heofonum] on þone heofen f[a]; on ðone heofeñ I

VIII, 4    [a] swyðe fægniende] fægniende and swyðe bliðe O; swyðe gefeonde] f[a], I    [b] to iosepe] ioseph f[a]    [c] nu] nu ioseph f[a], I    [d] mid] om. f[a], I    [e] þe] om. f[a]    [f] gemune] gemun f[a], I    [g] hit gelamp be] gelamp f[a]; lamp I    [h] hu] om. f[a], I    [i] eac] eac mid him f[a], I    [j] forhycge] forhoge I    [k] ac ic hy gehealde oðþæt ic ongyte Godes willan] om. I; *first* ic om. f[a]

there and gave each one his staff separately. There were three thousand men, but the dove did not come from any of the staffs. Then Abiathar the bishop put on the dress of the high-priests and went into the Sancta Sanctorum and burnt the sacrifice and uttered his prayer to the Lord. Then the angel of the Lord appeared to him and said to him: 'The smallest staff is still not given, the one you reckon as nothing. Take it and give it, then the sign which you are seeking there will come.' That was Joseph's staff. He had not been looked for because he was old and stood farthest off. Then the bishop called him in a loud voice and named him and he immediately received the staff from the bishop's hands. Behold, immediately a very white dove flew from it and flew through the highest part of the temple, and then she departed into the heavens.

VIII, 4   Then the people were very glad and said to Joseph: 'Blessed are you in your old age, now that God has so honoured you that you are to be the guardian of the pure virgin'. Likewise the bishops said: 'Receive her now, because you alone are chosen by God from your tribe to be her guardian'. Then Joseph said in a trembling voice: 'It is not for me to receive such a child, because I have many children and they are all older than she is'. Then the bishop said to him: 'Remember what happened to Dathan, how he perished, and many also who rejected God's will'. Then Joseph said: 'I do not reject God's will, but I will take care of her until I understand God's will concerning her; and God will then make known

God þonne gecyþeð hwilc iungra manna on minum cynne hyre wurðe bið.[68] Ac syle þam clænan fæmnan fultum þæt heo wunigen mid hig oðþæt ælice yldo.'[169] Ða cwæð se biscop: 'Fæmnan beoð hyre[m] on fultume oð þæne dæg eowra gemænunga,[n70] and ne mæg hig nan oðer onfon'.[o]

VIII, 5    Ða onfeng Ioseph Marian[a71] mid oðrum fif[b] fæmnum þe hyre wæron on fultume geseald to Iosepes hame. Ða wæron þus gehatene, ærest[c] Becca, Sephira, Susanna, Abugea and Sehel,[d] and se biscop sealde heom eallum godweb to wefanne of seolce and of mislicum hiwum wahrift to þam temple.[72] Ða onfeng Maria hwit godweb[e73] to wefanne and ða oðre mislices hiwes. Ða spræcon hi heom betwynan on gleo and ðus cwædon: 'Þu eart ure gingast, þe[f] miht wefan þæt hwite godeweb, and ðu miht beon ure cwen'. Ða þa hi[g] þas word spræcon,[h74] ða ætywde heom Drihtnes encgel and cwæð: 'Ne sceal eower word beon on[i] idelnyssa, ac hit sceal beon mid soðe[j] / gecyþed, forðan þe[k] witegan geare[l] sædon þæt heo scolde beon middaneardes cwen'.[75] Ða wæron hi ealle swiðe forhte[m] for ðæs engles gesihðe and his worde and ongunnon[n] hi wurþian and hyre eadmodlice hyran.[76]

IX    Þa gelamp hit sume dæge þæt heo stod be sumere wyllan. Þa ætywde hire þær[a] Drihtnes encgel and cwæð hyre to:[b] 'Eadig þu eart,[c] Maria, forðan[d] on þinum mode þu gearwodest[e77] Drihtnes eardunghus, and leoht cymð of heofonum on ðe and þæt lihteð ofer ealne middaneard'. Ða eft þæs[f] þriddan dæges Drihtnes heahencgel[g] hyre ætywde mid unasecgendlicre[h] beorhtnysse, and heo[i] ða wæs swyðe afyrht and abreged for ðæs engles gesihðe. Ða cwæð he[j] to hyre: 'Ne þearftu[k] ðe ondrædan,

---

[l] ac syle þam clænan fæmnan fultum þæt heo wunigen mid hig oðþæt ælice yldo] ac ic onfo þære clænan fæmnan þæt heo wunige mid me oððæt heo hæbbe ælite [sic] ylde f[a]; ac ic onfo þare clænen femnæn þæt heo wunie mid me oððet heo hæbbe ælycre ylde I    [m] hyre] mid hire f[a], I    [n] eowra gemænunga] incra gemunga f[a]; incra geamungæ I    [o] nan oðer onfon] nænig oþer wer onfon f[a]; nan oðer wer underfon I

VIII, 5    [a] Marian] f[a]; mariam I; hi O    [b] oðrum fif] f[a], I; oðrum O    [c] þus gehatene ærest] hatene þus ærest f[a]; ihatene ærest þus I    [d] and Sehel] ansehel f[a]    [e] hwit godweb] hwites godeswebbes f[a]; hwite godewebbes I    [f] þe] þu f[a], I    [g] ða þa hi] ða hig f[a]; ða I    [h] spræcon] f[a], I; spræcon on gleo O    [i] on] *om.* f[a]    [j] beon mid soðe] mit soðe beon I    [k] þe] *om.* f[a]    [l] geare] geo geara f[a]    [m] forhte] afyrhte I    [n] ongunnon] heo ongunnon I    IX    [a] hire þær] f[a], I; þær O    [b] cwæð hyre to] hire to cwæð f[a], I    [c] þu eart] eart þu f[a], I    [d] forðan] forðan ðe I    [e] gearwodest] gearcost I    [f] Ða eft þæs] ant eft þæs þy f[a]; and eft þæs on I    [g] heahencgel] engel f[a], I    [h] unasecgendlicre] secgendlicere f[a], I    [i] heo] he I    [j] he] f[a], I; se encgel O    [k] þearftu] þearft þu f[a], I

184

which of the young men of my tribe is worthy of her. But give support to the pure virgin that they may live with her until the legal age.' Then the bishop said: 'Virgins will be a support for her until the day of your marriage, and no one else can receive her'.

VIII, 5    Then Joseph received Mary with five other virgins who were given as a help to her in Joseph's home. They were called as follows – Becca first, Sephira, Susanna, Abugea and Sehel – and the bishop gave them all fine cloth of silk and of various kinds to weave a curtain for the temple. Then Mary received fine white cloth to weave and the others [received] various kinds. Then they talked amongst themselves in sport and said as follows: 'You, who can weave the fine white cloth, are the youngest of us, and you can be our queen'. When they spoke these words, then the angel of the Lord appeared to them and said: 'Your words are destined not to be in vain, but they shall be truly uttered because prophets said long ago that she should be queen of middle earth'. Then they were all very frightened because of the sight of the angel and his words and they began to honour her and to obey her humbly.

IX    Then it happened that one day she stood next to a certain well. Then the angel of the Lord appeared to her there and said to her: 'Blessed are you, Mary, because you have prepared the Lord's dwelling in your mind, and a light will come from heaven over you and that will give light throughout all middle-earth'. Then again on the third day the archangel of the Lord appeared to her with indescribable brightness, and she was very frightened then and terrified by the sight of the angel. Then he said to her: 'You need not be afraid, Mary. The grace of the Lord is

Maria. Drihtnes gifu is mid þe. Þu scealt acennan cyning se ah anweald heofonas and eorðan and his rice[l] ne bið nan ende.'

X, 1    On þa tid þe þis gelamp wæs Iosep on þam lande, þe Cafarnaum hatte, ymbe his cræft. He wæs smið and mænigteawa wyrhta. Ða þa[a] he þanon gecyrde to his agenum hame þa gemette he hi bearn hæbbende on hire / gehrife. Ða wæs he sona swyðe forht[b] and sorhfull[c] and ðus cwæð: 'Drihten, Drihten min, onfoh minum gaste; me is dead selre þonne lif'. Ða cwædon[d] þa fæmnan him to,[e] þe mid hyre wæron,[f] þæt hi geare wiston þæt hyre nan wer[g] ne onhran, ac heo wære onwelges[h78] mægðhades and unwemme: 'And we witon þæt heo wæs dæges and nihtes on halgum gebedum wuniende[i] and Godes encgel wið hyre[j] spræc and heo dæghwamlice of ðæs engles handum mete þigde. Hu mæg þæt gewurðan, þæt þæt sy swa,[k] forðan þe[l] we witon þæt hit man ne dyde ac Godes encgel?'

X, 2    Ða cwæð he[a] Ioseph: 'Nis[b] þæt na swa, nat ic, þeah heo beo beswicen þurh þæs engles hiw'. And he ða weop biterlice and ðus cwæð: 'Mid hwylcre byldu mæg ic æfre gan to[c] Godes temple oððe hu mæg ic geseon þa ansyne þara sacerda for sceame?' Ða þa[d] he þus cwæð þa þohte he digollice þæt he wolde hy forlæton and faran[e] him on oðer land.

XI    Ða on þære ilcan nihte, þe he þis þohte, / þa[a] ætywde him Godes encgel on slæpe and cwæð to him:[b] 'Ioseph, ne þearft þu ðe ondrædan.[c] Þu eart Dauides cynnes. Onfoh þinne gemæccan; hyre geeacnung is of ðam Halgan Gaste and heo cenneð[d] sunu and ðæs[e] nama is Hælend, forðam þe he gedeð hal his folc fram heora synnum.' He þa Ioseph aras of ðam slæpe swyðe gefeonde[f79] and Gode þancode and Marian sæde and þam fæmnum, þe mid hyre wæron, þa fægran gesyhðe þæs engles and ða frofre þara worda and ðus cwæþ: 'Ic singode mid gemynde þæs[g] facnes[80] þær nan næs'.[h]

---

[l] rice] rices f[a], I
X, 1    [a] þa] *om.* f[a], I    [b] forht] afurht I    [c] sorhfull] f[a], I; sorhfull on his mode O
[d] cwædon] sædon him f[a], I    [e] him to] *om.* f[a], I    [f] wæron] wæron þæt hi wæron
f[a]    [g] nan wer] nænig `wer´ f[a]    [h] onwelges] onweales f[a]; andwealdes I    [i] wuniende] *om.* f[a], I    [j] wið hyre] hyre wið f[a]    [k] sy swa] swa sy f[a]; swa beo I    [l] þe] *om.* f[a]
X, 2    [a] he] *om.* I    [b] nis] nis na I    [c] to] into I    [d] þa] *om.* f[a], I    [e] faran] gewitan f[a]
XI    [a] þa] *om.* I    [b] cwæð to him] him to cwæð f[a], I    [c] ne þearft þu ðe ondrædan] ne
ondræd þu þe f[a]    [d] cenneð] acennð I    [e] ðæs] his I    [f] gefeonde] I; f[a] *breaks off with* ge-;
gefeonde and swyðe bliðe O    [g] mid gemynde þæs] I; and gemunde þe O    [h] nan næs] I;
nanes O

with you. You shall give birth to the king who has power over heaven and earth and his kingdom will have no end.'

X, 1   At the time when this happened Joseph was in the country which is called Capharnaum, at his trade. He was a carpenter and a skilful worker. When he returned to his own home from there he found her with a child in her womb. Then he was immediately very frightened and sorrowful and spoke as follows: 'Lord, my Lord, receive my spirit; death is preferable to me than life'. Then the virgins who were with her said to him that they knew well that no man had touched her, but that she was of perfect and unblemished virginity. 'And we know that she persevered day and night at holy prayers and God's angel spoke with her and she received food daily from the hands of the angel. How can that happen, that it should be so, for we know that a man did not do it but the angel of God?'

X, 2   Then Joseph said: 'It is not so, I know, though she may be deceived by the appearance of an angel'. And then he wept bitterly and spoke as follows: 'How can I be so bold ever to go into the temple of God or how can I look at the faces of the priests for shame?' While he spoke like this he secretly thought that he would abandon her and go to another country.

XI   Then, on the same night that he was thinking this, an angel of the Lord appeared to him in his sleep and said to him: 'Joseph, you need not be afraid. You are of the family of David. Take your wife; she is pregnant by the Holy Spirit and she will give birth to a son for you and his name is Saviour, because he will save his people from their sins.' Then Joseph arose from his sleep rejoicing very much and he thanked God and told Mary and the virgins who were with her about the joyful vision of the angel and the consolation of his words and spoke thus: 'I sinned with the thought of a fault where there was none'.

The Old English Gospel of Pseudo-Matthew

XII, 1  Ða wearð æfter þisum mycel hlysa on þam folce þæt Maria
wæs geeacnod.[a] Ða sume dæge namon hine þa þegnas þæs temples and
læddon hine to ðam biscope and to þam heahsacerdum and cwædon to
him: 'To hwan forhæle ðu us þine gemænunge[b] swa clænre fæmnan, þe
Godes englas hy[c] feddan swa swa culfran on þam temple, and heo næfre
nolde[d] were[e] æthrinan,[f] ac heo wæs on Godes æ seo getydeste fæmne?
And gyf ðu nedinga hyre[g] on ne sohtest þonne wære heo clæne.' He ða
Iosep hine ladode / and cwæð þæt he hyre næfre ne æthrine.[h]

XII, 2–4  Hwæt,[a] þa biscopas[b] and ða heahsacerdas, on unarimdum
tacenum[c81] godcundre geryna be ðære ealdan æ, acunnodan soðlice þæt
hio wæren butu clæne fram eallum þam synnum þe þæt folc hi
oncuðe.

XII, 5  Hi ða ealle eadmodlice bædon hyre mildse[a] and heora
wohnyssa forgyfennysse, þæs þe hi þæs unrihtes hy oncuðan,[82] and hi[b]
and eall þæt folc and ða sacerdas læddon hi mid þam fæmnum to Iosepes
hame mid micclum gefean, and mid mycelre blisse clypodon and ðus
cwædon: 'Sy[c] Drihtnes nama gebletsod on worulda woruld, se ðe cuðlice
gecydde þine halignyssa on eallum Israhela[d] folce'.

Wæs seo halige fæmne, swa we ær cwædon,[e] of Iesses wyrtruman and
of Dauides cynne, and heo wæs[f] Drihtnes modor, ures Hælendes, and
heo is[g] hordfæt þæs Halgan Gastes and heo is cwen þæs heofonlican
cyninges[83] gecweden[h] and heo is engla hiht and ealra manna frofor and
fultum,[i] forðan þe ealles middaneardes hælo þurh hi becom on þas
woruld. And forðan hi nu englas[j] eadigað[84] / and ealle þeoda and ealle
cneorissa, gehwylc mancynnes geleafulra. And mid þisra bletsunga and
herenyssa[k] heo becom beforan þæt þrymsetl þæs heofonlican deman and[l]
beforan gesyhðe ealra haligra, þær heo nu dæghwamlice þingað for eall
þis mennisce cynn. Ac uton we nu hi[m] eadmodlice biddan þæt heo us

XII, 1  [a] wæs geeacnod] ieacnod wæs I  [b] gemænunge] gemungæ I  [c] hy] om. I
[d] næfre nolde] nolde næfre I  [e] were] followed by erasure of two letters O  [f] æthrinan]
arinæn I  [g] nedinga hyre] hire nydes I  [h] æthrine] arine I
XII, 2–4  [a] hwæt] om. I  [b] biscopas] biscopas þa I  [c] unarimdum tacenum]
unarimdum O, I
XII, 5  [a] mildse] bletsunge I  [b] hi þæs unrihtes hy oncuðan and hi] hi þæs unrihtes hy
acuðan and hi O; heo yfele wilnunge bi heom hæfdon I  [c] sy] beo I  [d] israhela]
israele I  [e] cwædon] sædon I  [f] wæs] wæs `and is´ O  [g] is] wæs I  [h] gecweden]
om. I  [i] frofor and fultum] om. I  [j] hi nu englas] englæs hire nu I  [k] herenyssa]
herunge I  [l] beforan . . . and] om. I  [m] nu hi] hire nu I

188

XII, 1    Then after this there was a great rumour among the people that Mary was pregnant. Then one day the servants of the temple took him and led him to the bishop and to the high-priests and said to him: 'Why did you conceal from us your union with such a pure virgin, whom God's angels fed like a dove in the temple, and who never wished to touch a man, but was the most skilled virgin in God's law? And if you had not attacked her by force then she would be pure.' Then Joseph defended himself and said that he had never touched her.

XII, 2–4    Behold, the bishops and the high-priests, by means of countless signs of the divine mysteries according to the old law, proved truly that they were both innocent of all the sins of which the people accused them.

XII, 5    Then they all humbly begged them for mercy and for forgiveness for their errors, for that of which they had wrongly accused them, and they and all the people and the priests led them, with the virgins, to Joseph's home with great joy, and with great bliss called out and said as follows: 'May the Lord's name be blessed forever, he who openly made known your holiness to all the people of Israel'.

The holy Virgin, as we said already, was from the root of Jesse and from the people of David, and she was the mother of the Lord, our Saviour, and she is the treasury of the Holy Spirit and she is called the queen of the heavenly king and she is the joy of angels and the consolation and help of all people, because through her the salvation of all middle-earth came into the world. And therefore angels call her blessed, as do all peoples and all generations, every one of the faithful of mankind. And with this blessing and praise she came before the throne of the heavenly judge and in sight of all of the saints, where she now daily intercedes for all this human race. But let us now humbly entreat her that she be a merciful

si[n] milde mundbora and bliðe þingere[o] to ðam heofonlican mægn-
þrymme. Nu we geare witan þæt heo mæg æt hire þam deoran sunu
biddan, swa hwæt swa heo wile, and[p] beon ðingere to urum Drihtne
þæt he us forgyfe[q] gesibsum lif[r] and ece eadignysse a butan ende. God
us to ðam gefultumige![s] Amen.

[n] si] beo I    [o] þingere] þingestre I    [p] and] I, *om.* O    [q] forgyfe] gife I    [r] lif] lif `for
hire bene´ O    [s] gefultumige] fylste I

protector for us and a gracious intercessor with the heavenly majesty. Now we know well that she can ask her dear son for whatever she wishes and be a intercessor to our Lord that he may give us a peaceful life and eternal blessedness without end. May God help us to [attain] that! Amen.

# Glosses to the Old English *Gospel of Pseudo-Matthew*

Hatton 114

fol. 201v
De natiuitate Sanctae Mariae apocrifum

weorþian] ueneremur; *illegible gloss*
hlæfdige] domina

201v
scypliðendum] nauigantibus
wearð] fuit
siðfæt] uia; uia
scuan] specu
yðum] undas
a] semper
fruman] originem
gebyrde] natiuitatem
þæs] cuius
heorda] pastor
gymene] curam
eowde] communam; oues
gode] deo

202r
gode] deo
hirede] familie; seruientibus
micclode] augebat
Ðas þing he ongan don] ista incepit
　facere

onsegednysse] sacrificium; sacrificium

202v
þæs] cuius
alyfed] licitum
onsegednysse] incensum; sacrificium
þæs] hoc
gewat] exiit
hweorfan] reuertere; turnen
fæce] spacium
gegearwie] preparo

203r
cauertune] cleoue; atrio; atrium
gebed] orationem
spearwan] passerum
byrðor] fetum
gefeoð] gaudent
ane] solam
atyndest] *illegible gloss*; exclusisti
gesinscipes] guweþe
gehet] uoui
geþeahte] consilio
fram] of

203v
gesihðe] uisione
gelaþode] conuocauit

192

þinene] ancillam; ancillam
ungeþwærlice] inconuenianter;
  peruerse; contrariando
gename] abstulit; abstulit
beluce] clausit; clausit
gehweorfan] reuertere
gemæccan] coniugem
geæswicod] *illegible gloss*; scandalizatus
gyfe] dona

204r
geeacnod] concepit; concepta
ana] sola
geeacnode] prengnans
geseted] dicta; constituta
wurþode] honorauit
efenþeowa] conseruus
wit] nos
fram] ab

204v
tihhie] disponis
onsægednysse] sacrificium; incensum
gedyrstig] audax
onsægednysse] sacrificium
ongeate] percepi
stence] incensum
to þam] so
ansyn] faciem
intingan] causam; causam
trymedon] edificabant

205r
gehwyrfde] reuerteret
þreodode] deliberauit
færinga] subito
gewit] perge
orsorh] securus
ingcer] uestra
gyt] uos

ingc] uobis
beorðre] onere; onere
ricene] cito; cito; mox; mox
gegan] igon
to ðam] so
feor] veor; longe
for] in
gecigde] notum fecit

205v
mægðe] kun; parentes
hlisan] famam
geeacnunge] conceptionis
ða] illa
gemanan] communitate;
  communitate
fæmnena] sanctimonialium
stæpas] gradus
on gange] ambulando; in gressu
worde] uerba
gebærum] gestu

206r
gebære] gestu
þa] tunc propfeticum anne;
  propfeticum anne
arisan] insurrexerunt
ontynon] aperire
mundbyrdum] protector
tuddor] peritus
mægna] uirtute
heanyssum] sullimi; summa

206v
onbirigde] accepit; sumsit; percepit
getyddre] perita
gestæðþig] grauis

207r
gebæran] gestu

tælan] contumeliam
teonan] contumelia
hi] eam
gesealde] daret

207v
gemæccan] coniugem
styrde] castigauit
anrædlice] instanter; mox
gewurð] absit
mægðe] tribu; tribu
arleaslice] impie; impie
hluttre] purum
onsegednysse] sacrificium
lichaman] corporis
alæded] ductus
geþeahtodon] consilium inierunt

208r
gehyrað] audite
ge] uos
witon] scitis
ælicre] legalia
ælicum] legalia
gyftum] nupciis; nubciis
endebyrdnysse] ordine
gemeted] iþuht
niwe] riht
endebyrdnysse] ordinem
uton secan þa andsware to gode]
    queramus responsa a deo
wæ'e're] uiro
gelicode] placuit; placuit
hlota] sortem
cyn] tribu; tribu
þonon] inde

208v
ðonne] tunc
foreweardre] summitate; summitate;
    summitate

onsægednysse] incensi
gegyrede] uestiuit
onbærnde] accendit; *illegible gloss*
onsegednysse] incensum
seleste] melior; melior; *illegible gloss*
unseald] non datur

209r
syle] da
fram] of; a
þa] qui

209v
forhycge] sperno
ælice] legal'
gemænunga] communione
ða] que
wahrift] uelum; uelum

210r
forhte] pauidi
gearwodest] preparasti
lihteð] illuminat
abreged] terita
þa] illa
bearnhæbbende] pregnantem

210v
sorhfull] tristis
geare] certe; certe
onwelges] ditata
hiw] specie
byldu] audacitate
ansyne] faciem

211r
ioseph ne þearft þu ðe ondrædan]
    Ioseps noli timere
onfoh] accipe
ðæs] illius
gedeð] fac

hal] saluum
fram] of
gefeonde] gaudens
gemunde] mem
facnes] dolum; dolum; fraudem
þær] ubi
nanes] non fuit
hlysa] opinio; fama
gemænunge] commnam
getydeste] peritissima
nedinga] ui
ladode] purgauit; excu. . .

211v
acunnodan] probauerunt; probauerunt
wæren] fuerunt; fuerunt
butu] ii ambe
hi] eam

212r
cneorissa] diligencia; studia; diligencia
herenysse] laude
si] sit
mundbora] protexorix
geare] *illegible*; bene

# Commentary on the Old English
## *Gospel of Pseudo-Matthew*

[1] The apocryphon is supplied with a homiletic introduction to make it suitable reading for the feast of the nativity of Mary on 8 September. Only f[a] marks the date of the feast, the sixth ides of September (8 September), but in O the text comes in a series of homilies for saints' days from 12 March to 1 November and in I in a series from St Laurence on 10 August to Martin on 11 November. The O version further highlights the text's function as a reading on 8 September by adding *on þissum dæge* in ch. IV, where Mary's birth is described.

[2] I replaces *cennystre* with *godes kenninge*. The word *kenninge* means 'a birth' or 'mother' and is attested in the latter meaning here and in the D assumption text.

[3] The word *sæsteorra* is a calque on the Latin *stella maris*, a title given to Mary in the belief that it expressed the Hebrew etymology of her Hebrew name, Miriam. This text is the only witness to the word in Old English and it does not occur again until the *Orrmulum* and the Trinity Homilies.

[4] I's reading *þeo sæsteorra*, with both article and the first element *sæ-*, appears preferable to O's *se steorra* or f[a]'s *sæsteorra* since a particular star is intended.

[5] f[a]'s reading *se rihtes þæt* appears to have arisen as a misreading of *se rihte siðfæt*, with the initial *s* of *siðfæt* becoming attached to the adjective and *f* perhaps being read as *þ*. An intended, but imperfectly executed, substitution of *þæð* for *siðfæt* is unlikely in view of the form of the adjective.

[6] I's '*Þeonne magen we nu hwylcen seogum wordum sæcgæn*' is clearly corrupt and Assmann, ed., *Angelsächsische Homilien und Heiligenleben*, p. 260, n. 1, suggests that *seogum* is 'vielleicht verderbt aus *feawum*'. Palaeographically, this seems plausible and there are parallels within the homiletic tradition, for example, the beginning of Belfour 6: 'Men þa leofeste we wyllæð her specan feawum wordum . . .' (*Twelfth Century Homilies in MS Bodley 343. Part I, Text and Translation*, ed. A. O. Belfour, EETS, os 137 (London, 1909)).

O's *and acenned* is probably not original. The subject *seo* refers back to *ðære gebyrde* and not to Mary, and *acenned* therefore does not fit the sense of the

196

passage, nor is it in the other two manuscripts. There is, however, a similar sort of mistake in I, which reads *hu heo iboren wæs*.

[7] I's reading *leorniæð*, meaning 'read', may be a non-West Saxon sense of the word and it is included in Vleeskruyer's list of dialect vocabulary in the life of Chad (*The Life of St Chad*, p. 31). See also Klaeber, 'Zur altenglischen Bedaübersetzung', pp. 267–8.

[8] *Pseudo-Matthew* does not give the birthplaces of Joachim and Anna and the information given here in O and f[a] is probably derived from the *De natiuitate Mariae*, which states: 'Domus paterna ex Galilae et ciuitate Nazareth, maternum autem genus ex Bethleem erat'. This information is not among the variants in Gijsel's edition of *Pseudo-Matthew* and was probably inserted by a scribal editor, as O and f[a] are related at this point of the text and I's text conforms to the Latin source.

[9] I's reading *nymðe*, 'except', an Anglian word, was probably not even understood by the scribe, to judge from the way it is written.

[10] I replaces *þeowodon* with *seruedæn*; the form *seruedon* appears in the homily on the temptation of Christ in the same manuscript (Irvine, ed., *Old English Homilies*, p. 145, n. 151). The verb *seruian* does not appear elsewhere in Old English, but is used in twelfth-century texts.

[11] See note 8 for a discussion of Anna's birthplace.

[12] I inserts *lac* before *onsægednesse* to read *heora lac onsægednysse*; that the scribe felt this type of gloss necessary suggests that the word was already passing out of use, even though it is faithfully copied for the rest of the text.

[13] O's reading is closer to the Latin's 'Quae dum fleret in oratione sua et diceret' than is that of the other two manuscripts, which state at this point that Anna bewailed her husband.

[14] The first part of Anna's speech is a question in the Latin, but the Old English makes it into a declaration. The Latin then reads 'nescio ubi mortuus sit ut uel sepulturam illi fecissem' [I do not know where he may be dead so that perhaps I should have made a burial for him], which, with its pluperfect subjunctive, seems closer to the past tense of f[a]'s 'þonne ne gegearwode ic him byrgenne' than the reading of O. O's 'þonne ne gegearwie', with its subjunctive present tense, presumably means 'then I may not prepare a burial for him', which, while it makes sense, is significantly different to the source. I's reading, 'þonne gearwode ic him byrigenne', is like f[a]'s, apart from the omission of the negative particle.

[15] This first occurrence of *gebed* is the only one to be replaced by *bone*, a twelfth-century variant of *ben*, prayer, in I.

[16] This curious and unexpected gratitude for her childlessness is part of the P version's revision of *Pseudo-Matthew*, which is concerned not to cast any doubts on the piety of the principal characters.

[17] The Latin reads *noli timere* here. O has *ne* and *ondrædan* written normally and *ðearft ðu þe* written over an erasure in a smaller script, and the other two manuscripts read *nylt þu ðe ondredan*. It is tempting to emend O to agree with the other manuscripts, even though their syntax is faulty, as they both have an indicative rather than imperative form, and would have to be emended to read *Nelle ðu* in order to translate the Latin correctly. The phrase *noli timere* appears twice more in the Latin, both times translated *ne ðearft þu þe ondrædan* in all three manuscripts (though f[a] substitutes *ne ondræd þu* for the last occurrence, in the angel's speech to Joseph). Rather, therefore, than emend the form offered by I and f[a] and incorporate it in the critical text, I have chosen to let the O reading stand, as it agrees with the translator's practice in the remainder of the text and is correct grammatically. The erasure in O makes this procedure somewhat problematical, of course, as it is tempting to suppose that the *-lt* or *-lle* of *nelt* or *nelle* was erased (and *-lt* or *-lle ðu þe* would fit the space in the script of the original hand), but there is, naturally, no proof of this.

[18] All of the Old English manuscripts agree on this reading, but the Latin reads 'in consilio dei est germen tuum', with no variants which could throw light on the Old English. Perhaps the translator felt that Anna's suffering was a more dignified object for God's plan than her pregnancy.

[19] The Latin reads *post haec* and the definition of time in the Old English is not paralleled, but it is self-evident from the narrative. O's reading here is undoubtedly correct; the alteration of *þæs* to *wæs* in I and in f[a] probably originated in a mistaken reading of *wyn* for thorn and *geworden* was presumably then added in an attempt to make sense.

[20] The rare agreement of O and f[a] in this part of the text would seem to guarantee the originality of this reading as against I's 'noldest me to foren cuman'. The Latin reads 'tu nec ingredi ad me uoluisti', which, while not mentioning consolation, implies it, as Anna is berating her maid-servant for leaving her alone in her distress.

[21] The Latin reads here: 'Et haec audiens Anna emittens uocem cum clamoribus flebat'. Although all three manuscripts agree on *ane* (f[a] *ana*; I *anæ*), the word does not really make satisfactory sense in the context and it is preferable to follow the source and to emend to *Anna*. The resulting construction *heo Anna*, pronoun followed by a proper name, is one which is common elsewhere in the text and the omission of an *-n-* at an early stage of transmission is not difficult to explain.

[22] O's *on þære ylcan tide* is closer to the Latin (*in ipso autem tempore*) than I and f[a]'s *on ðære ylcan nihte*, which latter reading has the added disadvantage of not being true to the morning setting of the preceding scene.

[23] Assmann emends the reading *þeowa* to *þeow*, but I have retained the manu-

script reading as it could be the accusative of the weak noun *þeowa* with loss of final nasal. Loss of final nasals is perhaps indicative of northern influence, though it is also found even in early West Saxon texts.

[24] The Latin reads 'Ego non essem ausus offerre holocaustum deo nisi tua iussio daret mihi pontificium offerendi'. All three Old English manuscripts read *næs* where one would have expected a subjunctive corresponding to *essem*.

[25] The Latin reads: 'Nec ego te ad offerendum inuitarem nisi uoluntatem domini cognouissem', rendered originally in O as 'Na ic ðe ne hete Gode sacerdlice onsægednysse bringan forðam gyf ic Godes willan to þan on þe ne ongeate'. The meaning of the second part of this is reversed in f[a] and in I, which read 'Na ic þe ne hete [I: hate] Gode sacerdlice onsægednysse bringan forþam þe ic Godes willan to þam ne ongeate'. The original reading in O corresponds to the Latin and has been retained in the edited text (apart from the word *forðam*) but it evidently puzzled either the scribe or a later reader, as *na* and the second *e* of *hete* have been erased, giving a reading which means 'I did not command you' rather than 'I would not have commanded you'. The manuscript punctuation and Assmann's edition have a point before *forðam* suggesting that it refers forward, but there is no plausible referent for it as an adverb and as a conjunction it does not give satisfactory sense in the context. Given the odd placing of *forðam* in the sentence, it is possible that it was inserted as a sort of gloss in the archetype of all the manuscripts as an alternative to *gyf* by someone unable to make sense of the sentence and that this intrusive *forðam* (augmented by *þe*) was copied by f[a] and I instead of *gyf*, whereas O mistakenly kept both *forðam* and *gyf*. The correction of *hete* to *het* in O was probably influenced by the presence of *forðam* in this manuscript. There is nothing in the Latin to correspond to *forðam*, which is another argument for its having been an addition at a later stage. The previous sentence is similar in structure, the Latin 'Ego non essem ausus offerre holocaustum deo nisi tua iussio daret mihi pontificium offerendi', being rendered by 'Næs ic na gedyrstig þæt ic Gode sacerdlice onsægednysse brohte, þær [gyf f[a], I] þu me ne hete', with the *nisi* translated correctly as *þær* or *gyf*, without *forðam*. I am most grateful to Dr Bruce Mitchell for advising me on this point.

[26] *swilce he dead wære* seems to be an independent addition in the Old English, as it is not in any of Gijsel's manuscripts.

[27] *and smeade* seems to be an independent addition in O, as it is not in the other two manuscripts, nor is it paralleled in the Latin, which reads *in suo animo discuteret*. It is possible that the scribe felt the need to supplement the relatively unusual word *þreodode*.

[28] There are problems with this sentence in the Old English. The *is* in O seems to have been inserted later and is contrary to sense, to the Latin source and to the evidence of the other two manuscripts and of O itself as first written. But

this is not the only difficulty, as comparison with the source shows. The Latin reads: 'quia misericordiae quas fecisti tu et uxor tua, in conspectu altissimi recitatae sunt'. An Old English text corresponding to the Latin would lack the repetition of *beforan Godes (Drihtenes) gesihðe* and would have no *ingcer nama* and would therefore read: 'and ingcer mildheortnyss þe gyt worhten was geraedd beforan Godes gesihðe on his þrymsetle . . .'. The idea of Joachim and Anna's names, as well as their good deeds, being read before the Lord is, however, the sort of minor addition to the Latin that one finds elsewhere in the Old English text and, as it is found in all the manuscripts, is probably original: the translator presumably wanted to make plain that the merciful deeds were attributed correctly to Joachim and Anna.

The repetition of *beforan Godes gesihðe* is more difficult to account for. It is just possible that the Latin source used by the translator had inadvertently repeated *in conspectu altissimi* and that the translator had then connected one instance of it with *fecisti* and the other with *recitatae*. Alternatively, and perhaps more likely, the repetition of *beforan Godes (Drihtenes) gesihðe* in O and in f[a] was due to corruption in the Old English archetype, with the translator or a later scribe inadvertently repeating the phrase. The phrase is not repeated in I, whose reading 'and eower mildheortnysse þe ge wrohton and eower nomæ was iræded beforæn Drihtnes isihðe on his ðreomsettle' is the most satisfactory of all three manuscripts. Since O and f[a] agree, as against the usual agreement of I and f[a] in this part of the text, however, it is difficult to account for their agreement except by supposing that the Old English archetype had this repetition and that it was corrected by scribal intervention in I. Both the I scribe and the O scribe had difficulty with the sentence, as the emendation in I and the addition of *is* in O testify. I have chosen to follow I in the edited text as it is closest to the Latin and, even though it is probably a scribe's conjecture, it at least has the authority of one Old English manuscript.

[29] The Old English here changes the sense of the Latin, in which Joachim's servants urge him to journey home slowly, grazing his sheep on the way. Presumably, obedience to the angel's command required a swift return for the translator.

[30] The speech of the angel ('Uade ad portam quae uocatur aurea . . .'), which was to give rise to one of the most popular scenes in medieval art, is here given only in indirect speech, with all mention of the famous Golden Gate omitted. The scene is first depicted in English art in the Winchester Psalter, London, British Library, Cotton Nero C. iv, from the mid-twelfth century (see F. Wormald, *The Winchester Psalter* (London, 1973), pl. 11). This psalter contains a picture-cycle obviously drawn from the *Gospel of Pseudo-Matthew*, depicting the refused offerings of Joachim, the Annunciation to Joachim and then to Anna, the meeting at the Golden Gate, the nativity of Mary and her

presentation at the temple. The artist appears not to have had a visual source for the Golden Gate scene, which is modelled on a scene with Christ and his parents, and seems to have been recycling motifs from the Winchester Infancy cycle (see K. E. Haney, *The Winchester Psalter: an Iconographic Study* (Leicester, 1986), p. 36, p. 92 and pl. 7).

O has mistakenly substituted *gecigde* for *gecydde* here and the reading has been emended to accord with that of the other two manuscripts.

31  I replaces O's Old English *hyrede* with the Middle English *hinene*, the only occurrence of this word in the *MCOE*, although the Old English word is allowed to stand in I, 1. I have been unable to find a satisfactory explanation for f$^a$'s *hærenne*.

32  O's *mægðe* is not the usual nominative form (*mægð*), but the oblique ending -*e* is sometimes extended to the nominative of feminine nouns (see Scragg, ed., *The Vercelli Homilies*, p. lxiii). The O scribe seems to have been replacing *magas* with *mægðe* (see note 48: the corresponding Latin word is *affinibus/affines* respectively). Anna's prayer of thanks in the Latin is omitted, as is the description of her hanging upon Joachim's neck.

33  'Hwæt, þa æfter þan wæron gefylde nigan monað hire geeacnunge' is not an independent addition of the O scribe, even though it is missing in the other two manuscripts, as it corresponds to the Latin 'Post haec autem expletis mensibus nouem'. Its omission from I and f$^a$ is presumably due to homoeoteleuton, the eye of the scribe of the common original of these two manuscripts having skipped from one occurrence of *geeacnunge* to the next.

34  O's *on þissum dæge* is not paralleled in the Latin or in the other two manuscripts and is therefore probably an independent addition introduced at some stage in the transmission of the text, presumably in order to increase its suitability as a homily for the feast of the nativity of Mary. It is not, therefore, included in the critical text.

35  *templ* is consistently neuter throughout the text, so O's *to ðære* is clearly an error, although, if the text is Anglian, gender confusion can be expected.

36  I and f$^a$'s *ne heo na ne taltrade* is probably an independent addition in the common original of these two manuscripts, as it is not in O or in the Latin source.

37  O's 'ne æfter hyre yldrum ne murnde' is roughly synonymous with I's 'ne æfter hire ealdre ne rymde' ( *hriman* means 'to lament', 'cry out'). f$^a$'s reading *myrde* can be explained as a corruption of either of these readings: as a corruption of *murnde*, with loss of *n*, or as a case of metathesis of *r* and *m* from I's *rymde*. As f$^a$ normally retains initial *h*, however, and should read *\*hmyrde* if derived from the reading which gave rise to that in I, it is more likely to have come from the O reading.

38  There is a departure here from the Latin sections as the Old English

anticipates what in the Latin is related after Anna's prophecy. The description of Mary's perfection and of her similarity to a thirty-year-old comes after Anna's prophecy in the Latin, rather than before, as here. It is possible that the translator inadvertently skipped a chapter of the Latin and then, realizing the mistake, kept what he had already translated but went back and translated the chapter with the prophecy. There is a slight similarity between the end of ch. IV and the beginning of VI, 1 which may have helped to cause the error, with *omnes stupore* (VI, 1) echoing *omnes stupor* at the end of IV. The Old English also combines the bishops from ch. IV with the people from ch. VI.

[39] O's *Sancta Marian modor*, with the first two words in capitals, is not paralleled in the Latin or in the other two manuscripts and so has been emended out of the edited text.

[40] There is confusion in the syntax here. The Latin means: 'with the result that he humbles the peoples who used to rise against us and turns their hearts towards himself. He has opened his ears to our prayers and has shut out from us the insults of our enemies.' *Conuertat*, a present tense subjunctive, has been translated as a past tense in the Old English and, instead of taking *drihten* as the subject of *gecyrdon*, the translator has made *þeode* the subject, producing a very unsatisfactory reading: 'so that they would turn to their own hearts'. The manuscripts then vary in the extent to which they continue with the mistaken subject. O's version seems to be the best in this respect, as it is possible to take *onynon* and *acerron* as infinitives dependent on *he wolde*, even though the way they are spelled makes them look more like present-tense subjunctives, parallel to the past-tense subjunctive *gecyrdon* and governed by *hi* (compare *forlæton* as infinitive in section X, 2). Taking them as infinitives results in a text which means 'he would humiliate the peoples who rose against us, so that they would turn to their own hearts, and [he] would open their ears to our prayers and would turn away from us the insults of our enemies'. Taking them as governed by *hi* results in 'he would humiliate the peoples who rose against us, so that they might turn to their own hearts and they may open their ears to our prayers and they may turn away from us the insults of our enemies'. Clearly, the first reading makes better sense, though even if the author meant them as infinitives he was still mistranslating, as *aperuit* and *exclusit* are perfect indicatives.

I reads *ontyndon* and *acyrdon* instead of O's *ontynon* and *acerron*, with the result that this version has consistently made *þa þeode* the subject of all the clauses in question, giving rise to the absurdity of the last clause, 'and þa bismernesse ure feondum from us acyrdon'. Here the plural past-tense verb seems to indicate that *þa þeode* is still the subject and the clause, therefore, must mean '[the enemy peoples] turned away from us the insults of our enemies'. O and I agree on the mistaken *feondum* for *feonda*, probably due to the scribe of the archetype of all the Old English manuscripts having been influenced by the *-um* of *benum* just above; the scribe of fᵃ presumably corrected this.

In fᵃ the verbs read *ontyndon* and *acyrran*; the scribe therefore seems to have continued to take *þa þeode* as the subject of *ontyndon*, even though to fit in *acyrran*, which seems to be an infinitive, one must return to *he wolde*, referring to *Drihten*. All three manuscripts, of course, agree on a reading in which *heora earan* refers to the enemy peoples and not, as in the Latin, to God.

The difficulty seems to go back, in part at least, to the translator, as it is unlikely that a reading corresponding to the Latin such as 'he ontynde his earan to urum benum' would be corrupted to 'heora earan ontynon to urum benum'.

41 The Latin reads here: 'Sterilis facta est mater et genuit exsultationem et laetitiam in Israel'. The only reading which can be correct here is that of fᵃ, 'On þam unbeorþrum ecere blisse tuddor for gefean on Israhelum', but even this manuscript appears to be missing an essential part of the sentence. The word *unbeorþrum* is not otherwise attested, but the related noun, *byrðre*, meaning 'mother', is. Here we must be dealing with a dative plural adjective, so the Latin singular, referring to Anna alone, has been translated as a plural, presumably referring to both Anna and her husband. The reading *mundbyrdum* of O presumably arose by the process of the *m* of the article becoming attached to the noun, possibly resulting in a form *munbyrðrum*, which a scribe then altered to *mundbyrdum*.

There is nothing in the Old English to correspond to *genuit* but the Old English sentence seems to require such a verb. There is no verb in fᵃ, O has an unsatisfactory verb, *forgeafon*, and I has *ðe þar i gefæn*, which is hard to interpret. It would be possible to emend *forgeafon* to *forgeaf*, but this is against the evidence of all three manuscripts which show that *on israhelum* was preceded by something ending in *-n*. It would also leave the subject (God?) unexpressed, as well as clumsily anticipating the *forgeaf* of the next clause. It seems more likely that the original verb, corresponding to *genuit*, was lost from the archetype of all three Old English manuscripts and that fᵃ's *for gefean* corresponds to the Latin *laetitiam* rather than being a corruption of *forgeaf*. Something like *wæs acenned* or *wæs geboren* therefore seems to be required and I have supplied *wæs acenned*. If this is correct, then the translator replaced 'genuit exsultationem et laetitiam' with 'ecere blisse tuddor wæs acenned for gefean', preferring the concrete *tuddor* to the image of Anna giving birth to rejoicing. *forgeafon* in O must, therefore, be a corruption of *for gefean*, as is I's reading.

42 This sentence is an independent addition by the Old English translator, who omits from this section the Latin description of Mary's shining face: 'et iam

203

resplendebat facies eius sicut nix ita ut uix potuisset in eius uultum quia intendere'.

[43] The Latin reads: 'Insistebat autem in lanificio, et omnia quae mulieres antiquae non poterant facere, ista in tenera aetate posita explicabat'. Although all three Old English manuscripts agree at this point, there is something obviously corrupt with the reading *heora bearn*. What is needed in the Old English is some parallel to *mulieres antiquae*. It is possible that the Old English should read 'ænig þara þe heora yldran wæron, wifa and fæmnena' and that *yldran*, 'older', was mistaken for *yldran*, 'ancestors', that this seemed nonsensical and that the scribe of the archetype, guessing desperately, substituted *bearn*, 'children'. I have emended accordingly. *yldran fæmnan* is used in the next section to translate *seniores uirgines*.

[44] The translator has failed to recognize the passive, *docebantur*, and, instead of having Mary being taught with the older virgins, has her teach them.

[45] The translator has here changed the order in which Mary's virtues are described. O's *and wisra* is not in the other two manuscripts or in the Latin and has, therefore, been excluded from the edited text. Presumably the adjective *wrætlicre*, translating *elegantior*, struck the scribe, or the scribe of an exemplar, as odd in the context and *wisra* was added to supplement it. f[a] has replaced *wrætlicre* with *wærlicre*, 'more carefully', and I has *wræsclicre*, probably an error for *wræstlicre*, a synonym for *wrætlicre*, 'more elegant'.

[46] Assmann reads *steaðig* in I here, but the manuscript clearly reads *sceaðig*, which does not occur elsewhere (and which is not in the *MCOE* as that follows Assmann) but which would have to mean something like the totally inappropriate 'injurious'. Presumably it is a scribal error for *steaðig*.

[47] f[a]'s and I's *hire* has been preferred to O's *heom* as the source clearly attributes the origin of the custom to Mary rather than the other virgins: 'Denique ab ipsa primum exiit ut cum resalutant homines sancti "Deo gratias" dicant'.

[48] The Latin reads here: 'Et dicebant ei pontifices et omnes affines eius'. This supports the reading of f[a] and I ('Ða andswaradon hyre þa biscopas and hire magas ealle þe on þam temple wæron') rather than that of O ('Ða andwyrdan þa biscopas hyre and hyre mægðe on þam temple'). The O scribe seems to have thought that Mary had support in her wish to remain a virgin, whereas it is clear from the source that she was alone. Again it looks very much as if the O scribe was substituting *mægðe* for *magas* (see note 32). As the detail of the *magas* being in the temple is not made explicit in the source, the Latin offers no help in deciding whether þe . . . wæron is original or not, but, if the O scribe was under the impression that *hyre mægðe* agreed with *hyre* rather than þa biscopas, then he might well have decided to omit þe . . . wæron. I have, therefore, included þe . . . wæron in the edited text.

[49] The Latin reads: 'Deus in filiis colitur et in posteris adoratur sicut semper fuit

The Old English Gospel of Pseudo-Matthew

in populo Israel'. O's *her ætforan* is clearly incorrect, but the other two manuscripts preserve the correct *eaforen*, which is largely a poetic word. All manuscripts share what seems to be a present-tense ending on *weorþian*, but the grammar of the clause calls for a past participle, paralleling *begangen*. Interchange of *d* and *ð* is, however, not uncommon and I have not, therefore, emended (see Muir, ed., *The Exeter Anthology*, I, 39, n. 106). O's *an* must be a corruption of *a*, from the source's *semper*; the other two manuscripts omit this, perhaps because the archetype of all the Old English manuscripts shared this corruption and *an* made no sense to the scribe of the common original of f ᵃ and I.

50 The first sentence of Mary's reply in the source has been omitted: 'Deus in castitate primo omnium probatur et colitur'. In the next sentence O reads *his broðor* where f ᵃ and I have *unwis*; the source supports neither, reading instead: 'Nam ante Abel nullus fuit iustus inter homines. Et iste pro oblatione placuit deo ab eo qui displicuit, nam inclementer occisus est.' Presumably the translator wished to be more explicit than the Latin's *ab eo qui displicuit*. O's reading seems more likely to be original; the other reading could be due to omission of *broðor*, followed by emendation of *his* to *unwis*. *Unwis* is otherwise a rather unlikely description of Cain, whom one would expect to be more unequivocally condemned; in addition, an adjective used substantively would usually be preceded by a demonstrative. The slightly strange word-order of *and hine arleaslice his broðor ofsloh* can be explained by the wish to give especial prominence to *hine*.

51 The Latin reads here: 'Denique et Helias cum esset in carne assumptus est, quia carnem suam uirginem custodiuit'. The reading of f ᵃ and I corresponds closely to the Latin and is, therefore, most probably original. O's reading may have been produced by a misreading of *on* for *of* and an expansion of the rest of the sentence to make sense of this. The Old English then omits Mary's repetition of her resolution to remain a virgin.

52 Despite the unanimity of the manuscripts in omitting *ne*, this should, of course, read *wunian ne sceolde* (Latin: *morari non posse*).

53 The omission of most of this sentence in I is presumably due to homoeoteleuton, the eye of the scribe jumping from one occurrence of *temple* to the next.

54 The Old English translator has slightly changed and expanded the Latin here. The Latin reads: 'Tamen uenientes ad legitimam aetatem uiros in coniugio adeptae sunt et secutae priorum suorum ordinem domino placuerunt', whereas in the Old English those who follow the example of their forefathers are the children of the now-married virgins, rather than the virgins themselves. O's reading, *gehyrsume to ælicum gyftum*, is preferable to the reading of the other two manuscripts, *æwfæston*, as it agrees more closely with the Latin.

The omission of *on* from f[a] and I in the last part of the sentence changes the sense and departs from the source.

55 The *nu þonne* with which this sentence begins in O is not supported by the Latin or the other two manuscripts and may well be due to the *nu is þonne* of the previous Old English sentence. It is not included in the edited text.

56 *ealre* is supported by the Latin, *omni synagogae*, and was, therefore, presumably omitted accidentally from O.

57 The Old English translation abbreviates this section of the Latin, in which the priest offers a sacrifice to God, who then makes known, in direct speech, how the custodian of the Virgin is to be decided upon. In handling the Latin freely here, the translator makes it seem as though the priest is giving the orders of his own volition, rather than at the command of God.

58 O follows the Latin in not naming Abiathar until two sentences later; the archetype of the other two manuscripts presumably brought his name forward here.

59 One would expect *nanre* here as *of* governs the dative (as in *of þære gyrde* in the previous paragraph). All three Old English manuscripts read *nan*, however, and the endingless form has therefore been retained.

60 *seo læste: seleste* in all three manuscripts must be an error of the archetype for *læste*. The Latin reads *breuissima* and the Old English sentence itself, like the Latin, ends *seo þe þu for naht ne telest*, an unlikely comment if it was the best rod.

61 *þe þu þær secest*: in keeping with his omission of the direct speech by God earlier, the translator here replaces the source's *quod locutus sum tibi*.

62 The Old English is compressing the Latin here and this makes it difficult to know which of the vernacular readings to accept. The relevant Latin passage reads: 'uoce magna clamauit ad eum Abiathar pontifex dicens: "Ueni et accipe uirgam tuam, quoniam tu exspectaris". Et accessit Ioseph expauescens, quod summus pontifex cum clamore nimio uocasset eum. Mox autem extendens manum suam uirgam accepit.' Where O has *and cydde him þæt*, f[a] reads *and hine cigde*, which is supported by I's *and hine nemnode*. The sense 'and named him' seems at least as good as O's 'and told him that', if not better, and is supported by the *uocasset eum* of the Latin. Moreover, O has earlier mistakenly replaced *gecydde* with *gecigde* (see note 30) and this lends some support to a similar error here. The f[a]/I reading has therefore been adopted.

Where O has 'and he ða sona onfeng þæra gyrda of ðæs bisceopes handum', f[a] and I have 'and him his gyrde sealde'. Does the Old English correspond to 'Ueni et accipe uirgam tuam' or the last sentence of this passage, 'Mox autem extendens manum suam uirgam accepit'? The f[a]/I reading could be thought to correspond more or less to the first of these Latin sentences and O to the last. I have retained the O reading because it is a more faithful translation of the Latin (apart from *of ðæs bisceopes handum*) than that of the other two manuscripts, rendering *mox autem uirgam accepit*, with the *manum* perhaps being mistakenly responsible for *ðæs bisceopes handum*. The form *þæra gyrda* looks, of course, like a genitive plural, whereas a dative singular (*þære gyrde*) is required, but the O scribe occasionally interchanges *-a* and *-e* endings and I have not emended.

63 O's *heannysse* corresponds to the source's *fastigium*, whereas the other two manuscripts have *hwæmmas*, 'corners'.

64 O's reading, *fægniende and swyðe bliðe*, must be an expanded substitution for the Anglian *swiþe gefeonde*, the reading of the other two manuscripts. I have, accordingly, emended to *swyðe fægniende*, keeping the replacement word but not including *bliðe*, which is a kind of gloss, in the edited text. *gefeoð* and *gefeonde* are preserved elsewhere in the text (but see note 79).

65 O's form *gemune* is a late West Saxon form: see A. Campbell, *Old English Grammar* (Oxford, 1959), p. 345, n. 1.

66 The reference is to Numbers XXVI. 9; the Old English omits the names of Korah and Abiram, supplied in the Latin.

67 There is omission through homoeoteleuton in I, the two occurrences of *willan* having misled the scribe.

68 The Old English translator here changes the mention of Joseph's sons to the more general kinsmen, although he has already included Joseph's statement *ic hæbbe fela bearna*. The existence of Joseph's children by a former marriage was one of the points in the apocrypha to which, for example, Jerome objected.

69 O's reading here is closer to the Latin than is that of the other two manuscripts. The source reads: 'Dentur aliquae ex sodalibus eius uirgines cum quibus interim degat'. The archetype of f ª/I must have rewritten this passage to place more emphasis on Joseph's obedience. Where the Latin merely has *interim*, all three Old English versions contain the notion of legal age. Presumably *ælice yldo* means 'marriageable age', but Mary is already of marriageable age and Joseph in the Latin asks that the virgins live with her until she is actually married.

70 O's reading is probably a replacement for the Mercian word *gemung*, 'marriage'.

71 I have emended O's *hi* to *Marian* to agree with the Latin and the readings of the other two manuscripts (f ª *Marian*, I *Mariam*).

72 The precious fabrics enumerated in the Latin ('sericum et iacintum et bissum et purpura et linum') are summarized in the Old English.

73 The Latin manuscripts are unanimous in giving Mary the royal purple to weave and this is very important iconographically. The Old English text, in giving her the *hwit godweb*, the 'white luxury textile', 'fine white cloth', appears to be ignorant of this tradition. *godweb* here appears to have the

meaning 'luxury textile', 'silken textile' rather than the meaning 'purple textile', though the word corresponds to Latin *purpura*. *Purpura* cloth was often purple in colour, but that is not its principal semantic force by the Middle Ages, and, although the majority of references to *godweb* which specify a colour indicate purple or red, there is a reference to *geolo godweb* as well as *hwit godweb*. I take *hiw* to be 'kind' rather than 'colour' as the Latin specifies the different fabrics given to the virgins – cotton, linen, silk – more than colours.

[74] This instance of *on gleo* is not supported by the Latin or by f[a] and I; it is most probably an addition by the O scribe or his exemplar and has, therefore, been omitted from the edited text.

[75] The Old English here alters the sense of the Latin, in which the virgins are the unintentional prophets.

[76] The Latin reads 'rogare coeperunt Mariam ut indulgeret eis et oraret pro eis'; the Old English alters this to 'ongunnon hi wurþian and hyre eadmodlice hyran'.

[77] I's reading here, *gearcost*, a scribal substitution for *gearwodest*, is a so-called 'Winchester word' (see Hofstetter, *Winchester*, p. 237), the only one in any version of the text.

[78] For O, Assmann read *orwelges*, 'pure'. However, the manuscript clearly has *n* rather than *r* and, accordingly, *BT Supplement* lists the occurrence under *onwealh*, 'physically perfect, whole, entire, uninjured'.

[79] O's *swyðe bliðe* is unsupported by I, which reads simply *swiðe gefeonde* (f[a] has finished just before this). O was probably supplying *bliðe* to augment the unfamiliar Anglian word *gefeonde* and I have not, therefore, included it in the edited text.

[80] I's reading is syntactically preferable and supported by the source's *suspitionem*. I have, accordingly, read *gemynde* rather than *gemunde*, as O has *gemunde* because the scribe thought it was a verb (hence his *and gemunde þe* rather than *mid gemynde þæs*).

[81] There is something wrong with the Old English text at this point. *unarimdum* is a adjective, either dative singular masculine or neuter or dative plural. It needs a noun with which to agree, probably a dative plural, as the sense is 'countless'. *godcundre* is an adjective (genitive or dative singular feminine, strictly speaking, but final *-a* and *-e* are often interchanged in texts of this period and it could therefore be intended as a genitive plural) and *geryna* is a neuter noun in the genitive plural. It is difficult to know whether *godcundre geryna* was originally dependent on the noun accompanying *unarimdum* or whether more than one word is missing at this point. *Unarimdum* corresponds to *dinumerari non potest* in the Latin sentence 'Tunc congregata est omnis multitudo Israel quae dinumerari non potest', but a noun meaning something

like 'multitude' does not seem to fit *godcundre geryna*. Perhaps an Old English equivalent to *signum* would fit the context better: the word occurs five times in the Latin accounts of the tests of Joseph and Mary in these chapters and it provides an appropriate summary of the Old Testament trials of the couple's innocence. I have accordingly supplied *tacenum*.

82 It is virtually impossible to choose here between the rival readings of O and I. The clauses, 'þæs þe hi þæs unrihtes hy acuðan' in O and 'þæs ðe heo yfele wilnunge bi heom hæfdon' in I, relate to '(rogantes eam) ut daret malis suspicionibus (eorum indulgentiam)' in the source, and both Old English versions could be regarded as rough equivalents of *malis suspicionibus*. I have chosen to follow O as it is the base manuscript. O's *acuðan* has been emended to *oncuðan* as the meaning (*accused, charged*) fits the context better than *acuðan* (*announced, showed*). The emendation is Assmann's.

83 Both manuscripts read *cyninges* and I have let it stand, but *regina regis coeli* is an unusual description, whereas *regina coeli*, queen of heaven, is of course common.

84 This echoes the liturgical antiphon 'Beatam praedicant omnes angeli', found in the devotional anthology *De laude Dei*, which was compiled by Alcuin at York *c.* 790 (R. Constantinescu, 'Alcuin et les "libelli precum" de l'époque carolingienne', *Révue d'histoire de la spiritualité* 50 (1974), 17–56, at 50).

# The Old English assumption homily in Cambridge, Corpus Christi College, 41

# Editorial introduction

This apocryphon was written and corrected by one scribe and is relatively straightforward from an editorial viewpoint. Corrections by the scribe have been incorporated in the text and are indicated in the apparatus. The text has been edited twice before, by Tristram, *Vier altenglische Predigten*, in 1970 and by Grant, *Three Homilies*, in 1982. Both are reliable editions. Tristram follows manuscript punctuation and capitalization and emends only when a letter or group of letters has been omitted or when a wrong letter has been written, so her text is not particularly easy for a modern reader to follow and does not attempt to supply obvious gaps in the manuscript (e.g. *ælces leohtnesse* where the lack of grammatical agreement indicates that something is missing). Grant intervenes only marginally more in the text, while indicating in his notes where he thinks something has been omitted. Both Tristram and Grant were working under the disadvantage of not knowing the precise Latin source of this text and had to rely on a combination of *Transitus B*[1], *Transitus W* and what Willard termed *Transitus E* (a variant version of *Transitus B* in Milan, Biblioteca Ambrosiana, L. 58), together with Blickling XIII. I have since identified the source as *Transitus B*[2] and this means that it is possible to be much more accurate in discussing how the Latin is handled in this translation and also that deficiencies in the text can be identified with some degree of certainty. As the text is an abbreviated rendering of the source, there is not a sentence for sentence correspondence between Latin and Old English, but there are passages where one can be reasonably sure that something which was originally in the Old English translation has been lost. In this edition I have, therefore, attempted to supply such lacunae in cases where the grammar of the Old English indicates that something is missing or where something is omitted which is necessary to the sense of

213

the text and where one can see how a mechanical error in copying could have occurred to cause such an omission. Each such case is discussed in the notes.

Chapter numbers are taken from the edition of the Latin *Transitus B*[2] by Haibach-Reinisch.

# The text

Her sagað ymbe þa halgan Marian, usses Dryhtnes modor:

1 Mid þy þe Dryhten Hælende Crist for ealre worulde alysnesse on rode gefæstnod hangode, he geseah under þære rode standan his modor and Iohannes þane godspellere, þone he beforan his oðrum halgum lufode forþon he ana unwemmed[a][1] in lychoman þurhwunode. Þa bebead he him þa halgan Marian and him to cwæð: 'Þis is þin modor', and æfter þon he cwæð to hire: 'Þis is þin sunu';[b] and of þære tide seo halie Maria on Iohannes gymnesse þurhwunode, swa lange swa hio on þissum life lyfede. Hwæt la, he sende ure Dryhten his apostolas geond ealne middangeard mancyn to læranne; þa sæt Maria in hire huse[2] be Oliuetes dune.

2 Ðy þriddan geare[3] æfter þon þe Drihten Crist in heofon astah, þa sume dæge wæs hio to þon swiðe gyrnende his ansine þæt hio angan wepan, and þa sona geseah hio Drihtnes[a] engel hire ætstandende. Ða grette he hi and cwæð: 'Hal wes þu, Maria, from Drihtne gebletsod. Hwæt la, þis palmtwig of niorhxnawonge[b] ic þe brohte þæt þu gedo þæt he sie boren beforan þinre bære. And nu, binnan þy ðriddan dæge, þu bist ferende of lichoman, and þin bideð þin sunu Drihten Hælende Crist mid his englum and mid eallum halgum and mid heahenglum.'[4] Ða cwæð Maria to þam engle: 'Ic þe bidde þætte syn to me gesomnode ealle apostolas mines Drihtnes Hælendes Cristes þæt ic hi geseo licumlicum eagum ær ðon þe ic swelte'. Ða / andswarode hire se engel and cwæð: 'Nu

---

Text from D, pp. 280–7

1   [a]  he ana unwemmed] he D, *with a deliberate gap of about twelve or fourteen letters in the manuscript after he*   [b]  sunu] *the final letter looks very like a, but the scribe seems to have intended* sunu *and to have inadvertently joined the tops of the ascenders.* a *is formed differently in the remainder of the text.*

2   [a]  Drihtnes] Drihnes D   [b]  niorhxnawonge] niorhxwonge D

# The translation

This tells about the holy Mary, our Lord's mother:

1    When the Lord and Saviour Christ hung fastened to the cross for the redemption of all the world, he saw, standing beneath the cross, his mother and John the evangelist, whom he loved more than his other saints because he alone had remained a virgin in body. Then he entrusted the holy Mary to him and said to him: 'This is your mother', and after that he said to her: 'This is your son'; and from that time on the holy Mary remained in John's care, as long as she lived in this life. Well then, our Lord sent his apostles throughout the whole world to teach mankind; during that time Mary resided in her house near the Mount of Olives.

2    In the third year after Christ the Lord ascended into heaven, she longed so much for his presence one day that she began to weep and then immediately she saw the angel of the Lord standing by her. Then he greeted her and said: 'Hail, Mary, blessed by the Lord. Behold, I have brought you this palm-branch from paradise so that you may have it carried in front of your bier. And now, within three days, you will go from your body, and your son the Lord and Saviour Christ will await you with his angels and with all the saints and with the archangels.' Then Mary said to the angel: 'I entreat you that all the apostles of my Lord the Saviour Christ be assembled with me so that I may see them with my bodily eyes before I die'. Then the angel answered her and said: 'This very

todæge hi beoð genumene of neorhxnawonges gefean[5] and her to ðe cumað'. Þa cwæð Maria eft to þam engle: 'Ic ðe bidde þæt þu sende þine bletsunge ofer me, þætte nænig geweald þæs wiðerweardan deofles me ongen ne yrne and þæt ic ne geseo þistro aldor me ongen cumende'. Se engel hire[c6] to cwæð: 'Þa ecean bletsunge þe sealde þin Drihten (Godes þeowa and ærenddraca ic eom) þætte[d] ðu þonne ne gesihst ðistra[e] aldor,[7] ac ne wene þu þæt ðe sy þæt from me seald, ac from him þone þu in þinum innoþe gebære; his anweald is in ealra worulda woruld'. And se engel þa mid micelre biorhtnesse ðanon gewat. And se palma scan swiþe leohte and his leaf[f] lihton swa se scinenda mergensteorra.[g] Maria hi ða gegirede mid hire selran gyrelan, and hio genam ðone palman þone þe hio of ðæs engles handa onfeng, and eode in Oliuete ða dune and hie þær gebæd and cwæð: 'Þancas[h] ic ðe dem, ælmihtig Domine, ealles þæs þu me to gemedomodest. Ic næs swa micelre weorðmyndu weorðe þæt þu me nære mildsiende.' And þa, ðus cweðende, in hire huse hio wæs gongende.[i8]

3   Mid þy ðe se halga Iohannes lærde þæt folc in Effessum on Sunnandæge æt underntide,[a] þa[b] þunorrada hlynedon and wæron swiðe micele ligetas gewordene[9] and he wæs ahafen[c] from þara ymbstandendra eagum[10] and he wæs aset beforan ðæs huses dura þær sio eadige Maria inne wunode. And, ingangende, he hie grette, mid þy þe hio ongan wepan.[11] And hio cwæð to Iohanne: 'Ic ðe bidde, min bearn Iohannes, þætte ðu wes gemindig þines lareowes worda þe he spræc ða he me þe ætfæste. And ic gehyrde Iudea geðeahtunge;[12] hi cwædon: "Uton onbidan hwænne[d] ðios swelte, þæt we mægen hire lichoman mid fyre forbærnan". Ac forðon gym þu mynre deaðþenunga.'[e13] And ða hio þis gecweden hæfde, hio him æteowde hire lichrægl and þone palman,[f14] þe hio of ðæs engles handa onfeng, and cwæð to him: 'Gedo þu þæt þes palma sie beren beforan minre bære þonne min lichoma sie to byrgene læded'.

4   Se halga Iohannes hire andswarode[a15] and cwæð: 'Hu mæg ic ðe ana gedefelice deaðþenunga[b] gegearwian, nymðe mine broþor and efne-

---

[c] hire] me D   [d] þætte] þætie D   [e] ðistra] ðistr[[e]]´a´ D   [f] leaf] *followed by erasure of* scan D   [g] mergensteorra] mergenst`e´orra D   [h] þancas] þa`n´cas D   [i] gongende] g[[e]]ongende

3   [a] underntide] undern[[y]]tide D   [b] þa] þæt þa D   [c] ahafen] ah[[æ]]´a´fen D   [d] hwænne] *first* n *altered from* o *by erasure*   [e] deaðþenunga] deaðþenuga D   [f] lichrægl and þone palman] lichrægl D

4   [a] andswarode] andwarode D   [b] deaðþenunga] deaðþenuga D

day they will be taken from the joys of Paradise and will come here to you'. Then Mary said again to the angel: 'I entreat you that you bestow your blessing on me, so that no power of the hostile devil may attack me and so that I may not see the prince of darkness coming against me'. The angel said to her: 'Your Lord gave you this eternal blessing (I am God's servant and messenger) that you will not see the prince of darkness then, but do not think that this is granted to you by me, but by him whom you bore in your womb; his power is forever and ever'. And then the angel departed from there with great splendour. And the palm shone very brightly and its leaves gave light like the shining morning star. Mary then dressed herself in her best garments, and she took the palm which she had received from the hand of the angel, and went to the Mount of Olives and prayed there and said: 'I thank you, almighty Lord, for all that of which you have deemed me worthy. I was not worthy of such a great honour unless you had mercy on me.' And then, saying this, she went into her house.

3    While St John preached to the people in Ephesus at the third hour on Sunday, peals of thunder resounded and there were great flashes of lightning and he was lifted up away from the eyes of the bystanders and was set down in front of the door of the house in which the blessed Mary lived. And, entering, he greeted her, while she began to weep. And she said to John: 'I entreat you, John my son, that you be mindful of the words of your master which he spoke when he entrusted me to you. And I have heard the consultations of the Jews; they said: "Let us wait until this woman dies, in order that we may be able to burn up her body with fire". Therefore let you take charge of my obsequies.' And when she had said this, she showed him her winding-sheet and the palm, which she had received from the hand of the angel, and said to him: 'Let you see to it that this palm be carried in front of my bier when my body is taken for burial'.

4    St John answered her and said: 'How can I alone prepare fitting obsequies for you, unless my brothers and fellow-apostles be assembled

apostolas hider sin gesamnode?' Þa, betweox þas word, ealle þa apostolas wæron of þam stowum, þe hie ær lærdon, in wolcnum ahafen and asette beforan duru þæs huses in þæm sio halige Marie wunude. And, ingongende,[16] hi gretton hi him betwunum and cwædon: 'For hwylcon þingon gesamnode us Drihten hider todæge?'

5    Mid þy þe[a] hi þæt spræcon and hi to Drihtne gebædon, Iohannes se apostol cwom[b] to him and he him sæde ealles þæs þe Maria him sæde.[c17] Ingongende, þa apostolas gretton Marian and cwædon: 'Bio þu gebletsod[d] from Dryhtne, se geworhte heofon and eorðan'. Hio him andswarode[e] and cwæð: 'Si Drihtnes bletsung ofer eow and sib sie mid eow in Drihtnes noman. Nu þonne, mine þa leofan broþor, secgeað me hu ge hider cwomon.' Hiere ða apostolas[f] sædon ealle hu hiera anra[g] gehwylc of ðere[h] stowe þyder com, þe he on lærde. Maria him to cwæð: 'Gebletsod[i] sie Drihten se gefylde mine gyrnesse, and he me ne bescyrede eowerre gesyhðe, ac he me forgeaf þæt ic eow licumlicum eagum gesio ær þon þe ic swelte. And ic eow ealle bidde þæt ge anmodlice wacien oð[j] ða tid þe Domine[k] cume.'[18]

6    Hie ealle þa hire geheton and mid hira wordum frefredon and in Godes hirnesse ðurhwunedon. And ða samnunga æt / underne[19] slæp com ofer ealle þa ðe wæron in þam huse, swa þætte nænig wacian ne meahte buton þa apostolas ane and ða þreo fæmnan þam Maria hire deaðþenunga bebead. And þa hraþe com Drihten mid micele engla werode and cwæð to þam apostolum: 'Sib sy mid eow, broþor'. Ða andswaredon and cwædon: 'Domine, sy þin mildheortnes[a] ofer us swa we gehyhtað in ðe'.

7    Maria hi þa astrehte in ðone flor and hi to Drihtne gebæd and cwæð: 'Wes þu min gemyndig, wuldres aldor, for þære stemne þinre þeowenne, þætte nænig geweald þæs wiðerweardan feondes me ongean ne yrne and þæt ic ne gesio þa sweartan gastas me ongean cumende'. Þa andswarode hire Domine and cwæð: 'Mid þy ðe ic sylf for mancynnes hælo deað þrowode, þystra ealdor to me com, and mid þy þe ðu æfter

5    [a] mid þy þe] mid þe D, *with e partially erased*    [b] cwom] c`w´om D    [c] sæde ealles þæs þe Maria him sæde] sæde D    [d] gebletsod] g̃ebletsod D    [e] andswarode] andswarod[[on]]`e´ D    [f] apostolas] aposto[[ ]]`l´as D, *one or two letters erased*    [g] anra] n *altered from* r *by erasure*    [h] ðere] *first* e *slightly blotched, possibly* ðære    [i] gebletsod] *abbreviation stroke over* b *rather than* g D    [j] oð] on D    [k] Domine] d`n´e D
6    [a] mildheortnes] mildheornes[[s]] D

here?' Then, in the course of these words, all the apostles were lifted up in clouds from the places where they had been preaching and were set down in front of the door of the house in which the holy Mary lived. And, entering, they greeted one another and said: 'For what reason did the Lord assemble us here today?'

5   While they were saying this and praying to the Lord, the apostle John came to them and told them everything which Mary had told him. Going in, the apostles greeted Mary and said: 'May you be blessed by the Lord, who made heaven and earth'. She answered them and said: 'May the Lord's blessing be upon you and peace be with you in the name of the Lord. Now then, my beloved brothers, tell me how you came here.' All the apostles told her how each of them had come there from the place in which he had been preaching. Mary said to them: 'Blessed be the Lord who fulfilled my desire and he did not deprive me of the sight of you, but he granted me that I should see you with my bodily eyes before I die. And I entreat you all that you should keep watch unanimously until the time when the Lord may come.'

6   Then they all promised her that and consoled her with their words and they continued in praise of God. And then suddenly at the third hour sleep overcame all those who were in the house, so that no-one could stay awake except the apostles alone and the three women to whom Mary had entrusted her obsequies. And then the Lord came immediately with a great host of angels and said to the apostles: 'May peace be with you, brothers'. Then they answered and said: 'Lord, may your mercy be upon us as we trust in you'.

7   Mary then prostrated herself on the floor and prayed to God and said: 'Be mindful of me, prince of glory, because of the voice of your servant, so that no power of the hostile enemy may attack me and so that I may not see the dark spirits coming against me'. Then the Lord answered her and said: 'When I myself suffered death for the salvation of mankind, the prince of darkness came to me, and when you, according to

manncynnes[a] æwe deaþes gafol agyldest, þu hine gesyhst.[b] Ac astih ofer[c20] þinre reste and[d] þone gedefan ende þines[e] lifes gefyl, forþon ðin bideþ se heofonlica camphad þæt he ðe inlædeþ in neorxnawonges gefean.' Mid þy þe[f] he Domine þus cwæð, heo astah ofer hire bedde and, Gode þanciende, hio onsende hire gast. And þa apostolas gesawon þære halgan Marian sawle swa micle leohte scinende swa þæt nænig man mid wordum asecgan ne mæg; seo beorhtnes oferswiðde æghwelces dæges hwitnesse and ælces snawes[g] leohtnesse.[21]

8  Þa ætfæste se Hælend þære haligan Marian saule Michaele þam heahengle, se is neorxnawonges hyrde, ealdormon Ebrea ðeode.[a22] Swylce he cwæð to Petre: 'Geheald ðu Marian lichoman and bringað[b] hine in þa swiðran healfe þære ceastre to eastdæle, and ge þær gemetað niwe byrgenne, in þære nu git nænig mon gelæd[c] wæs. Byrgeað[d] hi þær and onbidað þær oð þone þriddan dæg, and ic hweorfe eft to eow.'[23] And he ða Drihten mid sawle his modor and mid þam halgum englum / and in micelre[e] beorhtnesse onweg gewat. And ða englas eodon micele gefean hyhtende and Gode lof singende.

9  Hwæt la, þa þreo fæmnan genamon þone lichoman þære eadegan[a] Marian to ðon þæt hi woldon hie baðigean, swa hira þeaw wæs. Mid þy þe hine ongiredon, se haliga lichoma scean swa micele leohte þætte he ne[b24] meahte wesan gesewen. Hi hine þa gegyredon mid hire lichrægle and ða samnunga þæt leoht þanon gewat. And on ansine þære halgan Marian wæs swilce lilian blostman, and on micelre swetnesse swæc uteode of hire muðe.

10  And ða apostolas þa gesetton þone halgan lichoman in bære. And Iohannes cwæð to Petre: 'Þe gedafenað þysne palman to beranne and þæt þu gonge[a] beforan þas bære, forðon þe þu us ealle in geleafan þæs apostolhades forgæst'. Petrus him andswarode and cwæð: 'Hwæt þu unwemmast[b] from[c] us ealle from Drihtne eart gecoren,[d25] forðon æt þam æfengereordum ofer his breost ðu onhlinedest mid þy ðe he[e] us sæde þæt he þrowian wolde.[26] And ða he in rode gealgan gefæstnod hangode,[f] his

<hr />

7  [a] manncynnes] mann[[e]]cynnes D    [b] gesyhst] gesyhð D    [c] ofer] of D    [d] and] 'and' D    [e] þines] þine D    [f] mid þy þy] þe D    [g] ælces snawes] ælces D

8  [a] ðeode] ðeoden D    [b] bringað] b[[.]]r˙in˙gað D    [c] gelæd] ge[[s]]læd D    [d] byrgeað] byrg˙e˙að D    [e] micelre] micel˙r˙e D

9  [a] eadegan] geadegan D    [b] he ne] he D

10  [a] g[[e]]onge D    [b] unwemmast] nu wemmast D    [c] from] for D    [d] gecoren] ge˙cor˙ren D    [e] ðe he] ðe [[he]] he D    [f] hangode] hagode D

the law of mankind, pay your debt of death, you will see him. But get on to your bed and complete the fitting end of your life because the heavenly army awaits you that it may lead you into the joys of paradise.' While the Lord was saying this she got on to her bed and, thanking God, she sent forth her spirit. And the apostles saw the soul of the holy Mary shining with so great a light that no one can describe it in words; this brightness surpassed the radiance of every day and the light of every snow.

8    Then the Saviour entrusted the holy Mary's soul to the archangel Michael, who is the guardian of paradise, the chief of the Hebrew people. He also said to Peter: 'Guard Mary's corpse and bring it to the right-hand side of the city, towards the east, and you will find there a new sepulchre, in which no one has yet been laid. Bury her there and wait there until the third day, and I shall return again to you.' And then the Lord departed in great splendour with his mother's soul and with the holy angels. And the angels went exulting in great joy and singing praise to God.

9    Well then, the three women took the blessed Mary's corpse in order to bathe her, as was their custom. When they stripped it, the holy corpse shone with so great a light that it could not be looked at. Then they dressed it in her winding-sheet and then suddenly the light departed from there. And upon the face of the blessed Mary it was like lily blossoms and a fragrance of great sweetness came from her mouth.

10    And then the apostles placed the holy body on the bier. And John said to Peter: 'It is fitting for you to carry this palm and that you go in front of this bier, because you surpass us all in the faith of the apostleship'. Peter answered him and said: 'Indeed, you, most pure, have been chosen out of us all by the Lord, because at the [Last] supper you leaned on his breast when he told us that he intended to suffer. And when he hung fastened to the cross, he entrusted this woman to you with his gracious

þy arfæstan muðe þe þas ætfæste. Forðon þu þisne palman beran scealt;[g27] ic bere þisne halgan lichoman mid minum efnapostolum.' Paulus cwæð: 'Forþon þe ic eower ealra gingest eom in þan apostolhade, ic bere þa bære mid þe'. Petrus ahof[h] þa bære æt ðam heafdum, Paulus æt ðam fotum; and Petrus ongan singan, and ealle ða apostolas eodon ymb ða bære Gode to lof singende.

11 Eac swylce englas of heofnum him onefn sungon, swa þæt eal seo eorðe þæs sanges wynsumnesse and ðæs sweges swiðnesse wæs gefylledo, swa þæt gedafenode[a] to deaðþenunga Drihtenes cenninge. Ða þis ða gehirdon þara sacerda ealdormen, þa eodon hi mid micelre mænigo of þære ceastre and cwædon: 'Hwæt is þes sweg on þus micelre winsumnesse?' Him þa wæs sæd: 'Maria[b28] is forðferedo, and Cristes ðegenas[c] hire lichoman to byrgenne beoð[29] and ðas herenesse ymb hie singað'. Mitte þe ðara sacerda ealdorman[d] þis gehyrde,[e] þætte þa apostolas hyhtende and singende / eodon, þa wæs he swiðe mid yrre gefylled and cwæð: 'Þis is modor þæs ðe us gedrefde and ure cyn'. Eode to þære bære and hie wolde oferweorpan and to eorðan afyllan. Mid þy þe he hire onhran, hraðe his handa wæron fæste in þære bære,[30] and he hangode on þære bære swa he no eorðan æthran,[31] ac micele wite he wæs ðread. And ða apostolas eodon swiðe hyhtende Domine. Englas þa wæron in þære lyfte;[f32] hi slogon þæt folc mid micelre blindnesse þe of þære ceastre ut eode.[g]

12 Þara sacerda ealdorman, se wæs fæst in þære bære, he cwæð to Petre: 'Ic þe bidde, þu halga Petrus, þæt þu me ne forseoh in þisse nydþearfe, ac gemyne, mid þy ðe sio duruþiowen þe hearm spæc[a] and þe þære dura wyrnde, ic þe wæs wel specende. Forðon mildsa me þurh Domine.'[33] Cwæð him Petrus to: 'Gelyf in God, þone þeos gebær in hire innoþe, þæt is Drihten Hælende Crist'.

13 Petrus[a] het þa bære asettan, and þara sacerda ealdormon cwæð: 'Ic gelyfe on Godes sunu, urne Drihten Hælende Crist, þone þios gebær in hire[b] innoþe'. And þa sona his handa wæron alysed from þære bære and his earmas wæron ungefele,[c34] and þæt wite þa git ne gewat from him.

---

[g] beran scealt] beran D  [h] ahof] *altered from* abof *by erasure*
11  [a] gedafenode] gefenode D  [b] maria] marian D  [c] ðegenas] *altered from* ðegenan
[d] ealdorman] ealdormen D  [e] gehyrde] gehyrdon D  [f] lyfte] bære lyfte D  [g] eode] eode[[n]] D
12  [a] spæc] speceð D
13  [a] Petrus] *preceded by erasure, possibly of 7*  [b] in hire] `in hire´ D  [c] alysed from þære bære and his earmas wæron ungefele] ungefele D

mouth. Therefore you must carry this palm; I shall carry this holy corpse with my fellow-apostles.' Paul said: 'Because I am the most junior of you all in the apostleship, I shall carry the bier with you'. Peter lifted up the head of the bier, Paul the foot; and Peter began to sing, and all the apostles surrounded the bier singing praise to God.

11    Likewise the angels sang alongside them from the heavens, so that the whole world was filled with the beauty of the song and the immensity of the sound, as was fitting for the obsequies of the mother of the Lord. When the chief priests heard this, they went out of the city with a great multitude and said: 'What is this sound of such great loveliness?' They were told: 'Mary has died, and Christ's servants are carrying her corpse to the sepulchre and are singing these praises around her'. When the high-priest heard this, that the apostles were going rejoicing and singing, then he was greatly filled with fury and said: 'This is the mother of that man who vexed us and our people'. He went to the bier, intending to overturn it and to make it fall down to the ground. When he touched it, his hands were immediately stuck to the bier and he hung on the bier so that he was not touching the ground, but he was tormented with great punishment. And the apostles went on, greatly rejoicing in the Lord. There were angels in the clouds; they struck the people who came out of the city with severe blindness.

12    The high-priest, who was stuck to the bier, said to Peter: 'I entreat you, holy Peter, that you do not despise me in this distress, but remember that when the woman who kept the door accused you and refused you the door, I spoke well of you. Therefore have mercy on me through the Lord.' Peter said to him: 'Believe in God, whom this woman bore in her womb, that is the Lord the Saviour Christ'.

13    Peter commanded the bier to be put down and the high-priest said: 'I believe in God's son, our Lord the Saviour Christ, whom this woman bore in her womb'. And then immediately his hands were freed from the bier and his arms were numb, but the torment had not left him

Cwæð him Petrus to: 'Gong to þissum lichoman and cweð: "Ic gelyfe in Drihten Hælend,[d] þone þios gebær in hire innoþe and fæmne hio þuruhwunude æfter beorðre"'.[e] Mid þy ðe he þus dide,[f] hraðe his hælo him wæs agifen, and he wuldrode Drihten and herede God.

14 Cwæð him Petrus to: 'Genim þisne palman of Iohannes handa and gong in þas ceastre. Þonne gemetest þu þær micel folc ablended. Sete þone palman ofer hira eagan and cweð: "Gelyf in God Fæder ælmihtigne". And ðonne swa hwylce swa gelyfan / willað onfoð gesyhðe; þa ðe ne willað gelyfan, hi sweltað.'[a] And þa onfeng se ealdormon þane palman and eode in þa ceastre. Þa gemette he þær micel folc cigendra and cweþendra: 'Wa us, mid micelre blindnesse we syndon slagene.' Hie þa gehirdon word þæs ealdormonnes and in[b] God gelifdon;[35] and þa sona onfengon hi gesyhþe. Fife þara manna[c] þuruhwunedon[36] in hira ungeleaffulnesse;[d] sona hi wæron deaþ sweltende. And se ealdormon brohte þone palman to þam apostolum and him sæde ealle þa þing þe þær gedon wæron.

15 And ða apostolas brohton Marian lichoman to þære stowe þe him Domine bebead. Hi hine[a] alegdon in þa byrgenne, and mid stane þa byrgene behlidon and þæræt gesetton. And þa, þy þriddan dæge, on underne, com ure Hælend mid micele engla[b] werode and cwæð to þam apostolum: 'Sib si mid eow'. Þa gebædon hi him to Drihtne and cwædon: 'Wuldor þe, Hælend, þu ana wyrcest micel wundor'.[c][37] Cwæð him Hælend to: 'Hwæt la, þa ic lichomlice mid eow wæs, ic eow gehet, þe me fylgende wæron,[d] mid þy þe ic[e] sitte on þam dome ofer ðam setle mines mægenþrimmes, ge sittað ofer twelf heahsetlum demende twelf Israela mægða. And þa sona of Israhela mægðe ic geceas, forðon þe hio fæmne þurhwunode æfter þam beorðre[f] and fæmne[g] hio wæs ær ðam beorðre.[38] And nu þone gedafenan ende hire lifes hio gefilde.[h] Hwæt willað ge þæt[i] ic hire do?' Petrus and ða apostolas cwædon: 'Drihten, nu is geþuht þinum þiowum þætte, swa swa ðu deaþe oferswiðdum ricsast in wuldre, swa awece þu lichoman þinre modor and mid þe bliþne in hiofen[j] gelæd'.

---

[d] Hælend] hælend[[e]] D    [e] beorðre] beorð`r´e[[r]] D    [f] dide] d[[.]]ide D
14  [a] sweltað] s`w´[[þ]]eltað D    [b] in] *not in* D    [c] manna] manna and D
[d] ungeleaffulnesse] ungealffullnesse D
15  [a] hine] *altered from* hire *by erasure* D    [b] engla] engla [[wæron]] D    [c] wundor] wuldor D    [d] wæron] *possibly* weron, *second letter blotched*    [e] ic] he D    [f] beorðre] beorð[[r]]`r´e D, *with the first r of `rre´ blotched*    [g] fæmne] fæmne [[..]] D, *possibly* he *erased*    [h] gefilde] gefild`e´ D    [i] þæt] hwæt D    [j] hiofen] hiofen[[ū]] D

yet. Peter said to him: 'Go to this corpse and say: "I believe in the Lord the Saviour, whom this woman bore in her womb and she remained a virgin after the birth"'. When he did this, his health was immediately restored to him, and he glorified the Lord and praised God.

14 Peter said to him: 'Take this palm from John's hand and go into the city. Then you will find many people blinded. Put this palm on their eyes and say: "Believe in God, the Father almighty". And then whoever is willing to believe will receive sight; those who are not willing to believe will die.' And then the high-priest took the palm and went into the city. Then he found a great crowd of people there calling out and saying: 'Alas, we are struck with great blindness!' Then they heard the words of the high-priest and believed in God; and then they immediately received their sight. Five of the people persisted in their lack of belief; they immediately perished in death. And the high-priest brought the palm to the apostles and told them all the things which had been done there.

15 And the apostles brought Mary's corpse to the place which the Lord had commanded them. They laid it in the sepulchre and covered the sepulchre with a stone and sat down by it. And then, on the third day, at the third hour, our Saviour came with a great host of angels and said to the apostles: 'Peace be with you'. Then they prayed to the Lord and said: 'Glory to you, Saviour, you alone perform great miracles'. The Saviour said to them: 'Well, when I was with you physically, I promised you, who followed me, that, when I shall sit in judgement on the throne of my majesty, you will sit on twelve thrones judging the twelve tribes of Israel. And I chose her directly from the tribe of Israel, because she remained a virgin after the birth and she was a virgin before the birth. And now she has fulfilled the proper end of her life. What do you wish me to do with her?' Peter and the apostles said: 'Lord, now it seems to your servants that, just as you reign in glory, having overcome death, so you should raise up the body of your mother and lead it with you happy into heaven'.

16 Þa cwæð Drihten to þam apostolum: 'Sy þæt æfter eowrum worde'. And þa het Drihten Gabriel / þone heahengel þæt he wylede þone stan from þære byrgene dura.[39] And Michael[a][40] se heahengel brohte saule þære halgan Marian beforan Drihtene and[b] cwæð:[41] 'Aris, wuldres aldor and gecorenesse fæt and heofonlic tempel'. And mid þy aras sio halige fæmne of þære byrgene and hio hi onhylde to Hælende, and hine wuldrode, and cwæð: 'Ælmihtig Drihten, þe eal þes middangeard fullice gehiran ne mæg,[c][42] sy hwæðre þin nama gebletsod and upahafen[d] in worulda worold'.[e]

17 Hwæt la, ure Drihten hi up ahof and hi cyste. Bebead hi þa Michaele þam heahengle, and hio þa wæs sona upahafen beforan Drihtne in þæt wolcen mid þam englum. Þa cwæð he Hælend to þam apostolum: 'Gongað to me'. And mid þy ðe hi to him eodon, þa cyste he hi sona ealle and him to cwæð: 'Mine sibbe ic eow selle and toforlæte, and ic beo mid eow eallum dagum oþ þisse worulde ende'. And þa he þis gecweden hæfde, mid þam singendum englum and mid his meder he wæs onfangen[a] on neorxnawonge. And þa apostolas wæron þurh Drihtnes mægen up in þæt wolcn ahafen, and þanon hi wæron anra[b] gehwylc hiora eft aseted in þa stowe ðær he ær lærde; and hi wæron secgende Drihtenes word and ondettende Godes þa micelan mihte, se liofað and ricsað in ealra worulda[c] woruld a butan ende. Amen.

16   [a] Michael] Gabriel D   [b] and] `and´ D   [c] ne mæg] mæg D   [d] upahafen] upafen D   [e] worold] woro[[..]]`ld´ D
17   [a] onfangen] *altered from* orfongen *by erasure*   [b] anra] *altered from* arra *by erasure*   [c] worulda] woruda D

16 Then the Lord said to the apostles: 'Let it be according to your word'. And then the Lord commanded the archangel Gabriel to roll the stone away from the door of the sepulchre. And the archangel Michael brought the soul of holy Mary before the Lord and he said: 'Arise, source of glory and vessel of election and heavenly temple'. And with that the blessed virgin arose out of the sepulchre and bowed to the Saviour and glorified him and said: 'Almighty Lord, whom all the world cannot fully praise, may your name nevertheless be blessed and raised up world without end'.

17 Well, our Lord raised her up and kissed her. Then he entrusted her to the archangel Michael, and she was immediately raised up before the Lord into the cloud with the angels. Then the Saviour said to the apostles: 'Come to me'. And when they had come to him, he kissed them all immediately and said to them: 'My peace I give you and leave with you and I will be with you all the days until the end of this world'. And when he had said this, he was received into paradise with the singing angels and with his mother. And the apostles were raised up into the cloud, through the power of the Lord, and from there each one of them was set down again in the place where he had been preaching; and they went on proclaiming the word of the Lord and confessing the great power of God, who lives and reigns for ever and ever, world without end. Amen.

# Commentary on Cambridge, Corpus Christi College, 41

[1] There is a gap of about twelve letters in the manuscript, with no trace of an erasure, corresponding to a break in the sense of the sentence. The Latin reads here: 'eo quod ipse solus plus ex eis uirgo esset in corpore'. Grant (*Three Homilies*, p. 34) suggests *in unwemnesse* to supply the gap but this does not convey John's uniqueness among the apostles in his chastity. Tristram (*Vier altenglische Predigten*, p. 234) says of this passage: 'es fehlt offensichtlich ein Stück, möglicherweise zumindest ein Wort wie *fæmne*', but *fæmne* alone is open to the same objection as Grant's suggestion and would, moreover, not correspond to the gap in the manuscript. I have supplied *ana unwemmed* for the missing words, which may not have been legible in the scribe's exemplar or which may have puzzled him, as he later probably mistranscribes 'unwemmast' as 'nu wemmast' (ch. 10).

[2] The Old English *in hire huse* does not correspond to the Latin *in domo parentum illius*. Whereas the Latin agrees with John XIX.27, 'accepit eam discipulus in sua', the Old English has her living in her own house. The source of the Old English may simply have omitted 'parentum'.

The tradition that Mary lived in Jerusalem goes back to the Acts of the Apostles I.12–14, where Mary, after Christ's Ascension, is in a house in Jerusalem among the apostles. *Pseudo-Melito* is the only apocryphon to place Mary's house next to the Mount of Olives (see above, p. 89).

[3] *Transitus B²* reads *secundo igitur anno*, with one manuscript reading *quarto decimo*. The third year seems to be confined to the Old English.

[4] The Latin reads 'cum thronis et angelis et uniuersis uirtutibus caeli'. The Old English translator has replaced the Latin with a more accessible rendering, introducing the saints who, as Tristram points out (*Vier altenglische Predigten*, p. 237), do not then appear at Mary's assumption. Some Latin manuscripts do include the archangels at this point (Z, Stuttgart, Württembergische Landes-universität, Cod. theol. okt. 57, eleventh to twelfth century, and E, Einsiedeln, Stiftsbibliothek, Cod. 250, twelfth century).

230

[5] The Latin reads 'Ecce hodie omnes apostoli per uirtutem Domini assumpti huc uenient' and no variant reading casts light on the Old English reading, which also does not correspond to the remainder of the text, from which it is clear that the apostles are still alive. Grant (*Three Homilies*, p. 35), suggests that the translator 'caught sight of the words *de paradiso* already rendered . . . and retranslated them', but this does not account for *gefean*. The phrase *of neorhxnawonges gefean* translates *in paradisi gaudia* in ch. 7, but this Latin phrase does not occur here. Tristram, on the other hand, points to the Greek *Iohannis Liber de dormitione Mariae*, in which three of the apostles (Luke, Simon and Thaddeus) are dead at this point and have to be resurrected by the Holy Spirit in order to be present at Mary's death and assumption (see above, p. 29). The problem with this is that the Old English reading does not agree with this tradition either, in that it appears to suggest that all the apostles are dead, and that no extant manuscript of *Transitus B*[2] contains any hint of this motif (indeed, they are incompatible with it).

[6] D reads here 'se engel me to cwæð', while the Latin reads 'cui ait angelus'. It is tempting to take the *me* as an abbreviation of *Marie*, as Grant does, although there is no indication of an abbreviation, but the Old English is following the Latin speech introductions very exactly at this point and *hire* is therefore perhaps more likely. *Me* may have been introduced because the three-times repeated *me* of the preceding sentence was still in the scribe's mind.

[7] The syntax of the Latin has defeated the translator: 'Benedictionem aeternam dedit tibi Dominus Deus tuus, cuius ego sum seruus et nuntius; non uidendi autem principem tenebrarum . . . .'. The relative clause 'cuius ego sum seruus et nuntius' has become a parenthesis in the Old English, with the *Deus* of the main clause of the Latin becoming a genitive in the Old English.

[8] The end of ch. 2 is much abbreviated in the Old English, but it is not, as Grant (*Three Homilies*, p. 35), says, corrupt. Typically, it is the continuation of Mary's speech, which has no bearing on the story, that is omitted.

[9] The Latin reads: 'nubes candida cum tonitrui fragore descendit'. The cloud is omitted from the Old English, which has John raised up and deposited in front of Mary's house without specifying how this was accomplished.

[10] Haibach-Reinisch's manuscripts T, F, O[1], O[2] and V of the Latin read *ab oculis*, a reading reflected in the Old English, while the other Latin manuscripts read *ante oculos*.

[11] Grant's note (*Three Homilies*, p. 35), on the Old English translator's 'sounder knowledge of feminine behaviour' and Tristram's (*Vier altenglische Predigten*, p. 240, n. to line 58), on such differences between Latin and Old English being characteristic are both in error, as *Transitus B*[2] reads here 'coepit prae gaudio flere' and the Old English is therefore merely following its source in

having the Virgin cry at this point. Tristram and Grant were following a source which read *exultauit in gaudio*.

[12] The translation omits any equivalent of Mary's 'Ecce enim uocata ingredior uiam uniuersae terrae', so making her mention of the Jews' plan somewhat abrupt.

[13] *deaðþenunga* occurs four times in this text, twice spelt *deaðþenuga* and twice *deaðþenunga*. The word occurs only one other time in Old English, in a glossary, where it is spelled with an *n* in the suffix. (*Dictionary of Old English*, 'D'). Although *deaðþenuga* is listed as an alternative spelling in the *Dictionary*, it looks like a case of scribal error, with omission of a contraction mark, and I have, therefore, emended to *deaðþenunga* (compare *hangode*, MS *hagode* in ch. 10).

[14] The Latin reads: 'ostendit illi uestimenta sepulturae suae et palmam illam luminis, quam acceperat ab angelo'. In the Latin, therefore, it is the palm, not the winding-sheet, which Mary receives from the angel; the Old English has omitted the palm, but this is probably a scribal error, rather than the translator's, as Mary's next sentence refers to *þes palma*. The Old English narrative has not, of course, shown Mary receiving *hire lichrægl* from the angel, which also indicates that the omission of the palm is accidental. In ch. 10 the translator has rendered *palma luminis* simply as *palman*, so I have not introduced an Old English equivalent of *luminis* in supplying the omission here.

[15] Every other instance in this text (five other instances) has the form *ands-* and I have therefore emended here. Tristram (*Vier altenglische Predigten*, p. 242, n. to line 70), suggests that the manuscript form *andwarode* is possibly a 'Misch-form von *andswarian* und dem im Spätae. altertümlichen *andwyrdan*', but the unanimity of the other forms indicates rather an error. The form *andwarode* does not occur otherwise in the *MCOE*.

[16] There is no equivalent to *ingongende* at this point in the Latin, which reads 'Et salutantes se inuicem apostoli mirabantur dicentes'; *mirabantur* in the Latin is not translated, but it is difficult to see how this could result in *ingongende*. The entry of the apostles is repeated in the Old English at the correct point in ch. 5, where it translates *introeuntes*, giving two entries by the apostles to Mary's house.

[17] The Old English *he him sæde* seems very abrupt, while the Latin reads: 'indicauit illis omnia quaecumque dixerat illi Maria'. Eyeskip from one *sæde* to another is a very plausible explanation of the abrupt Old English sentence and I have, therefore, supplied *ealles þæs þe Maria him sæde*. The eyeskip must have happened in an Old English text with *sæde* translating both *indicauit* and *dixerat*, as such eyeskip would not occur in the Latin.

[18] The Latin reads 'Deprecor uos, ut omnes unanimiter uigiletis, usque ad

horam illam qua Dominus ueniat' and I have therefore emended the *on* of the Old English manuscript to *oð*. The remainder of the Old English narrative shows the apostles indeed keeping watch until Christ comes.

[19] The time indication that this is the third day of their vigil is omitted, perhaps due to the double mention of third in the Latin: 'ecce subito tertia die circa horam tertiam'. Only *circa horam tertiam, æt underne*, is translated.

[20] The Lord's command in the Latin reads 'ascende igitur super stratum lectuli tui', whereas the D reading, 'astih of þinre reste', commands that Mary get down from her bed. As Mary, however, in obedience to this command, 'astah ofer hire bedde', I have emended Christ's command to also read 'astih ofer þinre reste'.

[21] The Latin reads here: 'uincebat enim omnem candorem niuis et uniuersa metalla argenti radians magni luminis claritate'. *æghwelces dæges hwitnesse* in the Old English is not paralleled in the Latin. The *leohtnesse* of the next phrase is feminine and does not agree with *ælces*; a genitive noun seems to have been omitted, paralleling *dæges*. *Snawes*, corresponding to the Latin *niuis*, has been supplied. Grant (*Three Homilies*, p. 37) suggests that an Old English word meaning 'metal' has been omitted here, but comparisons of brightness in Old English generally feature the sun, snow, glass or daylight, not a metal (see *MCOE* under *beorhte*).

[22] The Latin reads 'custos paradisi et princeps gentis Hebraeorum', while the Old English manuscript has 'neorxnawonges hyrde, ealdormon Ebrea ðeoden'. As the Old English reads very awkwardly as it stands, leaving either *ealdormon* or *ðeoden* in isolation, and as it would be very easy to confuse *ðeoden* and *ðeode*, I have emended it to agree with the Latin.

[23] The Latin reads 'Et dixit apostolis: Petre . . .' and, like the Old English, has a singular verb first in Christ's speech, followed by plural. The Old English has omitted *apostolis* in the introduction, reading instead *Swylce he cwæð to Petre*, and the plural verbs are therefore unexpected.

[24] The sense of the Old English demands a negative, which the Latin has ('uideri autem prae nimia luce coruscante non posset'), and I have therefore emended accordingly. The omission of *ne* is presumably due to the similarity of *ne* and the preceding word, *he*. The passage on Mary's radiance is simplified and abbreviated in the Old English. In the first clause of this sentence, *Mid þy þe hine ongiredon*, it is probable that the pronoun *hi* has been omitted, due to the repetition of the same two letters in the following word, *hine*, but, as it does not cause difficulties of comprehension, I have not supplied it.

[25] The manuscript reading, *nu wemmast*, is very clear, but does not make very good sense and does not correspond to the Latin, which reads 'tu solus ex nobis uirgo electus a Domino'. Grant (*Three Homilies*, p. 38), suggests emending to *unwemmast*, which is not attested in Old English, although

*unwemmed* is. This fits the Latin and the overall context better than *wemmast* ('you speak foolishly'?), which is retained by Tristram (*Vier altenglische Predigten*, p. 246), and defended by her as 'allzu menschlich' (all too human).

26 There is nothing in the Latin to correspond to 'mid þy ðe he us sæde þæt he þrowian wolde', and it presumably reflects the translator's biblical knowledge (see especially John XIII.21–3, the passage which also mentions the disciple lying on Jesus's breast).

27 The manuscript reading is clearly incomplete here, lacking an equivalent of Latin *debes*; *scealt* has been supplied.

28 The nominative of *Maria* is otherwise *Maria* or *Marie* in this text, so I have emended the *Marian* of the manuscript here. All but one of Haibach-Reinisch's manuscripts read 'Tunc exstitit qui diceret: "Maria exiit modo de corpore . . ."', but her P³ has instead an accusative and infinitive construction: 'Mariam modo exisse de corpore . . .'; it is possible that the source of the Old English translation had such a construction and that it misled the translator here, in which case *Marian* would, of course, be the original reading.

29 There is nothing in any of the Latin manuscripts to correspond to 'hire lichoman to byrgenne berað'.

30 The Old English omits the drying up of the hands, 'statim aruerunt ambae manus eius ab ipsis cubitis'.

31 'swa he no eorðan æthran' corresponds to and clarifies the Latin 'pars eius pendebat et pars adhaerebat lecto'.

32 The manuscript reads *in þære bære lyfte*, while the Latin has *in nubibus*. I have emended to omit *bære*, which may possibly have been a result of the scribe's eye going to *in þære bære* two sentences back. *þære bære lyfte* is translated as 'the air over the bier' by Grant and Tristram, but the phrase is syntactically very awkward and it seems very unlikely that it would have been composed by the translator without any Latin source.

33 See the discussion of this scene, pp. 73–6 above.

34 The Latin reads here: 'Statimque solutae sunt manus eius a feretro; et erant brachia eius arida, et non discesserat ab eo supplicium'. The Old English, *sona his handa wæron ungefele*, has jumped from *manus* to the adjective going with arms, *arida*, and has therefore failed to say that the high-priest's hands were set free from the bier. Such an important point is unlikely to have been omitted and Grant suggests (*Three Homilies*, p. 40) that 'the Old English probably read 7 þa sona his handa wæron ungefeolene (from *feolan=adhaerere*, BT, p. 277, *s.v. feolan*) but the copyist's eye fell to *ungefele* and he made the omission'. The eyeskip, however, was probably from one *wæron* to the next and so it is not necessary to postulate a unique form such as *ungefeolene* as a translation of *solutae*. *alysed* seems a more probable choice and I have, therefore, supplied 'alysed from þære bære and his earmas wæron'.

35 Haibach-Reinisch reads here: 'Cum ergo audissent uerba principis sacerdotum narrantis magnalia Dei, crediderunt et receperunt uisum', but her manuscripts O¹, O² and V read 'crediderunt in Dominum Jesum Christum et imposita palma super oculos eorum receperunt uisum'. Though the Old English leaves out the clause about the palm, it is clearly based on such a reading. I have supplied *in*, as elsewhere in the text in the same context (chs. 12, 13, 14) *geliefan* is always accompanied by a preposition, either *on* or, more usually, *in*.

36 D reads *and þuruhwunedon* but the *and* seems redundant, although it is retained by Grant. Tristram (*Vier altenglische Predigten*, p. 250) suggests that: 'Da es eine Reihe von ae. Wörtern gibt die zwischen *an/on* und *and/ond* als Präfix schwanken ... and da bei Wörtern, die mit dem Element *and*-beginnen, in den Mss häufig dafür die tyronische Kürzel 7 geschrieben wurde, ist es möglich, dass hier durch Vertauschung 7 = *on* ist and so losgelöst für die Präposition steht. – *on* im Sinne von "weiter"'. There is nothing in the Latin sentence which 'weiter' could translate, however, and the argument seems rather forced. Grant (*Three Homilies*, p. 40), on the other hand, says '7 is a relative pronoun; see *BT Supplement*, p. 38, *s.v. and*, III'. While BT does give instances where *and* is a relative pronoun, they are in cases where the *and* connects coordinate clauses: '(1) in which the subject of the second is the object of the first, but is not expressed ... (2) where the object of the second is that of the first, but is not expressed'. Neither of these is the case here; there are in fact no coordinate clauses here. Because, therefore, it is difficult to find a satisfactory explanation for *and* here, it has been omitted from the edited text.

The number five is found in almost all of the manuscripts of *Transitus B²* but it originated in a mistaken copying of *quinque* instead of *quicumque*; see Haibach-Reinisch, *Ein neuer 'Transitus'*, pp. 143–4.

37 The Latin reads 'Gloria tibi, Deus, qui facis mirabilia magna solus' and I have therefore emended D's second *wuldor* to *wundor*. The error is easily explicable as repetition of *wuldor* from the beginning of the sentence.

38 The Old English has omitted some of the Latin here, resulting in a lack of logic, as Christ did not choose Mary as his mother because she remained a virgin after his birth. The Latin reads: 'Hanc ergo ex una tribu Israel elegit iussio Patris mei, ut sumerem carnem ex ea. Propter quod sanctificaui illam mihi templum inuiolabile castitatis, ut uirgo ante partum et uirgo post partum permaneret.' The *forðon ðe* in the Old English corresponds to the Latin *propter quod*, but is followed by a different clause. It is difficult to know whether the Old English translator introduced the lack of consequence or whether the scribe of D has omitted part of the Old English, corresponding to the Latin.

[39] Only T, F, O$^1$, O$^2$ and V among Haibach-Reinisch's manuscripts have the sentence: 'Gabriel archangelus reuoluit lapidem ab ostio monumenti', translated here, at this point in the text.

[40] No Latin manuscript has Gabriel alone present Mary's soul to Christ, as is the case in D; most Latin manuscripts have Michael only, and B, P$^2$ and P$^3$ have both Michael and Gabriel. I have therefore emended Gabriel to Michael in the Old English text, as the substitution of Gabriel would be an easy error to make in view of his role in the previous sentence. That Michael was the original reading in the Old English is supported by the fact that Christ then entrusts Mary's resurrected body to Michael, in both Old English and Latin versions, and Michael then departs with both soul and body. Michael is also always the psychopomp in Christian tradition. Grant also points out that the Old English text seems to have put Gabriel for Michael in error here.

[41] The speaker of this sentence is Christ, not the archangel. The Latin introduces the speech much more explicitly ('Tunc Saluator locutus est dicens') and such a clause is probably missing from the Old English. It is possible that the translation originally read 'and Drihten cwæð' and that *Drihten* was accidentally omitted because of the proximity of *Drihtene* in the preceding clause.

[42] The Old English requires the negative of the Latin sentence in order to make sense and I have emended accordingly.

# The Old English assumption homily
# in Cambridge, Corpus Christi College,
# 198 (Blickling XIII)

# Editorial Introduction

This Old English apocryphon survives in two versions, one in the
Blickling Homilies (B) and the second in CCCC 198 (F). The B version,
which lacks a page, was edited by Morris, without the benefit of the other
manuscript or knowledge of the exact source, in a volume without notes,
and the page which is missing from B was later edited from F by
Willard.[1] While Morris's edition is in many ways a remarkable achieve-
ment, given the nature of this peculiar text, it is, I think, time for a new,
complete edition which utilizes the source and which discusses the many
problems of this difficult work.

Of the two manuscripts of this second Old English assumption
apocryphon, B and F, I have chosen to edit this homily from the text in F
for a number of reasons. In the first place, B has already been edited by
Morris and a new edition of B as a whole, by Gatch and Stoneman, is in
progress, in which B xiii will be re-edited, whereas most of the text in F
has never before been edited. Secondly, as noted above, a page is missing
in B, unlike F, which has a complete text (apart from a few short
omissions). The two manuscripts are probably about a generation apart in
date, B dating from around the millennium and F from the first half of
the eleventh century, with the additions in Part II of the manuscript,
which include this homily, in nearly contemporary hands. The compilers
of F Part II, however, seem to have worked in an old-fashioned centre and
'had available to them only material known to have existed before the end
of the tenth [century]',[2] so perhaps minimizing any importance which
could be attributed to the difference in date. Scragg suggests that F Part

---

[1] Morris, ed., *The Blickling Homilies*, pp. 136–59; Willard, 'On Blickling Homily XIII'.
[2] Scragg, 'The Homilies of the Blickling Manuscript', p. 312.

II was probably not made in the same centre which produced Part I and that it is not unlikely that Part II was written in the same unknown centre in which B was produced.[3] While this cannot be proved, F seems to be close to B in its milieu of origin, despite its later date.

The two texts, apart from the lacuna in B, are very similar; as Willard observes, 'it is extraordinary how few variant readings are to be recorded in editing either with the other as a second text',[4] and the most common variant is *þ* in B where F has *ð*. Scragg points out that in this homily 'some unusual spellings (e.g. *góod*, 'good', *culufre*, 'dove') appear in both manuscripts, as do simple errors (e.g. *geongweardode* for *ge-ondweardode*, 'answered', *earan* for *earman*, *deoflum* for *deoflu*)'.[5] He points out also that the two manuscripts 'have upper-case letters, often of a distinctive shape, at the same points of the text, and have other paleographical details in common'.[6] But F could not have been copied from B because it preserves some better readings, such as *stengum* rather than B's *strengþum*, and better readings in some of the Latin quotations, even though this scribe had 'a very limited understanding of Latin'[7] and is unlikely to have corrected his source on his own initiative. F must, therefore, have been copied from a text behind B rather than B itself; and as the simple errors they share would not, Scragg argues, have survived a long transmission process, but would have been corrected, the two manuscripts must have a 'common ancestor lying at no great distance behind them'.[8]

The two copies of the homily were, therefore, probably copied from the same exemplar (or at the very least they share a common ancestor with very few intermediate copies), possibly at the same centre. As the F scribe of this homily was a 'mechanical and unthinking copyist',[9] we can assume that his version represents the common ancestor fairly accurately and this is, of course, supported by its agreement with B. He does make a number of 'mechanical errors (especially the omission of letters and short words)',[10] but B, too, is not immune to such mechanical errors, although they are less frequent than in F. Even though it is later in date, the F copy has a very similar status to that in B, therefore, and is, of course, superior in being a full text.

---

[3] *Ibid.*, pp. 309–16.     [4] 'On Blickling Homily XIII', p. 4.

[5] 'The Homilies of the Blickling Manuscript', p. 313, but note that *geondweardode* does not mean 'answered', but 'presented'.

[6] *Ibid.*     [7] *Ibid.*, p. 314, n. 68.     [8] *Ibid.*, p. 313.     [9] *Ibid.*

[10] *Ibid.*, p. 314.

F, therefore, has almost as good – or bad – a text as B, has some novelty value and is complete; it is, accordingly, the base text for this edition of the apocryphon.

This homily poses unusual problems for the editor. The translator's Latin was poor and his grasp of the role of Latin inflectional endings, in particular, was erratic and unreliable. This occasionally results in a translation which is almost nonsensical, but the nonsense is, in most cases, clearly original, not the consequence of a later scribe's intervention. Willard argued that the translator was also working from a poor Latin source and he summed up the state of the text very clearly:

> The Blickling assumption story is remarkable for its amazing treatment of its Latin original, for its frequent reversal of meaning, for its curious inability to follow the thread of the narrative, particularly in long passages of reported action, and for its strange readings, suggesting that the Old English translator possessed inadequate Latinity, and that, in addition, he worked from a Latin text already corrupt and difficult to read. . . . The morphological features of the Latin seem to have been as ineffectual with that Anglo-Saxon translator a millennium ago as they are with the schoolboy of today. Indications of number, gender, person, mood, case, voice and tense are disregarded as though they had not been.[11]

Willard argued further that the Old English text, faulty as it was to begin with, 'suffered much in transmission, so as to become very difficult to read; and that some scribe took it upon himself to improve this difficult text, often rendering confusion worse confounded'.[12] What he regarded as 'one of the most spectacular'[13] instances proving the intervention of this scribe is the reading *hlifigende ofer sæs brim*, which he convincingly traced back to an original *hlinigende ofer his bosm*.[14] As both manuscripts share this reading, this hypothetical revising scribe would have had to have worked on the text at the stage of or before the common ancestor of both F and B. In addition to such 'improvements', Willard also attributed the material from the Beatitudes inserted into the *Magnificat* to this revising scribe, as well as the other amplifications of the *Magnificat*. We have, therefore, according to Willard (1) a corrupt Latin source; (2) a translator with a very poor grasp of Latin; (3) a stage in which the Old English text became very difficult to read; and (4) a revising scribe, who sought to

---

[11] Willard, 'An Old English *Magnificat*', pp. 6–7.     [12] *Ibid.*, p. 23.     [13] *Ibid.*

[14] Discussed below, p. 43.

make some kind of sense out of the difficult passages in his exemplar and who also inserted a 'gratuitous admixture of extraneous matter'[15] into the version of the *Magnificat*.

Some of Willard's explanations for the state of the text are, however, open to question: indeed, only his stage 2 is beyond dispute, even though he claimed that his notes to the text proved all these stages.[16] Stage 1, the corruption of the Latin source, is not proved beyond doubt by Willard's notes to those parts of the text which he discussed in detail; very few of them indicate a fault in the Latin. He suggested at one point that *honorem* was missing from the Latin source,[17] at another that, '*Dominus* must have been missing in the Latin source; its absence there would deprive *dixit* of its proper subject'[18] and later that, '*Iussione patris* is represented by *he mines Fæder hæse*. The rest appears to be an interpretative substitution for an unintelligible reading in the source. The source here must have had a reading rather different in detail from what we find in *Transitus B*.'[19] *Transitus B*² does indeed have a different reading, which throws light on the Old English text,[20] and the source cannot, therefore, be regarded as having had 'an unintelligible reading' here. The possible omissions of *honorem* and *dominus* hardly seem sufficient to establish the faulty nature of the source, as Willard's other comments on the probable form of the Latin source suggest abbreviations and variant readings, but not corruptions. Except for these two cases, the strange readings in the Old English all appear to stem from the translator's feeble grasp of Latin, which is beyond question, or, in the case of the *hlifigende ofer sæs brim* reading, from a later scribe's alterations. The corruption of the Latin source is, therefore, very much open to doubt, rather than being proved by Willard's discussion. Stage (3) also seems to me to be of dubious validity, as only one piece of evidence is presented: once again that of the reading *hlifigende ofer sæs brim*, where insular *s* and *r* were probably confused. This single reading hardly seems sufficient basis on which to argue that the Old English text went through a stage in which the script was difficult to read.

Willard's last argument, that a revising scribe, rather than merely attempting to make sense of his difficult exemplar, 'has taken it upon

---

[15] *Ibid.*, p. 27.    [16] Willard, 'The Two Accounts', p. 5, n. 1.
[17] 'On Blickling Homily XIII', pp.14–15.    [18] 'The Two Accounts', p. 9, n. 9.
[19] *Ibid.*, p. 13, n. 2.    [20] See below, note 112.

himself to embellish his original as he copied it',[21] is also questionable. The *hlifigende ofer sæs brim* reading originated in an attempt to make sense of a mechanical error, and I would not agree with Willard's view: 'that a revising scribe has had a hand in shaping our Old English redaction of *Transitus C* [W] is revealed clearly by [this] reading'.[22] It seems to me that what we have here is an isolated attempt to make sense of a flawed reading which had originated, according to Willard himself, in a peculiarity of insular script, and there is nothing in the text, until we come to the *Magnificat*, which is more than this. The only other instance quoted by Willard, apart from the *Magnificat*, is the reading *ic gefille* and that does not seem to me to be a comparable case.[23] A 'revising scribe', with its suggestions of deliberate reworking, is a rather misleading description therefore, at least with regard to the assumption story itself. The problem of the expanded and interpolated form of the *Magnificat*, which cannot be explained by mechanical error, is, I believe, of a totally different nature, and it is only in the translation and amplification of this final section of the text that embellishment can be suspected.

Willard argued that the material from the Beatitudes interpolated into the *Magnificat* is not original and also believed that 'the Other-world material to be found in verses 7 and 8 [of the *Magnificat* translation] is due to the reviser'.[24] There can be no doubt that there is something radically wrong with the text here, as the Sermon on the Mount material is combined with the *Magnificat* in a very odd fashion. It could be argued, though, that Willard's solution of a very clumsy revising scribe who 'often render[ed] confusion worse confounded'[25] is not entirely persuasive. An original translator, whose grasp of Latin was very poor and who produced a muddled text, having the misfortune to have his errors compounded by an embellishing reviser, who was at least as inept as he, could be thought to strain the bounds of credibility somewhat, when the whole confusion could plausibly be laid at the door of the original translator. Willard does not attempt to explain why the insertion of the Beatitudes would have been carried out in so clumsy a fashion by his revising scribe and it seems to me that when this problem is looked at in detail, as I have attempted to do in the notes to the text, it makes more

---

[21] 'An Old English *Magnificat*', p. 21    [22] *Ibid.*, p. 21.

[23] See below, note 10.    [24] 'An Old English *Magnificat*', p. 23.    [25] *Ibid.*

sense to ascribe the form of the text, as it has come down to us in both manuscripts, to the original author.

In this edition, therefore, I am working on the basis that the entire text, excluding, of course, mechanical errors, was the work of one translator and I have not attempted to tamper with the additional matter in the *Magnificat*. I have emended only when the reading of the manuscript is manifestly in error and when the emendation is supported by the B reading; when comparison with B shows that something is omitted from F; when the reading of both manuscripts is faulty because of a mechanical error in their exemplar or at an earlier stage in the transmission of the work (e.g. the omission of *ongan*[26] or the omission of *-m* in *earman*);[27] or occasionally when a comparison with the source supports an emendation, as with *on* for *ond*.[28]

Punctuation, capitalization and word-division are modern, and rare or unique spellings are retained whenever they can be justified at all. So, for example, *eaðmoðnesse* is retained as it occurs twice and *ð* and *d* could be used to represent the same sound. I have also retained *ussun* (B *ussum*) and *swidram* (B *swiþran*), even though these do not appear in the *MCOE*, as *-m* and *-n* seem not to have been distinguished in the pronunciation of inflections. Abbreviations are silently expanded in the text. As *ond* occurs twice in F and *and* not at all, I have used *ond* throughout in expanding the nota 7. In the case of *se eadiga* and *on neorxnawange*, F twice reads *seadiga* and twice *oneorxnawange*, but I have in each case emended to the fuller forms. As B has been edited by Morris and is available, I have not presented a complete set of variants in the apparatus. Variant readings exclude spelling and inflectional endings, unless they have significance beyond their linguistic interest.

The paragraph divisions of the Latin sources have been followed in the Old English text to facilitate comparison, even though they occasionally fit very awkwardly with its sense divisions and the Old English also skips a paragraph. Wilmart's numbering of *Transitus W* is followed until the Old English skips a paragraph, after which Wilmart's chapter numbers are given in brackets after the Old English chapter numbers. When the source switches to *Transitus B²*, I have followed the chapter divisions of Haibach-Reinisch's text but have continued the sequence of Old English chapter numbers, giving Haibach-Reinisch's chapter numbers in brackets.

[26] See note 81.   [27] See note 131.   [28] See note 79.

The *Magnificat* section at the end forms the final chapter of the edited text.

In the translation I have sometimes used the Latin sources as a guide to meaning of the Old English text, as their sense was what the translator was striving towards: even where he did not succeed in reproducing the meaning of the Latin, he often produced a corruption of it, and the Latin is valuable in seeing what he was aiming at. My translation does not, however, always strive for a smooth sense, as Morris's does, because the translator often seems not to have thought beyond the level of the clause or the sentence. The effect is frequently that of someone struggling with a glossed text, which gave meanings for the Latin words but did not analyse them syntactically, and it seems at times to be only a matter of luck whether the sense is correct or not.

# The text

1    Men ða leofestan, gehyrað nu hwæt her segð on ðissum bocum be
ðære halgan fæmnan[a] Sancta Marian, hu be hire on ðas tid geworden wæs.
Heo wæs wæccende dæges ond nihtes ond hi gebiddende æfter Drihtnes
upstige.   Ða com hire to Drihtnes engel ond he wæs cweðende: 'Aris ðu
Maria ond onfoh[b] ðissum palmtwige ðe ic þe nu brohte, forðan ðu bist
soðlice ær ðrim dagum genumen of ðinum lichoman[1] ond ealle Drihtnes[c]
apostolas beoð sende þe to bebyrgenne'.[2]

2    Þa cwæð Maria to ðæm engle: 'Hwæt is ðin nama?' Ða cwæð se
engel to hire: 'Hwæt secestu minne naman, forðon he is mycel ond
wundorlic?'

3    Þa Sancta Maria ðis geherde, ða astah heo on ðone munt þe wæs
genemned[a] Oliuete. Ond þæt wæs soðlice swiðe scinende palmtwig ond
hit wæs ða swa leoht swa se mergenlica steorra, ðe heo ðær onfeng of ðæs
engles handa.[3] Þa wæs heo swiðe wynsumigende ond mid mycelre[b] gefean
gewuldrad; ond ealle ða ðe þær wæron[4] hi gesawon þæt se engel ðe ær
com to hire astah[c] on heofonas mid micclum leohte.

4    / Þa wæs Maria eft hweorfende to hire huse ond heo ða alegde þæt
palmtwig mid ealre eadmodnesse, ðe heo ær onfeng of ðæs engles handa;
ond heo eac alegde hire hrægl ðe heo mid gegyred wæs, ond þwoh hire
lichoman, ond heo hie gegyrede mid þon selestan hregle. Ond ða wæs

---

Text from F, fols. 350r–359r

1    [a] fæmnan] fe`æ´mnan F    [b] onfoh] on[[p]]`f´oh F    [c] Drihtnes] driht F
3    [a] genemned] `ge´nenned F, *with extra minim added to correct first* n *to* m; nemned
B    [b] mycelre] m[[i]]`y´celre F; mycle B    [c] astah] asta[[g]]`h´ F

246

# The translation

1   Beloved people, listen now to what it says here in these books about the holy virgin St Mary, [and] what happened to her at this time. She was watching and praying day and night after the Lord's ascension. Then the angel of the Lord came to her and said: 'Arise, Mary, and receive this palm-branch which I have now brought to you, because truly within three days you will be taken from your body and all the apostles of the Lord will be sent to bury you'.

2   Then Mary said to the angel: 'What is your name?' Then the angel said to her: 'Why do you ask my name, for it is great and wonderful?'

3   When St Mary heard this, she went up the hill which is called the Mount of Olives. And that was truly a very radiant palm-branch which she received there from the hand of the angel, and it was then as bright as the morning star. Then she rejoiced greatly and she was glorified with great joy; and all those who were there saw that the angel who had come to her ascended into the heavens with a great light.

4   Then Mary returned to her house again and, with all humility, laid down the palm-branch which she had received from the hand of the angel; and she also laid aside the garment in which she was clothed and washed her body and she dressed herself in her best garment. And then

247

swiðe gefeonde ond swiðe blissiende ond bletsode God ond wæs cweðende: *'Benedico nomen tuum et laudabile in secula seculorum.*[a] Ic bletsige ðinne þone halgan naman, forðon ðe he is micel ond hergendlic in worlda world. Ic ðe bidde, min Drihten, þæt ðu sende ofer me ðine bletsunga.' Ða wæs Maria cweðende: 'Mid ðy ðe ðu me hate of minum lichoman gewitan, ðonne onfoh ðu minre sawle'. Ða wæs se engel cweðende: 'Ne beo ðu, Maria, geunreted'.[5]

5 Mid ðy ðe heo ðis gehyrde,[6] ða wæs heo cleopiende ond cegende ealle hire magas, ða ðe þær neah wæron, ond wæs cwæðende: 'Gehera ð me nu ealle ond gelyfað ge ealle on God Fæder ælmihtigne, forðon ðys morgenlican dæge ic beo gangende of minum lichoman ond ic gange to minum Gode. Ond ic bidde eow ealle þæt ge anmodlice wacian mid me oð ða tid ðe on ðæm dæge bið mines gewinnes ende.'[7]

6 (7) Ond mid ðy ðe heo ðys gecweðen[a] hæfde, ða com ðær sona se eadega[b] Iohannes ond slog on ða duru ðæs huses, þæt heo onarn,[8] ond wæs ingangende to hire. Ond geseah þæt Sancta Maria wæs gedrefedu on hire gaste, ond heo sworette, ond heo ne mihte forhabban þæt heo ne weope. Ond wæs cweðende:[9] 'Fæder Iohannes, westu gemindig min, forðon ðe Drihten / is ðinra beboda lareow, ond þæt he me bebead þæt ic gefille. On ðissum dæge he gewat fram us þæt he wolde ðrowian for middaneardes hælo.'[10]

7 (8) Ond ða cwæð se halga Iohannes to hire: 'Hwæt wilt ðu þæt ic ðe doo?' Ða ondsworede him seo halige Maria ond wæs cwæðende: 'Ne bidde ic ðe nanes ðinges elles buton þæt ðu gehealde minne lichoman ond hine gesette on byrgenne, forðon ðe ic beo ær ðrim dagum[11] gongende of minum lichoman'. Ða gehyrde se halga Iohannes þæt ða Iudeas cwæðan:[12] 'Uton we nu gan ond acwellan ða apostolas[13] ond Marian lichoman geniman ond hine forbærnan'. Mid ðy ðe ðis gehyrde se eadiga Iohannes, ða wæs he cweðende: 'On ðissum dæge he wat fram us of lichoman'.[14] Ond he ða wes wepende on Godes gesyhðe ond cweðende: 'Eala, Drihten, hwæt syndon we ðe ðu gecyddest[a] swa micle sorge?'

8 (9) Ond ða cegde seo halige Maria to ðem halgan Iohanne on hire hordcofan[a] ond him æteowde ealne hire gyrelan ond þæt scinende

---

4   [a] seculorum] seculum F, B
6   [a] gecweðen] gecwæðen, *with* a *of* æ *partly erased* F; gecweden B   [b] eadega] *page missing after this in* B
7 (8)   [a] gecyddest] *first* d *altered from* ð *by erasure*
8 (9)   [a] hordcofan] h[[eortan]]`ordcofan´ F

248

she rejoiced greatly and was very glad and she blessed God and said: *'Benedico nomen tuum et laudabile in secula seculorum.* I bless your holy name, because it is great and praiseworthy, world without end. I beseech you, my Lord, that you bestow your blessing on me.' Then Mary said: 'When you command me to leave my body, then let you receive my soul'. Then the angel said: 'Do not be sad, Mary'.

5   When she heard this, then she called and summoned all her relations who were nearby, and said: 'Let you all listen to me now and all believe in God the almighty father, because tomorrow I shall depart from my body and I shall go to my God. And I ask you all that, with one accord, you watch with me until the hour of the day when there shall be an end to my toil.'

6 (7)   And when she had said this, then immediately the blessed John came there and knocked on the door of the house, so that it opened, and went in to her. And he saw that St Mary was troubled in her spirit, and she sighed, and she could not refrain from weeping. And she said: 'Father John, be mindful of me, because the Lord is the teacher of your commandments, and I shall fulfil that which he commanded me. On this day he departed from us in order that he might suffer for the salvation of the world.'

7 (8)   And then the holy John said to her: 'What do you wish that I should do for you?' Then the holy Mary answered him and said: 'I do not ask you for anything other than that you guard my body and lay it in the tomb, because within three days I shall depart from my body'. Then the holy John heard that the Jews said: 'Let us go now and kill the apostles and take Mary's body and burn it'. When the blessed John heard this, then he said: 'On this day he departed from us, out of the body'. And then he was weeping in the sight of God and said: 'O Lord, what are we, to whom you have revealed such great sorrow?'

8 (9)   And then the holy Mary called the holy John into her chamber and showed him all her clothing and the shining palm-branch which she

249

pealmtwig ðe heo ær onfeng of ðæs engles handa. Ond heo him æteowde ealle hire medomnesse[15] ond cwæð to him: 'Ic ðe bidde, fæder Iohannes, þæt ðu ðis palmtwig onfo, ond hit ðonne ber beforan minre bæran, mid ðy ðe ic sy gongende of minum lichoman'.

9 (10)  Ða cwæð se halga Iohannes to hire: 'Ne mæg ic þæt ana don; ac her[16] cumað mine efnapostolas to me, ond we ðonne beoð ealle on annesse gesamnode / on ðisse stowe, ðurh Drihtnes mægen, to alysnesse[17] ðines lichoman'.

10 (11)  Mid ðy ðe he ðis gecweden hæfde, ða wæs he gongende of hire hordcofan. Ða wæs semninga geworden mycel[a] ðunorrad, þæt eall seo stow wæs gedrefedu, ond ealle ða ðe ðær wæron on ðæm huse. Ond ða semninga ealle ða apostolas tugon hie upp mid wolcnum,[18] ond sume hie[19] wæron gesette beforan þæs huses dura[b] ðære halgan Marian. Ond hie gesawon be him tweonum þæt heo wæs gewuldrod[c][20] ond hie ða haletton on hie ond hie cwædon: '*Deo gratias*, forðon we wæron todæge ealle on annesse gemedemode.[21] Forðon is soðlice se cwide gefylled Dauides ðæs witgan ðe he cwæð: "*Ecce quam*[d] *bonum et quam*[e] *iocundum habitare fratres in hunum.* Hu good is ond hu wynsum þæt mon eardie on ðara gebroðra annesse."' Ond ða cwæð hira ælc to oðrum: 'Uton gebiddan us to urum Drihtne þæt he us þæt cuð gedo[22] þæt he us todæge wolde on ðisse tide[23] gesomnian'.

11 (12)  Ða cwæð Petrus to Paule[24]: 'Broðor Paulus, aris ðu ond gebide ðe ær, forðon ðu eart leohtes swer,[25] ond ealle ða ðe ymbe me standað hie syndon[a] beteran ðonne ic,[26] ond ðu eart forelærende on ðara apostola gebede ond ðu eart eall Drihtnes gyfe full'.[27] Ða wæron ealle ða apostolas gefeonde for Paules[b] eaðmodnesse.

12 (13)  Ond, swa swa Petrus gesette ðisum mænniscum cynne, ða aðenede Sanctus Petrus his handa to Gode[28] ond wæs cweðende: '*Domine* / *Deus omnipotens, qui sedes super cherubin et* p*rofundi.* Drihten ælmihtig God, ðu ðe sitest ofer cherubine ond ofer deopnesse ealra grunda,[29] ond we ahebbað ure handa to ðe on anlicnesse þinre rode, ond on ðinre cyððe we reste habbað, forðon ðe ðu sylest urum limun reste, forðon ðe hie on ðinum noman wunnon,[30] ond ðu eallum oferhydigum eaðmodnesse

---

10 (11)   [a] mycel] mi`y´cel F   [b] dura] B *resumes here*   [c] gewuldrod] gew[[o]]ʹuʹldrod F   [d] quam] B; quan F   [e] quam] B; quan F

11 (12)   [a] hie syndon] hie hie syndan B   [b] Paules] B; paulus F

had received from the hand of the angel. And she disclosed all her dignity to him and said to him: 'I ask you, father John, that you accept this palm-branch, and carry it then in front of my bier, when I shall go from my body'.

9 (10)   Then the holy John said to her: 'I cannot do that alone; but my fellow-apostles will come here to me, and then we will all be gathered in unity in this place, through the power of the Lord, for the redemption of your body'.

10 (11)   When he had said this, then he went out of her chamber. Then there was suddenly a great peal of thunder, so that all the place was disturbed, and all those who were in the house. And then suddenly all the apostles pulled her up in the clouds and some of them were set down before the door of the house of the holy Mary. And they saw among themselves that she was glorified and then they greeted her and they said: '*Deo gratias*, because we were all honoured today in unity. Because truly the word of the prophet David is fulfilled which he said: "*Ecce quam bonum et quam iocundum habitare fratres in hunum*. How good and how joyful it is that one should live in the unity of brothers."' And then each of them said to the others: 'Let us pray to our Lord that he should make known to us that for which he wished to gather us together today at this time'.

11 (12)   Then Peter said to Paul: 'Brother Paul, arise and pray first, because you are a pillar of light, and all those who are standing around me are better than I am, and you are the foremost teacher in the prayer of the apostles and you are all full of the grace of the Lord'. Then all the apostles rejoiced because of Paul's humility.

12 (13)   And, just as Peter appointed for this human kind, so St Peter stretched out his hands to God and said: '*Domine Deus omnipotens, qui sedes super cherubin et profundi*. Lord almighty God, you who sit above the cherubim and above the depth of all abysses, and we raise up our hands to you in the likeness of your cross; and in knowledge of you we have rest, because you give rest to our limbs because they have worked in your name and you give humility to all the proud and you conquer death. You

forgifest ond oferswiðest[a] deað. Ðu eart soðlice ure[b] rest ond ðu, Drihten, eart ure scyldend ond on ðe we cegeað,[31] ðu ðe wunast on Suna ond Fæder on ðe, ond ðu eart ana mid Halige Gaste on worlda[c] world.' Ða ondsweredon[d] him ealle ða apostolas ond cwædon: '*Amen*'.

13 (14)    Ða arn se eadiga Iohannes to eallum ðam apostolum ond wæs cweðende to him: '*Benedicite fratres*'. *Et dixerunt*[a32] *Petrus*. 'Bletsiað ge, broðor ða leofestan, urne Drihten.' Ða cwæð Petrus ond Andreas[b] to Iohanne: 'Ðu leafa Drihten,[33] gecyðe us hwylce gemete ðu come todæg to us'. Ða cwæð Iohannes:[c] 'Bletsiað, broðor ða leofestan, urne God ond gehyrað ge ealle þæt he wæs gongende todæg on ðas ceastre ond he wes lærende þæt ge eow gebædon to Gode on ða nigoðan tid ðæs dæges.[34] Ond ða semninga astag micel wolcen on ða ilcan stowe on ðære ðe we[d] wæron gesamnode, ðær we gehyrdon Godes word.'[35] Ond ða sæmninga ða embsealdon ealle ða apostolas ða halgan Marian ond hie gegripan on hire middel. Ond ða gesawon hie ond ealle ða ðe ðær wæron[36] þæt se eadiga[e] Michael genam ond ða slog on ðæs huses duru;[37] ond heo him ne forwyrnde,[38] ac heo hie ontynde. Ond he ðær gemette swiðe manig folc / ðe ðær ætstodan, ond ðær eac stod þære halgan Marian sweostor ond heo spræc to ðæm werode[f39] ond cwæð: 'Ðys mergenlicen dæge heo bið gongende of lichoman'.[40] Ond ða ælc ðara ðe ðis gehyrde wæs swiðe wæpende.[41] Ond ða wæs Maria cweðende: '*Nunc, fratres, audite*.[42] Broðor ða leofestan, geherað ge me nu ealle þæt ic beo ðys mergenlican dæge gongende of lichoman.' Þa cwædon ða apostolas to hire: 'Ne ceara ðu, Maria, ne ne wep, þæt ðin folc ne sy gedrefed. Forðon ðis cwæð ure Drihten[g] ond ure beboda lareow, mid ðy ðe he wæs hlinigende ofer his bosm,[h] ða he wæs æt his efengereordum. Forðon ic eow manige ealle þæt, ge ðis folc wepende þæt her hymb-standeð.' Þa þæt folc ongan tweogan on hire heortan ond hio cwædon: 'To hwan[i] ondrædeð[j] ðeos halige Maria hire deað ond mid hire syndon Godes apostolas ond oðre ða ðe hie bereð to hire æriste?' Ða cwædon ða apostolas to ðæm folce: 'Heo bið swiðor gestrangod be us tweonum ðurh Drihtnes gehat ond ne tweoge ðis folc be hire untrumnesse ne be hire geleafan'.[43]

---

12 (13)    [a] oferswiðest] ofo`e´rswiðest F    [b] ure] uru`e´ F    [c] on worlda] B; oworlda F    [d] ondsweredon] ondswered[[e]]`on´ F; ondswaredon B

13 (14)    [a] dixerunt] dix[[. . .]t F; dixerunt B    [b] Andreas] and`r´eas F    [c] iohannes] *bow of -e- partly erased* F    [d] ðe we] ðe F; þe we B    [e] se eadiga] seadiga F    [f] werode] weorode B; halgan werode F    [g] ure Drihten] *followed by erasure, probably of* ure drihten    [h] hlinigende ofer his bosm] hlifigende ofer sæs brim F, B    [i] hwan] hwom`an´ F    [j] ondrædeð] ondre`æ´deþ F

are truly our rest and you, Lord, are our protector and on you we call, you who live in the Son and the Father in you, and you are one with the Holy Spirit, world without end.' Then all the apostles answered him and said '*Amen*'.

13 (14)   Then the blessed John ran to all the apostles and said to them: '*Benedicite fratres*'. *Et dixerunt Petrus*. 'Bless our Lord, most beloved brothers.' Then Peter and Andrew said to John: 'You, dear lord, tell us in what way you came to us today'. Then John said: 'Bless our God, most beloved brothers, and let you all hear that he was going today into this city and he was teaching that you should pray to God at the ninth hour of the day. And then suddenly a large cloud descended on that same place in which we were gathered, where we heard the word of God.' And then suddenly all the apostles surrounded the holy Mary and they seized her waist. And they saw, as did all who were there, that the blessed Michael took and then he struck on the door of the house; and it did not refuse him but it opened of itself. And he found there very many people standing near there and there stood also the sister of the holy Mary and she spoke to the company and said: 'Tomorrow she will go from her body'. And then each of those who heard this wept very much. And then Mary said: '*Nunc, fratres, audite*. Most beloved brothers, let you all listen to me now that I shall go from my body tomorrow.' Then the apostles said to her: 'Do not worry, Mary, and do not weep, so that your people may not be troubled. Because our Lord and the teacher of our command-ments said this, when he was leaning over his bosom, when he was at his supper. Therefore I urge you all to that and this weeping people that are standing around here.' Then the people began to doubt in their hearts and they said: 'Why does this holy Mary fear her death, when God's apostles are with her and others who will bear her to her resurrection?' Then the apostles said to the people: 'She will be more comforted among us by the Lord's promise and let not this people doubt her weakness or her faith'.

14 (15)  Mid ðy ðe hie ðis gespræcen hæfdon, ða com ðær se eadiga Iohannes ond wæs ingongende on[a] ðære halgan Marian huse[44] ond halette on hie mycelre stefne ond wæs cweðende: '*Aue Maria gratia plena, Dominus tecum.* Hal wes ðu, Maria, þu eart geofe ful ond ðu eart gebletsod betuh ealle wifcyn ond[b] betuh ealle halige gastes.'[45] Ond hio ða ondswerede ond cwæð:[46]

15 (16)  'Broðor ða leofestan, ic eow bidde ealle þæt ge me secgen hwylce gemete ge coman ealle samod todæge to me, oððe hwa sægde eow þæt ic scolde beon ðys mærgenlican dæge gongende to heofenum?'[a47] / Ond swa anra gehwilc ðara apostola bið geseted to his synderlicre stowe þæt he bodige his godcundnesse ond hire geacnunge. Ond ða apostolas togon hie up ond hie gesetton on ðæm fægran[b] neorxnawange.[c48]

16 (17)  Ða wæs Maria wynsumigende[a] on hire gaste ond wæs cweðende: '*Benedico te qui dominaris super omnem benedictionem.*[b] Ic ðe bletsige, min Drihten, ðu ðe waldest ealra bletsunge,[49] ond ic bletsige eall ðin gehat ðe ðu me gehete. Ofer minre gecignesse ðu gesettest ealle ðine apostolas to minre byrgenne ond ic bletsige ðinne ðonne halgan naman,[c] ðe wunað in eallra worolda worold. Amen.'

17 (18)  *Et post hec uocauit Sancta Maria omnes apostolas*[a50] *in cubiculo suo et ostendit illis omne[b] indumentum.*[c] Ond ða æfter ðon ða cegde seo halige Maria to eallum ðæm apostolum[d] on hire hordcofan ond him æteowde ealne hire gegyrelean ðe heo[e] wolde æt hire byrgenne habban.

18 (19)  Ond wæs cweðende:[51] 'Ðis wæs se ðridda dæg geworden on ðæm heo gewat of lichoman fram us'.[52] Ond ða cwæð se eadiga Petrus to eallum ðæm apostolum ond to eallum ðæm folce: 'Broðor ða leofestan, ic eow bidde[53] ealle ða ðe on ðisse stowe syndon þæt ge wacian mid me ond we bærnan gastlico leohtfato oðþæt Drihten hider cume'.[a] Ond ða æfter ðysum wordum ða com ðær ure Drihten ond he hie gemette ealle anmodlice wæccende ond he hie onlyhte mid his ðæs Halgan Gastas gife. Ond he wæs cweðende to hiom: 'Broðor ða leofestan, ne sy eow nænigu[b]

---

14 (15)  [a] on] of F, B  [b] betuh ealle wifcyn ond] *om.* F; *supplied from* B
15  (16)  [a] heofenum] heofo`e´num  F  [b] fægran] fæ`g´ran  F  [c] neorxnawange] neorx`n´awange  F
16  (17)  [a] wynsumigende] wynsumigen`de´  F  [b] benedictionem] B; beneditionem F  [c] naman] `naman´ F
17  (18)  [a] apostolas] aposta`o´las  F  [b] omne] omne[[.]] F, m *probably erased*; omnem B  [c] indumentum] indumemtum F  [d] apostolum] apostolas`um´ F  [e] heo] `heo´ F
18 (19)  [a] cume] co`u´me F  [b] nænigu] nænige`u´ F

14 (15)   And when they had said this, then the blessed John came and entered holy Mary's house and greeted her in a loud voice, saying: '*Aue Maria gratia plena, Dominus tecum.* Blessed are you, Mary, you are full of grace and you are blessed among all women and among all holy spirits.' And then she answered and said:

15 (16)   'Most beloved brothers, I ask you all to tell me how you came to me today all together or who told you that I would have to go to heaven tomorrow?' And so each of the apostles will be set in his separate place so that he may preach his divinity and her conception. And the apostles drew her up and set her in the beautiful paradise.

16 (17)   Then Mary rejoiced in her spirit and said: '*Benedico te qui dominaris super omnem benedictionem.* I bless you, my Lord, you who rule over all blessings, and I bless all your promises which you promised me. Upon my entreaty you have appointed all the apostles to my burial and I bless your holy name, which will endure world without end. Amen.'

17 (18)   *Et post hec uocauit Sancta Maria omnes apostolas in cubiculo suo et ostendit illis omne indumentum.* And then after that the holy Mary called all the apostles into her chamber and showed them all her garments which she wished to have for her burial.

18 (19)   And said: 'This was the third day on which she departed from the body from us'. And then the blessed Peter said to all the apostles and to all the people: 'Most loved brothers, I ask you all who are in this place that you watch with me and that we burn spiritual lamps until the Lord comes here'. And then after these words our Lord came and he found them all watching with one accord and he illuminated them with the grace of his Holy Spirit. And he said to them: 'Most loved brothers, do not be concerned that you see that this blessed Mary is called to death and

cearo þæt ge geseon þæt ðeos eadiga Maria sy geceged to deaðe ond ne bið heo no to ðæm eorðlican deaðe ac heo bið gehered mid Gode, / forðon ðe hire bið mycel wuldor gegearwod'.[54]

19 (20)    Ond mid ði ðe he ðis gecwedon hæfde, ða ascan[a] samninga mycel leoht on hire huse þæt ealle ða fynd wæron oferswiðede, ða ðe ðær wæron,[55] ond ða ðe þæt leoht gesawon ða ne mihton asecgan for ðæs leohtes mycelnesse. Ond ða wæs geworden micel stæfn of heofonum to Petre[56] ond wæs cweðende: 'Ic beo mid eow ealle dagas oð ða gefylnesse ðisse worlde'. Ond ða ahof Petrus his stefne ond wæs cweðende: 'We bletsiað ðinne noman mid urum saulum ond we biddað þæt ðu fram us ne gewite. Ond we bletsiað ðe ond we biddað þæt ðu onlyhte ure world, forðæm ðe ðu eallum miltsast ðæm ðe ðe ongelyfað.'[b57]

20 (21)    Ond ðis wæs cweðende se eadiga[a] Petrus to eallum ðæm apostolum ond he trymede heora heortan mid Godes geleafan.[58]

21 (22)    Æfter ðyssum wordum gefylde,[59] ða wæs Maria arisende ond wæs utgangende of hire huse, ond hie gebæd to ðæm gebede ðe se engel hire[a] to cweð, ðe ðær com to hire. Ða ðis gebed wæs gefylled, ða wæs heo eft gangende on hire hus ond hio ða wæs hleonigende ofer hire reste.

22 (23)    Ond æt hire heafdan set se eadiga Petrus ond emb ða reste oðre Cristes ðegnas. Ond ða ær ðære syxtan tide ðæs dæges, ða wæs semninga geworden mycel ðunorrad ond ðær wæs ða[a] swiðe swete stenc, swa þætte ealle ða slepan ðe ðær wæron. Ond ða apostolas onfengon[b] ðære eadigan Marian[60] ond ða ðreo fæmnan ðe him ær Crist[c] bebead þæt heo wacedon buton forletnesse ond þæt heo cyðdon Drihtnes wuldor be hire ond ealle medemnesse be ðære eadigan / Marian.[61]

23 (24)    Ða slepan ða ealle ðe ðær wæron; ða com ðær semninga ure Drihten Hælend Crist ðurh wolcnum mid miccle mengeo engla ond wæs ingangende on ðære halgan Marian hus, on þæt ðe heo hie inne reste. Michael se heahengel, se wæs ealra engla ealdorman, he wæs ymen singende mid eallum ðæm englum. Mid ðy ðe Hælend wæs ingongende, ða gemette he ealle ða apostolas emb ðære eadigan Marian reste.

19 (20)    [a] ascan] asc[[e]]an F; ascean B    [b] ðe ðe ongelyfað] þe on þe gelyfaþ B
20 (21)    [a] se eadiga] B; seadiga F
21 (22)    [a] hire] ` hire´ F
22 (23)    [a] ða] *om.* B    [b] onfengon] B; ofengon F    [c] ær Crist] crist ær B

she will not be for earthly death but she will be praised with God, because great glory will be prepared for her'.

19 (20)   And when he had said this, then suddenly a great light shone in her house so that all the enemies who were there were overpowered, and those who saw the light could not tell of it because of the magnificence of the light. And then there was a great voice from the heavens to Peter and it said: 'I will be with you all the days until the end of the world'. And then Peter raised his voice and said: 'We bless your name with our souls and we entreat you not to depart from us. And we bless you and we entreat that you illumine our world, because you have mercy on all who believe in you.'

20 (21)   And the blessed Peter said this to all the apostles and he strengthened their hearts with faith in God.

21 (22)   After these words had been completed, then Mary arose and went out of her house, and she prayed according to the prayer which the angel, who had come to her there, said to her. When this prayer was finished, she went back into her house again and she lay on her bed.

22 (23)   And at her head sat the blessed Peter, and the other disciples of Christ were around the bed. And there before the sixth hour of the day, there was suddenly a great peal of thunder and there was then a very sweet scent, so that all who were there slept. And the apostles received the blessed Mary, as did the three virgins whom Christ had earlier commanded to watch without interruption and to testify to the glory of the Lord concerning her and all the dignity concerning the blessed Mary.

23 (24)   Then all who were there slept; suddenly our Lord the Saviour Christ came then through the clouds with a great multitude of angels and entered the house of the holy Mary, in which she was resting. Michael the archangel, who was the prince of all the angels, was singing hymns with all the angels. When the Saviour entered, then he found all the apostles around the blessed Mary's bed.

24 (25)   Ond he ða bletsode ða halgan Marian[62] ond wæs cweðende: *'Benedico te, quia quicumque promisisti.*[a] Ic þe bletsige, min Sancta Maria, ond eall[b] swa hwæt swa ic ðe gehet eal ic hit gesette.' Ond ða ondswarode him seo halige Maria ond wæs cweðende: 'Ic do a ðine gife, min Drihten, ond ic ðe bidde for ðinum noman þæt ðu gehwyrfe on me ealle eaðmodnesse ðinra beboda, forðon ðe ic mæg don ðine gife. Þu eart gemeodomed on ecnesse.'[63]

25 (26)   Ond ða onfeng ure Drihten hire saule ond he hi ða sealde Sancte Michaele ðæm heahengle ond he onfeng hire saule mid ealra his leoma eaðmoðnesse.[64] Ond næfde heo naht on hire buton þæt an þæt heo hæfde mennisce onlicnysse ond heo hæfde seofon[a] siðum breohtran saule ðonne snaw.

26 (27)   Ond ða fræng Petrus urne Drihten ond wæs cweðende: 'Hwilc is of us, Drihten, þæt hæbbe swa hwite saule swa ðeos halige Maria?' Ða cwæð ure Drihten to Petre ond to eallum ðæm mannum ðe ðær wæron:[65] 'Ðisse halgan / Marian saul bið a gewuldrod mid Gode ond heo bið aðwægen mid ðæm halgan ðweale.[a66] Ond oðre apostolas[b] beoð sende beforan hire bære, mid ðy ðe heo bið gongende of lichoman.' Ond hie ne gemetton nane swa hwite saule swa ðære eadigan Marian wæs, forðon heo[c] lufode ma ðeostru for hire synnum[d] ond heo wæs a ðeh[e] gehealden fram[f] hire synnum.[67] Ond hie gesawon ealle þæt seo eadige Marie hæfde[g] swa hwite saule swa snaw.

27 (28)   Ða cwæð[a] ure Hælend to Petre ond to ðære eadigan Marian lichoman:[68] 'Ðys mærgenlican dæge heo bið gangende on ðisse ceastre on ða swiðran healfe mines dæles, ond ge ðær gemetað niwe birgenne.[69] Ðonne asette ge ðone lichoman to ðære birgenne ond hine ðær healdeð, swa ic eow bebeode.'

28 (29)   Ða mid ðy ðe he ðis gecweden hæfde ure Drihten, ða clyopode semninga ðære eadigan Marian lichoma beforen him eallum ond wæs cweðende: 'Wes ðu min[a] gemindig, ðu gewuldroda cyning, forþon ic

---

24 (25)   [a] promisisti] w`p´romisisti F   [b] ond eall] eall F; ond eal B

25 (26)   [a] seofon] seofa`o´n F

26 (27)   [a] ðweale] ðw[[æ]]`e´ale F   [b] apostolas] apost[[a]]`o´las F   [c] heo] B; hie F
[d] synnum] B; synmin F *(one minim too few for* synnum*)*   [e] a ðeh] ðeh F; a þeh B   [f] fram]
fran *with attempted correction to* fram F   [g] hæfde] [[w]]`h´æfde F

27 (28)   [a] cwæð] `c´wæð F

28 (29)   [a] ðu min] ðu F, B

24 (25)   And he blessed the holy Mary and said: '*Benedico te, quia quicumque promisisti.* I bless you, my St Mary, and I will carry out everything which I promised you.' And then the holy Mary answered him and said: 'I always bestow your grace, my Lord, and I entreat you in your name that you confer upon me all the humility of your commands, because I can bestow your grace. You are honoured for ever.'

25 (26)   And then our Lord received her soul and he gave it to the archangel St Michael and he received her soul, with the humility of all his limbs. And she had nothing on her except that she had a human likeness and she had a soul seven times brighter than snow.

26 (27)   And then Peter asked our Lord and said: 'Lord, what one of us is there who has as white a soul as this holy Mary?' Then our Lord said to Peter and to all the people who were there: 'The soul of this holy Mary will always be glorified with God and it will be washed by the holy bath. And the other apostles will be sent in front of her bier when she shall depart from her body.' And they found no soul as white as that of the blessed Mary was, because she loved darkness more for her sins and nevertheless she was always preserved from her sins. And they all saw that the blessed Mary had a soul as white as snow.

27 (28)   Then our Saviour said to Peter and to the body of the blessed Mary: 'Tomorrow she will go into this city on the right-hand side of my part, and you will find there a new tomb. Then put the body in the tomb and guard it there as I command you.'

28 (29)   When our Lord had said this, then suddenly the body of the blessed Mary called out in front of all of them and said: 'Be mindful of me, you glorious king, because I am your handiwork and be mindful of

beo þin hondgeweorc ond wes þu min gemyndig,[b] forðon ic healde ðynra beboda goldhord'. Ond ða cwæð ure Drihten to ðære eadigan Marian lichoman: 'Ne forlæte ic ðe næfre, min meregrot, ne ic ðe næfre ne forlæte, min eorclanstan,[70] forðon ðe ðu eart soðlice[c] godes templ'.

29 (30)    Ond ða he ðis[a] gecweden hæfde, ða astah ure Drihten on heofonas.

30 (31)    Ða nam Petrus ond ða oðre apostolas hie, ond ða ðreo fæmnan ðe ðær wacodon, ond ðwogon ðære eadigan Marian* lichoman, ond hie ða asetton ofer hire bære. Ond ða æfter ðon ða arison ealle ða ðe ðær slepon.

31 (32)    Ond ða brohte Petrus ðær þæt palmtwig þæt seo eadigo Marie ær onfeng of ðæs ængles / handa. Ða cwæð se eadiga Iohannes:[71] *'Tu es uirgo; tu debes[a] procidere lectum.* Ðu eart seo clæneste fæmne, ond ðe gedafenað þæt ðu leore on ðine bære ond we beran ðis palmtwig ond cweðan Godes lof.' Ða cwæð eft se halga Iohannes: 'Ðu eart forelærende on ðara apostola gebede ond ðe gedafenað þæt ðu leore on ðine bære ond we ðe ðonne beran þæt we cuman[b] to ðære stowe ðær Drihten bebead.[72] Ond ne sy ure nan geunrotsod, ac we gesigefæstan ðine bære.'

32 (33)    Ond ða arison ða apostolas ond hio hofan ða bære ond hie bæron mid heora handum.

33 (34)    Ond Petrus ða soðlice onhof his stefne ond wæs cweðende: '*In[a] exitu[73] Israel de Egipto,[b] alleluia.* Israel wæs utgangende of Egyptum ond wæs singende alleluia.

34 (35)    Ond Drihten soðlice is[a] ðisse bære fultmiende.'[74] Ond ða apostolas wæron gangende on wolcnum.[75] Ond hie ða bæron ða bære ond hie cwædon Godes lof.

35 (36)    Ða þæt folc þa þæt[a] gehyrde ond ða Iudeas þæt[b] gesawon ða miclan mengeo engla ond heora stefn wæs swiðe hlud ond hie heredon God, ða wæron hie swiðe erre on heora mode.[76] Ond heora ða ongan ælc

---

[b] forþon ic beo þin hondgeweorc and wes þu min gemyndig] *om.* F; *supplied from* B    [c] soðlice] soðl[[o]]ʼ iʹce F

29 (30)    [a] ðis] ðʼiʹ[[o]]ʼ iʹs F; i *added both above and below* o

31 (32)    [a] debes] [[..]] ʼdebesʹ F    [b] cuman] B; cunnan, *with extra minim inserted above, giving* cumnan F

33 (34)    [a] in] Ii B    [b] de Egipto] ex egypto B

34 (35)    [a] is] *om.* F, *supplied from* B

35 (36)    [a] þa þæt] B; þæt F    [b] þæt] *om.* B

me, because I obey the treasury of your commands'. And then our Lord said to the body of the blessed Mary: 'I will never abandon you, my pearl, nor will I ever abandon you, my jewel, because you are truly the temple of God'.

29 (30)    And when he had said this, then our Lord ascended into the heavens.

30 (31)    Then Peter and the other apostles took her, and so did the three virgins who watched there, and they washed the body of the blessed Mary and put her on her bier. And then after that all who were sleeping there arose.

31 (32)    And then Peter brought there the palm-branch which the blessed Mary had previously received from the hand of the angel. Then the blessed John said: *'Tu es uirgo; tu debes procidere lectum.* You are the purest virgin, and it befits you that you should depart on your bier and we will bear this palm-branch and proclaim the praise of God.' Then the holy John said again: 'You are the foremost teacher in the prayer of the apostles and it befits you that you should depart on your bier and we will then bear you until we come to the place where the Lord commanded. And let none of us be grieved, but we will crown your bier.'

32 (33)    And then the apostles arose and they lifted the bier and carried it with their hands.

33 (34)    And then truly Peter raised up his voice and said: *'In exitu Israel de Egipto, alleluia.* Israel went out of Egypt and sang alleluia.

34 (35)    And the Lord is truly supporting this bier.' And the apostles were walking in clouds. And they then carried the bier and they proclaimed praise of God.

35 (36)    Then when the people heard this and the Jews saw the great multitude of angels and their voices were very loud and they were praising God, then they were very angry in their minds. And each of

cweðan to oðrum: 'Hwæt is ðeos mengeo ond ðis folc ðe her ðus hlude singeð?'[77]

36 (37)　Ða cwæð ðara apostola sum ðe ðær ætstod:[78] 'Maria is nu soðlice of lichoman gewitan[a] ond we cweðað lof ymb hie'.

37 (38)　Ond ða raðe eode Satanas þæt deofol on[a] ðara Iudea ealdormen[79] ond heora ongan ða ælc cweðan to oðrum:[b] 'Uton we nu arisan ond acwellan ða apostolas ond Marian lichoman geniman ond hine[c] ðonne mid fyre forbærnan, forðon ðe heo / gebær ðonne swican'.[d] Ond ða Iudeas þa arisan ond hie ða ongunnon mid sweordum[e] ond mid stengum[f] ðyder gan; ðohton þæt hie woldan ofslean ða apostolas. Ond ða, on ða ilcan tid, ða englas ða ðær wæron on ðæm wolcnum hie wurdon wyldran ðonne ða Iudeas ond ongunnon slean ða Iudeas.[80] Ond hie ða wurdon sona blinde ond feollan to eorðan ond heora heafdu slogan on ða wagas ond hie grapodan mid heora handum on ða eorðan ond nyston hwyder hie eodan.

38 (39)　Ond ða an ðe ðær wæs ðara Iudea ealdorman he ongan genealæcan[a][81] ðæm apostolum ond he wæs ða[b] geseonde þæt seo bær wæs gesigefæsted. Ond hie wæron soðlice ymen syngende ða apostolas ond wæron cweðende: 'Nu is gefylled þæt myccle hatheort ond þæt miccle yrre ðyses ealdormannes ond Drihten us sealde eardunga on ðisse stowe ond on eallum ussun cynne[c] ond he us sealde orsorh wuldor'.[82] Ond ða sona se arleasa gerefa cleopode mid mycelre stefne ond wæs cweðende: 'Ic me wille nu onhwyrfan to ðisse bære ond ðonne gegripan þæt palmtwig ond hit ðonne to eorðan afyllan ond forsearedum him begen dæles forbrecan ond forbærnan'.[d][83] Ða wæs he[e] gongende to ðære bære[f] ond ða onmiddan ðæm lichoman on ðære bære ða wearð he gefæstnod be ðære swidram handa to ðære bære,[g] þæt he hangode to eorðan.[84]

39 (40)　Ða clypode he micelre stefne ond wæs wepende mid tearum on ðara apostolo gesyhðe ond bæd[a] ond wæs ðus cweðende: '*Adiuro uos per Deum uiuum.*[b] Ic eow halsige ðurh ðonne lifgendan God þæt ge me ne[c]

---

36 (37)　[a] gewitan] `ge´witan F; gewiten B
37 (38)　[a] on] 7 (*Tironian nota*) F, B　[b] oðrum] oðrum [[. . .]] F　[c] hine] hie B　[d] swican] swican F, biswican B　[e] sweordum] swe`o´rdum F　[f] stengum] strengþum B
38 (39)　[a] ongan genealæcan] genealæcan F, B　[b] wæs ða] þa wæs B　[c] cynne] B; cynnum F　[d] forbærnan] bærnan F; forbærnan B　[e] wæs he] wæ`he´s F　[f] bære] *om.* F, *supplied from* B　[g] bære] *om.* F, *supplied from* B
39 (40)　[a] ond bæd] *om.* B　[b] uiuum] ui`u´um F　[c] ne] `ne´ F

them began to say to the other: 'What is this multitude and this people who are singing so loudly here?'

36 (37)   Then one of the apostles, who was standing near there, said: 'Mary has now truly departed from the body and we are proclaiming praise of her'.

37 (38)   And then the devil Satan immediately entered into the leaders of the Jews and each of them said to the other: 'Let us arise now and kill the apostles and take Mary's body and then burn it with fire, because she bore the traitor'. And the Jews arose then and went there with swords and with staves; they intended to kill the apostles. And then, at the same time, the angels who were there in the clouds became more powerful than the Jews and began to kill the Jews. And then they immediately became blind and fell to earth and struck their heads on the walls and they groped with their hands on the earth and did not know where they were going.

38 (39)   And then one who was the leader of the Jews there approached the apostles and he saw then that the bier was crowned. And truly the apostles were singing hymns and saying: 'Now the great rage and the great anger of this leader is satisfied and the Lord has given us a tabernacle in this place and among all our kin and he has given us secure glory'. And then immediately the impious official called out in a loud voice and said: 'I wish to turn now to this bier and then to seize this palm-branch and cast it to the ground and, when it is withered, to break both pieces and burn them'. Then he went to the bier and then, in the middle of the corpse on the bier, he was fastened by the right hand to the bier, so that he hung to the earth.

39 (40)   Then he called out in a loud voice and wept with tears in the sight of the apostles and prayed, saying: '*Adiuro uos per Deum uiuum*. I implore you by the living God that you do not despise me in this time of

forseon on ðisse / mycclan nedðearfe tide; ond ðe bidde ealra swiðost, min se halga Petrus, þæt ðu sy gemyndig hwæt min fæder ðe dyde ðaᵈ he wæs duruweard.' Ða frægn hine soðlice Petrus ond cwæð: 'Wære ðu mid ðynum fæder ða he me swa ladode þæt hie me ne gegripon?' Ond ða cwæð se aldorman eft: 'Ic eow nu bidde ealle þæt ge me ne forseon'.[85] Ond ða cwæð soðlice Petrus to him: 'Nis þæt soðlice min miht ne nænigesᵉ ures, ac gif ðu gelyfstᶠ on Hælende Crist, þæt he sy Godes sunu ðæs lifigendan, ond arise fram deaðe;[86]

40 (41)   gyf þuᵃ ðonne ne gelyfstᵇ þæt he sy Godes sunu, ðonne ne byst ðu asetted on eorðan.[87] Ac we wytan þæt ðyses menniscan cynnesᶜ fynd ablendeᵈ eowre heortan þæt Crist ne wære soð God

41 (42)   ond ðonne bist ðu gehæled fram him.[88] Ac gong ðu nu soðlice ond cys ðas bære ond cweð to ðysum lichoman þæt ðu gelyfe on God Fæder ond on Marian forðon hio bær Hælendne Crist.'[89]

42 (43)   Ond ða se ealdorman ðara sacerda bletsode Marian mid his tungan Ebreisceᵃ stæfne ðurh wuldor[90] ond heora nænig ða bære ða hwile ne ahof; ond ða æfter fyrstmearce ða bletsode he eft Marian lichoman[91] on Moyses boca gewytnesse ond ðurh swiðe manigfealde gewreotu, ond of eallum ðæm he wæs cweðende þæt Maria wære ðæs lifgendan Godes templ. Ða wæron ða apostolas swiðe wundrigende fram him ond wæron cweðende to him hwonon him ða wundorlican gereordo coman.[92] Ða cwæð Petrus to him: 'Arece ðine handa ond cweð þæt ðu gelyfe onᵇ ures Hælendes Cristes noman ond on ealra ðinre heortan, ðonne wesaðᶜ ðine handa sona geedniowode ond beoð swa hie ær wæron beforan ðe'.[93]

43 (44)   / Ond ða wæs hraðe geworden þæt he gelefde on his heortan.

44 (45)   Ond ða cwæð Petrus eft to him: 'Aris nu ond onfoh ðysum palmtwige ðe her is beforen ðisse halganᵃ Marian bære ond ðonne gong to ðissa Iudea ceastre to ðæm ðe ðær ofsleagene syndon mid blindnesse ond sprecᵇ to hiom ond cweð : "Swa hwilcᶜ swa ne gelyfeðᵈ on Hælend Crist, þæt he sy Godes sunu ðæs lifiendan, ðonne beoð ðæs eagan betinede".[94] Ond ðonne gif hwilc gelefe on God, ðonne æthrin ðu hire eagan mid

---

ᵈ ða] ð[[e]]ˋaʹ F   ᵉ næniges] næˋniʹges F   ᶠ gelyfst] gelyfˋsʹt F

40 (41)   ᵃ þu] ˋþuʹ F   ᵇ gelyfst] gelyfˋsʹt F   ᶜ cynnes] cyn[[d]]ˋnʹes F   ᵈ ablende] B; ablendan F

42 (43)   ᵃ ebreisce] ebreˋiʹsce F   ᵇ on] o *altered from* a   ᶜ wesað] weˋorʹþað F, *with* þ *corrected from* w, *by the addition of an ascender (the scribe originally wrote* wewað*)*; wesaþ B

44 (45)   ᵃ halgan] halgan [[.]] F   ᵇ sprec] spˋrʹec F   ᶜ hwilc] hwic F; hwylc B   ᵈ gelyfeð] g[[y]]ˋeʹlyfeð F

great necessity; and I entreat you most of all, my holy Peter, that you be mindful of what my father did for you, when he was door-keeper.' Then truly Peter asked him and said: 'Were you with your father when he excused me so that they did not seize me?' And the leader said again: 'I entreat you all now that you do not despise me'. And then truly Peter said to him: 'Truly that is not my power nor that of any of us, unless you believe in the Saviour Christ that he is the son of the living God and arose from death;

40 (41)   then if you do not believe that he is the son of God, then you will not be set down on the ground. But we know that the enemy of this humankind has blinded your hearts that Christ was not the true God

41 (42)   and then you will be healed by him. But truly go now and kiss this bier and say to this body that you believe in God the Father and in Mary, because she bore the Saviour Christ.'

42 (43)   And the chief of the priests blessed Mary with his tongue in the Hebrew language through glory, and meanwhile none of them raised up the bier; and then after an interval he blessed Mary's body again according to the testimony of the books of Moses and by means of very many scriptures, and from all of them he said that Mary was the temple of the living God. Then the apostles were greatly amazed at him and asked him from where he got the wonderful speeches. Then Peter said to him: 'Stretch out your hands and say that you believe in the name of our Saviour Christ with all your heart, then your hands will be restored immediately and will be in front of you as they were before'.

43 (44)   And it quickly happened that he believed in his heart.

44 (45)   And then Peter said again to him: 'Rise up now and receive this palm-branch which is here in front of the bier of this holy Mary and then go to the city of these Jews, to those who are struck with blindness there, and speak to them and say: "Whoever does not believe in the Saviour Christ, that he is the son of the living God, then will his eyes be shut". And then if any one should believe in God, let you touch their eyes with this palm-branch, which you receive here in your hand, then they

265

ðysum palmtwige, ðe ðu her onfenge on ðine hand, ðonne onfoþ[e] hie raðe gesyhðe. Se ðonne witodlice ne gelyfeð on God, ðonne ne gesyhð[f] se næfre on ecnesse.'

45 (46)    Ond ða eode se ealdorman ðara Iudea ond ðara sacerda ond wæs cweðende[95] swa him ær bebead se eadiga Petrus. Ond he gemette swiðe manige on ðæm folce wepende ond wæron cweðende: 'Wa us la, forðon be us is nu geworden[a] swa swa on Sodoma byrig wæs: ðær wæs geworden þæt ðær com ofer hie on fruman mycel broga[96] ond hie wæron mid blindnesse slegene; ond æfter ðon[b] ða sende Drihten fyr of hyofonum ofer hio ond hie mid[c] ealle forbærnde'. Ond hie ða wæron cweðende: 'Nu soðlice we syndon gefyllede mid eallra eaðmoðnesse'.[97] Ond ða soðlice him swa wependum ða cwom ðara sacerda ealdorman ðe Petrus him to sende ond he ða wæs sprecende to him[d] eallum ðæm ilcum wordum ðe him ær Petrus bebead. Ond he gehyrde heora ðrowunga[e98] ond he ða wundrode æfter ðære gesihðe[99] ond he wæs cweðende:[100] 'Swa hwilc swa gelyfeð on God ælmihtigne his wordum, ðonne wile he onfon rihtre andætnesse for Cristes[f] noman,[g] Godes / sunu ðæs lifygendan, ðonne onfehþ[h] se hraðe gesihðe;[i] se ðonne witodlice ne gelefeð on God ðonne wunað[j] he on blindnesse aa on ecnesse'. Ond hie ða wurdon hraðe gelyfde ond Crist him sealde gesihðe.[101]

46 (47)    Ond ða witodlice ða apostolas bæran Marian lichoman oðþæt hie coman to ðære byrgenne ðær Drihten him bebead, ond hie ða ðær bebyrigdon Marian lichoman. Ond ða setton hio æt ðære byrigenne duru swa swa Drihten Hælende Crist him bebead. Ond ða him swa sittendum ða com ðær semninga ure Drihten mid myccle mengeo engla ond cwæð to him: 'Sib sy, broðor, mid eow'.

47 (48)    Ond he ða bebead Michaele ðæm heahengla þæt he onfenge ðare eadigan Marian sawle[102] mid wolcnum.

48 (49)    Ond ða onfeng Michael ðære saule. Ond he[103] ða cwæð to ðæm apostolum oðþæt hie ealle genealeahtan[a] to Drihtne Hælendum Criste ond ðonne ðære saule onfeng on wolcnum.[104]

---

[e] onfoþ] B; onfoh`þ´ F    [f] gesyhð] gesyh`ð´ F
45 (46)    [a] geworden] gewu`o´rden F    [b] ðon] ðon[[..]] F    [c] mid] `mid´ F    [d] him] bim *written originally*, b *altered to* h *and superscript* h *above*    [e] ðrowunga] ðru`o´wunga F    [f] Cristes] crist`es´ F    [g] noman] nonam F; naman B    [h] onfehþ] onfeh`þ´ F; onfeh B    [i] gesihðe] ge[[.]]sihðe F    [j] wunað] w[[a]]`u´nað F
48 (49)    [a] genealeahtan] nealæhton B

will immediately receive their sight. Truly he who will not believe in God will never see for all eternity.'

45 (46)   And then the chief of the Jews and of the priests went and spoke as the blessed Peter had commanded him. And he found very many among the people weeping and they were saying: 'Alas for us, because it has now befallen us as it was in the city of Sodom: it happened there that a great fear came upon them first and they were struck with blindness; and after that the Lord sent fire from heaven upon them and burnt them up completely'. And they then said: 'Now we are truly filled with all humility'. And then indeed the chief of the priests, whom Peter sent to them, came to them, as they wept, and he spoke to them all in the same words that Peter had commanded him. And he heard their sufferings and then he was astonished at the sight and he said: 'Whoever believes in God almighty with his words will then receive true confession in the name of Christ, the son of the living God, and then he will receive sight immediately; but truly he who will not believe in God will continue in blindness for all eternity'. And they immediately became believing and Christ gave them sight.

46 (47)   And then truly the apostles carried Mary's body until they came to the tomb, to where the Lord had commanded them, and they buried Mary's body there. And then they sat at the door of the tomb as the Lord the Saviour Christ commanded them. And as they were sitting there suddenly our Lord came with a great multitude of angels and said to them: 'Peace be with you, brothers'.

47 (48)   And then he commanded the archangel Michael that he receive the soul of the blessed Mary into the clouds.

48 (49)   And then Michael received the soul. And then he spoke to the apostles until they all approached the Lord the Saviour Christ and then he received the soul into the clouds.

*The Old English assumption homily*

49 (50)   Ond Drihten bebead<sup>a</sup> ðæm wolcnum þæt hie eodan on neorxnawange<sup>b</sup> ond ðær asetton ðære eadigan Marian saule.<sup>105</sup> Ond on neorxnawange<sup>c</sup> bið a wuldor mid Gode ond mid eallum his gecorenum soðlice.<sup>106</sup>

50 (15)   Ond ða soðlice, æt ðære ðriddan tide ðæs dæges, ða com ðær Drihten mid micclum engla<sup>a</sup> menigeo ond halette ða apostolas ond wæs cweðende: 'Sib sy mid eow, broðor'. Ond ða ondsweredan him ða apostolas ond hie cwædon: 'Wuldor ðe sy, God, forðon ðe ðu dydest ana mycel wundor'.<sup>b107</sup> Ða cwæð ure Hælend to him: 'Ær ic wæs sænded fram minum Fæder<sup>108</sup> to ðæm þæt ic sceolde gefyllan mine ða halgan ðrowunga ond ða ic<sup>c</sup> wæs gehwirfed on minne lichoman,<sup>d109</sup> swa ic eow ær<sup>e</sup> gehet,<sup>110</sup> ond on eallum ðæm ðe me / fylgende wæron on ðissum mænniscan cynne.<sup>111</sup> Ond ic wæs sittende ofer manna bearnum on minum mægenðrimme ond wæs sittende ofer eow on minum heahsetle, ond ic demde twelf ðeodum on ðrim Israhela folcum ond of ðæm twelf mægðum ond be mines Fæder hæse ic wearð eft on lichoman geseted.<sup>112</sup> Ond for heora halignesse ic me gehalgode to ðæm unbesmitenan temple; ond heo is seo clæneste fæmne, ond heo wæs fæmne ær hire beorðre ond heo wunað fæmne æfter heora beorðre.' Ond ða cwæð se<sup>f</sup> Hælend to ðæm apostolum: 'Hwæt wille ge nu þæt<sup>g</sup> ic heora doo?'<sup>113</sup> Ond ða ondswerode him Petrus ond ealle ða apostolas ond cwædon: 'Drihten, ðu ðe gecure þæt fæt on to eardienne,<sup>h</sup> ond hio is ðin seo cleneste fæmne ær ealre worlde, ond ðu miht soðlice ond<sup>i</sup> gesewenlice ðine mihte gecyðan on Marian ðinra ðeowan. Ond ðu oferswiðdest<sup>j</sup> deað ond ðu eart rixiende on ðinum wuldre, swa ðu nu miht ðinra modor lichoman eft aweccan fram deaðe.'<sup>114</sup> Ond ða raðe wæs Drihten blissiende on heofonas.

51 (16)   Ond wæs cweðende to his apostolum: 'Wese hit nu be eowrum domum'. Ond ða hraðe<sup>a</sup> bead Drihten Gabriele ðæm heahengle þæt he wylede ðone stan fram ðære byrgenne duru.<sup>115</sup> Ond ða Michael se heahengel geondweardode<sup>b116</sup> ðære eadigan Marian sawle beforan<sup>c</sup>

---

49 (50)   <sup>a</sup> bebead] bead B   <sup>b</sup> on neorxnawange] oneorxnawange F; on neorxnawang B   <sup>c</sup> on neorxnawange] B; oneorxnawange F
50 (15)   <sup>a</sup> engla] *om.* B   <sup>b</sup> wundor] wuldor F, B   <sup>c</sup> ða ic] ic þa B   <sup>d</sup> lichoman] B; lichonam F   <sup>e</sup> eow ær] B; ær F   <sup>f</sup> se] *om.* B   <sup>g</sup> þæt] hwæt F, B   <sup>h</sup> eardienne] *second* n *corrected from* t   <sup>i</sup> ond] *om.* F; *supplied from* B   <sup>j</sup> oferswiðdest] oferswiðest F; oferswiþdest B
51 (16)   <sup>a</sup> hraðe] r *altered from* w (*wyn*) *and* r *superscript*   <sup>b</sup> geondweardode] geongweardode F, B   <sup>c</sup> beforan] befa`o´ ran F

49 (50)   And the Lord commanded the clouds that they should go to paradise and set down there the soul of the blessed Mary. And truly in paradise there is always glory with God and with all his chosen ones.

50 (15)   And then truly, at the third hour of the day, the Lord came there with a great multitude of angels and greeted the apostles and said: 'Peace be with you, brothers'. And then the apostles answered him and said: 'Glory be to you, God, because you alone performed great marvels'. Then our Saviour said to them: 'Formerly I was sent by my Father in order that I should fulfil my holy passion and then I was returned to my body, as I had promised you, and to all who had followed me among this humankind. And I was sitting above the children of men in my majesty and I was sitting over you on my throne, and I judged twelve nations among the three peoples of Israel and from the twelve tribes and by my father's command I was again placed in the body. And because of her holiness I consecrated myself to that immaculate temple; and she is the purest virgin and she was a virgin before her childbearing and she remains a virgin after her childbearing.' And then the Saviour said to the apostles: 'What do you wish now that I should do with her?' And then Peter and all the apostles answered him and said: 'Lord, you chose this vessel for yourself in which to dwell and she is your purest virgin before all the world and you are truly and evidently able to manifest your power in Mary your servant. And you conquered death and you are reigning in your glory, so that you are now able to raise up your mother's body again from death.' And then immediately the Lord rejoiced in the heavens.

51 (16)   And he said to his apostles: 'Let it be now according to your judgement'. And then immediately the Lord commanded the archangel Gabriel that he should roll the stone from the door of the tomb. And then the archangel Michael presented the soul of the blessed Mary before the

Drihtne ond ða wæs Drihten[d] cweðende to Marian lichoman: 'Aris ðu, min se nehste[e] ond min culufre ond mines wuldres eardung, ond forðon ðe ðu eart lifes fæt / ond ðu eart þæt heofonlice templ ond næron nænige leahtras[f] gefylde on ðinre heortan, ond[g] ðu ne ðrowast nænige ðrowunge on ðinum lichoman'.[117] Ond ða cwæð Drihten eft to ðæm lichoman: 'Aris ðu nu of ðinre byrgenne'.[118] Ond ða sona aras Maria of ðære byrgenne ond ymbfeng Drihtnes fet[119] ond ða ongan wuldrian on God ond wæs cweðende: 'Min Drihten, ne mæg ic ealle ða gife forðbringan ðe ðu me forgeafe for ðinum naman, ond hwæðere hi ne magon ealle ðine bletsunge gefyllan.[120] Ond ðu eart Israhela God ond ðu eart ahafen mid ðynum Fæder ond mid ðinum ðy Halgan Gaste on worlda[h] world.'

52 (17)    Ond ða ahof[121] Drihten hie up ond hie ða cyste ond hie[a] ða sealde Michaele ðæm heahengle, ond he hie ða ahof up on wolcnum beforan Drihtnes gesyhðe. Ond ða[b] cwæð Drihten to ðæm apostolum: 'Gangað nu to me on wolcnum'. Ond ða mid ðy ðe hie wæron gangende to him ða wæs Drihten hie cyssende ond wæs cweðende: *Pacem meam do*[c] *uobis, alleluia.* Ic forlæte mine sibbe to eow ðurh mines Fæder ðone Halgan Gast, ond ic eow sylle mine sibbe ðurh min þæt hehste lof.[122] Ond ic beo mid eow ealle dagas oð ða geendunga ðysse worlde.' Ond Drihten cwæð to ðæm englum: 'Singað nu ond onfoð minre meder on neorxnawange'.[123] Ond ða apostolas on heora mægene hofon Marian lichoman up mid wolcnum ond hine ða asetton on neorxnawanges[d] gefean.[124] Ond nu syndon gesette ða apostolas in hletæ:[e] hie bodian hire. Ond we nu onddetton Godes mycelnesse[125] ond singan on Marian naman:

53    / '*Magnificat anima mea*', forðon heo ðus cwæð ða heo *Magnificat*[a] sang: 'Min Drihten, gemyccla mine saule.[126] *Et exultauit.* Ond gedo þæt min gast wynsumige on ðinre hælo, forðon ðe ðu eart soð God.[127] *Quia respexit*,[b] forðon ðu nu sceawa ðines mægdenes[c] eaðmodnesse.[128] Ond min Drihten', cwæð Sancte Marie, 'gedo ðu þæt eall cyn cweðe þæt ic sy seo eadigoste fæmne.[129] *Quia*[d] *fecit*, forðon ðu me dydest mycel ond ðu eart mihtig ond ðin nama halig. *Et misericordia eius*, ond ðin mildheortnes is mid eallum ðæm cynne ðe ðe him ondrædað.[130] *Fecit potentiam*, ond he

---

[d] Drihten] *om.* F; *supplied from* B    [e] nehste] B; nehte F    [f] leahtras] leahtra`s´ F    [g] ond] on F; on`d´ B    [h] worlda] B; worda F
52    (17)    [a] hie] h`i´e    F    [b] ða] *om.* B    [c] do] da B    [d] neorxnawanges] neorxnawan[[d]]`g´es F    [e] hletæ] hlet æ F, B
53    [a] magnificat] magnificaþ B    [b] respexit] rexpecsit F; resp[[.]]exit B    [c] mægdenes] mægenes F, B    [d] quia] qui B

Lord and then the Lord said to Mary's body: 'Arise my nearest one and my dove and the dwelling of my glory, and because you are the vessel of life and you are the heavenly temple and no vices were felt in your heart, and you will not endure any suffering in your body'. And then the Lord said again to the body : 'Arise now from your tomb'. And then immediately Mary arose from the tomb and embraced the Lord's feet and began to glorify God and said: 'My Lord, I cannot cite all the favours which you have given me for the sake of your name, and nevertheless they cannot complete the sum of all your blessings. And you are the God of the Israelites and you are exalted with your father and with your Holy Spirit in eternity.'

52 (17)   And then the Lord raised her up and then he kissed her and then gave her to the archangel Michael, and he raised her up in the clouds in the sight of the Lord. And the Lord said to the apostles: 'Come now to me in the clouds'. And when they came to him the Lord kissed them and said: '*Pacem meam do uobis, alleluia*. I leave my peace with you through the Holy Spirit of my Father and I give you my peace through my highest glory. And I will be with you all the days until the end of this world.' And the Lord said to the angels: 'Sing now and receive my mother into paradise'. And the apostles in their power raised Mary's body up into the clouds and set it down in the joys of paradise. And now the apostles are set down in their lots: let them preach about her. And let us now confess the greatness of God and sing in Mary's name:

53   '*Magnificat anima mea*', because she spoke thus when she sang *Magnificat*: 'My Lord, magnify my soul. *Et exultauit*. And make my spirit rejoice in your salvation, because you are the true God. *Quia respexit*, therefore let you now see your handmaid's humility. And my Lord', said St Mary, 'make all people say that I am the most blessed virgin. *Quia fecit*, because you made me great and you are powerful and your name is holy. *Et misericordia eius*, and your mercy is with all the people who fear him. *Fecit potentiam*, and he has done great mighty works with his arms and he

dyde mycle mihte on his earman,[e][131] ond he todælde ealle ða ðe ðær wæron ofermode on heora heortan ond noldon on hine getrywan.[132] *Deposuit*, ond he asette ða mihtigan of heora setle, ond þæt wæs Satanas mid his deoflum, ða he wæs on heofona rice, ond he ða for his oferhygdun ond his deoflu[f] mid him wurdon aworpene on helle grund.[g][133] Ond Drihten ealle eaðmode upahefð on ecnesse. *Esurientes.*' Ond ða wæs Sancta Maria cweðende þæt Drihten ealle ða gefylde on heofona wuldres fægernesse ða ðe hie on eorðan leton hingrian ond ðyrstan for his naman. Ond elle ða men ða ðe onfengon welon ond on oferfylle swiðor gehyhton ðonne on God ond hie sylfe swa forleton on idelnesse, ðonne gegearwode he ðæm ece forwyrde.[134] *Suscepit Israel*, ond Israel onfehð eallum his cnihtum ond wæs gemindig ealra his mildheortnesse, swa Matheus wæs cweðende þæt Drihten astige on sume tid on anne munt / mid myccle werode his haligra ond ða gesæt[h] he on ðæm munte. *Sicut locutus est*, ond ða eodan his ðegnas to him ond ða ontynde se[i] Hælend his muð ond wæs sprecende to ussum fæderum ond to Abrahame ond wæs cweðende þæt his sæd oferweoxe ealle ðas weoruld ond he ða lærde his apostolas ond[j] him sægde ðurh hwæt seo saul[k] eadegust gewurde ond ðus cwæð:[135] 'Eadige beoð ðearfena gastes ond hie restað on heofona rice; ond eadige beoð ða ðe ðissa eorðwelena ne gymað. Ond eadige beoð ða ðe wepað nu for hiora synnum, forðon hie beoð eft gefrefrede[l] on heofona rice.'[136] Ac uton we biddan ða femnan Sancta Marian þæt heo us sie milde ðingere wið urne Drihten Hælendne Crist ondweardes rædes ond eces wuldres; to ðæm us gefultmige ure Drihten. AMEN.

---

[e] earman] earan F, B   [f] deoflu] deoflum F, B   [g] grund] [[d]]' g´rund F   [h] gesæt] B; gesette F   [i] se] *om.* B   [j] ond] *om.* B   [k] seo saul] B; saul F   [l] gefrefrede] afrefrede B

scattered all who were proud in their hearts and would not trust in him. *Deposuit*, and he put down the mighty from their seats, and that was Satan with his devils, when he was in the kingdom of heaven, and because of his pride he and his devils with him were cast down into the abyss of hell. And the Lord raises up all the humble for ever. *Esurientes.*' And then St Mary said that the Lord had filled in the beauty of heaven's glory all those who had allowed themselves to suffer hunger and thirst on earth for his name. And for all the people who received riches and who trusted in gluttony more than in God and so abandoned themselves to emptiness he has prepared eternal destruction. *Suscepit Israel*, and Israel receives all his servants and was mindful of all his mercy, as Matthew said that the Lord at a certain time ascended a mountain with a great company of his saints and then he sat on the mountain. *Sicut locutus est*, and then his disciples went to him and then the Saviour opened his mouth and spoke to our fathers and to Abraham and said that his seed should spread over all this world and then he taught his apostles and told them how the soul might become most blessed and spoke thus: 'Blessed are the spirits of the poor and they will rest in the kingdom of heaven; and blessed are those who do not care for these earthly riches. And blessed are those who weep now for their sins, because they will afterwards be consoled in the kingdom of heaven.' But let us entreat the virgin St Mary that she be a merciful intercessor for us with our Lord the Saviour Christ of present power and eternal glory; may our Lord help us to that. AMEN.

# Glosses to Cambridge,
# Corpus Christi College, 198

fol. 350r
secestu] quid queras
wynsumigende] iocunda
gefean] gaudia
hi [gesawon]] illi
ær] þer

fol.350v
hweorfende: conuertens
þwoh: lauit
hie [gegyrede]: illam
gegyrede: induit
hregle: ueste
gefeonde: gaudens
mid ðy ðe ðu me hate: cumque me
   iusseris
geunreted: contristata
cegende: uocauit
[gelyfað] ge: uos
ge [anmodlice]: uos
gewinnes: certaminis
slog [on]: pulsabant
onarn: aperuit
gedrefedu: turbata
sworette: suspirauit
forhabban: coibere
forðon: quia

fol. 351r
nu gan: eamus nunc

lichoman: corpus
he [ða wæs]: illa
cegde: uocauit
gyrelan: uestes; cleoue [ME]
medomnesse: dignitatem
mid ðy ðe: quando

fol. 351v
mægen: uirtutem
hordcofan: camera
semninga: repente
gedrefedu: turbatus
semninga: repente
wolcnum: nube
be him tweonum: inter eos
haletton on hie: se salutantes
todæge: hodie
swer [s *blotched*]: uir
gefeonde: gaudentes

fol. 352r
on anlicnesse þinre rode: in
   similitudine crucis
wunnon: certabant
oferhydigum: superbis
oferswiðest: uincis
scyldend: protector
[bletsiað] ge: uos
gemete: modo

[gehyrað] ge: uos
þis *inserted in inner margin, giving*
  gehyrað ge ealle þis þæt he . . .
ge [eow]: uos
wolcen: nubes
embsealdon: circumdederunt
hie [gegripan]: eam
ða [slog]: tunc
forwyrnde: non negauit
ontynde: aperuit
gemette: inuenit

fol. 352v
wæpende: stupens
ge me nu ealle: uos commune
gedrefed: turbatus
manige: admoneo
efengereordum: cena
tweogan: dubitare
hie [bereð]: eam
be us tweonum: inter nos
ne tweoge: non dubitet
halette: se salutauit
hwylce gemete: modo
ge [coman]: uos

fol. 353r
geseted: positus
synderlicre: specialiter
geacnunge: conceptionem
togon: traxerunt
hie [gesetton]: eam
wynsumigende: iocunda
gehat: promissum
gecignesse: uocatione
cegde: uocauit
gegyrelean: uestes
ge [wacian]: uos
ge [geseon]: uos
geceged: uocata

fol. 353v
ascan: lucebat
samninga: repente
fynd: inimici; demones
ðæm ðe: illis
hie [gebæd]: illa
reste: lecto
emb: circa
reste: lecto
ðæs [dæges]: illius
buton: sine
medemnesse: dignitas

fol. 354r
[heo] hie: eam
ymen: ymnum
reste: lecto
gemeodomed: dignatus
[he] hi [ða]: eam
leoma: luce
fræng: inquisiuit

fol. 354v
aðwægen: lota
ðweale: ablutione
hie [ne]: illi
hie [gesawon]: illi
ge [ðær]: uos
[asette] ge [ðone]: uos
semninga: repente
ðu [gewuldroda]: tu
meregrot: margareta
[apostolas] hie: eam

fol. 355r
gedafenað: decet
leore: migras
forelærende: doctrix
leore: migraris
we gesigefæstan: feramus uictoriosi
on wolcnum: nube

hie [heredon]: illi
erre: irati
[ymb] hie: eam
ongan: inceperunt

fol. 355v
biswican: seductorem
hie ða: illi
[englas] ða [ðær]: qui
wolcnum: nube
wyldran: forciores; gloriosiores
slean: percutere
slogan: illidebant
wagas: parietibus
gesigefæsted: uictoriosa
ussum cynne: nostra gente
onhwyrfan: conuertere
ðonne [gegripan]: tunc
forsearedum: aruit; aruit (*superscript and in margin*)
gefæstnod . . . to ðære bære: adhesit feretro
ge [me]: uos

fol. 356r
ablendan: excecauerunt
fyrstmearce: inducias
[fram] him: eo
wesað: offrede [ME]
geedniowode: renouati

fol. 356v
ðonne gong: tunc ite; tunc ite (*superscript and in margin*)
ofsleagene: percussi
blindnesse: cecitate
ðæs [eagan]: illius
betinede: ceci; clausi
ðonne: tunc
æthrin: tange
ðonne [witodlice]: tunc

wa us la: ue nobis
[ofer] hie: eam
broga: terror
slegene: percussi
ðrowunga: passionem
andætnesse: confessionem

fol. 357r
hie [ða wurdon]: illi
hraðe: cito
setton: sedebant
ðær: ubi
halette: salutauit
hie [cwædon]: illi

fol. 357v
ic me gehalgode to ðæm unbesmitenan temple: sanctificaui mihi inpollutum templum
beorðre: partum
beorðre: partum
fæt: uas
aweccan: excitare
wese: sit
wylede: reuolueret
geondweardode: presentauit; presentauit (*superscript and in margin*)
nehste: proxima
fæt: uas

fol. 358r
ðu [ne ðrowast]: tu
hie up: eam
andetton: confiteamur

fol. 358v
wynsumige: exultauit
mægdenes [mægenes MS]: uirtutem
earman [earan MS]: brachio
todælde: dispersit

ofermode: superbos

getrywan: confidere

oferhygdum: superbia

gehyhton: sperauerunt

forwyrde: interitum

fol 359r

werode: turbe

gesette: sedit

ontynde: aperuit

saul: anima

eadegust: beatior

ðearfena: pauperes

ne gymað: non curant

sie: sit

# Commentary on Cambridge,
# Corpus Christi College, 198

1 *genumen of ðinum lichoman* Transitus *W* reads here *adsumenda es* (with variants *adsumta eris* and *erit ascensio tua*), referring to the assumption as taking place after three days, whereas the Old English refers to the death. The Old English does not correspond to any of Wilmart's manuscripts and seems to have been revised to eliminate mention of Mary's assumption here.

2 The Latin reads here: 'Et ecce ego mittam omnes apostolos ad te sepeliendam, ut uideant gloriam tuam quam acceptura es'. This surprising reading in *Transitus W*, where the angel sends the apostles to Mary, may not be the original reading in this family of apocrypha; in other texts (*Transitus A* and the Old Irish text) it is the Lord who appears to Mary at this point (see Wenger, *L'assomption*, pp. 33 and 70, and above, pp. 52 and 67), going back to the appearance of the Christ-angel in the oldest texts. Wilmart's manuscript R inserts here *ait dominus omnipotens*. The Old English avoids attributing to the angel the power to send the apostles to bury Mary by using a passive construction; it is difficult to know whether this goes back to its source or is due to the translator. The final clause of the Latin sentence is not translated and is also missing from Wilmart's manuscript G; its omission is in line with a revision of the Old English (or, more probably, its source) to modify the exceptional nature of Mary's final destiny.

3 The simile of the morning star is not in any of Wilmart's manuscripts, but the text used by the translator must have had something similar to the reading at the parallel point in *Transitus B²*, or he himself may have supplied it from the version of *Transitus B²* which he used later in the homily: 'Palma autem illa fulgebat nimia luce; et erat quidem uirga illius uiriditati consimilis, sed folia illius ut stella matutina radio claritatis fulgebant'.

4 The translator has here, understandably, had difficulty with one of the confused and cryptic vestiges of older detail preserved in *Transitus W*. In the source of *Transitus W* the trees on the Mount of Olives bowed to Mary as she carried the palm, as is evident from the corresponding passage in Wenger's Greek text, R,

278

in John of Thessalonica and in the very literal Latin translation, *Transitus A*: 'et flecterunt capita omnes arbores et adorauerunt palmam que erat in manu angeli' (Wenger, *L'assomption*, p. 245). In *Transitus W* there is merely a relic of this: 'exultauit Maria cum magno gaudio, una cum omnibus qui ibidem erant'. The translator has connected the second clause of this sentence with the next sentence ('Angelus autem qui uenerat ad eam ascendit in caelis cum magno lumine'), thus creating an audience, not present in the Latin, to witness the angel's departure.

5  This is an excellent example of the translator's characteristic procedure with a long speech, which Willard described: 'whenever there is a long speech, and particularly if this speech contains a quotation from something said previously, the translator is sure to lose his way, to re-interpret the matter, and to make a conversation or a narrative account out of direct address' ('The Testament of Mary', p. 347). Here Mary in her prayer to God quotes the promise made to her by Christ: 'Peto domine ut mittas super me benedictionem tuam ut nulla potestas occurrat mihi inimici uel inferni, in illa hora cum me iusseris de hoc corpore recedere, siquidem ipse pollicitus es mihi, dicens: Noli tristis esse Maria'. Of this the translator makes two separate speeches by Mary, omitting 'ut nulla potestas occurrat mihi inimici uel inferni' and inserting instead an introduction to the second speech ('Ða wæs Maria cweðende'), and a reply by the angel, who is brought back after his departure to supply a speaker for the final clause. The translator has failed to realize that Mary is here quoting a former promise by her son.

6  The Latin reads 'Et cum haec dixisset' here, but the translator has altered this to *gehyrde* because he has finished the previous section with the angel rather than Mary speaking.

7  The translator has changed the description of Mary's death from the Latin 'usque in illam horam in qua sum recessura de hoc corpore' to 'oð ða tid ðe on ðæm dæge bið mines gewinnes ende'. He, or his source, has here omitted the remainder of Mary's speech in ch. 5, in which she describes how either the angel of good or evil carries off the soul of a dead person. Ch. 6 of the Latin, which describes the reaction of those listening to her speech, is also omitted. Wilmart's manuscripts F and G omit the same part of ch. 5 and his manuscripts B, G and R omit all of ch. 6, most of which is also missing in F. The existence of these truncated Latin versions suggests that the translator was working from a source which had already been abbreviated.

8  As Willard points out ('On Blickling Homily XIII', pp. 11–12), *þæt heo onarn* must go back to a variant like that of Wilmart's manuscript M, *et continuo aperuit*.

9  Wilmart's Latin text reads 'Et sic exclamauit uoce magna, dicens' but the first part is omitted in his manuscripts B and R, which read simply *dixit*. The source of the Old English was presumably such a reading.

<sup>10</sup> The Latin reads here: 'Pater Iohannes, memor esto sermonis domini mei magistri tui, quibus me tibi commendauit in qua die recessit a nobis, passus pro mundi salute'. As Willard shows ('On Blickling Homily XIII', p. 12), the translator has had considerable trouble with this passage and he was also most probably working from a variant like those in Wilmart's manuscripts G, M and T which replace *sermonis* with *praeceptis* (G) or *praeceptorum* (M and T), giving 'memor esto domini mei magistri tui praeceptis/praeceptorum'. This he seems to have understood as 'a garbled version of *memor esto mei, quia dominus est magister tuorum praeceptorum*' (Willard, 'On Blickling Homily XIII', p. 12) and he accordingly translated 'westu gemindig min, forðon ðe Drihten is ðinra beboda lareow'. In the next part of the Latin sentence, the translator seems to have misunderstood *commendauit* as *commandauit*, giving *bebead* (which, although it can also mean 'to entrust', seems to mean 'to command' here). Nothing in any of the Latin manuscripts provides an explanation for *þæt ic gefille*, which is therefore probably the result of the translator's wish to provide some context for *þæt he me bebead*; Willard suggests that *ic gefille* 'is to be attributed to the translator, or perhaps reviser, to whom the original meaning of the passage was obscure, and who, therefore, added this in the interests of intelligibility, only to succeed in making confusion worse confounded' (*ibid.*). This is perhaps slightly unfair, insofar as 'Fæder Iohannes, westu gemindig min, forðon ðe Drihten is ðinra beboda lareow, and þæt he me bebead þæt ic gefille' makes sense in itself, although not the same sense as the Latin. This translation, however, leaves the reference to the Crucifixion in the next sentence without any motivation in the Old English, which has now wiped out all trace of Mary's reminder to John of how she was entrusted to him on the day of her son's death. It would seem that the translator thought that the action of this passage took place on the day on which Christ had died; if he did, it shows, of course, utter ignorance of the liturgical year. I have been guided by the manuscript pointing and the syntax of the Latin in punctuating this passage (specifically in beginning a sentence with *on ðissum dæge* rather than ending the preceding sentence with it, as Willard does).

<sup>11</sup> The Latin reads *die crastina*, and no variant manuscript throws light on the Old English's *ær ðrim dagum*. At the beginning of the text, however, the translator has rendered the source's 'post tres dies adsumenda es' as 'ær ðrim dagum genumen of ðinum lichoman' and his alteration here may, therefore, have been the result of a concern for consistency.

<sup>12</sup> Again, the translator has broken up what is one long speech in the Latin, which here reads 'Siquidem ipsa audiui, dicentibus Iudaeis . . .' The translator has not realized that it was Mary herself who heard the Jews and he therefore attributes this part of the speech to John.

13 No variant throws light on the difference between the Latin's 'Sustineamus quando moriatur' and the Old English's 'Uton we nu gan and acwellan ða apostolas'. The Latin and Old English mention a plan to kill the apostles at a later point (ch. 37; 38 of the Latin) and it is possible that the source of the Old English contained a reference to it here. Alternatively, the translator may have thought *moriatur* meant 'to kill' rather than 'to die' and, searching for an object and knowing that the story later referred to the threat to the apostles, may have supplied it here.

14 The Old English is again very different from the Latin, because of the way in which the translator has misunderstood his source. In the Latin John is responding to Mary's speech about the Jews: 'Haec enim cum audisset beatus Iohannes, dicente illa quod esset recessura de corpore, fleuit in conspectu dei, dicens: "O domine, quid sumus nos, quibus demonstrasti tantas tribulationes?"'; in the Old English the *dicente* referring to Mary's speech has been taken as marking the beginning of John's, and the indication of what she had said becomes instead his speech: 'ða wæs he cweðende: "On ðissum dæge he wat fram us of lichoman"'. It is difficult to know where *on ðissum dæge* comes from; the line echoes 'On ðissum dæge he gewat fram us' in the preceding chapter, where the translator appears to be under the impression that the events he was recounting happened on the anniversary of the Crucifixion. Perhaps the translator wished to repeat this point for emphasis, once he had received this impression from his misunderstanding of the previous chapter. Willard says that the translator has 'interpreted the passage as alluding to the scene at the Crucifixion as Our Lord hung on the Cross, and committed his mother to St John' ('On Blickling Homily XIII', p. 13) and he regards the next speech (John's in the Latin) as that of the Virgin at the Cross, as this is how the tremulous hand glossator of F appears to have understood it. Willard therefore punctuates: *ða wæs he cweðende, 'Of* [sic] *ðissum dæge he* [sic] *gewat fram us of lichoman, and he ða wæs wepende on Godes gesyhðe, and cweðende, "Eala, Drihten, hwæt syndon we ðe ðu gecyddest swa micle sorge?"' (ibid.*, p. 9). This reading is not at all evident from the text, however, and means that one has to read the *he* of the manuscript's *he ða wes wepende* as feminine, as the glossator appears to have done with his *illa* gloss. But the glossator is by no means an infallible guide to the meaning of the text and *he* is not otherwise feminine in the text, so, rather than taking John's speech as containing a quotation from the Virgin within his speech, as Willard does, I have interpreted the Old English passage as presenting two separate speeches by John and have punctuated accordingly.

15 Once again there is a discrepancy between source and translation. The Latin reads: 'Tunc Maria rogauit sanctum Iohannem in cubiculo suo, et ostendit ei uestimenta sua quae ei poneret ad sepulturam, et ostendit ei illam palmam

luminis quam acceperat ab angelo qui ei apparuerat et eius adsumptionem ei praedixerat'. The first part of the Latin sentence is faithfully rendered, with the variant reading *uocauit* (Wilmart's manuscripts F, R and S) rather than *rogauit* and the omission of *quae ei poneret ad sepulturam*. Like Wilmart's S, the source of the Old English clearly had *de manu angeli* rather than *ab angelo*. *Qui ei apparuerat* is apparently omitted and *et eius adsumptionem ei praedixerat* seems to correspond to *heo him æteowde ealle hire medomnesse*. I quote Willard's comments at length:

> *Praedixerat* could, with some licence, be rendered as *heo æteowde*; but what is *medomnesse* and how does it correspond to *adsumptionem*? *Medomnes* occurs again in this homily, *Blickling Homilies*, p. 145, line 33. There it equals *benignitas*, which, however, hardly suits the present situation, where it is more likely to mean 'humility' or 'submissiveness'.
>
> A twelfth-century reader of the Corpus Christi manuscript has interpreted it to mean 'worth, virtue, excellence, dignity', since he has glossed *medomnesse* as *dignitas*. Remembering the great humility of Our Lady at the annunciation both of the birth of the Saviour and of her own death, one is tempted to render *medomnesse* as 'humility.' Could it possibly be a scribal error for *edmodnesse* (*ed=ead-*)? Or is it 'moderation'? The logical meaning, when the preceding clauses of the Latin are considered, is 'preparation', everything 'suitable for the occasion'. *Medomnesse* is unrecorded with this meaning, but *medume* does exist with the sense of 'proper, fitting', cf. Bosworth-Toller, *medume* III, and in this sense it approaches *dignus* in certain of its meanings. If it is taken as 'preparation', 'things fitting for the occasion', then the *ealle* of the Old English has some meaning. I have, therefore, so taken *medomnesse* in my translation of this particular passage. It is true that none of these meanings are in translation of the Latin as it comes to us in Wilmart's printed text or in the variant manuscripts. Possibly here the translator is introducing a comment of his own, by way of transition, as he omits a phrase or two of his original. ('On Blickling Homily XIII', p. 14)

Willard's discussion here, however, does not strike me as convincing, unlike so many of his other notes to this text; it is confused and inconclusive. In the first place, he fails to mention that at both occurrences of *medomnesse* in this text (*medemnesse* the second time), the corresponding Latin sentence mentions the assumption, suggesting that it was perceived as an equivalent or substitute term. In this case, the meaning *dignitas* given by the tremulous glossator is probably the most satisfactory of the possible meanings of *medomnesse.* He in fact repeats the same gloss at the second occurrence of the word and so Willard is not correct in saying that here 'it equals *benignitas*'. The gloss *benignitas* seems to come from the *Blickling Glosses*, part of the same manuscript as the *Blickling Homilies*; in the *Glosses*, *benignitatis tuae* equals *medemnesse þinre*, but meanings cannot be simply transferred from one text to another in this way and it is hard to see why Willard ignores the gloss *dignitas* underneath this second occurrence and turns to another text in B to supply the meaning. *Dignitas* is, in any case, one of the chief meanings of the word (see *BT* under *medumnesse*). Secondly, the verb *gemedemode* later in the text seems to mean 'honoured, deemed worthy' (see n. 21), which supports the meaning *dignitas* for the noun.

Either the translator deliberately chose a more general word than *adsumptio* (for which Ælfric, for example, uses *upstige* and *upfæreld*) or else the word *adsumptio* had been edited out of his Latin source; in this case it could have been replaced by a general word like *dignitas* which we see reflected in the Old English text.

16 The Old English has anticipated the future tense of the next clauses of the Latin sentence, rather than keeping the Latin conditional *nisi aduenerint*.

17 The Latin reads *ad reddendum honorem* here, to which the Old English version, *to alysnesse*, does not correspond. No variant reading in Wilmart helps, and Willard suggests that the source lacked *honorem* and that the translator 'had before him, or thought he had, or interpreted what he had as, *redimendum* instead of *reddendum*' ('On Blickling Homily XIII', p. 15).

18 It is difficult to be sure of what the translator intended this to mean. The source reads: 'Et sic subito omnes apostoli cum nubibus rapti sunt, et depositi sunt ante ostium domus beatae Mariae'. Willard comments that '*rapti sunt* of the Latin is rendered by *tugon hie upp*; cf. German *zogen sich empor*' ('On Blickling Homily XIII', p. 15), and he translates 'and then suddenly all the Apostles went up in clouds' (*ibid.*, p. 11), taking *hie* as a reflexive pronoun. However, this is not the usual meaning of *teon*, which generally means 'to draw' or 'to pull'. While *teon* is close to *rapere* in some of its meanings, there is a big difference between the passive *rapti sunt* and the active *tugon hie upp*, with *hie*, if it is a reflexive, seeming to imply that the apostles were responsible for lifting themselves up. *teon up*, moreover, is a common enough phrase, but not with a reflexive pronoun. An alternative, and to my mind better, reading is to take *tugon hie upp* as 'pulled her up', with *hie* referring to Mary rather than the apostles themselves. This would be more in accordance with normal Old English syntax and could be an example of the translator's tendency to translate phrase by phrase, often without taking the overall context into account (cf. n. 48). Here he may well have assumed that the source's mention of the apostles being taken up by clouds could only refer to

Mary and he therefore interpreted the apostles as the subject of an active rather than a passive verb and supplied a pronoun object.

19 *Sume hie* is problematic as there is no indication in the source, or elsewhere in the Old English, that not all of the apostles have been set down in front of Mary's house, and the first part of the Latin sentence refers to all of the apostles being taken up. If all of the apostles are not present, then the 'Deo gratias, forðon we wæron todæge ealle on annesse gemedemode' in this chapter is also nonsense. As Willard points out, there is a story about Thomas arriving late at Mary's house ('On Blickling Homily XIII', p. 15), but this belongs to a different tradition and cannot lie behind this passage of the Old English text. The Latin simply reads: 'et depositi sunt ante ostium domus beatae Mariae'. The explanation may lie with the translator's treatment of *tugon hie upp* in the first part of this sentence: if he did not realize that what was being described was the transport of the apostles to Mary's house and thought that the phrase referred instead to the apostles lifting Mary, then it is quite likely that he would have thought it necessary to insert a new subject for the passive *wæron gesette*, which clearly referred to the apostles (as Mary would hardly have been merely set down before her own door). As *ealle ða apostolas* and *sume hie* now referred to separate events in his mind, not the lifting up and setting down of the apostles, but the lifting up of Mary and the setting down of the apostles, then *sume hie* was probably not intended to imply that the remainder of the apostles were taken elsewhere. It may simply have been an inept response to the immediate need to make a new subject explicit.

20 This corresponds to the source's 'et uidentes se inuicem, admirantes salutauerunt', but, with a slight change of meaning, the translator seems to have made the *admirantes* into a clause referring to Mary, who is, of course, not mentioned in the Latin.

21 The source reads: 'Deo gratias, qui nos hodie dignatus est in unum congregare.' The translator was presumably working from a source which, like Wilmart's manuscripts B, F and R, read *quia* instead of *qui*; hence the *forðon*. All the Latin manuscripts, however, have *congregare* or a variant, but this appears to be omitted from the Old English. 'Because he has deigned to gather us all together today in unity' is therefore rendered 'forðon we wæron todæge ealle on annesse gemedemode'. Morris (*The Blickling Homilies*, p. 139) translates this as 'that we were today all in unity and in humbleness', but this is introducing the new idea of humility. *Gemedemode* seems to correspond to *dignatus* in the Latin, despite the plural subject in the Old English, and would therefore seem to have its Old English sense of 'to honour', 'to deem worthy' rather than 'to humble'. Ælfric also uses *gemedemige* as the translation of *dignor* (see *BT* I, under *medumian*).

22 Something seems to be missing in the Old English, which lacks a translation of *quae sit causa*. *causa* is omitted in Wilmart's M.

23 The translator was clearly working from a text which, like Wilmart's manuscripts F, G and T, read *in hac hora* or a variant.

24 The Latin reads simply *Et dixit Petrus*, but Wilmart's R has 'Et dixit Petrus apostolus ad beatum Paulum'; the translator's source presumably had something like 'Et dixit Petrus ad Paulum'.

25 Something is missing here in the Old English, as is evident from the end of this chapter, which describes Paul as 'forelærende on ðara apostola gebede' (it should, of course, be Peter) and where the apostles rejoice at Paul's humility even though he has said nothing. The Latin reads: 'Et dixit Petrus: "Frater Paule, surge et ora prior, quoniam ualde laetata est anima mea, uidens te". Et dixit Paulus: "Quomodo ego prior potero orare, cum tu sis columna luminis?" Eyeskip from *prior* to *prior*, if the mistake is the source's or translator's, or from *ær* to *ær*, if it is a later scribe's, is doubtless the cause of the omission. I have not attempted to supply the gap in the text, partly because we do not know whether it arose in the Latin or the Old English, partly because a straightforward translation of the Latin would run the risk of totally misrepresenting the normally convoluted Old English.

26 The Latin reads here 'qui circa me stant fratres meliores me sunt', but Wilmart's manuscripts B and R omit *fratres*; the source of the Old English presumably did too.

27 Again, the translator has altered the sense of the Latin, which reads: 'Tu ergo qui nos praecedis in apostolatum, ora pro nobis omnibus, ut gratia domini sit nobiscum'. *Ora* (apparently understood as a noun) seems to be attached to *apostolatum* in the Old English, giving 'ðu eart forelærende on ðara apostola gebede', and 'pro nobis omnibus' is omitted in the Old English, which then makes 'ut gratia domini sit nobiscum' into a description of Paul, omitting *nobiscum*.

28 A confusion of *genibus* with *gentibus*, or a source which had confused the two words, is at the root of the difference between the Latin and the Old English here. The Latin reads: 'Et sic Petrus, positis genibus, expansis manibus, orauit'. The two ablative clauses describing Peter's position of prayer in the Latin become a description of the position he prescribed for prayer: 'swa swa Petrus gesette ðisum mænniscum cynne, ða aðenede Sanctus Petrus his handa to Gode'.

29 The Latin has *et profundum abyssi intueris*, but the translator has omitted, or his source lacked, *intueris*.

30 'forðon ðe ðu sylest urum limun reste, forðon ðe hie on ðinum noman wunnon' corresponds to 'quoniam tu das requiem membris laborantibus', but

*on ðinum noman* has been introduced by the translator, who has made *laborantibus* into an independent clause.

[31] The Latin reads 'tu protectio omnibus inuocantibus te', but the translator again makes an independent clause.

[32] *Dixerunt* has been altered to *dix{{. . .}}t* in the manuscript; B reads *dixerunt*. There can be little doubt that the translator wrote *dixerunt*; his source reads: 'Et . . . beatus Iohannes occurrit omnibus, dicens: "Benedicite, fratres". Et dixerunt Petrus et Andreas . . .'. What has happened is that the translator has given too much in his Latin tag, including part of the following sentence, before going back to translate *Benedicite, fratres*. The erasure is clearly to be explained as an attempt to bring the verb into agreement with what now appears to be its sole subject, *Petrus*.

[33] Most of Wilmart's manuscripts read *Dilecte domini*, but G and S have the vocative *domine* and V reads *dominus*. The translator may have been following such a text.

[34] The apparent discontinuity in the sense of this passage led Morris to believe that there was a break in the text after *gehyrað ge ealle* and he says 'A leaf or more is missing here' (*Blickling Homilies*, p. 141), but a comparison with the source, as Willard has shown, proves that nothing is missing. The Latin reads here 'Et dixit ad eos Iohannes: "Benedicite deo, fratres. Audite quid mihi contigerit. Factum est dum essem in ciuitate Agathen docens. Erat hora circiter nona diei. Subito descendit nubes in eodem loco ubi erant congregati populi audientes uerbum dei."' Willard's discussion of this passage can hardly be bettered:

> *quid mihi contigerit* n'a pas de pendant en Blickling; *gehyraþ ge ealle* (écoutez tous) suggère un original qui lit: *Audite (uos) omnes*. *Factum est dum essem* n'est pas reconnaissable dans *þæt he wæs gongende todæg* (qu'il allait aujourd'hui) bien que ceci puisse bien être une tentative de rendre une variante de cela, peut-être *factum est* tout seul. *In ciuitate* est *on þas ceastre* (dans cette ville) et *docens* ou peut-être *docens* combiné avec le mot suivant *erat* est *& he wæs lærende* (et il enseignait). Mais qu'est-ce qui a donné naissance à *þæt ge eow gebædon to Gode* (que vous priiez Dieu)? Pourrait-on trouver là un écho d'un conflit avec quelque forme de *agathen* ou *agathe*, comme je l'ai proposé ailleurs? Si *agathe* se présentait dans la source sous une orthographe telle que l'*agathe* du ms. R, il pourrait avoir soufflé *agite* à l'esprit d'un traducteur troublé et *agite* aurait inspiré à son tour une phrase du genre de *gratias agite* ou *preces, orationes agite* pour arriver à la lecture, autrement inexplicable, de Blickling, *þæt ge eow gebædon to Gode*.
>
> ('La ville d'Agathé?' p. 349)

As Willard has suggested also, the 'sudden appearance of the third person', where the source has John speaking in the first person, 'is, perhaps, to be explained as a misreading of the Latin. If *essem* were in an abbreviated form, the translator, or some scribe before him, might have misexpanded it as *esset*, which would explain the translation *þæt he wæs gongende* ('On Blickling Homily XIII', p. 17).

[35] The translator was presumably working from a text which, like Wilmart's manuscripts F, G, M and T, omitted *populi* from 'Subito descendit nubes in eodem loco ubi erant congregati populi audientes uerbum dei'. He has translated *erant* as *we wæron*, demonstrating again that 'le traducteur avait la main facile pour traiter les flexions finales des verbes et qu'il accommodait à sa convenance nombres et personnes' (Willard, 'La ville d'Agathé?' p. 350).

[36] The source reads: 'Subito circumdedit me nubes et rapuit me de medio eorum, uidentibus omnibus qui ibidem erant', which seems at first to bear little relation to the Old English: 'Ond ða sæmninga ða embsealdon ealle ða apostolas ða halgan Marian ond hie gegripan on hire middel. Ond ða gesawon hie ond ealle ða ðe ðær wæron . . . .'. *Nubes* is missing in Wilmart's manuscripts F, G, M and T and presumably was also absent from the source of the Old English. The translator, clearly not realizing that it was understood from the previous sentence, went in search of a subject, deciding on the apostles. John himself is the object of this sentence in the Latin (*me*), but in the Old English sentence he is now part of the collective subject, and the translator has to find an object. *ða halgan Marian* makes no sense in terms of the Latin story at this point, as the Virgin should not even be present in the city where John is preaching, but it is possible that the translator understood *me* as an abbreviation for *Maria*, giving 'ða embsealdon ealle ða apostolas ða halgan Marian' (see Willard, 'La ville d'Agathé?' p. 350). 'ond hie gegripan on hire middel' obviously goes back to 'rapuit me de medio eorum' and Willard suggests that the original translator may have written *of hire middel*, 'qui serait un équivalent passable du latin' (*Ibid.*, p. 350). This is possible but, given that the subject of the Old English is the apostles rather than the cloud, it is also very likely that he wrote *on hire middel*, the reading of both manuscripts. While the Latin, therefore, describes the cloud seizing John, the Old English, absurdly, has all of the apostles grasping Mary's waist. 'uidentibus omnibus qui ibidem erant' is then attached to the next clause by the translator.

[37] 'þæt se eadiga Michael genam and ða slog on ðæs huses duru' corresponds to 'et adtulit me hic, et statim percussi ostium'. The Latin does not mention Michael, but in his search for a subject for *adtulit*, the translator seems to have seized on *me hic* and understood it as an abbreviation for Michael, although the archangel has no place at all in the story at this point (see

Willard, 'La ville d'Agathé?' p. 350). Willard's explanation of the appearance of Mary and Michael at this point in the narrative seems to me far more convincing than that of Nellis, who argues that this passage would 'fit into the source narrative at the point when the apostles lift Mary's dead body for the angel to carry to Paradise' and that 'if, before combining the different accounts of the assumption into one narrative, the Old English translator wrote out a complete translation of his sources, then the fragments displaced in combining the material might have been available to be slipped into the text' ('Misplaced Passages', pp. 400–1). It is difficult to know what meaning is intended for *genam*, for which there is no object; the misunderstanding of *me hic* as Michael has resulted in a subject instead of an object and the translator has not attempted to remedy the deficiency.

38 No variant reading throws light on this; it is possible that it is the translator's expansion of *sine mora*, which is otherwise not translated.

39 The manuscript reads *halgan werode* here, but there is no adjective in the Latin and nothing in B; as it is unlikely that the crowd would have been independently described as *halgan* by the translator, I have omitted it from the edited text. The word was probably in the scribe's mind because of *þære halgan Marian* in the previous line.

40 The Latin reads: 'et inueni hic populum multum adstantem circa sororem et dominam nostram Mariam, et adloquentem eam turbis, dicentem se de corpore exituram'. The translator makes Michael, introduced in the last sentence, into the subject here; in the Latin it is still John speaking in the first person. He appears to have understood *circa* as an adverb, 'round about', rather than as a preposition, and then to have construed *sororem* as a nominative, thereby introducing another character, Mary's sister, not found in the source. His source, like Wilmart's manuscripts G, M and T, presumably omitted *et dominam*. The translator then rendered *dicentem* as *cwæð* and *se de corpore exituram* as a speech by Mary's sister, adding *ðys mergenlicen dæge*, for which there is no Latin equivalent.

41 John's description of how he wept on hearing Mary announce her death here becomes the crowd's reaction to Mary's sister's announcement of it, the translator again ignoring indications of person ('ego uero haec audiens uehementer sum lacrimatus'). The Latin, of course, has no sister of Mary.

42 In the Latin John interjects 'Nunc ergo, fratres, audite me' in his speech to the apostles; the translator makes this into the start of a speech by Mary, joining his translation of it on to the beginning of the next sentence in the Latin.

43 In the Latin John, in this continuation of his speech, exhorts the apostles not to lament Mary if she dies the next day, lest the people doubt: 'Si exierit sequente die domina nostra de corpore, nolite eam flere, ne turbetur populus,

quoniam mihi ante dixerat dominus noster et magister illa nocte dum recumberem super pectus eius, dum cenaremus. Et ideo admoneo uos ne uideant nos populi flentes et incipiant dubii esse et dicant in cordibus suis: Ut quid isti timent mortem, dum sint apostoli dei et aliis praedicent resurrectionem? Sed magis confortemur nos inuicem de domini promissionibus, ut omnis populus possit firmus esse in fide et non dubius.' Ignoring indications of mood, tense and person, and adding extra introductions to speeches, the translator turns this speech by John into a conversation between Mary, the apostles and the crowd, which turns the hypothetical doubt into actual. *illa nocte* is omitted in Wilmart's G, M, T and V, as it presumably was in the source of the Old English text. 'mid ðy ðe he wæs hlifigende ofer sæs brim' must correspond, because of its position in the text, to 'dum recumberem super pectus eius', and Willard's brilliant conjectural reconstruction of the process by which it was arrived at deserves to be quoted in full:

It is barely possible that the translator has misread *pectus* as *pontus*. This would give a word which could account for sea. I believe, however, that the key to the problem is the *lectio difficilior, brim*. It must be remembered that in insular script *s* and *r* are very much alike. The translator, if he rendered his Latin anywhere nearly correctly, must have written *bosm*, 'bosom', in translation of *pectus*; the notion underlying *recumberem* would be satisfactorily represented in *hlinigende*, 'leaning'. If, in some later copy, the word *bosm* stood as *bsm*, through accidental omission of the *o*, the reading would puzzle the scribe. It would look very much like *brm*, and would suggest *brim*. The *brm*-reading would then be accounted for as the result of his predecessor's having written one short downstroke too few: three minims (*m*) instead of four (*im*). *Brm* would then naturally be emended to read *brim*. *Sæs* could be added in amplification. But the resultant reading, 'when he was reclining on the sea's flood, when he was at his evening meal', with its suspicion of *mal de mer*, would be intolerable under the circumstances, and would call for improvement. What could be easier than to change *hlinigende*, 'leaning', to *hlifigende*, 'towering up'? Though not making much sense, this reading would at least obviate any undignified notion of seasickness.                    ('An Old English *Magnificat*', pp. 22–3)

Following this the Old English has Mary herself fear her death, while in the Latin it is the apostles who, in the hypothetical speech of the people, fear it. Again, the grammar of the Latin is entirely disregarded. In the last sentence in this section, the translator seems to have construed *non dubius* as a verb, *ne tweoge*, and to have understood *firmus* as *infirmus*, giving *untrumnesse*; this results in an unlikely rendering of 'ut omnis populus possit firmus esse in fide et non dubius' as 'ond ne tweoge ðis folc be hire untrumnesse ne be hire geleafan'.

44 This translates 'Cum uero haec locutus fuisset beatus Iohannes, omnes pariter apostoli ingressi sunt in domum Mariae'; presumably *apostoli* was missing from the translator's source, as it is in Wilmart's manuscripts B, R and V. As the translator has failed to grasp that it was John who spoke what in the Latin is the long preceding speech, he changes the singular of the Latin into a plural and then has John arrive a second time and enter Mary's house alone. I have emended the two manuscripts' reading of *of* to *on*, as the Latin reads *in* and *ingongende of* makes little sense, despite Morris's ingenious translation 'and entered therein from the house of the holy Mary' (*The Blickling Homilies*, p. 142).

45 The source versions have only 'Aue Maria gratia plena, dominus tecum', but the translator has omitted to translate *dominus tecum* and has continued with the familiar prayer.

46 *Et uobiscum* has been omitted from the Old English, probably because it does not make sense in the immediate context where only John, rather than all the apostles, has addressed Mary.

47 'þæt ic scolde beon . . . gongende to heofenum' seems to be the translator's rendition of 'quod ego exitura sum de corpore', unless his source had a reading which has not been preserved in any of the extant manuscripts of *Transitus W*.

48 The Latin reads here: 'Et sic omnes apostoli exposuerunt quemadmodum unusquisque de locis suis ubi praedicabant diuina praeceptione fuerunt rapti et ibidem sunt depositi'. The translator has here, with some licence as to exact meaning, understood *exposuerunt* literally rather than figuratively (as 'to set down', *bið geseted*, rather than 'to set forth', 'explain'), *bodige* is obviously *praedicabant*, and *diuina*, instead of being taken as an adjective, becomes *godcundnesse* and is preceded by a *his* which seems to refer to Christ. *Praeceptione* seems to have been confused with *conceptione*, resulting in *hire geacnunge*, which presumably refers to Mary's conception of Christ. The second Old English sentence then appears to continue the reference to Mary, unless *togon hie* and *hie gesetton* are reflexive and refer to the apostles pulling themselves up and placing themselves in paradise (cf. n. 18). Either way, of course, we have a *non sequitur*, as it is clear immediately after Mary's next speech that both she and the apostles are still in her house, where she shows them the clothes in which she wishes to be buried. This particular 'assumption', then, is limited to this one sentence, in a manner typical of the translator's tendency to construct a meaning for a small section of the text which is sometimes at odds with the overall direction of the narrative. Given his emphasis throughout on the

Virgin, however, it seems more likely that what was in his mind at this point was getting Mary into paradise and I therefore take both occurrences of *hie* to refer to her. In the last clause of the Latin the translator perhaps took *ibidem* as a reference back to *his godcundnesse* and introduced paradise to make explicit the idea that the apostles placed Mary with Christ. The controlling idea behind the translation seems to have been the translator's desire to relate Mary's assumption, even though this is not what the Latin is about at this point.

Nellis ('Misplaced Passages', pp. 401–2) again interprets this passage as being misplaced and argues that it properly belongs to the end of the translation narrative. She suggests that the translator 'first translated at least one entire Latin narrative on his subject in writing', that 'gaps were left in the translation at difficult points; since the gaps are filled with material rejected from the integrated text, the translation had not been finished when the two versions were integrated, and therefore the translator was almost certainly the person who attempted to combine the two versions of the assumption, rejecting the fragment material'. This rejected material was, she then postulates, inserted into the text by a second individual: 'This person found a nearly complete homily, with at least two gaps left in the text and some fragmentary passages that seemed to be rough drafts of the difficult passages lying near it, and probably the Latin source for the first part as well. . . . The reviser, noticing a resemblance between the beginning of the Latin and parts of the Old English, simply plugged in the most likely fragment, probably looking at the Latin source enough to check for the appearance of a few easily recognizable words, since the sentences filling the second gap are rearranged' (*ibid.*, p. 402). This complicated procedure is not convincing to me, as the way in which this passage translates the Latin does not appear to be so fundamentally different to the rest of the text as to require such a different explanation.

[49] In the Latin this is followed by 'Benedico habitaculum gloriae tuae', but this is omitted in the Old English.

[50] All Wilmart's manuscripts apart from R read *et duxit eos* after *apostolos*; presumably the source of the Old English agreed with R in omitting this.

[51] There is no speech at this point in the Latin, which begins *Et cum factus*; it is hard to see how the translator took this as the introduction to a speech.

[52] This speech is part of the narrative in the Latin: 'Et cum factus fuisset dies tertius in quo recessura erat de corpore . . .'. Once again, the translator has ignored case, person and tense indicators; it is also difficult to decide who is intended to speak this sentence in the Old English. The only person suggested by the context is Mary, but she is referred to in the third person. Morris suggests Peter and takes the sentence as indirect speech, though one

would then expect a *þæt*; Peter has not been mentioned by name for a long time, however, even though he is the speaker of the following sentence and is there introduced properly. The translator has also not grasped the future nature of the statement in the Latin and has rendered *recessura erat* as *heo gewat*, resulting in 'wæs cweðende: "Ðis wæs se ðridda dæg geworden on ðæm heo gewat of lichoman fram us."' It requires very special pleading to translate, as Morris does, '[he? Peter] said this, that the third day was come, in which she would depart from the body [and] from us' (*The Blickling Homilies*, pp. 142–4). It is more natural to take this as a statement of Mary's death, although, of course, in the source she has not yet died.

53  Only T of Wilmart's manuscripts has *rogo* at this point.

54  Again, the translator has broken up what is one long speech by Peter in the Latin and has rendered as narrative what was only anticipated in Peter's account. The speech assigned to the Lord in the Old English is also still part of Peter's speech in the source: 'Fratres qui conuenistis in hunc locum, ut uigiletis nobiscum, sint omnium nostrum lampades accensae, et uigilemus animo et spiritu [et corpore], ut, cum uenerit dominus, inueniat nos omnes unianimiter uigilantes, et inluminet nos gratia spiritus sui sancti. Fratres karissimi, nolite suspicari hanc uocationem beatae Mariae esse mortem. Non est enim illi mors, sed uita aeterna, quoniam mors iustorum laudatur apud deum, quia haec est gloria magna.' Transitions between narrative and speeches are provided by the translator as they are, naturally, absent from the Latin.

55  It is difficult at first sight to see what the impetus for the introduction of the *fynd* was: the Latin reads 'ita ut uix aliquis aut conspicere posset aut enarrare prae magnitudine luminis'. The key is possibly the word *uix*: the translator may have confused this with *uis*, which can mean 'hostile strength', 'force', 'violence', and may have translated it as *fynd*. Once this idea was introduced in his mind, he seems to have felt it necessary to stress that the enemies or fiends were overcome. Alternatively, the source of the Old English may have had a variant reading, not preserved in any of Wilmart's manuscripts, which could account for its divergence here. There has been no prior mention of *fynd* in the Old English. It is, of course, just possible that the translator was influenced by standard depictions of saintly deaths, where the devils are vanquished, and decided to incorporate this motif in his text.

56  There is nothing in any of the Latin manuscripts to correspond to *of heofonum to Petre*; again, it may go back to an unpreserved variant reading or it may be the translator's own addition.

57  Peter's speech could not be regarded as rendering accurately the syntax of the Latin, but the meaning is more or less the same.

58  Most of a very long section of the Latin, containing Peter's speech, is omitted here; the whole section is omitted in Wilmart's P and his manuscripts B, G,

P and R have an omission corresponding to the Old English, which preserves only the last sentence. Only Wilmart's G, like the Old English, has the reading *apostolos*; the other manuscripts all read *populus*.

[59] There is no Latin equivalent to this phrase in any of Wilmart's manuscripts.

[60] The Latin manuscripts at first sight have nothing to correspond to 'onfengon ðære eadigan Marian' and it is difficult to fit into the context, as the apostles are already sitting at Mary's bedside. It is possible that the verbs *excipio* and *accipio* have been confused, so that the *exceptis* in 'exceptis apostolis et tribus uirginibus' has been translated *onfengon*, ignoring, of course, the Latin ending, and that Mary has been supplied as an object. See n. 64 also.

[61] The last clause is again different from the Latin, which reads: 'et testificarent de illa gloria adsumptionis eius in qua adsumpta est beata Maria'. *heo cyðdon Drihtnes wuldor* obviously corresponds to the first part of the Latin sentence, apart from *Drihtnes*, and, as with the occurrence discussed in n. 15, *medemnesse* seems to be in some way an equivalent or a substitute for *adsumptio* or *adsumpta*, probably with the meaning *dignitas*, as is given in the tremulous hand gloss.

[62] In the Latin the previous section ends 'inuenit apostolos circa lectum beatae Mariae, et dixit eis: "Pax uobis"' and this section begins 'Et subito apertum est os beatae Mariae et benedixit dominum, dicens: "Benedico te, quia quaecumque mihi promisisti praestitisti"'. There appears to have been eyeskip from one *Mariae* to the next, either by the translator or in his Latin exemplar. The translator then either failed to see that *dominum* was the object, not the subject, of *benedixit*, or it was omitted from his source, and this, together with the eyeskip, results in Christ speaking the speech which is assigned to Mary in the Latin. Wilmart's manuscripts P and M[2] add *sancta maria* (P) and *beata maria* (M[2]) after *benedixit*, and the source of the Old English probably did also, although the translator translated it as an accusative rather than a nominative form. In keeping with the change of speaker, the Old English adds *min Sancta Maria* and replaces *mihi* with *ðe*, even though the speech is quoted in Latin without any *Sancta Maria*.

[63] In the Latin this is the continuation of Mary's speech, but, as the translator has made the previous sentence into a speech by Christ, here he inserts an introduction attributing it to Mary. The Latin reads: 'Non enim ego possum tanta gratiarum actione nomini tuo referre quanta in me conferre dignatus es'. The Old English is so different that it seems to reflect a variant reading not preserved in any of the Latin manuscripts, although it was clearly similar in part to Wilmart's text, with *gife* reflecting *gratia*. *gemeodomed* presumably translates *dignatus* (see n. 21), but there is no equivalent in any of the Latin manuscripts to the Old English *on ecnesse*.

[64] The Latin reads here *exceptis omnibus membris*, a phrase which is explicable only

by reference to other texts of the same family. These show that what is meant is that Mary's soul had a human form but without sexual differentiation, as in, for example, Wenger's Greek text *R*, which reads in Wenger's French translation (*L'assomption*, p. 233): 'Et nous les apôtres, nous vîmes l'âme de Marie remise entre les mains de Michel dans une apparence humaine parfaite, à l'exception de la forme d'homme ou de femme, n'ayant rien d'autre que la ressemblance de tout le corps et une clarté sept fois plus grande que celle du soleil'. The Old English translator has transferred the description to Michael and has rendered the clause 'mid ealra his leoma eaðmodnesse', prefacing it with 'he onfeng hire saule', a phrase which has no parallel in any of Wilmart's manuscripts, unless we have once again some confusion between *excipio* and *accipio*, as in n. 60. If, as would seem to be the case, he understood *exceptis* as some form of the verb 'to accept', he supplied *saule* as an object and then had to provide some context for *ealra his leoma*, which he did with *eaðmodnesse*. R. Willard (*Two Apocrypha in Old English Homilies*, Beiträge zur englischen Philologie 30 (Leipzig, 1935), p. 80) suggests 'in all humility' as a translation for 'mid ealra his leoma eaðmodnesse'.

65 The Latin reads: 'Et dixit illi dominus: "Petre, omnium electorum meorum . . ."'. The Old English has understood the beginning of the Lord's speech as part of the introduction to it, rendering it: 'Ða cwæð ure Drihten to Petre and to eallum ðæm mannum ðe ðær wæron . . .'.

66 The speech is not about Mary in the Latin, but about the souls of all those who are baptized. In terms of position in the text, the Old English corresponds to 'et missi sunt ad me, animae eorum tales sunt . . .'. It is hard to see how this could give 'Ðisse halgan Marian saul bið a gewuldrod mid Gode' and no variant in Wilmart's manuscripts throws light on the Old English or mentions Mary or God. It is just possible that *me* was taken as an abbreviation for *Mariae* (cf. n. 36), with *me animae* giving *Marian saul* and the rest of the Old English sentence being invented by the translator to provide a context for this. 'cum de sancto lauacro lotae [processerint]' clearly gives 'heo bið aðwægen mid ðæm halgan ðweale', again without taking the grammar of the Latin into account.

67 There is no mention of the apostles or of the bier in the Latin, which is still dealing with the souls of all the baptized. *Processerint*, the last word of the previous sentence in the Latin, has become attached to this sentence in the Old English and the attempt to find a subject and a context for it seems to have resulted in 'Ond oðre apostolas beoð sende beforan hire bære . . .'. Zupitza, ('Kritische Beiträge', p. 212) suggests that *ond opre apostolas* (B reading) must be incorrect: 'der anschluss mit *ond* ist ungeschickt und *opre* in diesem zusammenhange auffallend: nach dem folgenden beteiligen sich alle apostel zu dem begräbnis. ich schlage vor zu schreiben: *þu and þa opre*

*apostolas'*. While Zupitza is undoubtedly correct in pointing out the clumsiness of the passage, the fact that the translator seems to be somewhat at a loss in this passage makes it hard to know whether anything has been lost here. Knowledge of the Latin is of no help in choosing between the manuscripts and Zupitza's suggestion.

In the next Old English sentence the infelicity of Mary loving darkness for her sins results from the translator's misunderstanding of the content and person endings of the Latin and his application to Mary of the description of the sinners, which he then hastily contradicts. While the Latin, therefore, has 'Sed cum de corpore exeunt, non inueniuntur sic candidae, quoniam aliter datae sunt et aliter inueniuntur, quia dilexerunt magis tenebras quam lucem, proper multa peccata sua', the Old English reads: '"Ond oðre apostolas beoð sende beforan hire bære, mid ðy ðe heo bið gongende of lichoman"'. Ond hie ne gemetton nane swa hwite saule swa ðære eadigan Marian wæs, forðon heo lufode ma ðeostru for hire synnum and heo wæs a ðeh gehealden fram hire synnum.' Although this is all part of the Lord's speech in the Latin, the translator seems to have judged that the speech ended with *lichoman*. Zupitza (*ibid.*) suggests that '*ma* für *na* verschrieben ist', but the source supports the manuscript reading.

68 The Old English has misplaced the beginning of the Lord's speech and has included the first words in the introduction. The Latin reads: 'Et iterum dixit ad eum dominus: "Petre, tuta corpus Mariae . . ."', while the Old English, ignoring the *tuta* (which may have been omitted in the source), has: 'Ða cwæð ure Hælend to Petre and to ðære eadigan Marian lichoman'. Wilmart's M reads *totum* and his B[2] *tutum* instead of *tuta*.

69 There seems to be nothing in the Latin which could have prompted *ðys mærgenlican dæge* in the Old English. The Latin has simply 'egredere in dexteram partem ciuitatis' and no variant reading has any indication of time. 'in dexteram partem ciuitatis' becomes 'on ðisse ceastre on ða swiðran healfe mines dæles' in the Old English, but it is difficult to see what the function of the possessive is here. Zupitza ('Kritische Beiträge', pp. 212–13) suggests that '*in mines dæles* muss irgend eine form von *eastdæl* stecken. ich vermute *wið eastdæles.*' He refers to Tischendorf's edition of *Transitus B*, which has *orientem* at this point in the narrative, but none of Wilmart's manuscripts of *Transitus W*, the source the translator is following here, mentions the East. It does not seem very probable, moreover, that *wið eastdæles* would be corrupted to *in mines dæles*.

The Old English has translated the command to the apostles as third-person future narrative ('Ðys mærgenlican dæge heo bið gangende on ðisse ceastre on ða swiðran healfe mines dæles'), even though the rest of the Lord's speech is rendered as an address to the apostles (plural rather than the singular of the

Latin). The change of person from *heo bið gangende* to *ge ðær gemetað* is also odd; in the Latin the whole speech is an address to Peter, apart from the last sentence which is addressed to the apostles ('Et custodite illud sicut mandaui uobis').

70 *min eorclanstan* suggests a Latin source which read *gemma*, but none of Wilmart's manuscripts has this reading.

71 The Latin reads *et dixit ad Iohannem*, with Peter as the subject; but the Old English has made this into a speech by John, apparently addressing the Virgin's body. The *uirgo* of the Latin, which refers to John, has clearly led the translator astray here. This means that the person endings of the Latin again have to be ignored in the rest of the Old English speech.

72 The confusion of the previous speech is continued here, as the translator has not realized that this is a conversation between John and Peter. John's reply in the Latin is here made into a second speech by John to Mary's body, so that what, in the Latin, Peter says about John and what John says about Peter both become John's addresses to Mary's body in the Old English. Hence the 'Tu es praecedens nos in apostolatum' becomes, with the addition of *gebede* (for which there is no Latin source and which was presumably inserted to avoid including Mary among the apostles), 'Ðu eart forelærende on ðara apostola gebede'. Morris has inadvertently repeated a passage here ('beran ðis palmtwig ond cweðan Godes lof. Ða cwæð eft se halga Iohannes: "Ðu eart forelærende on ðara apostola gebede ond ðe gedafenað þæt ðu leore on ðine bære ond we"' is printed twice).

73 Most of Wilmart's manuscripts read *Exiit*, but F, G and V have *in exitu*. The quotation is from Psalm 113.

74 In the Latin this is not part of Peter's speech, as the translator clearly understood it to be, but a resumption of the narrative.

75 The Latin reads: 'Dominus uero protexit lectum et apostolos nube'. As the translator has included the beginning of this sentence in Peter's speech, he is left with *apostolos nube* and has to supply a verb, which he takes from the beginning of the next sentence, *et ambulantes*.

76 The Latin reads: 'et a nullo uidebantur, nisi tantummodo uoces audiebantur, tamquam populi multi. Et cum audissent principes sacerdotum [R: turbe] Iudaeorum uoces magnas laudantium deum, turbati sunt uehementer . . .'. The translator may have been working from a version which had only the second of these sentences, although there seem to be vestiges of the first here also. Wilmart's manuscript V is the only one to mention angels in this passage ('de nube angeli canebant laudem desuper') but in a different context to the Old English, and it is hard to know whether or not the translator introduced the angels independently, as they feature in the next passage in both Latin and Old English. Case endings are again mangled, with *Iudaeorum* apparently becoming nominative.

77 There is no equivalent to *ðe her ðus hlude singeð* in any of Wilmart's manuscripts.

78 In none of Wilmart's manuscripts is it one of the apostles who answers the people: 'Et dixit quidam ex adstantibus: "Maria exiit de corpore. Modo uero apostoli circa illam laudes dicunt."' Either the translator was following a variant text or he was unusually consistent in altering *apostoli* to *we* in the next sentence in order to fit in with the first change.

79 Although both Old English manuscripts read 'eode Satanas þæt deofol ond ðara Iudea ealdormen', I have emended *ond* (7 in both manuscripts) to *on*, as the Latin reads 'Satanas introiuit in illos principes sacerdotum'. Faulty Latin is unlikely to have been the cause of the mistake and it is therefore more likely to have been a later transcription error than one made by the translator.

80 No Latin manuscript throws light on the Old English account of the angels becoming more powerful or wilder than the Jews. The Latin reads: 'Eadem uero hora angeli qui erant in nubibus percusserunt illos Iudaeos caecitate'. The translator seems not to have connected the *percusserunt* with *caecitate* and has introduced instead a new verb, *wurdon*: 'Ond ða, on ða ilcan tid, ða englas ða ðær wæron on ðæm wolcnum hie wurdon wyldran ðonne ða Iudeas and ongunnon slean ða Iudeas. Ond hie ða wurdon sona blinde . . .'. Zupitza ('Kritische Beiträge', p. 213) suggests that *wyldran* is not 'wilder', as Morris translates it, but 'stronger': 'dieses zu *wealdan* gehörige *wylde* = me. *welde* führt Ettmüller 116 mit der bedeutung potens, dominans, an'.

81 Although both manuscripts share the reading *he genealæcan* I have emended to *he ongan genealæcan*; *ongan* with an infinitive is a characteristic construction in this text and the omission of *ongan* is an easy mechanical error, as it shares the *-an* ending with *genealæcan*. This emendation is proposed by Zupitza, 'Kritische Beiträge', p. 213.

82 *dicentes* in the Latin has confused the translator, who assumed that this signalled the beginning of a speech, whereas in the Latin the speech begins with *dixit* in the next clause. The Latin reads: 'apostolos uero hymnum dicentes, repletus furore et [magna] ira dixit: "Ecce tabernaculum illius qui nos predauit et omne genus nostrum: qualem gloriam accepit."' What in the source is a speech by the Jewish leader becomes the apostles' hymn in the Old English and the translation is slanted to fit in with this attribution. As is often the case with this text, many of the key words of the source are translated, but the meaning of the Old English is very far from that of the Latin, as well as being totally inconsequential. I have not emended F's *ussun* to *ussum*, even though *ussun* is not attested in the *MCOE* and B reads *ussum*, as *-m* and *-n* seem not to have been distinguished in the pronunciation of inflectional endings in this period. I have, however, emended F's *cynnum* to agree with B's *cynne*, as the Latin is also singular.

[83] Again, words denoting speech (*clamans uoce magna*) have been taken, mistakenly, to signal the beginning of a speech; the Latin reads: 'Et subito faciens impetum, clamans uoce magna, uoluit euertere lectum. Mittens uero manum, uoluit conprehendere palmam illam et ad terram deducere.' This becomes in the Old English a first-person account of what the Jewish leader wishes to do to the palm. *euertere*, 'to overturn', has been rendered as *me onhwyrfan to*, which means 'to turn to'. The continuation of the Old English description of what the Jewish leader wishes to do with the palm corresponds to a description in the Latin of what happens to his arms: 'Statim uero manus eius ambae aruerunt ab ipsis cubitis'. *Forsearedum* corresponds to *aruerunt* and *ambae* to *begen*, but the rest of the Old English is difficult to explain, and the Latin has nothing about burning, unless *aruerunt* was translated twice, once as *forsearedum* and the second time as *ardeo*, 'to burn', rather than *areo*, 'to be dry', 'withered'. *Forbrecan* may go back to a variant like that of Wilmart's R, which replaces 'manus eius ambae aruerunt' with 'fracte sunt manus eius', although the translator's exemplar would then have to have had a version combining both readings here. Alternatively, the translator could have amplified his source himself, given that he was under the impression, despite two allusions to the Jewish leader's hand in this chapter, that the passage related to the palm. As it is never withered, the curing of the hand later in the Old English seems odd to a reader who does not know the Latin; conversely the notion that the Jewish leader, in the heat of anger, would wait for the palm to wither is equally strange.

[84] 'Ða wæs he gongende to ðære bære' seems to have been added independently by the translator, unless it was his rendering of 'adhaeserunt ad lectum'. None of Wilmart's manuscripts has the detail of the Jewish leader hanging by the right hand and the hand is not mentioned in the corresponding sentence in the Latin, which reads: 'Et pars eius media corporis ad lectum tenebatur, pars uero altera ad terram pendebat'. Although, therefore, the translator did not refer to the hand in his rendering of the corresponding section of the Latin (see previous note), he included it here. As with the previous sentence (see n. 82), he may well have been composing more independently than usual at this point. 'pars uero altera ad terram pendebat' is the source for 'þæt he hangode to eorðan', with the translator ignoring the 'pars uero altera'. I have not emended F's *swidram* to *swidran* or *swiþran* (B reads *swiþran*), even though the form *swidram* is not attested in the *MCOE*, as -*an* and -*am* seem to have more or less fallen together as inflectional endings in late Old English. Since *swidran* does occur and could presumably have been pronounced in the same way as *swidram*, there seems no necessity to emend.

[85] The Latin reads: 'Rogo te praecipue, sancte Petre, ut memor sis quid tibi praestiterit pater meus, quando ostiaria illa interrogauit te et dicebat: Uere tu

cum illo eras, quomodo te excusauit, ne conprehendereris. Et ego modo rogo uos ut non me despiciatis.' In the Old English the doorkeeper (female in the Latin) becomes the father of the Jewish leader. The *interrogauit te et dicebat* of the Latin is then understood as the introduction to a question which is assigned to Peter, rather than being the continuation of the Jewish leader's narrative of what happened on the night when Christ was arrested. In keeping with this different understanding of the passage, *cum illo* becomes *mid ðynum fæder*, instead of referring to Christ, and the inflectional ending on *conprehendereris* is ignored, becoming third-person plural rather than second-person singular. The final sentence of the Jewish leader's speech is then correctly assigned to him, with an introduction supplied by the translator, *Ond ða cwæð se aldorman eft*. The Latin reading itself, which has the high-priest's father assist Peter, arose from a misunderstanding of its source text, in which *pater* was probably originally a vocative: *Pseudo-Melito* has in the equivalent place 'tunc ego locutus sum pro te bona' (Haibach-Reinisch, ed., *Ein neuer 'Transitus'*, ch. 12, p. 81, and see above, pp. 73–5).

[86] For *super quem exsurrexistis*, the Old English reads *ond arise fram deaðe*, as the translator, not heeding the inflectional endings, has understood this as a reference to Christ's Resurrection.

[87] Either the source used had a very different reading here to any of Wilmart's manuscripts or the translator has ignored the indication in his source of a speech by the Jewish leader and has also disregarded the inflectional ending of *credimus*: 'Et respondit dicens: "Numquid non credimus quod filius dei est?" ' Instead, he has made of the Jewish chief's question a continuation of Peter's speech, 'gyf þu ðonne ne gelyfst þæt he sy Godes sunu', and has therefore been obliged to supply a suitable ending, 'ðonne ne byst ðu asetted on eorðan'. No known Latin manuscript has an equivalent to this last clause.

[88] The Latin reads here: ' "Sed quid faciemus, quia inimicus generis humani obcaecauit corda nostra? Sed uos nolite malum pro malo reddere. Hoc enim mihi ideo contigit, quia me uult dominus uiuere." Tunc Petrus iussit deponi lectum et dixit ad eum: "Si credis ex toto corde tuo quia poteris a deo sanari, accede et osculare lectum . . .".' The Old English sentence seems to combine elements from the first and last sentences here, one spoken by the Jewish leader and the other by Peter: 'inimicus generis humani obcaecauit corda nostra' clearly lies behind 'ðyses menniscan cynnes fynd ablende eowre heortan' and 'a deo sanari' behind 'bist ðu gehæled fram him'. The middle part of the Old English sentence, 'þæt Crist ne wære soð God', is harder to trace and may have been composed freely by the translator, guided by his belief that this whole passage was spoken by Peter rather than the Jewish leader. Eyeskip from 'corda (nostra)' to ('ex toto) corde tuo', either by the translator or in his exemplar, seems to have been responsible for the jump

from the Jewish leader's speech to Peter's speech. The eyeskip may well have been in the translator's exemplar and he may therefore have supplied 'þæt Crist ne wære soð God' in an attempt to make sense. Morris smoothes over the difficulty by misrepresenting the Old English text in his translation: 'But we know that the enemy of mankind hath blinded your hearts, lest you should believe that Christ were true God, and you should be saved by him'. I have emended F's *ablendan* to B's *ablende* as the Latin is also singular; Old English *fynd* is morphologically ambiguous and could be singular or plural.

89 Wilmart's text reads 'et dic: Credo in hoc corpus et in eum quem portauit', but M reads 'dic ad corpus: Credo in deum patrem et in eum quem haec portauit iesum christum'. A reading like this was probably in the translator's source, although his version is by no means identical in meaning: 'cweð to ðysum lichoman þæt ðu gelyfe on God Fæder ond on Marian forðon hio bær Hælendne Crist'.

90 There appears to be a double translation of *lingua*, as *tungan* and *stæfne*, in the phrase 'mid his tungan Ebreisce stæfne'. 'per trium horarum spatium' seems not to be reflected in the Old English, but it occurs at the same point in the sentence as *ðurh wuldor* and the rather unusual combination of *wuldor* with the preposition *ðurh* suggests that *ðurh* goes back to the Latin *per*. Could *per trium horarum* somehow have been confused with some form of *triumphare* or *triumphus* (perhaps *triumphorum?*), resulting in *ðurh wuldor?*

91 There is nothing in the Latin to correspond to this clause; it reads 'et neminem permisit lectum leuare, de libris Moysi testimonium dans . . .' It is tempting to see *spatium* from the preceding Latin clause reflected in *fyrstmearce*.

92 The source reads 'ita ut ipsi apostoli mirarentur ea quae ab eo dicebantur', but the translator has taken the *dicebantur* as referring to the apostles and then seems to have supplied 'hwonon him ða wundorlican gereordo coman'.

93 Again, some of the inflectional endings are unheeded as the source reads: 'Conleua manus tuas et dic: In nomine domini nostri Iesu Christi, cui modo ex toto corde credo, restaurentur manus meae et fiant sicut antea'.

94 The Latin reads 'whoever believes in the Lord will have his eyes opened' ('Quicumque crediderit in dominum Iesum Christum, quoniam ipse est filius dei uiui, aperientur oculi eius'), whereas the Old English has instead 'whoever does not believe will have his eyes closed'. *Aperire*, 'to open', and *operire*, 'to close', are easily confused and may not have been easy to distinguish in the translator's Latin exemplar. The Old English, however, makes perfect sense and the translator adds a clause to the next sentence, 'Ond ðonne gif hwilc gelefe on God', which is necessary for the sense there. The translator then nevertheless retains the last sentence of this section, beginning 'Se ðonne witodlice ne gelyfeð on God', even though this duplicates 'swa hwilc swa ne gelyfeð . . .'.

95  Wilmart's Latin reads 'et fecit secundum quod illi mandauerat beatus
    Petrus', but his manuscripts B, G, M and P read *dixit* instead of *fecit*; the
    source of the Old English must also have read *dixit*.

96  There is no Latin equivalent to *mycel broga* in any of Wilmart's manuscripts,
    which read 'quoniam illi quidem in primis percussi sunt caecitate'.

97  The Latin reads 'ecce enim nos repleti sumus omni iniquitate', and there is
    no variant which could throw light on *eaðmoðnesse*.

98  This clearly originates in the Latin '(et exposuit eis omnia) quae audiuit et
    passus est', but there it refers to what the Jewish chief, not the people, heard
    and suffered.

99  The equivalent at this point in the Latin is 'quomodo respexit illum deus';
    perhaps the translator was led astray by *respexit* in the sense 'to look'
    (resulting in *gesihðe*) rather than what is intended here, 'to have regard for',
    although this does not explain *wundrode* or the absence of *deus*.

100 Only V among Wilmart's manuscripts has here *et dixit eis quia*; presumably
    the source followed by the Old English had such a phrase.

101 There is no equivalent to this last sentence in the Latin, but it is necessitated
    by the translator's rendering of the previous sentence in direct speech, unlike
    his source where it is third-person narration.

102 Mary's soul has, of course, already been received into heaven, and the Latin
    reads *corpus* here, but, as this version of the apocryphon is augmented by
    another account of the reception of Mary's body, body has here been altered
    to soul. The difficulty arises from the fact that the translator, as Willard
    pointed out, continued to render *Transitus W* beyond the point at which he
    should have switched to translating *Transitus B²*, if he wished to avoid
    contradictions in his narrative:

> in taking up his new source, he went back to Christ's coming for
> the assumption, and he told the story over again according to the
> supplementary source [*Transitus B²*], with the result that Christ
> is made to appear at the tomb twice on this day and Mary's body
> is twice taken up to heaven. But the absurdity of this was
> apparent to the joiner, for in that passage which he still retained
> from *Transitus W* and which he failed to eliminate he altered the
> word 'body' to 'soul', so that it is only Mary's soul that is taken to
> heaven at Christ's first appearance on this occasion, and her body
> at the second. But in solving one difficulty he raised another, that
> of the double transport of Mary's soul to heaven: the first, and
> properly, at her death, and this second three days later, at what
> should have been the time of her assumption on the very day
> when, in fact, the soul must be brought back from heaven that it
> may rejoin its body.                     ('The Two Accounts', p. 6)

Although Willard specifies that Mary's soul went to heaven at Mary's death, the text never says this.

[103] The Lord is the subject of *dixit* in the Latin; as Willard states '*Dominus* must have been missing in the Latin source; its absence there would deprive *dixit* of its proper subject. In such a case Michael would be understood as the translator has actually done here' ('The Two Accounts', p. 9, n. 9).

[104] The translator seems not to have realized that 'ipsi suscepti sunt in nubibus' refers to the apostles being taken up into the clouds and this becomes in the Old English a further repetition of the reception of Mary's soul. There is no mention of *anima* in the source, although Wilmart's S and R add 'cum sanctissimo corpore sancte marie' and it is possible that the translator's source had such a reading and that he, or his source, again replaced body by soul.

[105] The translator has again altered *corpus* to *sawle*, in keeping with his earlier change.

[106] This is where *Transitus W* ends in Wilmart's G and P: 'Et sic deposuerunt nubes corpus beatae Mariae in paradiso, et est ibi glorificans deum cum omnibus electis eius'. In the Old English *in paradiso* is rendered with the succeeding rather than the preceding clause and the meaning of the second clause has been altered in a characteristic fashion, by ignoring the grammar of the Latin. The next sentence in the Old English is translated from *Transitus B²*. In the other manuscripts *Transitus W* ends differently, with the resurrection of Mary's body; see above, pp. 78–80.

[107] The Latin reads: 'Gloria tibi, Deus, qui facis mirabilia magna solus'. I have emended both manuscripts' reading *wuldor* to *wundor*, as the error is an easily explicable one; a scribe at some stage in the transmission of the text has repeated the *wuldor* at the beginning of the sentence. Exactly the same error is made in the D assumption apocryphon.

[108] Willard's notes on the section of the text translated from *Transitus B²* rely on a reconstruction of the source which, in the light of subsequent scholarship, is not always accurate; here, for example, the source reads 'Antequam ego missus a Patre', not 'Antequam ascenderem ad patrem meum'. The Old English is not, therefore, 'the exact opposite . . . of the Latin' ('The Two Accounts', p. 11, n. 5).

[109] The Latin reads 'cum adhuc corporaliter conuersarer uobiscum', with the verb *conuersor* meaning 'to live with'. The translator appears to have confused *conuersor* with *conuerso*, 'to turn round', or *conuerto*, 'to turn around' or 'to change', and has translated it as *wæs gehwirfed*, presumably intended to mean something like 'was turned to' or, perhaps, given the next *on* clause, 'was returned to'. Morris (*The Blickling Homilies*, p. 154) renders it 'was restored', as does *BT*. *Corporaliter* here becomes a noun clause *on minne lichoman* and the

verb *gehwirfed* also seems to govern the preposition *on* in the clause 'on eallum ðæm ðe me fylgende wæron on ðissum mænniscan cynne'.

110  The *ær* is inserted by the translator, in accordance with his different understanding of this passage (see previous note).

111  This passage in the Old English is translated from 'quod uos qui secuti estis me, in regeneratione'. *Regeneratione* is clearly confused with *generatione*, giving *on ðissum mænniscan cynne*. Nothing in the variant manuscripts of *Transitus B*² explains *on eallum ðæm ðe*, which was perhaps inserted because of the context created by the translator's rendering (or misrendering) of his source in this passage.

112  This renders 'cum sederit filius hominis in sede maiestatis suae, sedebitis et uos super thronos duodecim, iudicantes duodecim tribus Israel. Hanc ergo ex una tribu Israel elegit iussio Patris mei, ut sumerem carnem ex ea.' The translator has ignored the *cum* and has transferred Christ's third-person speech into the first person. *Filius hominis*, by ignoring the nominative singular ending, is then rendered as *ofer manna bearnum*. 'Sedebitis et uos super thronos duodecim', referring to the apostles' co-enthronement with Christ, becomes instead 'wæs sittende ofer eow on minum heahsetle', the translator failing to recognize Christ's honouring of the apostles, and rendering a third person plural future tense with a first-person singular past tense, and adding *minum*. He has obviously not realized that this passage is ultimately dependent on Matthew XIX.28 and no reader could guess from it that Christ was impressing on the apostles the power with which he had endowed them. *iudicantes*, similarly, becomes a first-person singular referring to Christ and, as Willard notes, *ðrim Israhela folcum* 'looks like a double translation of *tribus*, once as "three" and again as "tribes". It is probably to be explained as the confusion of *tribus*, as the ablative plural of *tres*, "three", with *tribus*, in the accusative plural, meaning "tribes" ' ('The Two Accounts', p. 12, n. 9). The *twelf* in *of ðæm twelf mægðum* can probably be explained as a translation of the reading *de tribubus* which both Haibach-Reinisch's English manuscripts O¹ and O² share (her edited text reads *ex una tribu*), with *duodecim* perhaps added because the first *duodecim* of the Latin had erroneously been connected with *iudicantes* rather than with *thronos*, leaving a floating *duodecim*. *Hanc ergo* and *elegit* do not seem to appear at all in the Old English but *ut sumerem carnem ex ea* presumably lies behind *ic wearð eft on lichoman geseted*.

113  The translator replaces the first part of the Latin sentence ('Ecce iam debito naturae completo') with 'Ond ða cwæð se Hælend to ðæm apostolum', perhaps because he found the meaning of the Latin obscure. Mitchell notes that 'Andrew (SS, para. 60) is right when he says that in *BlHom* 155. 35 *Hwæt wille ge nu? hwæt ic hire doo?* the second *hwæt* can only be a scribal error for *þæt*' (*OE Syntax*, para. 1868). I have emended accordingly.

114 The Old English is different in detail to the Latin, but recognizably derived from it and very similar in import. *Transitus B²* reads: 'Domine, tu elegisti uasculum istud in tabernaculum mundissimum tibi, omnia autem ante saecula praescisti. Si ergo potuisset fieri ante decretum tuae potentiae, uisum fuerat nobis famulis tuis, ut, sicut tu deuicta morte regnas in gloria, ita resuscitans matris corpusculum, tecum eam deduceres laetantem in caelum.' 'in to eardienne' appears to be the translator's addition and 'hio is ðin seo cleneste fæmne ær ealre worlde' seems to combine the *mundissimum* of the source with *ante saecula* of the next clause to produce a description of Mary, rather than the Latin's reference to Christ. 'ðu miht soðlice ond gesewenlice ðine miht gecyðan on Marian ðinra ðeowan' seems to render elements of the Latin (*potuisset, potentiae, famulis tuis*), but again with different grammatical forms and in a very different context. The next Old English sentence alters the verbal forms to produce: 'Ond ðu oferswiðdest dead ond ðu eart rixiende on ðinum wuldre, swa ðu nu miht ðinra modor lichoman eft aweccan fram deaðe'. The last clause of the Latin, 'tecum eam deduceres laetantem in caelum', is attached to the next sentence in the Old English and becomes a description instead of Christ's emotions, 'Ond ða raðe wæs Drihten blissiende on heofonas', with the result that the apostles do not ask for Mary's assumption, but only her resurrection.

115 Only Haibach-Reinisch's manuscripts T, F, O¹, O² (the last two English) and V have the clause 'Et ecce Gabriel archangelus reuoluit lapidem ab ostio monumenti et', inserted after *accedens* in the sentence 'Statimque iubente Domino accedens Michael archangelus, praesentauit animam sanctae Mariae coram Domino'. The Old English clearly followed a text like this.

116 F. Holthausen, 'Beiträge zur Erklärung und Textkritik alt- und mittelenglischer Denkmäler', *Englische Studien* 14 (1890), 393–401, suggested that this should read *geong and weardode*, with *geong* as an adjective referring to Michael, but, as the word translates *praesentauit*, this is not a convincing emendation.

117 The Latin reads 'et dum [quia O¹, O², V, P¹] non sensisti labem delicti per coitum, non patiaris resolutionem corporis in sepulchro'. The Old English scribe or his source must have read *cor tuum* for *coitum*, resulting in *on ðinre heortan*, but no variant reading accounts for the replacement of *resolutionem* with *nænige ðrowunge* and the omission of *in sepulchro*.

118 There is nothing in *Transitus B²* to account for this sentence.

119 *ymbfeng Drihtnes fet* renders *aduoluta pedibus*; the translator seems to have understood *aduoluta* in its sense 'roll to' rather than 'to prostrate oneself', and he must have interpreted it as something like 'to roll around', thus giving *ymbfeng*.

120 The translator has muddled Mary's speech of thanks somewhat. The Latin

reads: 'Non ego condignas gratias possum rependere tibi, omnipotens Domine, quem totus mundus plene non praeualet laudare'. Haibach-Reinisch's B reads *referre* rather than *rependere* and her Z and E *reddere* and it is probably one of these readings which lies behind the *forðbringan* of the Old English. The translator did not realize that *gratias referre* or *gratias reddere* was a set phrase and rendered the two words separately, *gratias* as 'grace', OE *gife*, rather than 'thanks', and the verb as *forðbringan*, which seems to mean 'to adduce', 'to cite', as both *referre* and *reddere* can mean 'to report'. *totus mundus* is not represented in the translation.

121 Willard has a long note on *ahof*, attempting to relate it to the Latin of his reconstructed source, which at this point reads *recessit*. He therefore postulates confusion of *recessit* and *recepit*: 'Because of the similarity of insular *s* and *p*, *recessit*, and particularly if it happened to have been written *recesit*, may have suggested *recepit* to him instead of *recessit*' ('The Two Accounts', p. 18, n. 1). *Transitus B*[2], however, reads *Elevans eam*, vindicating the translator here.

122 The Latin reads: 'Pacem meam do uobis, pacem meam relinquo uobis'. The Old English quotes the first part of this sentence in Latin, but then translates the second part first, followed by the first part. None of Haibach-Reinisch's manuscripts has anything corresponding to 'ðurh mines Fæder ðone Halgan Gast' or to 'ðurh min þæt hehste lof'.

123 The Latin reads: 'Et haec dicens Dominus, cum canentibus angelis et matre sua receptus est in paradiso'. The translator again seems to have confused inflectional endings and has made this third-person narrative into a command by the Lord to the angels to sing and to receive his mother into paradise. *canentibus*, an ablative adjective, is rendered as an imperative verb and *receptus est*, a perfect indicative, as another imperative.

124 The source reads here: 'Apostoli autem in uirtute Christi rapti in nubibus . . .' ('but the apostles, having been seized up into the clouds by the power of Christ . . .'). The translator's rendition, apart from misrepresenting the source, also does not quite agree with his own previous sentence, in which the angels were commanded to receive Mary into paradise. There is nothing corresponding to *Christi* in the Old English, in which it is the apostles' own power which allows them to raise Mary up; the word may have been missing in the source used, as it is in Haibach-Reinisch's manuscript P[1]. More importantly, of course, the source has no mention of Mary's body at this point, but the translator clearly did not realize that the verb was a passive one and he rendered it as an active, *hofon*, which then needed an object. Since the context of the previous sentence suggested Mary, the translator probably supplied *Marian lichoman*. Even without the difference between passive and active, *hofon* is not an accurate translation of *rapti*, but it is possible that at

this point the translator felt that the only possible object in seizing Mary was to raise her up and he therefore supplied this in his version; he may also have felt that the command to receive the body (which, of course, originated in a mistranslation) should be carried out. Having gone so far, he then appears to have concluded the sentence independently (or at any rate none of the Latin manuscripts surviving has anything comparable) with 'ond hine ða asetton on neorxnawanges gefean'; probably the mention of receiving Mary *on neorxnawange* in the previous sentence prompted him to make explicit Mary's being placed here.

[125] The first part of this sentence is difficult as both manuscripts read 'nu syndon gesette ða apostolas in hlet æ hie bodian hire'. The Latin reads: 'Apostoli . . . depositi sunt unusquisque in sorte praedicationis suae, narrantes et confitentes magnalia Dei'. *depositi sunt* is clearly *syndon gesette* and *confitentes magnalia Dei* (confessing the mighty works of the Lord) is *onddetton Godes mycelnesse*, while *hlet* means 'lot, share', as does *sors*, but the passage as a whole causes problems. *æ hie bodian hire*, while obviously related to *praedicationis suae*, does not appear to make sense. Willard suggests different possible solutions:

> Something, I believe, has happened to the Old English. *In sortem* [sic] *praedicationis suae* should have given *in hlet hira* (or *heora*) *bodunge*, or *in hlet þær hie bodien* (or *bodian sceoldon*). *Hlet æ* of Blickling has caused trouble. Morris and Toller took *æ* as a variant of *a*, 'ever', which phonologically is extremely unlikely. It may be a mutilated form of *æt* [*æt hire bodunge*] with the *t* lost by some scribal error. If so, this hypothecated accident must have occurred by the time of the archetype of our two Old English manuscripts, since both Blickling and MS. CCCC 198 show the same reading. It is equally possible, however, that *æ* may be the word 'law', as the second element of a hitherto unrecorded compound, *hlet-æ*, with the meaning 'divine law or disposition revealed through the casting of lots'. Surely it could not have been mere chance that governed the dispersal of the Apostles to their missionary stations, for the Divine Will must certainly have guided the fall of the lot, and thereby have made known His Providence. An analogous *æ*-compound can be found in *tungol-æ*, literally 'star-law', but more precisely the working out of Divine Providence through the influence of the stars, or the revelation of the Divine Will through the stars. . . . To a medieval churchman, *æ* meant not only human but, even more, divine law: cf. *Cristes æ*, 'Gospel', and *æ* in the sense of 'scriptures, revelation'. The religious character of Anglo-Saxon law is apparent in every

page of their legal compilations. *Hie bodian hire*, of Blickling, cannot be correct, but must represent some mangled version of *praedicationis suae*. *Hire* should not be a genitive or dative singular, with reference to the Virgin, but must originally have been a genitive plural, *hira*, or *heora*, etc., which in the form *hira* could easily be confused with *hire*, particularly by the time of Blickling and later, and so could become mistaken for the singular, *hire*. Thus, a reading which originally referred to the Apostles, as it should, has by some accident of transmission come to refer, though erroneously, to Mary instead. In case of any ambiguity, this would be but natural, since the whole homily is about her. In all probability *praedicationis suae* was originally translated *heora*, or *hira*, *bodunge*. But, as has happened to many another passage in this text, the translation, once clear and correct, has since become obscured, either through accident or revision, or both. ('The Two Accounts', p. 19, n. 1)

One problem with Willard's discussion is that it introduces a new, quite sophisticated concept, *hlet-æ*, a procedure not typical of this translation. His confidence that *heora* or *hira bodunge* was the original translation may also be misplaced. The translator seems to have understood *praedicationis* as a verb, not a noun, and the verbal form with which it could be most easily confused is probably the present participle, *praedicantes*, especially as there were other present participles in the immediate vicinity (*narrantes et confitentes*). When faced with a present participle the translator often translates with a finite verbal form, as he did with *confitentes* (*ond we nu onddetton*). If he did this with *praedicationis suae*, it could result in a clause like *hie bodian hire*, as it would be entirely consistent with the translator's practice to take *suae* as referring to Mary (thus the *hire*). It is possible that the only corruption here is the form *æ* and that could perhaps be explained by reading *hlete*, accounting for the *æ* as an *e* with a misplaced hook under it which then became detached from the noun or *hletæ*, with the *-æ* as the case ending. Hardy (*Die Sprache der Blickling Homilien*, p. 53) suggests *hletæ*, with *-æ* as the dative or instrumental ending instead of *-e*. While it seems to me that no certainty is possible, I have adopted this reading as it does least violence to the text of both manuscripts, while giving a reasonably satisfactory reading. As manuscript punctuation clearly (in B particularly) begins a new sentence with *Ond hie bodian hire*, I have also done so.

The Latin source ends: 'qui in Trinitate perfecta et una deitatis substantia uiuit, dominatur et regnat in saecula saeculorum'. This is not rendered in the Old English, which instead uses *confitentes magnalia Dei* as a transition to its version of the *Magnificat*.

126  Willard has commented at length on this Old English version of the
*Magnificat* 'somewhat farsed by blending with the Beatitudes' ('An Old
English *Magnificat*', p. 5) and I draw on his discussion. He pointed out that:

> Noteworthy in the Old English is the complete reversal of aspect
> evident in the first five verses of the *Magnificat*. In the Latin the
> verbs are all 3rd person, singular, and may be termed historical,
> in that they scan past action as they contemplate God's mercy to
> Mary at the Annunciation, – and this, of course, is the immediate
> impulse for this hymn. . . . The Old English, on the other hand,
> looks forward: it is concerned with the future and eternity. Two
> important grammatical changes are noticeable: the first five
> verses, those concerned with Mary, instead of being about God,
> are addressed directly to God, with the change of the verb from
> the 3rd person singular to the 2nd; furthermore, instead of being
> in the indicative, and expressions of Mary's exaltation of God's
> grace to her, they are in the imperative, as commands, or
> emphatic petitions, that God magnify her soul, that He make her
> spirit rejoice in Him, that He behold her humility, and that He
> bring it to pass that she be known to future ages as the most
> blessed virgin. All this implies unawareness of the translator of
> the spirit of the canticle he is translating, and of the traditional
> great humility of Our Lady as she sang 'magnificat with tune
> surpassinge sweete'. He makes her appear as *dom-georn* and as *tir-
> hwæt* as any figure in heroic tradition, so that she cries out like a
> prima donna hungry for publicity, demanding that the Lord
> extol her soul and make sure that all generations call her blessed.
>
> (*Ibid.*, pp. 16–17)

Willard's summary is rather unjust to Mary's requests in this text, which
are much more Christocentric than he implies, but it is, nevertheless, a very
surprising version of the canticle. In attempting to explain this extraordinary
reversal, Willard suggests three factors probably at work here: the form of
the verb *magnificat*, the word-order in the first verse and the fact that Mary
speaks of herself in these first verses, using first-person pronouns. The form
of *magnificat* could have suggested the subjunctive to the translator, who
then rendered it as an imperative, and he also seems to have understood
*anima mea*, the subject of the Latin, as the object of *magnificat*, and *dominum*,
the real object, as the subject. Word-order was probably instrumental in this
confusion. The following verbs could have then been affected by this initial
decision, though this version may also be the result of a much more
deliberate process than the rather haphazard one which this implies.

127  The second verse of the *Magnificat* reads: 'Et exsultauit spiritus meus in Deo

salutari meo'. The third-person singular past tense *exsultauit* is translated as a second-person singular imperative *gedo þæt min gast wynsumige* and *salutari meo* becomes *on ðinre hælo*. The translator was hardly unable to distinguish *meo* from *tuo*, but he may have felt that, as Mary was addressing the Lord, salvation was properly to be attributed to him rather than to her. *Deo* of the *Magnificat* becomes a full clause, *forðon ðe ðu eart soð God*.

[128] The same alteration in the verb is apparent here, with *respexit* becoming *ðu sceawa*. Both manuscripts read *mægenes* instead of *mægdenes*, and the glossator has glossed it *uirtutem*, 'all three evidently unconscious of the error in this passage' (Willard, 'An Old English *Magnificat*', p. 24).

[129] *Marie*, a reading shared by both manuscripts, should, as Willard points out, read *Maria*: 'It is probably due to a short-range misinterpretation, whereby *Sancta Maria*, the postpositive subject of *cwæð*, was taken to be the indirect object of *cwæð*' ('An Old English *Magnificat*', p. 24). However, *Marie* as a nominative occurs twice elsewhere in this homily and I have, therefore, not emended. Again, an imperative is substituted for the future verb of the *Magnificat*, resulting in Mary calling upon the Lord to make every generation call her the most blessed Virgin.

[130] The Latin tag *Et misericordia eius* is given first, but it is then rendered *ðin mildheortnes*. Willard argues that this, along with other details of the translation, suggests that these changes 'are in the main to be credited to the original translator, who rearranged his matter in direct address and in livelier fashion' ('An Old English *Magnificat*', p. 25).

[131] Both manuscripts share the reading *earan*, but should, clearly, read *earman*.

[132] The last clause here is an addition to the source, probably by the translator.

[133] The translator identifies the *mihtigan* as Satan and his angels, rather than the powerful of this world, as is implied in the *Magnificat*. Both manuscripts share the reading *ond his deoflum mid him*, of which the *-m* ending on *deoflum* is presumably, as Willard points out, due to the phrase *mid his deoflum* earlier in the sentence ('An Old English *Magnificat*', p. 25).

[134] Part of this is loosely translated from, or at least suggested by, the *Magnificat*, 'Esurientes impleuit bonis et diuites dimisit inanes' ('Drihten ealle ða gefylde . . . ða ðe hie on eorðan leton hingrian . . . Ond elle ða men ða ðe onfengon welon . . . hie sylfe swa forleton on idelnesse, ðonne gegearwode he ðæm ece forwyrde'); its import, however, is very different because of the change of setting from this world to the next, as was also the case with the previous verse. Willard argues that this 'universal direction given to the action of verses 7 and 8' of the *Magnificat* (this and the preceding sentence) is part of the 'fondness of the Anglo-Saxon homilist for themes treating of the Other-world' ('An Old English *Magnificat*', p. 20). It is open to question whether the original translator was freely amplifying this and the preceding

verse, or whether we have here a revising scribe at work, which is Willard's view: 'The insertion of the transitory 7 *ða wæs Sancta Maria cweðende*, "and then was St. Mary saying", immediately after the Latin tag *Esurientes*, suggests, to me at least, that this is the work of the revising scribe, who has taken it upon himself to embellish his original as he copied it' (*ibid.*, p. 21) and 'I believe also that the Other-world material to be found in verses 7 and 8 is due to the reviser' (*ibid.*, p. 23). Against this it could be argued that the translator has already inserted 'forðon heo ðus cwæð ða heo *Magnificat* sang' and 'cwæð Sancte Marie', so there seems little reason to assume that he did not also include this phrase, which, moreover, has the characteristic *wæs* plus present-participle form (*wæs cweðende*) which occurs so often in this text (thirty-seven times; see G. Nickel, *Die Expanded Form im Altenglischen* (Neumünster, 1966), p. 201). It seems to me, therefore, that this expansion of verses 7 and 8 of the *Magnificat* is more likely to be the work of the original translator than that of a revising scribe who expertly mimicked the style of the original translator. It is true that the translator did not embellish his version of the assumption narrative in the same way, but the *Magnificat* is a fundamentally different type of text and one much more suited to devotional glossing, as we have here.

<sup>135</sup> The verse from the *Magnificat* which is the source for the first of these Old English sentences reads 'Suscepit Israel puerum suum, recordatus misericordiae suae', with *Israel* and *puerum suum* in apposition to each other, but in the Old English *Israel* is taken to be the subject and *puerum suum* the object, while *suscepit* becomes present or future tense (*onfehð*). Israel is also the subject of 'ond wæs gemindig ealra his mildheortnesse' in the Old English, although in the Latin 'recordatus misericordiae suae' modifies the implied subject of *suscepit*, the Lord. The clauses 'Sicut locutus est' and 'ond wæs sprecende to ussum fæderum ond to Abrahame ond wæs cweðende þæt his sæd oferweoxe ealle ðas weoruld' in the next Old English sentence are based on the last verse of the *Magnificat*, 'Sicut locutus est ad patres nostros, Abraham et semini eius in saecula', though the notion that Abraham's seed will spread over the whole earth is, of course, not in the canticle. This is presumably derived from Genesis XVII.5–6 and XXII.17.

With 'swa Matheus wæs cweðende', in the middle of the first of these Old English sentences, material from the Sermon on the Mount, Matthew V, is introduced. The way in which the material from Matthew is inserted is extremely peculiar, interrupting the translation of the *Magnificat* in mid-stream. As Willard said, we have here and in the next lines 'alternate utilization of the last two clauses of the *Magnificat* and the opening lines of Matt. 5, as a passus from The Sermon on the Mount is brought in almost by main force' ('An Old English *Magnificat*', pp. 26–7). The manner in which they are combined results in neither *Magnificat* nor Sermon on the Mount material making much sense as they now stand. The *Magnificat* is interrupted by Matthew's account of the Lord climbing a mountain with his followers and sitting down and again by the retainers going to him and Christ opening his mouth, while the narrative introduction to the Sermon on the Mount in this and in the next sentence is interrupted by *Sicut locutus est* from the *Magnificat*, which is then not translated until later in the sentence, and by 'ond wæs sprecende to ussum fæderum and to Abrahame ond wæs cweðende þæt his sæd oferweoxe ealle ðas weoruld'. Without these extracts from the canticle, the Matthew passage is more coherent, reading 'swa Matheus wæs cweðende þæt Drihten astige on sume tid on anne munt mid myccle werode his haligra ond ða gesæt he on ðæm munte. Ond ða eodan his ðegnas to him ond ða ontynde se Hælend his muð ond he ða lærde his apostolas ond him sægde ðurh hwæt seo saul eadegust gewurde ond ðus cwæð . . .'. This is a fairly faithful rendition of Matthew V.1–2: 'Uidens autem Iesus turbas, ascendit in montem, et cum sedisset, accesserunt ad eum discipuli eius, et aperiens os suum docebat eos dicens . . .'. Conversely, without the clauses from the Sermon on the Mount, the *Magnificat* material is also somewhat more coherent, reading '*Suscepit Israel*, ond Israel onfehð eallum his cnihtum ond wæs gemindig ealra his mildheortnesse. *Sicut locutus est*, ond wæs sprecende to ussum fæderum and to Abrahame ond wæs cweðende þæt his sæd oferweoxe ealle ðas weoruld'. This last sentence would leave *wæs sprecende* without a subject other than Israel, which is not very satisfactory from the point of view of sense, though it is easy to see how the translator could have arrived at it; in the manuscripts the subject is *se Hælend* from the Sermon on the Mount material, but this, of course, also results in defective sense as we then have the unlikely scenario of Christ speaking 'to ussum fæderum and to Abrahame'.

The awkwardness of the combination naturally begs the question of whether the Sermon on the Mount material was original or not. Willard believed not, arguing, as he did with verses 7 and 8 of the *Magnificat*, that the present state is the result of inflation by a revising scribe. He suggested that this scribal editor was 'inspired by the association in his mind of "He hath filled the hungry with good things" from the *Magnificat* with the Beatitude, "Blessed are they that hunger and thirst after righteousness, for they shall be filled"' ('An Old English *Magnificat*', p. 23). This beatitude, Matthew V.6, reads 'Beati qui esuriunt et sitiunt iustitiam: quoniam ipsi saturabuntur', of which *esuriunt* could, clearly, call the *esurientes* of the *Magnificat* to mind. A problem here is that Matthew V.6 is not then translated or alluded to anywhere, as one might expect had it provided the impetus for the inclusion of the Beatitudes. The passage from Matthew does not, moreover, begin with this verse of the *Magnificat*, but two sentences later.

Willard argued also that the ease with which the *Magnificat* can be separated from the Sermon on the Mount material and the way in which the Latin tag *Sicut locutus est* is divided from its translation by extraneous matter and in which, 'when finally translated, it results in the absurd situation that Christ on the Mount of the Sermon is made to open his mouth and speak to the patriarchs and promise Abraham that his seed should cover the earth' (Willard, 'An Old English *Magnificat*', p. 20) all suggest a scribal editor. That absurdity is a hallmark of the original translator also is not proof of his responsibility for this passage, as the 'nonsense' of the translator 'all represents struggle with recalcitrant Latin originals' (*ibid.*, p. 27), whereas this nonsense is of a fundamentally different nature.

There is, clearly, much to be said for this view, as removing the Matthew material would undoubtedly make the passage far more coherent, but there are also arguments against it. In the first place, the very beginning of the Matthew text has the characteristic *wæs cweðende* structure, so typical of the text as a whole and found also in the expansion of verse 8 of the *Magnificat*. Secondly, the Beatitudes quoted seem to have an application to Mary as she is depicted in this assumption text, although it must be admitted that many of the Beatitudes could be applied to the Virgin, and they lead, too, quite naturally into the concluding prayer. The present ending ('Ond eadige beoð ða ðe wepað nu for hiora synnum, forðon hie beoð eft gefrefrede on heofona rice. Ac uton we biddan ða fæmnan Sancta Marian þæt heo us sie milde ðingere wið urne Drihten Hælendne Crist ondweardes rædes ond eces wuldres; to ðæm us gefultmige ure Drihten') seems more appropriate than the abrupt one which we would have if we removed the Matthew passages: '*Sicut locutus est*, ond wæs sprecende to ussum fæderum and to Abrahame ond wæs cweðende þæt his sæd oferweoxe ealle ðas weoruld. Ac uton we biddan ða fæmnan Sancta Marian . . .'. We have to reckon, then, with the possibility that the Matthew passages were translated by the person who was responsible for the bulk of the text. It seems to me that they can be defended as a devotional gloss on both the assumption story and on the *Magnificat*, rather than being simply gratuitous, as Willard believed ('An Old English *Magnificat*', p. 27), and could, therefore, be the work of the original translator, rather than that of a revising editor. The real problem, in my view, is not that the two biblical passages should be combined, but the way in which this combination is effected. This is a problem which demands explanation whether we think the connection was made by the translator or a later scribe, and to which Willard does not provide an answer. Why could not the *Magnificat* be completed and the Sermon on the Mount material introduced at that point, providing a transition to the concluding prayer?

If we were to rearrange the text in this way, however, *Magnificat* followed by Sermon on the Mount, this would not solve the problem of a lack of a logical sequence, in that this would give '*Sicut locutus est*, ond wæs sprecende to ussum fæderum and to Abrahame ond wæs cweðende þæt his sæd oferweoxe ealle ðas weoruld, swa Matheus wæs cweðende þæt Drihten astige . . .'. This leaves *swa Matheus* without any toe-hold at all on the *Magnificat* text and, despite the repetition here of *wæs cweðende*, it is difficult to think of any mechanical error which would explain the sentence sequence. It is possible that the translator realized that *Magnificat* followed by Sermon on the Mount was too clumsy and instead tried to make the transition somewhat less sudden by introducing the Matthew material more gradually. Transitions were not his strong point, however, as can be seen also from the way in which he joined the two versions of the assumption story in this text, if he was responsible for that combination. He may well, then, have begun the introduction to the Sermon on the Mount immediately after 'ond Israel onfehð eallum his cnihtum and wæs gemindig ealra his mildheortnesse' as this at least provided some kind of continuity, however illusory, with the Beatitudes. He then interrupted the Matthew material to insert *Sicut locutus est*, following it with both vernacular speech indications, that from the Sermon on the Mount and that from the *Magnificat*, before continuing with the Beatitudes. It seems to me that such a process is more likely to have been the work of the translator than that of a later scribe who, had he wished to add the Matthew material, would most probably simply have tagged it on as a block. The tortuousness of the text as we have it in both manuscripts seems to testify to its original status.

136 The source here is the Sermon on the Mount, Matthew V.3–5. 'Beati pauperes spiritu' ('Blessed are the poor in spirit', Matthew V.3) is rendered 'Eadige beoð ðearfena gastes' ('Blessed are the spirits of the poor'). Willard pointed out that the Latin 'could be rendered nicely as *ðearfan gastes*, 'poor of spirit', which may well have been the original reading' ('An Old English *Magnificat*', p. 27), although both manuscripts share *ðearfena gastes*. Willard took the next sentence, 'ond eadige beoð ða ðe ðissa eorðwelena ne gymað', as a rendering of the verse 'Beati mites: quoniam ipsi possidebunt terram' (Matthew V.4), but it does not correspond to the meaning of the Latin, as he was aware, with the crucial word *mites* not being represented in the Old English. He thought that the negative of the Old English 'suggests that the translator took *quoniam*, probably in abbreviation, as signifying *qui non*; hence *gymað* does not properly translate *possidebunt*, but must represent some difficult struggle with a half-comprehended Latin original' ('An Old English

*Magnificat'*, p. 27). On the other hand, this clause may well be the translator's expansion of his own rendering of Matthew V.3, a variation rather than an attempt at the next verse; the *ðearfena gastes* are expanded to include 'ða ðe ðissa eorðwelena ne gymað'. He amplifies his rendering of Matthew V.5 in the next sentence, adding *nu for hiora synnum* and *on heofona rice*; this supports the hypothesis of a similar amplification of Matthew V.3, with Matthew V.4 not being translated. There is much manuscript support in early bibles for the transposition of Matthew V verses 4 and 5, so the translator may simply have been rendering the first two Beatitudes in his version of the New Testament.

# Latin apocryphal texts from Anglo-Saxon England

This appendix presents Latin texts of Marian apocrypha from manuscripts written in Anglo-Saxon England. Three such texts are included: a Latin adaptation of part of the Greek *Proteuangelium* on fols. 119v–122r of Cambridge, Pembroke College, 25 (P), a variant version of *Transitus W* from 113v–117v of the same manuscript, and the text of part of the *Gospel of Pseudo-Matthew* from British Library, Cotton Nero E. i, fols. 116v–118r (N). All three texts are presented in the manuscripts as readings for the feasts of Mary, the two infancy stories for her Nativity on 8 September and the death narrative for her assumption on 15 August. There is no text of *Transitus B* in a manuscript from Anglo-Saxon England.

I have not attempted to provide a full critical edition for any of these texts. All are extant in other manuscripts, though not in any other from Anglo-Saxon England, but in no case can the text printed here be considered the closest to the Old English texts. All of the texts are set out in accordance with the conventions of modern punctuation, and abbreviations have been silently expanded. The texts have been corrected where they are obviously corrupt and such editorial interventions are noted in the apparatus criticus, but omissions which do not affect the sense of what remains have not been supplied.

## THE *PROTEUANGELIUM IACOBI*

This version of the story of the birth and childhood of Mary, found in the copy of the Saint-Père homiliary in Cambridge, Pembroke College, 25, fols. 119v–122r, is extant also in two later English manuscripts of this homiliary, Cambridge, St John's College 42, fols. 50r–51r (twelfth century) and Oxford, Balliol College, 240, fols. 107v–109r (fourteenth century).[1] It is a text of a Latin adaptation corresponding to Chapters I to VIII, 1, of the Greek *Proteuangelium*. There is another copy of this text in the twelfth-century manuscript Vatican City, Biblioteca Apostolica Vaticana, Reginensis lat. 537 (R), fols. 31v–32v, printed by Vattioni,[2] and an unpublished copy in Karlsruhe, Badische Landesbibliothek, K 506, of *c.* 1200.[3] The Karlsruhe text has been interwoven with the *Gospel of Pseudo-Matthew*.

The chapter divisions here correspond to those in Strycker's edition of the Greek *Proteuangelium* and in the text printed by Vattioni.[4] The Vattioni text omits part of ch. II through eyeskip, skipping from *arbore* in II, 4 to *arbore* in III, 1 and repeating part of III. Unless otherwise noted the emendations here agree with the text of R, Vattioni's manuscript. Variant readings from Vattioni's text are not given unless they are used to correct the Pembroke text.

Gijsel suggests that this adaptation of the *Proteuangelium* descends from the same version from which the texts in Montpellier, Bibliothèque Universitaire, Section de Médecine 55, that are used in the infancy gospel published by James and the text in Karlsruhe, Augiensis LXIII, stem, but that the Vatican/Karlsruhe K 506 (and Pembroke) version has been reworked.[5] The scene of the naming of Mary by the voice from above in ch. V is not found in the Greek *Proteuangelium* or in the Latin *Gospel of Pseudo-Matthew*, but is also a feature of the Latin *Proteuangelium* in Montpellier 55, published by Canal,[6] and of the version in Paris, Bibliothèque Sainte-Geneviève, 2787.[7] These texts are from different branches of the stemma constructed by Gijsel, with the Sainte-Geneviève text, according to him, going back to a different translation from the

[1] As signalled by J. E. Cross, *Cambridge Pembroke College MS 25*, p. 37. Neither of these later versions has been printed.

[2] Vattioni, 'Frammento latino', pp. 507–8.

[3] Signalled by J. Gijsel, 'Les "Evangiles latins de l'enfance" de M. R. James', *Analecta Bollandiana* 94 (1976), 289–302, at 293, and 'Het *Protevangelium Iacobi* in het Latijn', *Antiquité Classique* 50 (1981), 351–66, at 354.

[4] Vattioni, 'Frammento latino', and Strycker, *La forme*.

[5] 'Het *Protevangelium Iacobi*', pp. 365–6. See also pp. 16–18.

[6] J. M. Canal, 'Antiguas Versiones latinas del Protoevangelio de Santiago', *Ephemerides Mariologicae* 18 (1968), 431–73, at 439.

[7] See Gijsel, 'Het *Protevangelium Iacobi*', p. 362, n. 25. This text has not yet been published.

Greek than that from which the Montpellier and Vatican/Karlsruhe texts descend.

This adaptation of the *Proteuangelium* has been provided with a short introduction to make it suitable for reading on the feast of Mary's nativity and a conclusion based on responses for the feast.[8]

## THE GOSPEL OF PSEUDO-MATTHEW

The text presented here from British Library, Cotton Nero E. i, fols. 116v–118r, (N), corresponds to chs. I to VI, 3, of the *Gospel of Pseudo-Matthew*, in Gijsel's numbering.[9] This is the only manuscript from Anglo-Saxon England to contain a text of part of *Pseudo-Matthew*. Cotton Nero's text, like that of the Old English version, belongs to the P family of Latin texts.[10] Evident corruptions have been corrected with reference to Gijsel's P text.

## TRANSITUS W

This text, a homily for the feast of the assumption in the copy of the Saint-Père homiliary in Cambridge, Pembroke College, 25, fols. 113v–117v, is a variant, abbreviated text of *Transitus W*. It is not found in the other copies of the Saint-Père homiliary, although it is noted in the index to Oxford, Balliol College, 240, and was presumably part of the original collection.[11] The closest parallel is the text printed by Marocco from the twelfth-century manuscript Ivrea, Cathedral Library, 59, a fragmentary text which covers chs. 1 to the end of ch. 17 of the text printed here, and which is very similar to Pembroke 25.[12] While this text is unmistakably a text of *Transitus W*, it has some details unparalleled in

---

[8] As noted by Cross, *Cambridge Pembroke College MS 25*, p. 36, these correspond to those in the Pseudo-Gregory *Liber Responsalis*, PL 78, cols. 798–99, and in *Corpus Antiphonalium Officii*, III and IV, ed. R.-J. Hesbert, Rerum Ecclesiarcarum Documenta, Series Maior, Fontes IX, X (Rome, 1968, 1970), III, nos. 1566, 2762 and 3105, and IV, nos. 6165, 6851 and 6867.

[9] *Libri de natiuitate Mariae: Pseudo-Matthaei Euangelium.*

[10] See pp. 22–3 and 137–8.

[11] See Cross, *Cambridge Pembroke College MS 25*, p. 51.

[12] Marocco, 'Nuovi documenti', pp. 449–52.

Wilmart's manuscripts, such as the mention of Jehoshaphat. Instead of saying that Mary's body was carried to paradise, this text says that the apostles did not know where Mary's body was taken; the liturgical responses which conclude the text say that she ascended to heaven, but without specifying whether this was in body as well as soul. I have numbered the chapters according to Wilmart's edition to facilitate comparison, but Pembroke 25 omits some chapters and inserts ch. 14 at a later point. The text corrects any obvious errors, very few in this instance, but makes no attempt to detail deviations from Wilmart's text.

The apocryphon is provided with a short introduction and a slightly longer conclusion, very similar to the introduction and more substantial conclusion provided for the text of the adaptation of the *Proteuangelium* in the same collection.[13] Both conclusions make free use of responses for the feasts of Mary, and the same procedure can be observed in the homily for the feast of Mary's purification in the collection, although this is not based on an apocryphal text but on passages from a Pseudo-Hildefonsus sermon, Ambrose's *Commentary on Luke* and an insular commentary on Luke.[14] Other texts in the collection also make use of responses (e.g. no. 5, for Christmas and no. 55, for the feast of St Michael). This suggests that the two texts in their present form were probably compiled by the compiler of the Saint-Père collection and Cross argues that the entire collection in Pembroke 25 was composed by one author who was using and adapting material from existing sources.[15] Cross dates the compilation of this collection to after 822 but before the second half of the tenth century, in the British Isles or in a continental centre influenced by insular texts.[16]

---

[13] The conclusion, again as noted by Cross, *Cambridge Pembroke College MS 25*, p. 37, is based on responses for feasts of Mary, as in *Liber Responsalis*, PL 78, cols.798 and 802, and in Hesbert, *Corpus Antiphonalium*, IV, nos. 7455, 7199 and 6854.

[14] Cross, *Cambridge Pembroke College MS 25*, p. 25.

[15] *Ibid.*, pp. 52–5.

[16] *Ibid.*, pp. 88–90.

PROTEUANGELIUM IACOBI

*LI. Omelia: In natiuitate Sancte Mariae*

Inquirendum est, fratres karissimi, et explanandum per ordinem de origine generis Mariae et natiuitatis eius solemnitate.

I, 1 Quidam uir nobilis[a] fuit in tribu Iuda, Ioachim nomine, ex genere Dauid, honorabilis ualde in .xii. tribubus[b] Israel. Diues quippe erat et ideo offerebat frequenter munera duplicia, dicens in semetipso: 'Erit quod superhabundat mihi dandum omni plebi et propitius ero.' 2 Appropinquauit autem magnus dies festus Domini secundum legem et offerebant[c] filii Israhel munera sua. Ioachim autem prior obtulit sed restituit ei Ruben sacerdos, dicens: 'Non licet tibi offerre munera in templo Dei, quoniam non suscitasti semen Israel'. 3 Et, contristatus ualde, abiit intra semetipsum, dicens: 'Meditabor ergo ut sciam si ego solus non suscitaui semen Israel'. Et rememoratus[d] est patriarchae Abrahae, quoniam in nouissimo tempore dedit ei Dominus filium, Isaac nomine, ex Sarra sterili. 4 Dehinc non intrauit[e] Ioachim ad uxorem suam, sed contulit se in desertum et fixit sibi[f] tabernaculum in montem et fuit ibi .xl. diebus et .xl. noctibus, dicens intra se: 'Non discedam hinc neque ad manducandum neque ad bibendum[g] donec uisitet me Dominus[h] Deus meus'.

II, 1 Vxor autem eius, Anna nomine, lamentabatur, dicens: 'Lugens lugebo uiduitatem meam;[a] humiliauit enim me nimis Dominus meus'. 2 Appropinquante[b] autem die festo pasche, ancilla sua dixit ei: 'Quare humilias animam tuam? Noli lugere, sed indue te uestimenta tua regalia et ad diem festum propera, ornata et leta.' 3 Anna uero dixit ei: 'Recede, recede, quare conturbas me?' Et dixit ei ancilla: 'Quid amplius possum tibi dicere? Deus enim conclusit uuluam tuam ut non dares semen Israel.' 4 Pro hac autem uoce deposuit uestimenta lugubria et lauit caput suum et induit se regalia et descendit[c] in ortum suum circa horam nonam et sedit sub arbore laurea et orauit ibi, dicens: 'Deus patrum meorum, aufer

---

I  [a] nobilis] nobis P  [b] tribubus] tribus P  [c] et offerebant] ecos forebant P
[d] rememoratus] remoratus P  [e] intrauit] intrant P; introiuit R  [f] sibi] filii P
[g] ad manducandum neque ad bibendum] ad bibendum P  [h] dominus] domine P
II  [a] uiduitatem] induitatem P  [b] appropinquante] appropinquantem P
[c] descendit] descedit P

opprobrium meum et exaudi precem meam, sicut exaudisti Sarram et dedisti ei filium'.

III, 1　Et dum haec praecaretur, uidit nidum passeris supra se in arbore et adiecit lamentationem, dicens: 2 'Domine, cui assimilabor? Non sum enim similis auibus caeli, quia pullos habent, nec bestiis terrae, quia generant, 3 nec aquis, quia producunt ex se pisces, neque huic terrae, quia producit ex se fructus secundum tempus, et de donis tuis benedicunt te omnia.'

IV, 1　Et cum haec miserabiliter dixisset, ecce angelus Domini adstitit iuxta illam, dicens: 'Anna, exaudiuit Dominus Deus orationem tuam. Concipies enim et paries et audietur nomen tuum in uniuersa terra.' Et dixit Anna: 'Viuit Dominus Deus meus, si genuero siue masculum siue feminam offeram illud munus Domino meo et seruiet Domino Deo omnibus diebus uitae suae'. 2 Et ecce iterum angelus Domini descendit ad Ioachim, dicens: 'Exaudiuit Dominus preces tuas. Descende hinc. Ecce Anna uxor tua concipiet et pariet tibi.' 3 Descendit ergo Ioachim gaudens et arcessiuit pastores suos, dicens eis: 'Cito adferte mihi .xii. oues immaculatas et .xii. uitulos saginatos et erunt munus sacerdotibus habitantibus in templo Dei'. Et iterum uocauit principes pastorum, dicens eis: 'Adducite mihi uitulum primitiuum immaculatum et erit in oblationem Deo altissimo'. Et ecce adduxerunt pastores permixtos greges ad Ioachim,[a] dominum suum, 4 et ipse exultans in Domino ueniebat cum gregibus suis. Et annuntiatum est Annae quo Ioachim ueniebat cum gregibus suis. Processit de domo et stetit ante ianuas et uidit uirum suum uenientem. Et ipsa, repleta gaudio, cito uenit ad eum et, complectens eum, dixit: 'Nunc scio, Domine, quia benedixit me Deus meus et abstulit a me inproperium hominum'. Et dixit Ioachim: 'Gratias altissimo'. Et requieuit die primo in domu sua.

V, 1　Postero autem die, sumens munera, processit ad templum Domini et obtulit ibi. Et respexit ad sacerdotem et sacerdos ascendit ad altare Domini et, cum non[a] inuenisset in eum delictum, nuntiauit ei. Et dixit Ioachim: 'Nunc scio uere quia indulsit mihi Dominus omnia peccata mea'. Et descendit de templo Domini iustificatus et abiens in domum cognouitque uxorem suam. 2 Completo autem mense septimo conceptionis, peperit Anna et interrogauit obstetricem, dicens: 'Quid peperi?' Et

IV　[a] Ioachim] iacim P
V　[a] non] *second* n *corrected from* m *by erasure* P

dixit ei: 'Feminam genuisti'. Et dixit Anna: 'Gratias ago Deo altissimo quia abstulit a me ignominiam et opprobrium hominum'. Cum autem consummassent .vii. dies a natiuitate eius, inuitauit Ioachim omnes sacerdotes et multitudinem puellarum et dixit coram eis: 'Tu Domine, qui neminem despicis sed audis gemitum humilium et depressorum, da huic puelle nomen in isto die'. Et cum hoc dixisset, accesserunt sacerdotes ad epulationem in domum eius et, edentibus illis, audita est subito uox desuper, dicens: 'Maria erit nomen eius et honorificatum est nomen huius puellae ab altissimo Deo'. Et ammirati sunt uniuersi et dixerunt: 'Fiat, fiat'. Et obtulit eam pater sacerdotibus et benedixerunt illam, dicentes: 'Deus Abraham, Deus Isaac, Deus Iacob, benedic istam puellam et da illi nomen in aeternum in omnes generationes'. Et respondit omnis populus: 'Amen'.

VI, 2    Et iterum, completo primo anno natiuitatis eius, inuitauit Ioachim omnes sacerdotes et principes sacerdotum et scribas et seniores populi et uniuersum coetum filiorum Israel ad caelebrandum diem natiuitatis eius. Et obtulit eam sacerdotibus et principibus sacerdotum et benedixerunt eam, dicentes: 'Deus excelse, respice super puellam istam et da ei benedictionem tuam, ut sit sancta et immaculata in conspectu tuo hic et in futuro saeculo'. Et responderunt, dicentes: 'Amen'. Anna autem ministrabat gloriose sacerdotibus et omni populo Israel.

VII, 1    Maria autem crescebat cotidie et conualescebat Domino uolente. Et dixit Ioachim ad Annam: 'Deducamus puellam illam in templum Domini et reddamus promissum nostrum quod promisimus Deo, ne forte indignetur nobis[a] Deus et non sit acceptum munus nostrum'. Et dixit Anna: 'Sustineamus adhuc annum ut sit trina, ne forte inquirat patrem aut matrem, et sic constituamus eam postea in templum.' Et[b] dixit Ioachim: 'Sic fiat'. 2 Et completo tertio anno detulerunt eam in templum Domini et susceperunt sacerdotes eam de manibus eorum et osculabantur eam, dicentes: 'Benedixit te Dominus[c] Deus omnipotens et magnificauit nomen tuum in uniuersis nationibus. Per te enim notum faciet saluatorem mundi uniuerse plebi.'

VIII, 1    Et statim discesserunt parentes eius ab ea, mirantes et gratias agentes et Dominum benedicentes quia post se regredi nolebat, sed mitis sedebat in templum Domini sicut columba, accipiens frequenter escam de manu angeli, sicut scriptum est: 'Panem angelorum manducauit homo'.

VII    [a] nobis] *preceded by* deus *crossed out* P    [b] et] ex P    [c] dominus] domine P

Et diligebant eam omnes filii Israhel, sicut propriam filiam, pro constantia et mansuetudine et pulchritudine eius, dicentes: 'Quae est ista que processit sicut sol et formosa tamquam Hierusalem? Viderunt eam filiae Sion et beatam dixerunt et reginae laudauerunt eam.' Conuenire ergo et nos hodie debemus, fratres karissimi, ad sollemnitatem hodiernae natiuitatis beatae Mariae perpetuae uirginis et genitricis Dei, de qua processit Dominus Dominorum et rex angelorum, sicut de illa scriptum est: 'Natiuitas tua, Dei genitrix$^a$ uirgo, gaudium annuntiauit uniuerso mundo. Ex te enim ortus est sol iustitiae Christus Deus noster qui, soluens a nobis maledictionem Euae, per te dedit benedictionem uitae et, confusa morte, donauit nobis uitam perpetuam.' Deuotissime ergo caelebrare debemus, fratres karissimi, natiuitatem felicissimae Mariae et congaudere omnes in Domino diem festum caelebrantes sub honore natiuitatis eius. Per quam salus mundi credentibus apparuit ut ipsa intercedente pro nobis semper ad Dominum Iesum Christum mereamur et nos et omnes populi Christiani possidere gaudia sempiterna, prestante eodem Domino nostro Iesu$^b$ Christo, qui cum patre et spiritu sancto uiuit et regnat per infinita saecula saeculorum. AMEN.

VIII    $^a$ genitrix] *erasure of one letter between first* i *and* t P
$^b$ Ihesu] iuu, *with first* u *crossed through and abbreviation mark over it* P

## THE *GOSPEL OF PSEUDO-MATTHEW*

*Incipit sermo de natiuitate Sanctae Mariae*

I, 1   Erat uir in Israel nomine Ioachim ex tribu Iuda, et hic erat pastor ouium suarum, timens Deum in simplicitate sua, cui cura nulla erat alia nisi gregum suorum, de quorum fructu pascebat omnes timentes Deum, duplicia offerens munera in timore Dei egentibus et pauperibus et in doctrina laborantibus. Siue in agnis, siue in lanis, siue in omnibus rebus suis, quecumque possidere uidebatur tres partes faciebat. Vnam partem dabat uiduis et orphanis et peregrinis atque pauperibus, alteram partem dabat colentibus Deum, tertiam partem sibi et omni domui sue.

I, 2   Haec autem illi faciente multiplicabat Dominus greges suas, ita ut non esset similis homo in populo Israel. Haec autem inchoauit facere a quintodecimo[a] anno aetatis sue; cum autem esset annorum uiginti accepit Annam uxorem suam, filiam Achar, ex tribu sua, id est ex tribu Iuda, ex genere Dauid. Cum qua moratus est per annos uiginti et filios ex ea non accepit.

II, 1   Factum est autem in diebus festis inter eos qui offerebant incensum Domino, staret Ioachim parans munera sua in conspectu Domini. Et accedens ad eum scriba templi, nomine Ruben, ait ad eum: 'Non tibi licet inter sacrificia Dei consistere, quia non te benedixit Deus ut daret tibi semen in[a] Israel'. Passus itaque uerecundiam in conspectu populi, abscessit de templo Dei plorans et non est reuersus in domum suam, sed abiit ad pecora sua ut duxit secum pastores[b] in longinquam terram, ita ut per .v. menses nec nuntium[c] de eo audire potuisset Anna uxor eius.

II, 2   Que dum fleret in oratione sua et diceret: 'Domine Deus Israel fortissime, iam quia filios non dedisti mihi, uirum meum[a] quare tulisti a me? Ecce enim .v. menses fluxerunt et uirum meum non uideo, et nescio ubi mortuus est ut uel sepulturam[b] illi fecissem.' Et dum[c] fleret nimis ingressa est in uiridario domus sue, et cadens in orationem preces Domino fundere coepit. Et post haec surgens ab oratione eleuans oculos ad Deum, uidit nidum passeris in arbore[d] lauri et emisit uocem ad Dominum cum

---

I, 2    [a] a quintodecimo] quinta N
II, 1    [a] in] *om.* N    [b] pastores] pastori N    [c] nuntium] mentium N
II, 2    [a] meum] in eum N    [b] sepulturam] sepultura N    [c] dum] eum N [d] arbore] arborem N

gemitu et dixit: 'Domine, Deus omnipotens, qui omni creature donasti filios, bestiis et iumentis, serpentibus et piscibus et uolucribus, et gaudent super filios, tibi gratias ago soli quod uoluisti, ita ordinasti, ut me solam a benignitatis tuae donis exclauderes.[e] Tu enim nosti, Domine, cor meum, quia ab initio coniugi meae hoc uouisse me[f] confiteor ut, si tu, Domine, dedisses[g] mihi filium aut filiam, obtulissem tibi eam in templo sancto tuo.'

II, 3    Et dum ista dixit, subito apparuit angelus Domini ante faciem eius, dicens ei: 'Noli timere, Anna, quoniam in consilio Dei est germen tuum, et quod ex te natum fuerit, erit in admirationem omnibus saeculis usque in finem'. Et cum hoc dixisset, ab oculis eius elapsus est. Illa autem tremens et pauens quod talem uidisset uisionem et talem audisset sermonem, ingressa est cubiculum suum et iactauit se in lectum, iacens quasi mortua, et totam diem atque totam[a] noctem in tremore nimio et in oratione[b] permansit.

II, 4    Post haec uocauit ad se puellam suam et dixit ad eam: 'Vidisti uiduitate me deceptam et in angustia positam[a] et tu nec ingredi ad me uoluisti?' Tunc illa in murmuratione respondit, dicens: 'Si conclusit Deus uterum tuum et uirum tuum a te abstulit, ego tibi quid factura sum?' Et haec audiens Anna cum clamoribus emittens uocem flebat.

III, 1    In ipso autem tempore apparuit quidam iuuenis inter montes ubi Ioachim pascebat gregem suum et dixit ad Ioachim: 'Quare non reuerteris ad domum tuam et ad uxorem tuam?' Et dixit Ioachim: 'Per .xx. annos habui eam. Nunc uero, quia noluit Deus dare mihi filios ex ea et cum uerecundia[a] de templo Dei exprobratus exiui,[b] ut quid reuertar ad eam semel abiectus atque dispectus? Hic ero cum ouibus meis quamdiu uoluerit me uiuere Deus. Per manus autem puerorum meorum pauperibus et uiduis et orphanis et colentibus Deum partes suas libenter restituam.'

III, 2    Et cum haec dixisset, respondit ei ille iuuenis, dicens: 'Angelus Dei ego sum, qui apparui hodie flenti et oranti uxori tuae et consolatus sum eam, quam scias ex semine tuo concepisse filiam, quod tu nesciens relinquisti eam. Haec in templo Dei erit et spiritus sanctus requiescit in ea[a] et erit beatitudo eius super feminas sanctas, ita ut nullus possit dicere

---

[e] exclauderes] et clauderis N    [f] uouisse me] uouissem N    [g] dedisses] aedisses N
II, 3    [a] totam] nutam N    [b] in oratione] moratione N
II, 4    [a] positam] posita est N
III, 1    [a] uerecundia] uerecudia N    [b] exiui] *om.* N
III, 2    [a] ea] eam N

quia fuit talis ante eam aliqua, sed postea numquam erit ei similis uentura in hoc saeculo. Propter quod descende de montibus et reuertere ad coniugem tuam, et inuenies eam habentem in utero. De quo gratias referas Deo et semen eius erit benedictum, et mater benedictionis aeterne constituitur.'

III, 3    Et adorans eum Ioachim dixit:ᵃ 'Si inueni gratiam ante oculos coram te, sede modicum in tabernaculo meo et benedic seruum tuum'. Et dixit angelus: 'Noli dicere seruum sed conseruum tuum. Vniusᵇ enim Domini serui sumus. Nam cibus meus et potus meus ab hominibus mortalibus non est uisa. Et ideo non debes me tu hoc rogare, ut intrem in tabernaculo tuo, sed quod daturus es mihi offerᶜ holocaustum Deo.' Tunc Ioachim accepit agnum inmaculatum et dixit ad angelum: 'Ego non essem ausus offerre holocaustum Deo nisi tua iussio daret mihi pontificum offerendi'. Et dixit angelus: 'Nec ego te ad offerendum inuitarem nisi uoluntatem Domini hanc cognouissem'. Factum est autem cum offerret sacrificium Ioachim, simul cum odore sacrificii quasi cum fumo perrexit ad caelos.

III, 4    Tunc Ioachim cecidit in faciem suam, ab ora diei sexta usque ad uesperum iacuit. Venientes autem pueri eius et mercennarii, nescientes quid causa esset, et expauerunt atque putantes quod ipse uelletᵃ interficere, accesserunt ad eum et uix eleuauerunt eum a terrra. Quibus cum enarrasset quid uidisset, stupore nimio et admiratione inpulsi hortabantur eum, ut sine mora iussumᵇ angeli perficeret atque uelociter ad suamᶜ coniugem remearet. Cum haec Ioachim in suo animoᵈ discuteret, si reuerti deberet annon, factum est ut sopore teneretur. Et ecce angelus Domini qui ei apparuit uigilanti, apparuit ei in somnis, dicens: 'Ego sum angelus qui a Deo tuo tibi datus sum custos. Descende securuseᵉ et reuertere ad Annam, quia misericordiasᶠ quas fecisti in conspectu altissimi et uxor tua recitati sunt.ᵍ Et talis uobis datum est germen, qualem numquam ab initio nec prophete nec sancti habuerunt neque habituri sunt.' Et factum est cum euigilasset Ioachim a somno, uocauit ad se gregariosʰ suos et indicauit eis somnium suum. At illi adorauerunt Dominum et dixerunt ei: 'Vide ne ultra iam contemnas angelum Dei. Sed surge, proficiscamur, lentoⁱ gradu pergentes eamus.'

III, 3    ᵃ dixit] dicit N    ᵇ unius] un`i´us N    ᶜ offer] *followed by erasure* N
III, 4    ᵃ uellet] uellit N    ᵇ iussum] iusu N    ᶜ suam] sua N    ᵈ animo] amore N
ᵉ securus] securos N    ᶠ misericordias] miscordias N    ᵍ sunt] *om.* N
ʰ gregarios] gregios N    ⁱ lento] lentu N

III, 5   Cumque .xxx. dies ambulassent et essent iam prope, apparuit Annae in oratione[a] stanti angelus Domini dicens ei: 'Vade ad portam que uocatur aurea et occurre uiro tuo quoniam uenit ad te hodie'. At illa festinanter perrexit cum puellis suis et coepit[b] in ipsa porta stans orare. Et cum diutius expectaret et longa expectatione deficeret, eleuans oculos suos uidit Ioachim uenientem cum pecoribus[c] suis. Et occurrit Anna et suspendit in collo eius agens gratias Deo, dicens: 'Vidua eram[d] et ecce concepi'. Et factum est gaudium omnibus notis et[e] afinibus eorum, ita ut uniuersa terra Israel de ista fama gratularetur.[f]

IV   Post haec autem expletis mensibus .viiii. peperit Anna filiam et uocauit nomen eius Maria. Cum autem tertio anno[a] perlactasset eam, abierunt simul Ioachim et Anna uxor eius ad templum Domini.[b] Et offerentes hostias Deo tradiderunt infantulam suam MARIAM in contubernio uirginum que die noctuque uirgines in Dei laudibus permanebant. Que cum posita esset ante templum, .xv. gradus templi ita cursim ascendit ut penitus non respiceret retrorsum et ut solitum[c] est infantiae[d] parentes requirere. In quo facto omnes stupor tenebat, ita ut ipsi pontifices[e] templi mirarentur.

V   Tunc Anna repleta[a] spiritu sancto in conspectu omnium dixit:[b] 'Domine, Deus exercituum memor factus uerbi sui et uisitauit Deus populum suum uisitatione sancta sua. Et ecce poteram offerre munera Domino meo, et quare me prohibuere uolebant inimici mei? Dominus enim auertit eos a me et dedit mihi gaudium sempiternum.'

VI, 1   Erat autem Maria in admiratione omni populo quia, cum trium esset annorum, tam maturo[a] gressu ambulabat, et ita perfectissime in Dei laudibus loquebatur, ut omnes stupore atque admiratione subiacebant et quia non ut infantula putabatur esse sed magna, et quasi iam .xxx. esset annorum, ita in orationibus insistebat; etiam splendebat facies eius sicut nix et uix potuissent in eius uultum[b] adtendi. Insistebat autem et lanificio et omnia que mulieres antique non poterant facere, ista in tenera[c] aetate posita explicabat.

III, 5   [a] oratione] orationem N   [b] et coepit] *om.* N   [c] pecoribus] pecopibus N
[d] eram] coram *with* co *subpuncted and* 'e' *superscript* N   [e] et] *om.* N
[f] gratularetur] gratuletur N
IV   [a] tertio anno] tres annos N   [b] domini] domi`n´i N   [c] solitum] solutum N
[d] infantiae] infantia N   [e] pontifices] pontifici N
V   [a] repleta] repletus N   [b] dixit] dicit N
VI, 1   [a] maturo] mature N   [b] uultum] uultu N   [c] tenera] tenere N

VI, 2    Hanc autem regulam sibi ipsa statuerat ut a mane usque ad horam tertiam orationibus insistebat, a tertia usque ad nonam textrino opere se occuparet. A nona uero hora iterum ab oratione non recedebat, donec illi angelus Domini apparet de cuius manu escam acciperet, ut melius atque melius in Dei amore proficeret. Denique[a] cum seniores uirgines in Dei laudibus docebantur ita ut nullus in uigiliis prior ei inueniretur, in sapientia legis eruditior, in humilitate humilior, in carminibus dauiticis[b] elegantior, in caritate gratior, in puritate purior, in omni uirtute perfectior. Erat enim constans, inmobilis, inmutabilis atque cotidie ad meliora proficiebat.

VI, 3    Hanc irascentem numquam nullus uidit, hanc maledicentem nullus audiuit. Ita erat gratia plena, ut cognosceretur in lingua Deus. Semper in oratione et scrutatione legis Dei permanebat. Et erat sollicita circa socias suas, ne aliqua ex eis uel uno sermone peccaret, et ne aliqua in risu exaltaret uocem suam, ne[a] aliqua iniuriis aut superbia[b] circa patrem suum aut matrem existeret. Sine intermissione benedicebat Deum et, ne forte salutatione[c] sua a laudibus Domini tolleretur, si quis ad eam salutationem dicebat, 'Deo gratias' respondebat. Denique ab ipsa primum exiit ut cum salutant homines sancti[d] 'Deo gratias' dicant. Cotidie autem escam quam de manu angeli accipiebat, ipsa tantum reficiebat; escam uero quam pontificibus templi consequebatur, pauperibus diuidebat. Frequenter uidebantur cum ea angeli loqui et quasi karissimi eius obtemperabant ei. Si quis autem de infirmantibus tetigisset eam, saluus ad domum suam eadem hora reuertebatur.

Explicit de natuitate Sanctae Mariae.

---

VI, 2    [a] denique] dinique N    [b] dauiticis] dauiticas N
VI, 3    [a] ne] me N    [b] superbia] superbiam N    [c] salutatione] a salutione N
[d] sancti] *above subpuncted* dei N

## TRANSITUS W

### XLVIIII: *In Assumptione Sanctae Mariae*

1  Sciendum est, fratres karissimi, et omnibus exponendum fidelibus, quod post ascensionem Domini nostri Iesu Christi saluatoris mundi cum magna gloria ad alta[a] caelorum, descendit angelus Domini ad sanctam Mariam, cum esset in templo Dei diebus ac noctibus uigilans et orans in secretis locis cum ceteris sanctis uirginibus, dicens ad eam: 'Exsurge Maria et accipe palmam luminis quam nunc tibi detuli et scito quoniam post tres dies de hoc mundo assumenda es. Et ecce mittam omnes apostolos.'

2  Et dixit illi Maria: 'Peto, domine, ut dicas mihi nomen tuum'. Et dixit ei angelus: 'Quid quaeris nomen meum, quod est magnum et mirabile?'

3  Et cum hoc audisset Maria, ascendit in montem Oliueti et orauit ibi, tenens palmam in manu quam acceperat de manu angeli, et gauisa est gaudio magno cum omnibus qui ibidem erant. Angelus autem qui uenerat ad eam ascendit in caelum cum magno lumine.

4  Maria uero reuersa est in domum suam, et recondit palmam cum magno honore, et deposuit uestem qua induta erat, et lauit secreto corpus suum et induit se ueste obtima. Et postea gaudens benedicebat Dominum et dicebat: 'Benedico nomen tuum, Domine, sanctum et laudabile in aeterna saecula, et peto ut des super me benedictionem ut nulla potestas possit inimici occurrere mihi in illa hora cum me iusseris de hoc saeculo recedere'.

5  Et cum haec dixisset, inuitauit uicinos et propinquos, dicens eis: 'Audite me nunc omnes et credite quod dico, quoniam cras egrediar de corpore et uado ad[a] Dominum meum Iesum Christum. Et ideo peto uos ut uigiletis usque in illam horam qua sum recessura. Hoc enim scitote quod quando exit unusquisque homo de corpore, occurrunt ei duo angeli, unus iustitiae et alter iniquitatis. Et si inuenerit angelus iustitiae in illo homine opera bona, deducet gaudens animam eius ad locum iustorum. Et tunc deflet angelus iniquitatis, quia nihil operis sui potuit inuenire in eo. Et si iterum angelus iniquitatis inuenerit opera mala in illo, gaudet et

---

1  [a] ad alta] ab alto P
5  [a] ad] a *on line erased,* ad *inserted superscript by a different hand in very much lighter ink* P

assumet secum alios et deducunt animam eius ad locum poenarum. Et tunc angelus iustitiae recedet tristis.'

6   Et dixerunt qui cum illa erant: 'Quid nos acturi sumus, si tu contristaris de hac re, cui certum est regnum aperire caelorum?'

7   Et cum loquerentur, ecce subito aduenit beatus Iohannes et percussit hostium domus Mariae et ingressus est. At ubi uidit eum Maria, suspirans fleuit et clamauit uoce magna, dicens: 'Pater Iohannes, memor esto praeceptorum Domini mei magistri tui, quibus me tibi commendauit, in die qua recessit a nobis, passus pro nostra salute'.

8   Et dixit ad^a eam Iohannes: 'Quid uis, mater, ut faciam tibi?' Respondit Maria: 'Hoc quaero et postulo ut custodias corpus meum et componas illud in monumento, quoniam die crastina recessura sum de corpore. Audiui enim Iudaeos dicentes: "Sustineamus quando moriatur, ut possimus corpus eius inuenire, et igne comburamus"'. Et cum haec audisset sanctus Iohannes, quod esset recessura de corpore, fleuit in conspectu Domini, dicens: 'O Domine, quid sumus, quibus demonstrasti tantas tribulationes?'

9   Et tunc ostendit ei Maria uestimenta quae poneret ad sepulturam eius, ostendit ei et palmam luminis quam dederat ei angelus et dixit ad eum: 'Rogo te, pater Iohannes, ut portes hanc palmam ante lectum meum, cum de hoc corpore fuero assumpta'.

10   Et dixit Iohannes: 'Hoc non possum, Maria, facere solus, nisi aduenerint fratres et coapostoli mei'.

11   Et ecce subito ad hanc uocem omnes apostoli cum nubibus deducti sunt et depositi ad hostium domus Mariae. Et uidentes, salutauerunt se inuicem, dicentes: 'Domine, tibi gratias agimus, quia completum est hodie dictum prophetae dicentis: "Ecce quam bonum et quam iocundum habitare fratres in unum".' Et dixerunt ad inuicem: 'Oremus ad Dominum, ut ostendat nobis causam congregandi in unum'.

12   Et dixit Petrus: 'Surge, frater Paule, et ora prior pro nobis'. Et respondit: 'Quomodo potero prior orare, cum sis tu columna luminis et princeps apostolorum? Sed et omnes qui constant fratres meliores mei sunt. Tu ergo ora pro nobis omnibus, ut gratia Dei sit nobiscum.' Et tunc gauisi sunt apostoli propter humilitatem Pauli.

13   Et sic Petrus, expansis manibus, orauit, dicens: 'Domine Deus omnipotens, qui sedes super cherubin et abyssos intueris, ad te leuamus

8   ^a ad] *superscript* P

manus nostras in similitudinem tuae crucis, ut requiem tecum habeamus, quia tu es requies nostra et protectio inuocantibus te in ueritate, qui manes in patre et pater in te, cum sancto spiritu. Amen.'

15 Et tunc ingressi sunt omnes ad sanctam Mariam et salutauerunt eam magna uoce, dicentes: 'Aue, gratia plena, Dominus tecum'. Et illa dixit: 'Et uobiscum, fratres.

16 Rogo uos, ergo, ut reueletis mihi quomodo hodie hic pariter conuenistis et quis annuntiauit uobis quod recessura sum de corpore?'

[14] Et sanctus Iohannes primum dixit: 'Ego cum essem in ciuitate docens, circa horam nonam descendit nubes[a] praeclara in eodem loco in quo eramus et circumdedit me et rapuit de medio eorum, uidentibus cunctis qui ibidem erant, et attulit hic. Et inueni populum multum circa Mariam, dicentem se de corpore exituram. Et ideo ammoneo uos, nolite flere coram populo ne incipiant dubii esse, dicentes in cordibus suis:[b] "Vt quid timent hi mortem, cum sint apostoli et aliis praedicent resurrectionem?" Confortemus nos ergo inuicem, ut omnis populus possit firmus esse et non dubius in fide et opere.'

[16] Et sic omnes apostoli exposuerunt quemadmodum unusquisque de suis locis ubi praedicabant diuina praescentia Dei rapti sunt et ibidem depositi.

17 Et gaudens Sancta Maria in spiritu sancto dixit: 'Benedico te, Domine, qui ad meam commutationem omnes apostolos uocasti. Benedico nomen tuum sanctum quod est et permanet in saecula saeculorum, amen.'

18 Post haec inuitauit eos Maria in cubiculo suo et ostendit eis omne indumentum sepulture in quo recessura esset de corpore.

19 Et tunc beatus Petrus praecessit apostolis et omni populo, dicens: 'Sint omnium lampades accense, fratres, et uigilemus animo et spiritu ut, cum uenerit Dominus, inuenerit nos omnes unanimiter uigilantes, et inluminet nos diuina gratia spiritus sancti'. Et iterum dixit eis: 'Nolite suspicari mortem esse Mariae. Non enim illi est mors, sed uita, quoniam mors sanctorum laudabilis est apud Deum.'

20 Et cum haec diceret, subito lumen magnum refulsit in domum illam, ut uix posset aliquis conspicere aut narrare prae magnitudine luminis. Et facta est uox ad Petrum apostolum dicens: 'Ecce, ego uobiscum sum omnibus diebus usque ad consummationem saeculi'.

14   [a] nubes] e *inserted superscript in light ink* P   [b] *followed by a crossed out* Confortemus nos ergo inuicem P

Petrus uero, haec audiens et eleuans uocem suam, dixit: 'Benedicimus ergo te, Domine, gubernator animarum nostrarum, et petimus ut a nobis non discedas, sed miserearis semper nostri et omnium christianorum in tuo nomine credentium.'

21   Et cum haec et multa his similia dixisset beatus Petrus,

22   surgens Maria exiuit foras, et orationem orauit quae ei praedicta fuerat ab angelo. Et completa oratione reuersa est in domum, et sic decubuit super lectum suum.

23   Et beatus Petrus sedebat ad caput eius, et circa lectum alii apostoli. Circa autem horam diei sextam subito factum est tonitruum magnum et odor suauissimus uenit et totam domum repleuit, ita ut prae nimia suauitate omnes obdormirent qui ibidem erant, exceptis apostolis et tribus uirginibus quibus mandauerat Maria sine intermissione uigilare ut uiderent gloriam assumptionis eius et testificarentur aliis.

24   Post haec autem, omnibus dormientibus, subito uenit Dominus noster Iesus Christus per nubem cum multitudine angelorum et ingressus est domum in qua iacebat Maria. Et Michael, princeps angelorum, coepit ymnum dicerere cum multitudine angelorum et cum choris omnium sanctorum.

25   Et cum uidisset Maria filium et Dominum suum, benedixit eum dicens: 'Benedico te, Domine, quia implesti quaecumque promisisti mihi. Non enim possum tantam gratiarum actionem nomini tuo rependere quae in me conferre dignatus es.'

26   Et sic placide et benigne suscepit animam eius et tradidit eam sancto Michaeli angelo, niue candidiorem.

27   Et interrogauit Petrus dominum, dicens: 'Quis de nobis, Domine, habet animam candidam sicut Maria?' Et dixit ei Dominus: 'Scito, Petre, quoniam omnium electorum meorum animae tales sunt qualem uidisti animam eius'.

28   Et iterum dixit ad eum saluator: 'Accipe, Petre, corpus Mariae et ingredere in dexteram partem ciuitatis, et inuenies ibi monumentum nouum, et in ipso monumento componite corpus. Et custodite illud sicut mandaui uobis, [29] quoniam templum est Dei uiui.'

31   Deinde post haec tres uirgines quae uigilauerunt sine intermissione lauerunt corpus eius, et posuerunt illud super feretrum. Et omnes qui dormierant prae suauitate odoris surrexerunt.

32   Petrus autem attulit palmam quam acceperat Maria de manu angeli, et dixit ad Iohannem: 'Virgo es et tu debes precedere lectum et

hanc palmam portare et dicere laudem Deo'. Et dixit Iohannes: 'Tu precedis nos in apostolatu, tu debes precedere et portare illam, donec offeramus eum ad locum ubi praecepit Dominus'.

33 Et sic surgentes apostoli leuauerunt lectum, portantes eam in manibus suis.

35 Dominus uero protexit lectum et apostolos in nube. Et portantes lectum laudem dicebant.

34 Petrus coepit: 'Exiit Israhel de Egypto alleluia'. Alii dicebant: 'qui conuertit aridam[a] petram in stagnum aquae et rupem in fontes aquarum' et iterum 'Dominus uirtutum, ipse est rex gloriae'.

35 Illi autem a nullo uidebantur infidelium dum laudabant Dominum.

36 Cum autem audissent principes sacerdotum uocem laudantium, conturbati uehementer coeperunt dicere ad inuicem: 'Quae est haec turba et populi multitudo?'

37 Et dixit quidam ex asstantibus: 'Maria exiit[a] de mundo et apostoli circa illam laudes dicunt.'

38 Et statim Satanas introiuit in eos et dixerunt[a] ad inuicem: 'Interficiamus apostolos istos et corpus Mariae igne comburamus, quae portauit illum seductorem.' Et abierunt obuiam eis cum gladiis et fustibus occidere eos. Eadem uero hora angeli qui erant supra eos in nubibus percusserunt Iudaeos caecitate. Et cadentes in terram percutiebant capita sua circa parietes et, palpantes manibus suis terram, nesciebant ubi ambularent.

39 Vnus autem ex ipsis, princeps sacerdotum, cum appropinquasset et uidisset lectum Mariae et apostolos ymnum dicentes, repletus furore et ira magna dixit: 'Ecce tabernaculum illius qui nos damnauit et omne genus nostrum'. Et subito faciens impetum, uoluit euertere feretrum et comprehendere palmam uictoriae et ad terram deducere. Sed statim manus eius ambae aridae facte sunt et una pars corporis eius tenebatur ad feretrum et altera pendebat ad terram.

40 Tunc autem, flens et heiulans,[a] deprecabatur apostolos ut soluerent eum et praecipue Petrum, dicens: 'Memor esto, Petre, quid tibi fecerit

---

34   [a] aridam] *with superscript* vel solida P
37   [a] exiit] exi`i´t, *with second* i *inserted by original hand, and* e *altered from* i *by a later hand and preceded by erasure* P
38   [a] dixerunt] dixere *originally, superscript* vel runt, *giving* dixerunt P
40   [a] heiulans] heulans P

pater meus, quando te interrogauit ancilla, dicens: "Vere et tu cum Iesu eras", quia tunc excusauit[b] pro te, ne conprehendereris. Et ego[c] modo[d] rogo uos ne me despiciatis.' Tunc Petrus dixit: 'Non est nostra potestas quid dicis, sed si credis quod Iesus filius Dei uiui est, solutus eris'.

41    Et respondens dixit: 'Credimus quidem quod Iesus filius Dei est, sed inimicus generis humani obcaecauit corda nostra'.

43    Et dixit ad eum Petrus: 'Tolle manus tuas et fiant sicut antea.

45    Et nunc credens exsurge et accipe palmam uictoriae quae est ante lectum Mariae et ingredere ciuitatem et ammone Iudaeos qui percussi sunt caecitate, dicens eis: "Quicumque crediderit in Dominum Iesum Christum, quoniam ipse est filius Dei uiui, aperientur oculi eius. Et hanc palmam pone super oculos eorum, et statim recipient uisum. Qui autem non crediderit[a] non uidebit in aeternum."'

46    Et abiens princeps sacerdotum inuenit multos in populo, gementes et flentes, nichil uidentes, et exposuit eis omnia quae passus fuerat et quecumque a Petro audierat hortamenta et quomodo respexisset illum Deus et soluisset. Quicumque ergo crediderunt uerbis eius statim receperunt uisum, qui autem non crediderunt caeci permanserunt

47    Verumptamen apostoli portantes corpus Mariae peruenerunt ad monumentum, ubi praedixerat eis Iesus, et sepelierunt eam in ualle Iosaphath. Et sedentibus iuxta monumentum, subito aduenit Iesus cum multitudine angelorum et ait eis: 'Pax uobis, fratres'.

48    Et sic iussit angelis tolli corpus Mariae, nescientibus apostolis ubi transtulerunt illud.

50    Ipsi autem in nubibus translati sunt per aera ad loca unde uenerant, praedicantes uerbum Dei.

Hodie quidem exaltata est sancta Maria Dei genitrix super choros angelorum ad caelestia regna. Hodie uirgo uirginum caelos ascendit, quae regem gloriae in aluo gestare meruit. Gaudete quia cum Christo regnat in aeternum et ipsa intercedat pro nobis ad Dominum Iesum Christum ut mereamur uitam possidere aeternam, per omnia saecula saeculorum. Amen.

---

[b] excusauit] *with second* s *erased before* a P
[c] ego] *preceded by erasure of one letter* P    [d] modo] mundo P
45    [a] crediderit] crediderint P

# The Transitus of Pseudo-Melito
# (Transitus B²)

### Edited by Monika Haibach-Reinisch

## Prologus

Melito, seruus Christi, episcopus Ecclesiae Sardensis, uenerabilibus in Christo fratribus Laodiceae constitutis in pace Christi salutem.

Dum uobis de uita prophetarum uel de incarnatione dominica duo opuscula condidissem, denuo poscitis, ut uobis de Ecclesia librum unum conderem atque, quid de obitu Genitricis Domini certum haberem, uobis litteris indagassem, ob hoc maxime, quia, sicut illa Christum corporaliter pariens, uirgo permansit post partum, ita Ecclesia Christo per fidem filios spirituales gignens, uirginitatis meritum pariendo custodit.

Saepe namque scripsisse me memini de quodam Leucio, qui nobiscum et cum apostolis conuersatus, alieno sensu et animo temerario discedens a uia iustitiae, plurima de apostolorum actibus in libris suis inseruit: et de uirtutibus quidem eorum multa uera dixit, de doctrina uero eorum plurima mentitus est, asserens eos aliter docuisse, stabiliens quasi ex eorum uerbis sua nefanda commenta.

Nec hoc solum sibi sufficere arbitratus, uerum etiam transitum beatae semper uirginis Mariae ita deprauauit stilo, ut in Ecclesia Dei non solum legi, sed etiam ridiculum sit audiri.

Nos ergo uobis petentibus quae ab apostolo Iohanne exinde audiuimus, hoc in libri capite simpliciter scribentes uestrae fraternitati direximus, credentes non aliena dogmata ab haereticis pullulantia, sed Patrem in Filio et Filium in Patre, Spiritum Sanctum cum Patre et Filio, unius deitatis et indiuisae substantiae, trina manente persona; neque duas naturas boni et mali conditas, sed unam naturam tantum bonam a bono Dei conditam, quae dolo antiqui serpentis est uitiata per culpam, et Christi est reparata per gratiam.

# The Transitus of Pseudo-Melito (Transitus B²)

## Cap. 1

Igitur cum Dominus et Saluator noster Iesus Christus pro totius saeculi uita affixus clauis crucis penderet in ligno, uidit iuxta crucem matrem suam stantem et Iohannem euangelistam, quem prae ceteris apostolis ideo peculiarius diligebat, eo quod ipse solus plus ex eis uirgo esset in corpore.

Tradidit igitur ei curam sanctae Mariae dicens ad eum: 'Ecce mater tua', et ad ipsam inquiens: 'Ecce filius tuus'.

Ex illa hora sancta Dei Genitrix in Iohannis cura permansit, quamdiu uitae istius incolatum transegit.

Et dum apostoli mundum suis sortibus in praedicatione sumpsissent, ipsa in domo parentum illius iuxta Montem Oliueti consedit.

## Cap. 2

Secundo igitur anno postquam Dominus caeli alta conscendit, die quadam desiderio eius succensa, lacrimari sola in domus illius receptaculo coepit.

Et ecce angelus magni luminis habitu splendens ante eam astitit et salutationis uerba persoluit dicens: 'Aue, benedicta a Domino, suscipiens illius salutem qui mandauit salutem Iacob per prophetas suos. Ecce, inquit, ramum palmae de paradiso Dei attuli tibi; quem portare facies ante feretrum tuum, cum in die tertio fueris assumpta de corpore. Ecce enim expectat te Filius tuus cum thronis et angelis et uniuersis uirtutibus caeli.'

Tunc Maria dixit ad angelum: 'Peto ut congregentur ad me omnes apostoli Domini mei Iesu Christi et uideam eos corporalibus oculis et illis praesentibus emittam spiritum'.

Ait ad illam angelus: 'Ecce hodie omnes apostoli per uirtutem Domini assumpti huc uenient. Facillimum est enim omnipotenti Deo, sub euangelici temporis gratia, ueterana iterare miracula et Noui Testamenti ministros repente in unum colligere, cui facillimum fuit, temporibus Veteris Testamenti, prophetam manu angeli de Iudea in Babilonem per cincinnum capitis subito cum prandio transportare.'

Ait autem Maria ad angelum: 'Peto ut mittas super me benedictionem tuam, ut nulla potestas Satanae uel inferni occurrat mihi, et ne uideam tetros spiritus obuiantes mihi'.

Cui ait angelus: 'Benedictionem aeternam dedit tibi Dominus Deus tuus, cuius ego sum seruus et nuntius; non uidendi autem principem tenebrarum, non a me tibi dandum putes effectum, sed ab eo quem in tuo utero baiolasti; ipsius est enim potestas omnium in saecula saeculorum'.

Et haec dicens angelus, cum magna claritate discessit.

Palma autem illa fulgebat nimia luce; et erat quidem uirga illius uiriditati consimilis, sed folia illius ut stella matutina radio claritatis fulgebant.

Tunc Maria exuens se, induit se melioribus uestimentis. Et accipiens palmam illam, quam sumpserat de manu angeli, perrexit in Montem Oliueti praefulgente sibi luce Spiritus Sancti et coepit orare et dicere: 'Gratias tibi ago, omnipotens Domine, qui me dignatus es humilem ancillam tuam eligere et archanum tui mysterii commendare. Non enim digna fueram tantum a te honorari, nisi tu misertus fuisses mei et propitius ancillae tuae; at tamen custodiui thesaurum creditum mihi. Si enim throni et angeli ante te tremunt cotidie, quanto magis homo de terra conditus, cui nihil resedit boni nisi quantum acceperit de tua pia largitione. Tu es enim Deus uiuens et regnans cum benedicto Patre et glorioso Spiritu Sancto in una diuinitatis substantia trina manente persona qui uiuis et regnas in saecula saeculorum.'

Et haec dicens, reuersa est in domum suam.

## *Cap. 3*

Et ecce subito, cum praedicaret sanctus Iohannes in Epheso populum, die dominico, hora diei tertia, caelum repente intonuit et nubes candida cum tonitrui fragore descendit, et raptum ante oculos circumstantium sustulit atque hoc ordine eleuatus Iohannes in nube a Domino raptus est et depositus ante ostium domus, in qua habitabat Maria. Et ingressus domum, salutauit eam in Domino.

Videnfque eum Maria, coepit prae gaudio flere et dicere: 'Rogo te, fili Iohannes, memor esto uerborum magistri tui Domini Iesu Christi, quibus me commendauit tibi. Ecce enim uocata ingredior uiam uniuersae terrae; audiui enim consilia Iudaeorum dicentium: "Expectemus diem quando moriatur quae portauit Iesum Nazarenum, et corpus eius igne comburamus." Nunc ergo curam habeto exequiarum mearum.'

Et haec dicens ostendit illi uestimenta sepulturae suae et palmam illam luminis, quam acceperat ab angelo, monens eum ut illam faceret ferri ante feretrum suum cum iret ad monumentum.

# The Transitus of Pseudo-Melito (Transitus B²)

## Cap. 4

Tunc dixit ad eam sanctus Iohannes: 'Quomodo ego solus possum tibi parare exequias, nisi uenerint fratres et coapostoli mei ad reddendum honorem corpusculi tui?'

Haec eo dicente omnes apostoli de locis, in quibus praedicabant uerbum Domini, eleuati in nubibus rapti sunt, et depositi ante ostium domus in qua erat Maria. Inter quos etiam et Paulus erat nuper ex circumcisione conuersus, qui assumptus fuerat cum Barnaba in ministerium gentium. Et salutantes se inuicem apostoli mirabantur dicentes: 'Quae nam est causa propter quam nos Dominus hic hodie congregauit in unum?'

Cumque inter eos esset pia contentio, quis ex eis prior oraret ad Dominum, ut ostenderet illis causam conuentus ipsorum, et Petrus Paulum admoneret ut ipse prior oraret, ille respondit: 'Tuum est istud officium inchoare, maxime cum sis columna luminis electus a Deo, et praecedas nos omnes in apostolatu. Nam ego minimus omnium uestrum sum, cui tamquam abortiuo uisus est Christus. Gratia Dei sum id quod sum, nec me uobis aequare praesumo.'

## Cap. 5

Tunc omnes apostoli gaudentes super humilitate Pauli unanimiter consummauerunt orationem. Cumque dixissent Amen, uenit ad eos Iohannes apostolus et indicauit illis omnia quaecumque dixerat illi Maria.

Introeuntes ergo apostoli Domini, salutauerunt Mariam dicentes: 'Benedicta tu a Domino, qui fecit caelum et terram'. Quibus illa respondit: 'Benedictio Domini super uos et pax uobiscum in nomine Domini. Nunc ergo, fratres electi a Deo, dicite mihi quomodo huc uenistis.'

Tunc omnes apostoli narrauerunt ei, quomodo unusquisque de sorte praedicationis suae eleuatus in nube in uirtute Domini ibidem aduenisset.

Tunc ait ad eos Maria: 'Benedictus Dominus qui impleuit desiderium meum, quin potius non me fraudauit a conspectu uestro, sed permisit me, uidere uos corporalibus oculis antequam moriar. Ecce enim uiam patrum ingrediar. Deprecor uos, ut omnes unanimiter uigiletis, usque ad horam illam qua Dominus ueniat et ego recessura sum de corpore. Nec dubito, quin immo Dominus uos huc adduxerit in solatium ferendum angustiis quae uenturae sunt mihi. Ideo rogo, ut breue tempus praesentis uitae quod residuum habeo, una uobiscum in Dei deducam seruitio.'

## Cap. 6

Cumque consensissent omnes et consolantes eam, triduo in Dei laudibus uacarent, ecce subito tertia die circa horam tertiam sopor irruit super omnes qui erant in domo illa et nullus uigilare potuit nisi soli apostoli et tres tantummodo uirgines quibus illa praeceperat obsequium praestare corpusculo suo.

Et ecce subito aduenit Dominus Iesus cum magna multitudine angelorum et dixit apostolis: 'Pax uobiscum, fratres'. At illi responderunt: 'Fiat misericordia tua, Domine, super nos, sicut sperauimus in te'.

## Cap. 7

Tunc Maria prostrauit se in pauimento et coepit orare Dominum dicens: 'Memor esto mei, rex gloriae, cuius nomen sanctum et laudabile cum Patre et Sancto Paraclito in una permanet dignitate. Deprecor te ut audias uocem ancillae tuae, ut nulla potestas Satanae occurrat mihi et ne uideam tetros spiritus obuiantes mihi, neque conspiciam principem tenebrarum.'

Cui Saluator respondit: 'Dum ego a Patre missus pro totius saeculi uita acerbae mortis sustinerem supplicia, ad me princeps tenebrarum uenit; sed cum nullum sui operis uestigium in me inuenisset, uictus abscessit. Tu igitur uidebis eum quidem communi lege humani generis, per quam sortita es finem mortis; non autem nocere poterit tibi, quia ego tecum sum, ut adiuuem te. Ascende igitur super stratum lectuli tui et comple debitum terminum uitae iuxta legem Adae. Veni igitur, ne timeas, pretiosissima margarita mea, ueni, proxima mea, intra in receptaculum uitae aeternae, expectant te enim caelestes militiae, ut introducant te in paradisi gaudia.'

Et haec dicente Domino, accumbens Maria super lectum suum, et gratias agens Domino, emisit spiritum.

Viderunt autem apostoli animam eius tanti candoris esse, ut nulla mortalium lingua digne possit effari; uincebat enim omnem candorem niuis et uniuersa metalla argenti radians magni luminis claritate.

## Cap. 8

Tunc Saluator commendauit animam sanctae Mariae Michaeli archangelo, qui erat custos paradisi et princeps gentis Hebraeorum. Et dixit apostolis: 'Petre, serua corpus Mariae et deferentes illud in dexteram partem ciuitatis ad orientem, inuenietis ibi monumentum nouum, in quo nondum quisquam positus fuit, et sepelientes eam ibidem, expectate me triduo, donec reuertar ad uos'.

Et haec dicens Dominus, cum anima Genetricis suae et angelis sanctis in magna claritate discessit. Et ibant angeli in magna exultatione magnas laudes Domino concinentes.

## Cap. 9

Tres autem uirgines quae ibidem erant susceperunt corpus beatae Mariae, ut lauarent illud more funereo.

Cumque eam expoliare cepissent, subito sanctum corpus tanta claritate resplenduit, ut tangi quidem posset pro obsequio, uideri autem prae nimia luce coruscante non posset, nisi tantummodo sentiebatur corpus dum lauaretur mundissimum et nulla humana sorde infectum.

Cumque eam induissent uestimentis mortalibus, subito lux illa quae emissa fuerat abstracta recessit. Et erat facies beatae Mariae similis flori lilii, et odor suauitatis magnae egrediebatur ex ea.

## Cap. 10

Sanctum igitur corpus uenientes apostoli imposuerunt feretro.

Dixitque Iohannes ad Petrum: 'Te condecet palmam hanc portare et praecedere nos, qui meruisti nos omnes merito fidei in apostolatu praecedere'.

Cui Petrus ita respondit: 'Tu solus ex nobis uirgo electus a Domino, tantam gratiam meruisti, ut super pectus eius in cena recumberes. Et dum ipse pro salute nostra in crucis stipite penderet, hanc tibi ore proprio commendauit. Tu igitur portare debes hanc palmam luminis ad exequias sanctitatis, qui potatus es poculo lucis de fonte perpetuae claritatis. Et ego portabo sanctum corpus cum feretro, ceteri uero fratres et coapostoli nostri circumdantes feretrum laudes referant Domino.'

Cui Paulus ait: 'Et ego, qui iunior sum omnium uestrum, portabo tecum'.

Cumque ita placuisset omnibus, eleuans Petrus a capite feretrum coepit cantare et dicere: 'Exiit Israel de Aegypto, alleluia'. Portabat autem cum eo et Paulus ad pedes illius, ceteri uero apostoli laudes circa feretrum Domino referebant.

## *Cap. 11*

Et ecce nouo miraculo apparuit corona nubis super feretrum magna ualde, sicut apparere solet magnus circulus iuxta splendorem lunae; et angelorum exercitus erat in eo canticum suauitatis emittens.

Canentibus ergo apostolis et concinentibus angelis ut decebat ad exequias dominicae Genitricis, replebatur terra sonitu mirae dulcedinis.

Quod cum audissent principes sacerdotum, exierunt cum populo multo de ciuitate dicentes: 'Quid nam est sonitus tantae suauitatis?' Tunc exstitit qui diceret: 'Maria exiit modo de corpore, et discipuli Iesu circa eam laudes dicunt'.

Cumque uidisset princeps sacerdotum Iudaeorum, qui erat pontifex anni illius in ordine suo, lectum coronatum et discipulos Domini circa feretrum cum exultatione canentes, repletus furore et ira, dixit: 'Ecce tabernaculum illius qui nos turbauit et omne genus nostrum, qualem gloriam accipit?' Et haec dicens, uoluit euertere lectum et ad terram deducere. Et statim aruerunt ambae manus eius ab ipsis cubitis et adhaeserunt feretro.

Portantibus ergo apostolis feretrum, pars eius pendebat et pars adhaerebat lecto, et torquebatur supplicio uehementi ambulantibus apostolis cum exultatione et laudem canentibus Domino.

Angeli qui erant in nubibus percusserunt populum caecitate qui egressus fuerat a ciuitate.

## *Cap. 12*

Tunc princeps sacerdotum qui adhaerebat feretro coepit clamare et dicere: 'Deprecor te, sancte Petre, ne despicias me in tanta necessitate. Memento quando ancilla ostiaria calumniabatur tibi, ego locutus sum pro te bona. Sed nunc quaeso te, ut misererais mei per Dominum.'

Tunc Petrus ait ad eum: 'Nobis mundana uicissitudo non imminet, sed si credis in Deum et in eum, quem ista portauit, Iesum Christum Dominum nostrum, soluentur a feretro manus tuae'.

Cui ille respondit: 'Numquid non credimus? Sed quid faciemus? Quia inimicus humani generis excaecauit corda nostra, ut non confiteamur magnalia Dei, maxime cum ipsi nos malediximus contra Christum clamantes: "Sanguis eius super nos et super filios nostros". Et macula tanti sceleris adhaeret nobis.'

Cui Petrus respondit: 'Illis haec maledictio nocebit, qui infideles perstiterint, conuertentibus autem ad Dominum misericordia non negabitur'.

## Cap. 13

Cumque Petrus fecisset stare feretrum, dixit princeps sacerdotum: 'Credo in Dei filium, quem ista portauit in utero, Iesum Christum Dominum nostrum'. Statimque solutae sunt manus eius a feretro; et erant brachia eius arida, et non discesserat ab eo supplicium.

Tunc Petrus dixit ad eum: 'Accedens ad corpus, osculare lectum et dic: "Credo in Dei filium Iesum Christum Dominum nostrum, quem ista portauit in utero et uirgo permansit post partum"'.

Cumque fecisset ita, statim redditus est sanitati. Et coepit magnifice Deum collaudare et de libris Veteris Testamenti Mariae testimonium reddere, quod ipsa sit templum Dei, ita ut etiam apostoli admirantes flerent prae gaudio.

## Cap. 14

Tunc dixit ad eum Petrus: 'Accipe hanc palmam de manu fratris nostri Iohannis, et ingrediens ciuitatem, inuenies populum multum caecatum, et pones palmam super oculos eorum. Quicumque uoluerint credere, recipient uisum; qui autem infideles perstiterint, morientur.'

Cumque fecisset ita, inuenit populum multum plangentem et dicentem: 'Vae nobis, quia similes facti sumus Sodomitis caecitate percussi'.

Cum ergo audissent uerba principis sacerdotum narrantis magnalia Dei, crediderunt et receperunt uisum. Quinque tantum ex eis permanentes in duritia cordis mortui sunt. Princeps autem sacerdotum retulit palmam ad apostolos narrans eis omnia quae facta fuerant.

## Cap. 15

At illi portantes Mariam, uenerunt ad locum monumenti, sicut praeceperat eis Dominus, et posuerunt eam in monumento et clauserunt lapide. Ipsi uero sederunt ante ostium monumenti, sicut mandauerat Dominus.

Et ecce tertia die circa horam diei tertiam uenit Dominus Iesus cum multitudine angelorum et salutans apostolos, ait: 'Pax uobis'. At illi adorantes dixerunt: 'Gloria tibi, Deus, qui facis mirabilia magna solus'.

Tunc Saluator dixit eis: 'Antequam ego missus a Patre passionis sacramenta complerem, cum adhuc corporaliter conuersarer uobiscum, pollicitus sum uobis, quod uos qui secuti estis me, in regeneratione, cum sederit filius hominis in sede maiestatis suae, sedebitis et uos super thronos duodecim, iudicantes duodecim tribus Israel. Hanc ergo ex una tribu Israel elegit iussio Patris mei, ut sumerem carnem ex ea. Propter quod sanctificaui illam mihi templum inuiolabile castitatis, ut uirgo ante partum et uirgo post partum permaneret. Ecce iam debito naturae completo, quid nunc uultis, ut faciam ei?'

Respondens autem Petrus et apostoli, dixerunt: 'Domine, tu elegisti uasculum istud in tabernaculum mundissimum tibi, omnia autem ante saecula praescisti. Si ergo potuisset fieri ante decretum tuae potentiae, uisum fuerat nobis famulis tuis, ut, sicut tu deuicta mortis regnas in gloria, ita resuscitans matris corpusculum, tecum eam deduceres laetantem in caelum.'

## Cap. 16

Dixitque apostolis Dominus: 'Fiat iuxta uestram sententiam'. Statimque iubente Domino accedens Michael archangelus, praesentauit animam sanctae Mariae coram Domino.

Tunc Saluator locutus est dicens: 'Surge, proxima mea, columba mea, tabernaculum gloriae, uasculum uitae, templum caeleste; et dum non sensisti labem delicti per coitum, non patiaris resolutionem corporis in sepulcro'.

Protinus surrexit Maria de tumulo et aduoluta pedibus Domini, coepit glorificare Deum et dicere: 'Non ego condignas gratias possum rependere tibi, omnipotens Domine, quem totus mundus plene non praeualet laudare; at tamen sit nomen tuum, Deus Israel, benedictum et superexaltatum cum Patre et Spiritu Sancto in saecula'.

## Cap. 17

Eleuans eam Dominus osculatus est eam, tradidit eam Michaeli archangelo, et eleuata est coram Domino in nube cum angelis.

Et dixit apostolis Dominus: 'Accedite ad me in nube'. Et cum accessissent, osculatus est eos dicens: 'Pacem meam do uobis, pacem meam relinquo uobis. Quoniam ego uobiscum sum omnibus diebus, usque ad consummationem saeculi.'

Et haec dicens Dominus, cum canentibus angelis et matre sua receptus est in paradiso.

Apostoli autem in uirtute Christi rapti in nubibus, depositi sunt unusquisque in sorte praedicationis suae, narrantes et confitentes magnalia Dei, qui in Trinitate perfecta et una deitatis substantia uiuit, dominatur et regnat in saecula saeculorum. Amen.

# Bibliography

Aldama, J. de, 'Fragmentos de una versión latina del Protevangelio de Santiago y una nueva adaptación de sus primeros capítulos', *Biblica* 43 (1962), 57–74

Amann, E., ed., *Le Protévangile de Jacques et ses remaniements latins* (Paris, 1910)

Arras, V., ed., *De transitu Mariae Apocrypha Æthiopice*, Corpus Scriptorum Christianorum Orientalium 342 and 343 (Louvain, 1973)

Assmann, B., ed., *Angelsächsische Homilien und Heiligenleben*, Bibliothek der angelsächsischen Prosa, 3, repr. with a supplementary introduction by P. A. M. Clemoes (Darmstadt, 1964)

Bagatti, B., 'Le due redazioni del "Transitus Mariae"', *Marianum* 32 (1970), 279–87

Bately, J., 'Old English Prose Before and During the Reign of Alfred', *ASE* 17 (1988), 93–138

Beyers, R., ed., *Libri de natiuitate Mariae: Libellus de natiuitate santae Mariae*, Corpus Christianorum Series Apocryphorum 10 (Turnhout, 1997)

Bishop, E., *Liturgica Historica* (Oxford, 1918)

Brou, L., 'Restes de l'homélie sur la Dormition de l'Archévêque Jean de Thessalonique dans le plus ancien antiphonaire connu, et le dernier Magnificat de la Vierge', *Archiv für Liturgiewissenschaft* 2 (1952), 84–93

Capelle, B., 'Les anciens récits de l'Assomption et Jean de Thessalonique', *Recherches de théologie ancienne et médievale* 12 (1940), 209–35

'La fête de la Vierge à Jérusalem au v^e siècle', *Le Muséon* 56 (1943), 1–33

'Vestiges grecs et latins d'un antique "Transitus de la Vierge"', *AB* 67 (1949), 21–48

*Travaux liturgiques de doctrine et d'histoire* III (Louvain, 1967)

Charlesworth, J. H., and Mueller, J. R., *The New Testament Apocrypha and Pseudepigrapha: a Guide to Publications, with Excursus on Apocalypses*, Atla Bibliography Series 17 (Metuchen, NJ, and London, 1987)

Clayton, M., 'Blickling Homily XIII Reconsidered', *Leeds Studies in English* 17 (1986), 25–40

344

## Bibliography

'Delivering the Damned: a Motif in Old English Homiletic Prose', *Medium Ævum* 55 (1986), 92–102

'Homiliaries and Preaching in Anglo-Saxon England', *Peritia* 4 (1985), 207–42

'Ælfric and the Nativity of the Virgin Mary', *Anglia* 104 (1986), 286–315

'The Homily on the assumption in CCCC 41', *Notes and Queries* 234 (1989), 293–5

*The Cult of the Virgin Mary in Anglo-Saxon England*, Cambridge Studies in Anglo-Saxon England 2 (Cambridge, 1990)

Cothenet, E., 'Marie dans les apocryphes', in *Maria*, ed. du Manoir, VI, 71–156

'Le Protévangile de Jacques: origine, genre et signification d'un premier midrash chrétien sur la Nativité de Marie', *Aufstieg und Niedergang der römischen Welt* II, 25, 6 (1988), 4252–69

Cross, J., *Cambridge Pembroke College MS 25*, King's College London Medieval Studies 1 (London, 1987)

Deshman, R., *The Benedictional of Æthelwold*, Studies in Manuscript Illumination 9 (Princeton, 1995)

Dobschütz, E. von, ed., *Das Decretum Gelasianum de libris recipiendis et non recipiendis im Kritischen Text herausgegeben und untersucht*, Texte und Untersuchungen 38 (Leipzig, 1912)

Donahue, C., ed., *The Testament of Mary: the Gaelic Version of the Dormitio Mariae together with an Irish Latin Version* (New York, 1942)

Elliott, J., *The Apocryphal New Testament: a Collection of Apocryphal Christian Literature in an English Translation* (Oxford, 1993)

Erbetta, M., ed., *Gli Apocrifi del Nuovo Testamento*, I, 2 (Turin, 1981)

Evelyn White, H., *The Monasteries of the Wadi 'N Natrun, I, New Coptic Texts from the Monastery of Saint Macarius* (New York, 1926)

Förster, M., 'A New Version of the Apocalypse of Thomas in Old English', *Anglia* 73 (1955), 6–36

Frantzen, C., *The Tremulous Hand of Worcester* (Oxford, 1991)

Gatch, M. McC., *Preaching and Theology in Anglo-Saxon England: Ælfric and Wulfstan* (Toronto, 1977)

Geerard, M., *Clauis Apocryphorum Noui Testamenti* (Turnhout, 1992)

Gijsel, J., 'Zu welcher Textfamilie des Pseudo-Matthäus gehört die Quelle von Hrotsvits Maria?' *Classica et Mediaevalia* 32 (1980), 279–88

*Die unmittelbare Textüberlieferung des sogenannten Pseudo-Matthäus*, Verhandelingen van de Koninklijke Academie voor Wetenschappen, Letteren en Schone Kunsten van België, Klasse der Letteren 43, Nr 96 (1981)

Gisel, J., ed., *Libri de natiuitate Mariae: Pseudo-Matthei Euangelium*, Corpus Christianorum Series Apocryphorum 9 (Turnhout, 1997)

Godden, M., ed., *Ælfric's Catholic Homilies. The Second Series. Text*, EETS ss 5 (Oxford, 1979)

Grant, R., ed., *Three Homilies from Cambridge, Corpus Christi College, 41* (Ottawa, 1982)

Gribomont, J., 'Le plus ancien Transitus Mariae et l'encratisme', *Augustinianum* 23 (1983), 237–47

Haibach-Reinisch, M., ed., *Ein neuer 'Transitus Mariae' des Pseudo-Melito*, Bibliotheca assumptionis B. Virginis Mariae (Rome, 1962)

Harbison, P., 'Two Panels on the Wirksworth Slab', *Derbyshire Archaeological Journal* 107 (1987), 36–40

Hardy, A., *Die Sprache der Blickling Homilien* (Leipzig, 1899)

Hawkes, J., 'The Wirksworth Slab: an Iconography of *humilitas*', *Peritia* 9 (1995), 246–77

Herbert, M., and McNamara, M., eds., *Irish Biblical Apocrypha: Selected Texts in Translation* (Edinburgh, 1989)

Hofstetter, W., *Winchester und der spätaltenglische Sprachgebrauch: Untersuchungen zur geographischen und zeitlichen Verbreitung altenglischer Synonyme*, Texte und Untersuchungen zur Englischen Philologie 14 (Munich, 1987)

Holder-Egger, O., ed., *Vita Willibaldi episcopi Eichstetensis*, MGH Scriptores 15.1 (1887)

Irvine, S., ed., *Old English Homilies from MS Bodley 343*, EETS os 302 (Oxford, 1993)

Jackson P., and Lapidge, M., 'The Contents of the Cotton-Corpus Legendary', in *Holy Men and Holy Women: Old English Prose Saints' Lives and their Contexts*, ed. P. Szarmach (Albany, 1996), pp. 131–46

James, M., ed., *The Apocryphal New Testament* (Oxford, 1924)

Jugie, M., *La mort et l'assomption de la Sainte Vierge: Etude historico-doctrinale*, Studi e Testi 114 (Rome, 1944)

'Saint Jean, Archévêque de Thessalonique (mort vers 630), Discours sur la Dormition de la Sainte Vierge', *Patrologia Orientalis* 19 (1925), 375–436

Junod, E., and Kaestli, J.-D., *L'histoire des actes apocryphes des apôtres du III<sup>e</sup> au IX<sup>e</sup> siècle: Le cas des actes de Jean* (Geneva, 1982)

Junod, E., and Kaestli, J.-D., eds., *Acta Iohannis*, CC Series apocryphorum 1 and 2 (Turnhout, 1983)

Ker, N. R., *Catalogue of Manuscripts Containing Anglo-Saxon*, repr. with supplement (Oxford, 1990)

Klaeber, F., 'Zur altenglischen Bedaübersetzung', *Anglia* 25 (1902), 257–315; 27 (1904), 243–82 and 399–435

Kotzor, G., ed., *Das altenglische Martyrologium*, 2 vols., Bayerische Akademie der Wissenschaften, Phil.-hist. Klasse, Neue Folge, 88.1 (Munich, 1981)

Lafontaine, J., *Peintures médiévales dans le temple dit de la Fortune Virile à Rome*, Etudes de Philologie, D'Archéologie et d'Histoire anciennes publiées par l'Institut Historique Belge de Rome 6 (Brussels, 1959)

# Bibliography

Lafontaine-Dosogne, J., *Iconographie de l'enfance de la Vierge dans l'empire byzantin et en Occident*, 2 vols. (Brussels, 1964–5)

Laistner, M. L. W., ed., *Bedae Venerabilis expositio actuum Apostolorum et retractatio* (Cambridge, MA, 1939); repr. CCSL 121 (Turnhout, 1983)

Lausberg, H., 'Zur literarischen Gestaltung des *Transitus Beatae Mariae*', *Historisches Jahrbuch* 72 (1953), 25–49

Lees, C., 'Working with Patristic Sources: Language and Context in Old English Homilies', in *Speaking Two Languages: Traditional Disciplines and Contemporary Theory in Medieval Studies*, ed. A. Frantzen (Albany, 1991), pp. 157–80

Machan, T., *Textual Criticism and Middle English Texts* (Charlottesville and London, 1994)

Manns, F., *Le récit de la dormition de Marie (Vatican grec 1982): Contribution à l'étude des origines de l'exégèse chrétienne*, Studium Biblicum Franciscanum, Collectio Maior 33 (Jerusalem, 1989)

Manoir, H. du, ed., *Maria*, 8 vols. (Paris, 1949–71)

Marocco, G., 'Nuovi documenti sull'Assunzione del Medio Evo latino: due "transitus" dai codici 59 e 105 di Ivrea', *Marianum* 12 (1950), 449–52.

Mimouni, S. C., 'Genèse et évolution des traditions anciennes sur le sort final de Marie: Etude de la tradition litteraire copte', *Marianum* 42 (1991), 69–143

'Les Transitus Mariae sont-ils vraiment des apocryphes?' *Studia Patristica* 25 (Louvain, 1993), 122–8

*Dormition et Assomption de Marie: Histoire des Traditions anciennes*, Théologie Historique 98 (Paris, 1995)

Mitchell, B., *Old English Syntax*, 2 vols. (Oxford, 1985)

Moeller, E. E., ed., *Corpus benedictionum pontificalium*, 4 vols., CC Series Latina 162, 162A–C (Turnhout, 1971–9)

Moraldi, L., ed., *Apocrifi del Nuovo Testamenti*, 2 vols. (Turin, 1986)

Morris, R., ed., *The Blickling Homilies of the Tenth Century*, EETS os 58, 63 and 73 (Oxford, 1874–80, repr. as one vol., 1967)

Muir, B., ed., *The Exeter Anthology of Old English Poetry: an Edition of Exeter Dean and Chapter MS 3501*, 2 vols. (Exeter, 1994)

Nellis, M. K., 'Misplaced Passages in Blickling Homily XIII', *Neuphilologische Mitteilungen* 81 (1980), 399–402

Pope, J., ed., *Homilies of Ælfric: a Supplementary Collection*, EETS os 259 and 260 (Oxford, 1967–8)

Prescott, A., 'The Structure of English Pre-Conquest Benedictionals', *British Library Journal* 13 (1987), 118–58

Rivière, J., 'Le plus vieux Transitus latin et son dérivé grec', *Recherches de théologie ancienne et médiévale* 8 (1936), 5–23

'Rôle du démon au jugement particulier: Contribution à l'histoire des

"Transitus Mariae"', *Bulletin de littérature ecclésiastique* 48 (1947), 49–56 and 96–126

Roberts, A., and Donaldson, J., eds., *Apocryphal Gospels, Acts, and Revelations,* Ante-Nicene Christian Library 16 (Edinburgh, 1870)

Robinson, F., ed., *Coptic Apocryphal Gospels*, Texts and Studies 4.2 (Cambridge, 1896)

Robinson, P., 'Self-contained Units in Composite Manuscripts of the Anglo-Saxon Period', *ASE* 7 (1978), 231–8

Santos Otero, A. de, *Los evangelios apocrifos* (Madrid, 1956)

Schabram, H., *Superbia: Studien zum altenglischen Wortschatz,* Teil I: *Die dialektale und zeitliche Verbreitung des Wortguts* (Munich, 1965)

Schiller, G., *Ikonographie der christlichen Kunst, iv, 2: Maria* (Gütersloh, 1980)

Schneemelcher, W., ed., *New Testament Apocrypha, I: Gospels and Related Writings,* English translation ed. R. McL. Wilson, rev. edn. (Cambridge and Louisville, KY, 1991)

Scragg, D. G., 'The Corpus of Vernacular Homilies and Prose Saints' Lives before Ælfric', *ASE* 8 (1979), 223–77

'The Homilies of the Blickling Manuscript', in *Learning and Literature in Anglo-Saxon England: Studies Presented to Peter Clemoes on the Occasion of his Sixty-Fifth Birthday,* ed. M. Lapidge and H. Gneuss (Cambridge, 1985), pp. 299–316

'The Corpus of Anonymous Lives and their Manuscript Context' in *Holy Men and Holy Women: Old English Prose Saints' Lives and their Contexts,* ed. P. Szarmach (Albany, 1996), pp. 209–30.

Scragg, D. G., ed., *The Vercelli Homilies and Related Texts,* EETS os 300 (Oxford, 1992)

Sisam, K., *Studies in the History of Old English Literature* (Oxford, 1953)

Smid, H., *Protevangelium Jacobi: a Commentary,* trans. G. E. Van Baaren-Pape (Assen, 1965)

Smith-Lewis, A., ed., *Apocrypha Syriaca. The Protevangelium Jacobi and Transitus Mariae,* Studia Sinaitica 11 (London and Cambridge, 1902), 22–115

Strycker, E. de, *La forme la plus ancienne du Protévangile de Jacques* (Brussels, 1961)

'Une ancienne version latine du Protévangile de Jacques avec des extraits de la Vulgate de Matthieu 1–2 et Luc 1–2', *AB* 83 (1965), 365–402

'Die griechischen Handschriften des Protevangeliums Iacobi', in *Griechische Kodikologie und Textüberlieferung,* ed. D. Harlfinger (Darmstadt, 1980), pp. 577–612

Temple, E., *Anglo-Saxon Manuscripts 900–1066* (London, 1976)

Teviotdale, E. C., 'The Cotton Troper (London, British Library, Cotton MS Caligula A. xiv, ff. 1–36): a Study of an Illustrated English Troper of the Eleventh Century', unpubl. PhD dissertation, University of North Carolina at Chapel Hill (1991)

# Bibliography

Tischendorf, C., ed., *Apocalypses Apocryphae* (Leipzig, 1866)

*Evangelia Apocrypha*, 2nd edn. (Leipzig, 1876)

Torkar, R., 'Die Ohnmacht der Textkritik, am Beispiel der Ausgaben der dritten *Vercelli-Homilie'*, *Anglo-Saxonica: Festschrift für Hans Schabram zum 65. Geburtstag*, ed. K. Grinda and C.-D. Wetzel (Munich, 1994), pp. 225–50

Tristram, H., ed., *Vier altenglische Predigten aus der heterodoxen Tradition* (Freiburg, 1970)

Van Esbroeck, M., *Aux origines de la Dormition de la Vierge: Etudes historiques sur les traditions orientales*, Variorum Collected Studies Series 472 (Aldershot, 1995)

'Nouveaux Apocryphes de la Dormition conservés en géorgien', *AB* 90 (1972), 363–9

'L'Assomption de la Vierge dans un Transitus Pseudo-Basilien', *AB* 92 (1974), 125–63

'Les textes littéraires sur l'Assomption avant le x^e siècle', in *Les Actes apocryphes des Apôtres: Christianisme et monde paien*, ed. F. Bovon *et al.* (Geneva, 1981), pp. 265–85; reprinted in *Aux origines de la Dormition de la Vierge*

Van Lantschoot, A., 'L'assomption de la Sainte Vierge chez les Coptes', *Gregorianum* 27 (1946), 493–526

Vattioni, F., 'Frammento latino del Vangelo de Giacomo', *Augustinianum* 17 (1977), 505–9

Vleeskruyer, R., ed., *The Life of St Chad: an Old English Homily* (Amsterdam, 1953)

Wenger, A., *L'assomption de la très Sainte Vierge dans la tradition byzantine du vi^e au x^e siècle*, Archives de l'Orient chrétien 5 (Paris, 1955)

Wenisch, F., *Spezifisch anglisches Wortgut in den nordhumbrischen Interlinearglossierungen des Lukasevangeliums*, Anglistische Forschungen 132 (Heidelberg, 1979)

Willard, R., 'On Blickling Homily XIII: the Assumption of the Virgin', *RES* 12 (1936), 1–17

'The Testament of Mary: the Irish Account of the Death of the Virgin', *Recherches de théologie ancienne et médiévale* 9 (1937), 339–64

'The Two Accounts of the Assumption in Blickling Homily XIII', *RES* 14 (1938), 1–19

'La ville d'Agathé? Note sur le Transitus Mariae C', *Echos d'Orient* 38 (1939), 346–54

'An Old English *Magnificat'*, *Studies in English* (University of Texas, 1940), 5–28

Wilmart, A., 'L'ancien récit latin de l'Assomption', in *Analecta Reginensia. Extraits des manuscrits latins de la Reine Christine conservés au Vatican* (Vatican, 1933), pp. 323–62

# Bibliography

Wright, W., ed., *Contributions to the Apocryphal Literature of the New Testament, Collected and Edited from Syriac Manuscripts in the British Museum* (London, 1865)

'The Departure of my Lady Mary from this World', *The Journal of Sacred Literature and Biblical Record* 6 (1865), 417–48; 7 (1865), 108–60

Zupitza, J., 'Kritische Beiträge zu den Blickling Homilies und Blickling Glosses', *Zeitschrift für deutsches Alterthum und deutsche Literatur* 26 (1882), 211–24

# Index